Speaking Out

Speaking Out

Out *The Reagan*

Presidency from Inside

the White House

LARRY SPEAKES with Robert Pack

CHARLES SCRIBNER'S SONS   NEW YORK

Charles Scribner's Sons
Macmillan Publishing Company
866 Third Avenue, New York, N.Y. 10022
Collier Macmillan Canada, Inc.

Library of Congress Cataloging-in-Publication Data

Speakes, Larry.
  Speaking out.

  1. United States—Politics and government—1981–
2. Reagan, Ronald. 3. Speakes, Larry. I. Pack, Robert,
1942–   II. Title.
E876.S65 1988 973.927   88–3247
ISBN 0–684–18929–1

Macmillan books are available at special discounts for bulk purchases for sales promotions, premiums, fund-raising, or educational use. For details, contact:

Special Sales Director
Macmillan Publishing Company
866 Third Avenue
New York, N.Y. 10022

10 9 8 7 6 5 4 3 2 1

Designed by Jack Meserole

Printed in the United States of America

Especially for
Laura,
Jeremy, Scott, and Sandy

and to the staff of
THE OFFICE OF THE PRESS SECRETARY,
1981–1987,

Pete Roussel, Marlin Fitzwater, Rusty Brashear, Mort Allin, Les Janka, Bob Sims, Ed Djerejian, Dan Howard, Karna Small, Connie Gerrard, Sally McElroy, David Prosperi, Anson Franklin, Dale Petroskey, Mark Weinberg, Kim Hoggard, Robin Gray, Denny Brisley, Liz Murphy, Mike Guest, Roman Popaduik, Jeanne Winnick, Flo Taussig, Sandy Sidey, Mary Kayne Heinze, Jan Farrell, Caroline Rhoden, Betsy Strong, Jane Thomas, Delores Granberg, Debbie Bird, Bill Hart, Sheila Dixon, Ben Jarratt, the staff of the White House News Summary—and to Jim Brady.

The authors gratefully acknowledge the help of our agent, Mel Berger, of William Morris, and of our editor, Edward T. Chase, of Scribners.

Contents

Perspectives

In my six years as White House spokesman, I did what I could to contribute to the success Ronald Reagan enjoyed during that time. On the other hand, I helped make Al Haig what he is today.

This book is my account of those years, from 1981 until 1987, of what went on in the Reagan White House and what my role was in those events. For most of my six years as spokesman, President Reagan's relationship with the press corps was better than that of any other President since John F. Kennedy. Ronald Reagan is justifiably known as "The Great Communicator," which made my job easier than it otherwise would have been. Nevertheless, there was no doubt that he was on the hot seat—and so was I. It's no exaggeration to say that the White House spokesman is the second most visible person in the country, which can be not only an honor but a headache. Certainly, we had both our triumphs and our failures, as you will read here.

You might call my impact on the Reagan presidency and on Alexander Haig the best and worst parts of my job. The Haig episode occurred at the most tension-filled moment of Ronald Reagan's two terms as President. On March 30, 1981, just seventy days into the Reagan presidency, bullets fired from the gun of John W. Hinckley, Jr., seriously wounded my boss, White House Press Secretary Jim Brady, and his boss, the President of the United States. Those gunshots thrust me from a relatively obscure job as deputy press secretary into the spotlight as the spokesman for the President, the White House, and the nation.

About four o'clock that afternoon, an hour and a half after the President and Brady had been shot, I found myself in the press briefing room at the White House, trying to give the news media what few details were known within the White House about the assassination attempt. After telling the assembled reporters that Reagan had been shot in the chest and that I did not know whether he had already gone into surgery, I was asked, "Has the U.S. military been placed on any higher alert readiness?" My response was, "Not that I'm aware of." One reporter followed up by asking me, "Who's running the government right now?" but before I could answer, another reporter shouted, "If the President goes into surgery and goes under anesthesia, would Vice President Bush [who was then flying back to Washington from Texas] become the acting President at that moment?" In the hectic events that had followed the gunshots, no one had considered passing the reins of power, so all I could say was, "I cannot answer that question at this time."

As I would learn so often in the six years that followed, anything I said to the press was often broadcast instantly around the world. During the hijacking of a TWA airliner in the Middle East in June 1985, I would be communicating directly via live television and radio with the terrorists who had seized 153 hostages, including 104 Americans. When I met Soviet leader Mikhail Gorbachev at the Geneva summit later that year, he knew me on sight, and when Queen Sofia of Spain visited the United Nations several years ago, she picked me out of a crowded room and said, to my surprise, "Oh, Mr. Speakes, I wanted to meet you. I see you on television all the time."

My words were transmitted immediately not just around the world, but all over the United States and even within the White House. What I said might make news right there at the center of government, and now, on that fateful afternoon, that was exactly what was happening.

Watching me on live television in the Situation Room—the super-secure headquarters in the basement of the White House from which the nation's most sensitive commands are issued in times of crisis—Secretary of State Alexander M. Haig, Jr., lost control. Until then I had greatly admired Haig, for whom I had worked in the last few months of the Nixon presidency, and I had even considered signing on for his abortive 1980 presidential campaign. But after seeing me on television, Haig bolted from his chair in the Situation Room, rushed up to the press room, seized the microphone, and informed the press that the Cabinet had gathered in the SitRoom and was in touch with George Bush, who would be landing in Washington in about two and a half hours, and that "absolutely no alert measures . . . are necessary at this time." Then, asked by a reporter, "Who is making the decisions for the government right now? Who's making the decisions?" a nervous and uptight Haig gave his unfortunate reply:

"Constitutionally, gentlemen, you have the President, the Vice President, and the Secretary of State, in that order, and should the President decide he wants to transfer the helm, he will do so. He has not done that. As of now, *I am in control here* [emphasis added] in the White House, pending return of the Vice President and in close touch with him. If something came up, I would check with him, of course."

Haig didn't realize it, but from a political standpoint he had just become history. Back downstairs in the Situation Room, an angry Caspar Weinberger, the Secretary of Defense, took issue with Haig's claim to be in charge, prompting Haig to compound his mistake by glaring at Weinberger and declaring, "You'd better read your Constitution, buddy." Turning to White House counsel Fred Fielding, who had been Haig's subordinate when Haig was President Richard Nixon's White House chief of staff, the Secretary of State asked, "Isn't that right, Fred?"—only to be informed, "No, Al, it isn't." The Constitution made the Vice President next in line to the President, and congressional legislation directed that the line of succession proceed from the Vice President to the Speaker of the House to the President Pro Tempore of the Senate to the Secretary of State.

I have had a passion for government and the study of politics ever since 1968, when I came from the rural Mississippi Delta country, where I was born and reared, to be press secretary to Mississippi Senator James O. Eastland. And I have always been struck by the impact that a few well-chosen or ill-chosen words or a brief moment recorded on film can have on someone's political career. President Kennedy set the course for his New Frontier with his electrifying inaugural message, "Let the word go forth . . . that the torch has been passed to a new generation of Americans." Barry Goldwater's 1964 remark that "extremism in the defense of liberty is no vice"; George Romney's complaint in 1968 that he had been "brainwashed" over the Vietnam War; and a picture of Edmund Muskie sobbing over an insult to his wife in New Hampshire in 1972 doomed their presidential campaigns. President Nixon's statement in November 1973 at the height of Watergate—"I'm not a crook."—helped convince the nation that he *was* a crook. Ronald Reagan's brilliant off-the-cuff comment at a debate among Republican presidential contenders in New Hampshire in

1980—"I'm paying for this microphone!"—effectively won him the nomination right on the spot. Reagan staged a repeat performance, ending whatever slim hope Walter Mondale might have had of defeating him in 1984, when Reagan, seventeen years older than Mondale, ridiculed suggestions that he was too old to be reelected by declaring during a debate with Mondale, "I'm not going to exploit for political purposes my opponent's youth and inexperience."

And now Al Haig had written his own political epitaph: "Gentlemen, . . . as of now, I am in control here." Moreover, Haig seemed to panic under pressure; the beads of perspiration on his forehead and his out-of-breath declaration gave a concerned public reason to worry. From then on, other members of the Reagan team would be viewing him with suspicion, and within fifteen months their hazing would drive him out of the White House. He would launch a campaign for the presidency in 1988, a campaign that obviously (to almost everyone but Haig) never had a chance.

All because a kid from Merigold, Mississippi (population 714), in his first at-bat before the world, the nation, and the top players within the White House, had gone before the cameras and microphones without being afraid to say, "I don't know."

Back in Mississippi I had been a newspaper reporter and editor, and also had some experience in law enforcement. All of that seasoning came in handy in the White House; not only was I in charge of relations with the press, but as part of my duties, I would ride in a decoy limousine, pretending it was the President's car, in case terrorists launched an attack on the motorcade.

Looking back over my years in the White House, no day stands out in my mind so much as the one when I received a battlefield promotion to replace Brady as press spokesman. Suddenly, there I was—the fellow whom "the Bear," Jim Brady, had dubbed "the Catfish"—propelled into the most sensitive public relations job in the world. Every statement of mine, every sentence, every word, every nuance, could literally make history. In large measure, what I said to the public could shape world perception of the Reagan administration. Moreover, in doing my best to answer a difficult question, I could inadvertently change history, as I did when I set in motion the events that would bring an early end to the political career of someone as formidable as Al Haig.

Throughout the nearly nine years I worked for Presidents Nixon, Ford, and Reagan, my small-town background stood me in good stead. I did cultivate the good-ole-boy image to some extent. Being a southerner, I was underestimated by some people. I found it to be true under Nixon, under Ford, to some extent under Reagan, and even now that I'm senior vice president for communications at Merrill Lynch. Just because you're southern, and you talk slow, people think you may think slow and you may not be very bright. At meetings people would just try to walk right over you when you had to say something, and they would be amazed when you would interject a strong point. They would look around in amazement that a country bumpkin like this could have anything worthwhile to say.

Working in the White House would be heady stuff for anyone, but more so, I think, for someone with a background like mine. I sat in the Oval Office hundreds of times, but never got over my sense of awe at being there with the leader of the Free World, at looking up and seeing the Presidential Seal set in plaster relief in the ceiling, at the sight of the historic paintings, furniture, and other artifacts that were scattered through the room. All of a sudden it hits you that you're making history, that you're part of two hundred years of tradition, that you're in the very room where FDR, Eisenhower, Kennedy, and all the rest worked. Imagine the voices that have filled this office, the decisions that have been made here, I always said to myself.

Little did I know when I replaced Jim Brady on March 30, 1981, that I would end up briefing the White House press corps 2,000 times and that I would serve five years, ten months, and one day—longer than any other presidential spokesman since President Eisenhower's press secretary, Jim Hagerty. Every time I faced the press was like the seventh game of the World Series—I was only one pitch away from disaster. The potential for screwups was greater than it was in almost any other job in the world.

But the work was extremely rewarding, as well as challenging. My approach to the job was, "Let's enjoy this while we're doing it. Let's do our job well, but let's have fun, too." On January 19, 1981, those of us who had worked in the press office during the Reagan campaign prepared to move into the White House. There had been grumbling about job titles, who would have which office, and how much the staff would be paid. As the only one who had worked previously in the White House, I felt it was my right and my duty to convene our people in a conference room at Reagan transition headquarters and give them a little speech that summarized how I felt:

"I want all of you to understand that you are about to be given a rare privilege in life. You're about to embark on something that will forever be the highlight of your life. Once you leave the White House, everything you do will seem somewhat less by comparison. There are 200 million Americans out there who would give their right arm to do what you are about to do. You need to set aside your bickering and you need to be thankful for the privilege of serving in the White House."

I still feel the same way, to this day, and I always will.

Speaking Out

1

"The President

Has Been Shot"

"Do you want to go with the President or should I go?" I asked Jim Brady as we finished lunch in the White House dining room one day not long after we had come to work at the White House. The date was March 30, 1981.

Brady had just given the midday briefing to the press, informing the White House reporters that the President had taped a statement to be broadcast on the Academy Awards that night and that Reagan would be traveling to Springfield, Illinois, two days later to address a joint session of the state legislature. All in all, it was a fairly routine day, ten weeks into Reagan's first term, if there was ever a routine day for us in the White House. President Reagan was scheduled to leave the White House at quarter of two and ride over to the Washington Hilton Hotel, a mile or so away, to give a speech to the National Conference of the Building and Construction Trades Department of the AFL-CIO. It was to be a quick trip, with the President to give his speech at two o'clock, depart from the hotel at two-thirty-five, and return to the White House in plenty of time for a 3:10 P.M. meeting with Republican members of the House Ways and Means Committee.

"I guess I'll go," Brady replied. As it turned out, those were the most fateful words of his life—or of mine.

Brady had invited me to lunch that day for the first time. Although

I was his deputy and right-hand man, we had not worked that closely together before then. Brady had been spending most of his time getting to know the President, leaving me to conduct many of the daily press briefings. We barely had our feet on the ground in the new Reagan press office, and Brady was having so little contact with the press in comparison to previous press secretaries that some of the reporters were getting upset about it. Six weeks earlier, an article had appeared in the *Washington Post* under the sarcastic headline, "In a Peculiar Twist, Brady Reappears to Brief Press." One unidentified White House official was quoted as telling a writer who was doing a story on Brady, "You must be an investigative reporter." Brady himself acknowledged in the *Post* story, "I have found it hard to find time to be press secretary." He was experiencing the press secretary's dilemma: serving two masters, the press and the President.

So, when Brady suggested we have lunch on March 30, I wondered if he had something important he wanted to discuss about the way I was doing my job. He never brought anything up, and as we were eating dessert I asked him, "Was there something you wanted to talk about?" "No," he answered, "we just ought to have lunch more often." Then, as we headed back to our offices, he repeated what he had said earlier, "I'll go with the President."

After President Reagan and Jim Brady left for the Washington Hilton, I went ahead with final planning for a meeting between press office staffers and the Secret Service that I had scheduled ironically, for four o'clock that afternoon. The topic: how the press office should handle an assassination attempt against the President. I knew from my own experience how chaotic that could be. President Ford had been shot at on two different occasions when I worked for him in the White House press office. The first time, on September 5, 1975, when he was in Sacramento, I had not been with him but back in Washington, where I caught some of the brunt of the press questioning. But I was in San Francisco seventeen days later, working in the makeshift White House press office on the second floor of the St. Francis Hotel, when Thym Smith, an assistant on our press staff, burst in and shouted, "You won't believe what just happened!" In an incredible repeat performance of what had occurred in Sacramento, a woman later identified as Sara Jane Moore had fired at Ford and barely missed him as he left the hotel. As Ford was hustled off to the airport in his limousine, radio silence from the motorcade was put into effect; we couldn't get any information from Secret Service agents or from the San Francisco Police. As a result, it was not until Ford's limousine raced across the tarmac to a revved-up Air Force One that we could determine exactly what had happened and inform the press.

If the unthinkable occurred again and someone made an attempt on President Reagan's life, I wanted our office to be prepared to gather all the facts and get them out to the press and the public fast. That is why I had arranged for our staff to meet with several Secret Service agents that afternoon—a meeting that was not held and would never be rescheduled.

As the afternoon wore on, I went to a budget meeting across the hall from my office in the White House. As I returned to my office just after two-thirty, my secretary, Connie Gerrard, thrust the phone at me, saying, "David Prosperi," an aide in the press office who had gone with Brady and the President. I took the phone at Connie's desk, and an out-of-breath Prosperi exclaimed, "Shots have been fired. Brady is down. I don't know about the President." I replied, "Thanks, David. Keep us posted," and hung up.

From what Prosperi had told me, I had no way of knowing if the President had been harmed. My first inclination was to go to the South Portico of the White House, where the motorcade would return, to make sure the President was all right. On my way I ran into several reporters in the briefing room and gave them, off the record, just what Prosperi had told me.

Before I reached the South Portico, I whirled in my tracks, deciding I should tell White House Chief of Staff James Baker what I had heard from Prosperi. The Secret Service had informed him that something had happened, but Baker had little more information than I had. At that moment, Baker's phone rang. Deputy Chief of Staff Mike Deaver, who had accompanied Reagan to the Washington Hilton, was calling. "The President appears to be all right," said Deaver. I passed that along to the reporters who had remained in the White House during Reagan's speech, and the story that the President appeared to be unharmed moved on the wire services at two-thirty-five—the first official words from the White House, and they were wrong.

A few minutes later we received the ominous word that Reagan's limousine had been diverted to George Washington University Hospital, six blocks up Pennsylvania Avenue from the White House. The "locator," a computer-like screen in Baker's office that kept senior staff informed of the whereabouts of top administration officials, clicked: "En route hospital." One of the Secret Service agents had noticed blood trickling from the President's mouth, and ordered the driver to go to the hospital instead of back to the White House.

Baker, White House counselor Edwin Meese, longtime Reagan aide Lyn Nofziger, and I made a quick decision. We got in Meese's car with the sirens and lights going, and threaded our way through traffic to the emergency room at GW. We rushed in and found the President in the emergency suite, just to the left as you walk in the door.

I started taking notes, which still give me shivers when I read them: "Doctors believe bleeding to death. Can't find a wound. 'Think we're going to lose him' [one doctor said]. Rapid loss of blood pressure. Touch and go." It had initially appeared that the President had suffered nothing more than a bruised or broken rib from being pushed into his limousine by a Secret Service agent. After arriving at the hospital, however, Reagan had collapsed to one knee, evidently going into shock due to the loss of about two pints of blood. He also complained of difficulty in breathing—which turned out to be from a collapsed left lung—and started coughing up blood. The entry hole from the bullet was so tiny that the emergency room crew had trouble finding it. Consequently, the emergency room team was initially at a loss to spot the cause of Reagan's symptoms. His blood pressure appeared dangerously low, and I watched a nurse strain to get a reading amid the growing pandemonium around her. After a few minutes the medical team did locate the bullet wound in the side of his chest under his left arm, and then they knew what had happened. One of the doctors or nurses, I have no idea who, told us, "The President has been shot," the most frightening in a long series of shockers that day. Once the doctors knew what they were dealing with, they were able to stabilize his condition with blood transfusions and intravenous fluids. But it was a crisis we would deal with for a long time.

Jim Brady was lying on the other side of the same room, separated from President Reagan by a curtain. Brady had a severe head wound, and it appeared it would be difficult for him to survive. I thought to myself that he was only forty, almost exactly a year younger than I. And I might have been lying there instead of him, but for his decision to accompany the President that day.

Returning to the area where Reagan lay, I stood by the foot of his bed. He was conscious and making jokes, and his shirt had been taken off. Looking at him without his shirt, I was struck by his rugged-looking physical condition. He appeared quite robust for a man of seventy, although at the same time I could see that in some ways he had the body of an older man, with a bit of flab and withered muscles that are dead giveaways that the body is not quite what it used to be.

During the next few years, I was excluded from a number of key meetings until I won membership in the inner circle, and I would often think back to the experience of being in the emergency room and seeing the President. There was no substitute for being present, no way I could fully inform the press without being a participant.

After a few minutes the President was wheeled out of the emergency room, with Mrs. Reagan walking beside him, holding his hand and talking to him, and taken to the surgical suite. "Honey, I forgot to duck," he said in a quip that was to set the tone for a remarkable recovery from a grave gunshot wound. Baker and Nofziger and Meese and I followed, but we were not allowed to enter the surgical suite, where surgery to remove the Devastator bullet—flattened after it ricocheted off the presidential limousine—and close his wound began at 3:24 P.M. and lasted for two hours.

Jim Baker told me to go back to the White House to manage the press there. As I left the hospital, reporters gathered around me. It was pouring rain and a U.S. Park Policeman mercifully held an umbrella over me, providing shelter from the downpour. Even so, I was soaking wet, my hair plastered down, my suit soaked, my notes splattered with rain. I answered the reporters' questions, finding myself shocked by the anxiety and concern etched on their faces as they strained to get my every word. I told them all I knew, which was that the President had been wounded in the left side and was undergoing surgery, but the outlook was good.

Back at the White House, I walked into my office; it was wall-to-wall people, bedlam reigned, and everyone was shouting questions. I suggested that we move downstairs to the briefing room, where there was more space, and I repeated what I had said at the hospital.

I had no idea that Haig and many other Cabinet members and top presidential aides had gathered in the Situation Room and were watching television. As far as I was concerned, the command center was wherever Baker and Meese were—which, at that time, was at the hospital. Then the question came up, were U.S. forces on any increased alert? My answer, "Not that I am aware of," is a standard press secretary reply. "What's *he* doing there?" Haig blurted out. He shot out of his chair, really bolted up, I heard later. "We've got to straighten this out," he said over his shoulder to Dick Allen, the national security adviser. Haig burst through the door out of the Situation Room and bounded up the stairs to the press room. By that time I had been handed a note at the podium that said "Come to the Situation Room." As I went out the press room door, Haig burst in, practically shouldering me aside. The rest is well-known: He announced, "I am in charge here."

Meanwhile, I quickly went down to the Situation Room, and in a few minutes, Haig and Allen came back. Puzzled by Haig's behavior, I leaned over and said, "Did I make a mistake?" And Haig reached over and grabbed my arm and said, "No, no, no, you're all right." I sensed that

Haig, by that time, was uneasy about his own performance in the briefing room. Before we could continue, the angry discussion over who was in charge erupted, with Haig and Weinberger glaring at each other across the table.

As a matter of fact, Weinberger had put his Strategic Air Command pilots on alert status. Soviet submarines, sailing off the Atlantic Coast, made some moves that seemed suspicious to us during the next few hours. It turned out that those Soviet subs had no hostile intentions, but no one was taking anything for granted.

In the Situation Room, most of the top officials of the government were present: Haig, Weinberger, Allen, Meese, Attorney General William French Smith, Secretary of the Treasury Donald Regan, CIA director William Casey, as well as Interior Secretary James Watt and a number of lesser officials. Those directly involved in the investigation of the assassination attempt were receiving reports from their people—the attorney general hearing from the FBI, Casey getting word from intelligence sources worldwide, and Haig and Weinberger monitoring diplomatic and military reaction. Around four-thirty, Don Regan, who as treasury secretary was in charge of the Secret Service, got a report from his agents that Brady had died. Regan announced solemnly, "I've just received some sad news. Jim Brady is dead." Stunned, Dick Allen, a close friend of Brady's, said, "Let's have a moment of silent prayer." And all of us bowed our heads for a minute. Regan, meanwhile, relayed the word to Senate GOP leader Howard Baker.

In the bedlam of the day, all three television networks reported a few minutes later that Brady had died. Word leaked out from Baker's office on Capitol Hill—and to add to the credibility, ABC reported that the White House was confirming Brady's death. What happened was that a group of reporters surrounded David Prosperi, who had returned to the White House, and was on the phone making arrangements for Brady's family to fly from their home in Centralia, Illinois, to Washington. In the midst of this pandemonium, Bill Greenwood of ABC asked Prosperi if Brady had died, and Prosperi, juggling the phone and the question, answered yes. Greenwood thought David was answering his question—when Prosperi was actually giving that answer to a different question from another reporter—and ABC went on the air with it. At 5:41 P.M., some forty-three minutes after Brady's death was first announced on television, I received a denial from the hospital, and I promptly went up to the press briefing room to announce that Jim was still alive. Another false rumor reported by the press that day was that the hospital had no blood of Reagan's type. At a time like that, though, you have to expect that untrue stories will circulate, through no one's fault.

My wife, Laura, was visiting her mother in Mississippi on March 30, and was due to come back that day. Just as Laura was putting her bags in the car to drive to the airport, her mother called out to her that the President had been shot. The first thing Laura saw on television was a body lying on the ground, and she heard a report that a White House press officer was down. Knowing that I sometimes accompanied the President outside the White House, she quickly dialed Connie Gerrard in my office to make sure I was okay. Back in the White House, a thought shot through my mind. Our son, Jeremy, who was ten, would be alone at our home in Annandale, Virginia, after school. How would a kid that age react, knowing that something bad had happened and that his dad was involved? Fortunately, a friend of ours, Sis Jones, reassured Jeremy that I was all right and kept him at her house until Laura got home.

Inside the Situation Room the drama continued for the rest of the afternoon and on into the evening. There was discussion of the Twenty-fifth Amendment on presidential succession, and we were in constant communication with Vice President Bush aboard Air Force Two as he returned from Texas. It was decided that we would not formally invoke the Twenty-fifth Amendment, because it would have alarmed the American people and our allies, giving them reason to believe that the President was much more seriously wounded than he now appeared to be. We also decided that Vice President Bush would make a short statement to the press after he had arrived at the White House and met with those of us in the Situation Room, and then I would follow with full details as we knew them.

Bush landed at Andrews Air Force Base outside of Washington at 6:30 P.M. Arriving at the White House, he took his seat at the head of the table in the Situation Room at six-fifty-nine and began presiding over a crisis-management meeting that lasted half an hour. The seal of the President hung on the wall behind the Vice President, and a wooden-paneled wall was opened to reveal a now-silent television set. Haig sat to Bush's left, and seated around the table were Jim Baker; Admiral Dan Murphy, Bush's chief of staff; Regan; Weinberger; William French Smith; Secretary of Transportation Drew Lewis; Dick Allen; and, immediately to Bush's right, Meese. The rest of us were seated throughout the room. I have never been so impressed with Bush as I was that night, the way he instantly took command. After announcing that he would hold cabinet and congressional leadership meetings the next day, the Vice President declared:

"The more normal things are, the better. If reports about the President's condition are encouraging, we want to make the government function as normally as possible. Everybody has to do his job."

As the meeting continued, Al Haig said he was sending messages to many foreign governments, stressing that the U.S. government continued to operate as usual, and he also reported that we had received numerous messages of sympathy and support from foreign leaders like Margaret Thatcher and Helmut Schmidt. Don Regan, drawing on his many years of Wall Street experience, expressed concern about the effect that the wounding of the President would have on the stock market. David Gergen, chief aide to Jim Baker, wanted to "stop the conspiracy talk" that developed in the wake of any attack on a President. William French Smith had the most information from his reports from the FBI. He reported that Reagan's assailant, John W. Hinckley, Jr., had a similar psychological profile to Arthur Bremer, the troubled young man who had shot George Wallace in 1972, and disclosed that Hinckley had stalked President Carter during the 1980 campaign. He described the weapon Hinckley had shot Reagan with as a Saturday Night Special. Vice President Bush said he thought he had once received a letter from the gunman. The best news was provided by Jim Baker, who said the President was in good condition and was expected to recover quickly.

After that meeting, Bush and I and a few others walked up to Bush's office on the main floor of the White House, discussing what he would say to the press and what I would say. Still feeling very much an outsider in the Reagan camp, I turned to Dave Gergen as we walked down the hall and said to him, "Tell these people—Baker and Deaver and Meese—that I can do this job." There had been indecision immediately after Brady was shot as to whether Lyn Nofziger or I would take over; Nofziger had briefed the press at the hospital, while I briefed at the White House. Nofziger, then the White House political director, had been one of Reagan's leading press operatives since Reagan was elected governor of California fifteen years earlier, and Nofziger and I had crossed swords in 1976, when I was in the Ford campaign and he was part of the Reagan campaign. But, in the late afternoon, as the chaos began to subside, Baker and Meese told me that I was the deputy and I should take over in place of Brady. Later that night, just outside the Oval Office, Lyn said to me, "I just want you to know one thing, you are the press secretary. I don't want that job. You're good at it, you know what you're doing." I said, "I really appreciate that. I know we've had our differences, but I really appreciate your support, and I'll always count on it." Lyn at that moment became a strong supporter of mine and any rivalry that had existed between us ended.

At eight-twenty Bush and I went to the briefing room. I introduced him, announcing that he would make a brief statement and would not take questions. "I can reassure this nation and the watching world that the American government is functioning fully and effectively," Bush declared.

Answering questions myself, I was asked why six hours had elapsed before Bush had reassured the nation that everything was under control. I was perhaps unduly kind to Haig, replying that Bush had been away, but "we were constantly reassuring the nation through Secretary Haig." Haig was already in trouble; after I gave details about the succession of command authority, one reporter pointed out that Haig was "completely wrong when he thought he was in command here when Weinberger was in the building." And there were many other questions about Haig's performance that afternoon. Haig's conduct that day would become a source of gallows humor; at one of my press briefings several months later, I ducked a question and a reporter asked, "Is it true, Larry, that anytime you don't answer our questions, Haig will come out?" Haig's image never recovered from the events of March 30. Typical of the press treatment of Haig was a column by William Safire in *The New York Times* a few days later. Safire wrote that Haig was the only top White House official to "choke up" in those critical hours. I felt that Haig's briefing room blunder had marred an otherwise credible White House performance in the immediate aftermath of the assassination attempt.

By ten o'clock or so on the night of March 30, things wound down and there was little left for me to do. The White House was suddenly quiet, with a few reporters staying around the clock as a presidential "death watch," and the day's events being played over and over on television. I felt it was important that I stay at the White House to provide a link between the hospital and the press, should something occur during the night, and I lay down for a few hours on Brady's couch. I turned off the light and drew the curtains, but a strange light still shone through from the North Lawn. The light and the silence—so strange after a chaotic day—added to my very eerie, empty feeling. Brady lay near death at the hospital a few blocks away, and the President, although apparently out of danger, was recovering there. And here I was sleeping in the White House for the first time, on Brady's couch. There was a certain numbness, as well as the slow realization of how important my role had become.

I awoke the next morning at five-thirty, knowing that my world had changed forever. Until someone told me differently, I was now the principal spokesman for the Reagan administration. I understood very well that what I said and did in the days ahead would have worldwide impact. By the day after the assassination attempt, my main task was to spearhead the administration effort to make sure that everyone knew the President was recovering and was in charge of the government, even though he would be in the hospital. That first morning he signed a dairy support bill and we copied it and distributed it to the press. I went into the briefing room and told the reporters that the President was fine, was meeting with Baker, Meese, and others, and that he had signed this bill. Of course, his signature was shaky, and Lesley Stahl of CBS said, "This isn't the President's signature." Somewhat taken aback, I pointedly informed her that it was in fact his signature, asking, "Are you the handwriting expert?" It was the first of many run-ins I had with her.

The next few days were a blur, like trying to read the words on a boxcar of a fast freight train while standing too close to the tracks. By week's end, we had settled into a routine. During a slow moment I had a chance to go out and sit in the Rose Garden under the ancient magnolia planted by Andrew Jackson, and let the enormity and the magnitude of what had happened sink in on me. The momentum of the events that followed the assassination attempt had carried me through until then. As I sat there on a beautiful spring day, I thought about Brady lying there in the hospital and what had been thrust on me, and I prayed, both for his recovery and for the strength to see me through this crisis and to handle the responsibility that I now carried. The warm sunshine of that Saturday afternoon seemed to ease my weariness.

The awkwardness of my position was on my mind for a long time, and a month or two passed before I could even bring myself to move into Jim's office. There was always the slim chance that he would be coming back, and even if he didn't, the thought of taking over his office and sitting at his desk made me uncomfortable. I kept operating out of my much smaller quarters until Jim Baker finally insisted that I move into Brady's office because mine simply wasn't large enough for me to do the job properly.

One of the hardest things for me to do was to go and see Brady. I just could not bear to see him in the condition I knew he was in. I suspect it was a feeling of guilt that it was him and not me, although I had volunteered to go to the Hilton that day. Brady, the affable "Bear," had been struck down for doing his duty, gravely wounded just as he reached the pinnacle of his profession. I did go to George Washington Hospital the first time the President visited him, two months after the shooting, but I stayed outside the room, glad that I was relieved of the chore of having to go in and see Jim as he was. I have a lot of respect for him, a lot of admiration for him, a lot of friendship for him.

The first time I saw Jim was several months later, his initial weekend visit home. I was at my house late on a Saturday afternoon when my White House phone rang and the operator told me that Brady's wife, Sarah, was calling. She was in a cold panic and tears, and she said, "Can you come do something? The press, they won't leave us alone. They're looking in the windows. They're continuing to harass us." I said, "Sarah, don't do anything, I'm on my way." I didn't even know where Brady lived, but I got the address from the White House switchboard. Laura and I were about to go out to dinner with *Los Angeles Times* reporter Rudy Abramson and his wife, Joyce, but we all loaded up in our car and headed for Brady's house in Arlington. By the time I got there the press had moved back to the corner. Sarah met me at the front door and said, "I'm so sorry I panicked, but they were just absolutely looking in the windows and we couldn't get a moment's peace in here." She invited me in to see Jim. I went in there, shook hands with him, and sat with him. I had prepared myself for what he would be like, and he quickly did his best to put me at ease. At that point Jim was difficult to understand, his voice high-pitched, sort of like a wail. But he still had his sense of humor. "Catfish," as he used to call me, "what's going on in Mississippi?" he asked. "Still got slaves down there?" I was glad I had finally crossed the bridge and had at last seen him. Seeing him in the future would be much easier.

Brady retained the title of White House press secretary, while I was designated as principal deputy press secretary and chief spokesman. Although it appeared initially that he might be able to return to work after a few months, he never did. But Jim retained the title of press secretary— certainly this was one of the most generous and gracious acts of the Reagan presidency. He and Sarah are the most courageous couple I have ever met.

Although Brady has never recovered completely, President Reagan made a miraculous recovery. By the early morning hours of March 31, about twelve hours after he was wounded, he was alert and joking with the doctors and nurses. A few hours later, he was moved from the intensive care unit to his own suite, which included a room for Mrs. Reagan and working offices for White House aides. And that night he stayed up late and watched the Academy Awards, which had been postponed for twenty-four hours because of the shooting. Twelve days after the assassination attempt, on April 11, he returned to the White House, telling reporters he felt great.

A few days later, in the Diplomatic Reception Room, where FDR gave his fireside chats, we were preparing for Reagan's first interview after the shooting, with reporters from AP and UPI. The President told me about his feelings in the minutes after he was shot: "Was I in mortal danger? That seems unreal to me. My first thoughts, I knew I was hurt, it was paralyzing pain. It was like I had been hit with a hammer. I sat up and the pain wasn't going away. [I was] coughing up blood, which I thought was a broken rib that maybe had punctured the lung. My main concern was the more I breathed, I seemed to get in less air. It diminished to where I was not going to get any." It struck me as odd that the President didn't seem to realize how close he had come to death, although when Terence Cardinal Cooke, archbishop of New York, visited him on April 17, Reagan declared, "The Lord spared me and what time I have left I will devote to Him."

We in the White House were shocked to learn later that the news media had obtained the President's emergency room records. Certainly, the press and the public have a right to know about the President's health, but the President also has a right to some privacy. Because of our experience in the aftermath of March 30, we would go to great lengths to preserve Reagan's privacy four years later, when he was operated on at Bethesda Naval Hospital for cancer of the colon. The media's demands to know everything and the insistence of the President and, more particularly, Mrs. Reagan, on revealing as little as possible would lead to major clashes between me and the press.

2 *Mississippi*

Born and Bred

There were many times during my White House years when I sat in the Oval Office with President Reagan, Vice President Bush, and the Secretary of State or another top official and felt a cold shudder going down my spine and a tingling in my stomach. What's a kid from a dusty little cotton town in Mississippi doing here? I would think to myself. This is the White House, and that's the President of the United States.

I never got used to it.

Now, in New York, I live in an apartment building that's forty-three stories high. In Merigold, the tallest building was three stories. That was the old Merigold Hotel, and they tore it down back in the mid-1950s when I was in high school.

More often than not, I'm still that kid who climbed the neighbor's tree to swipe the sour green apples and eat them until he got a stomach ache, or the second baseman for the Merigold Wildcats—not the White House spokesman or a Wall Street executive.

I spent the first eighteen years of my life in Merigold, a onetime sawmill town about one hundred miles south of Memphis. I would have been born there, too, except that Merigold was too small to have a hospital of its own, so I was born in the next town, Cleveland.

Nor was there ever a last picture show in Merigold, because the town wasn't even large enough to have a movie theater. The closest one, like the hospital, was in Cleveland.

Aside from a hospital, a movie theater, a barber shop, or a respectably sized restaurant, Merigold also lacked street signs. My parents and I lived on South Street; when I printed my own stationery as a teenager, I made up the street number: 410. Since there were no street signs, I would tell strangers that in order to find my house, you would come down Route 61 from Memphis until you got to the only traffic light in town (more often than not, it wasn't working), turn right, cross the Illinois Central railroad tracks, and look for the first house on the left, a little green house with yellow shutters. Or you could just ask anybody in town where the Speakeses lived, but, careful, don't get them mixed up with my grandfather, who lived on the other side of town. I lived in that house from birth until I went away to college, and my mother lives there to this day.

Merigold, named after the man who founded it around the turn of the century, Frank Merigold, is in a flat flood plain mistakenly called the Delta. The real Mississippi River delta is far to the south, below New Orleans, where the river flows into the Gulf of Mexico. Merigold is in the heart of cotton country, and blues country as well. My family settled there about seventy years ago, but my ancestors had come to Mississippi long before that. The story goes that my great-great-great grandfather, who was a horse trader in Virginia down near the North Carolina border, arrived in Mississippi sort of by accident back in the 1840s: he was on the trail of a man who had stolen a horse from him.

My grandfather, Earl Speakes, moved to Merigold about the time of World War I, shipping his belongings on a railroad flat car, and went to work as a clerk in a grocery store. Eventually he opened his own store, Speakes' Grocery. That was one of about a half dozen little grocery stores in Merigold.

My father, Harry Earl Speakes, grew up working in the store. He went to business school in Bowling Green, Kentucky, for a year or two, returned to Merigold, and went to work in his father's store again. Then in 1932 an opening came up and he became a one-man operation in the local branch of the Cleveland State Bank. He was the branch manager of the bank for over forty years before he retired in 1977. He died in 1986.

My mother, Ethlyn Fincher, was also born in Merigold. Her father was a bookkeeper for a plantation owner, and he owned a little farmland in his own right. None of them were wealthy, but they were solidly middle class, and we never wanted for much of anything.

My parents lived in a tiny apartment on the second floor above my grandfather's store from the time they were married in 1934 until shortly before I was born in September 1939, when they moved into our house. There used to be one house between us and the railroad, but the other house is gone now. The main line from Memphis to Vicksburg ran right down the middle of town. You'd go to sleep listening to the steam engines and the whistle in the night, and my earliest ambition was to be the man who waved the lantern on the train, the conductor who shouted, "Allll 'board."

I learned about hard work from my father. He would open his father's grocery at seven-thirty in the morning, work there until nine, when he walked across the railroad tracks to open the bank, work in the bank until noon, when he would shut the bank, and come home for lunch—dinner, we called it—our big meal of the day. He would always whistle for me from up the street, and I would run out to meet him. Every day of his life he took a short nap after lunch. At ten minutes to one he'd pop up and go back to work, then he'd close the bank about two, go back to my grandfather's store, work there until six, come home for supper, and then go back to the store and stay until it closed at eight-thirty. At night, while he was still at work, I'd shine my shoes and leave them out, and in the morning there'd be a nickel in each. I still think of those shiny nickels every time I shine my shoes now. On Saturdays the store was open until eleven at night, and on Sundays until 11:00 A.M., when church began. My father's only time off was Sunday afternoon after church.

Merigold was Middle America, the heartland, Norman Rockwell's America. It was an ideal place to grow up, and an ideal time, between the dark days of World War II and the complexities of the 1960s. We were kind of a John Boy Walton family. The three of us, my parents and I, were always very close. And like the Waltons, my mother went to every church service, but my father went only on Christmas and Easter, and sometimes on Sundays. He used to complain that there were too many hymns, and he "had to stand up and sit down too much." On Sundays, my mother would linger at the church and Dad and I would be home ready for Sunday dinner. Daddy would joke, "We've got to go get the key to the church. I know she's locked up in there."

My dad and I often went fishing or hunting for squirrels and deer. Those quiet days in the woods were our best times. I walked to school across town, across the railroad tracks, the highway, and the bayou. Many of the roads outside town weren't paved or even graveled, and we got what they called "rainy day holidays" any time there was a hint that the school buses wouldn't be able to get the kids to school and back without getting stuck on a muddy road.

I went to Merigold Consolidated School all the way from kindergarten to twelfth grade. It was a yellow brick schoolhouse, with one side for the elementary, one side for the high school, and the auditorium in between. There were about thirty kids in each class, and of course all of them were white. Desegregation didn't take place in Mississippi until I was out of college. You had one teacher for each grade, plus an art teacher, a music teacher, and the phys. ed. teacher, who also coached all three major sports and taught history on the side.

I played baseball, basketball, and football all through school. My senior year there were only thirteen of us on the football team. I was the captain, a 150-pound halfback, playing with a 110-pound guard in front of me. Talk about living dangerously!

My high school coach, James Merritt, was one of the first people who made a deep impression on me. He taught me the value of fair play, and he was the one who influenced me not to use profanity. He said, "You don't have to curse to make your point. I don't use it and I expect you not to use it."

At one time I wanted to be a professional baseball player, but in the ninth grade I found my future calling. I was a member of the Future Farmers of America and we rode up to the Mid-South Fair in Memphis on a rickety old school bus. I wrote a piece about it for our high school newspaper, which was a mimeographed publication, *The Wildcat.* I wrote kind of a tongue-in-cheek narrative and everyone liked it. I enjoyed hearing people say, "I liked what you wrote," and so I started stringing for the local weekly newspaper in Cleveland, the *Bolivar Commercial.* Then I became a stringer for the *Commercial Appeal* in Memphis at fourteen cents a column inch. And from then on a reporter was what I wanted to be.

It was also while I was in high school that I first got interested in politics. A bunch of us from civics class went to a friend's house to watch Eisenhower's second inauguration in 1957. The closest television stations were in Memphis, and even though my friend's house had a fifty-foot antenna, a lot of the time all you could get on the screen was snow. Occasionally you'd get a flicker of a picture.

My other big interest was music. When I was fourteen, three of my friends and I formed a little band we called the Cottonchoppers, made up of a singer, two guitar players, and a bass player. We were state hillbilly band contest winners three or four years in a row. I played the guitar, a Martin, which was not only expensive but almost impossible to come by. When I was eleven or twelve my parents had gone to Memphis and searched high and low in the music stores until they finally found one for $100 in a pawnshop. I still play the same old Martin today, and it has become a true collector's item.

We played on what you might call the Class D Grand Ole Opry Circuit in Mississippi and across the river in Arkansas. For a while we played in a show called the Southland Jamboree in Hamburg, Arkansas, in a shed used for cattle shows, and we got five bucks. That was for the whole band. We wore blue pants and white shirts and string ties, and finally invested in matching western straw hats.

Then in 1954 Elvis came along. We saw him first at the Clarksdale City Auditorium, about thirty miles from Merigold, and we were immediate fans. We watched his blossoming career, copied his songs, tried to sound like him. We played on the radio on Saturday mornings at ten-thirty, station WCLD, 250 watts in Cleveland, when we were juniors in high school. We'd sing, tell jokes, and read the mail. In fact, we'd write ourselves letters to show the radio station owner we had a following. If the three Presidents of the United States I later worked for had known about that, they might have assigned me to the White House correspondence office instead of the press office. Our show was a typical small-town Saturday morning radio show. I didn't sing, but I did do the announcing.

We actually played on the same stage as Elvis one time, at Ellis Auditorium in Memphis, one Saturday afternoon in an amateur contest prior to his performance that night at the same auditorium. It was 1956, when we were juniors in high school. This was our big break. I still have a picture of me and my girlfriend, who became my first wife, with Elvis. Elvis is wearing a white sportcoat, a black shirt, and white shoes. We went backstage and I got to talk to him, which was a thrill. Music was and is a big part of my life, and more than a quarter century after that time I met Elvis, I livened up dull moments in the White House briefing room by holding Elvis trivia contests for the press corps.

When I was a junior in high school and we were raising money for our senior class trip to Washington, I tried to get Elvis to play at our high school. I called his manager, Bob Neal. He was a disc jockey in Memphis and also a local promoter who managed Elvis before Colonel Tom Parker came in and took over. Elvis was unavailable for any of our dates; he was already too big by that time. But Neal offered us a double-barreled show: Carl Perkins and Johnny Cash, Perkins being the lead on the show. He had just come out with "Blue Suede Shoes." We brought 'em to Merigold High School, sold out the auditorium—about four hundred people were there—and raised $400 toward our trip. About twenty-five years later I met Johnny Cash at the White House and told him I'd given him his start. He got a kick out of my story.

By the time I was a senior in high school there were only seventeen of us in my class. We raised $1,122 for our trip to Washington, from the Carl Perkins–Johnny Cash concert, selling Christmas cards, and making hamburgers in home economics class that the girls would sell at the games while we boys played in them.

That trip to Washington caused a political controversy in Merigold. It was 1957, just three years after the Supreme Court ordered public schools to be integrated, and there had been a number of racial incidents in Washington that were prominently played in the newspapers down South. The school board, made up of probably the most conservative element of the community, opposed our going to Washington. My best friend, Bubba Jones, and I concocted an effort to outsmart the school board. Bubba was vice president of the class, and I was class president. Bubba and I wrote a letter to U.S. Senator James O. Eastland, knowing that he was revered by these people, and asked him, did he think it would be safe for our senior class to come visit Washington? Eastland wrote back saying that if we stayed together in groups we would be very safe coming to Washington. We presented that to the school board, and they could not go in the face of what Senator Eastland said was all right. I still have Eastland's letter saying it would be okay for us to come to Washington.

Washington was tremendously exciting for me. We toured the White House and the Capitol, and visited Senator Eastland's office. I can remember sitting in the visitors' gallery of the Senate, looking at the reporters, and saying, "That's what I want to do. I want to cover the Senate." Eleven years later I became Senator Eastland's press secretary.

You hear a lot about the value of a college degree, and of course it's true. But I never got one. A college education, yes. A college degree, no. It happened this way:

Three months after I graduated from high school I got married. It was in August 1957, when I was seventeen, turning eighteen in September. My girlfriend, Jenell Robinson, and I had dated since the tenth grade. Her father ran a country grocery store not far from Merigold, and, like my father, he had succeeded his father. Being shy, I had not dated much before Jenell, and she and I went steady all through high school. I was getting ready to go to Ole Miss—the University of Mississippi—and study journalism. She was afraid that if I went away she'd never see me again, so we got married. Her parents were ambivalent and mine definitely did not approve of it, although they came to accept it in time. I didn't really run away, I just simply went to the little country church, and her parents and a few relatives and friends were there, and we got married.

The Sunday I got to Ole Miss in September, the first thing I did was to head for the student newspaper office, where I presented myself and said, "Here I am, I want to work for the paper." A couple of editors were there and I helped them put out the first edition of the year. A few days later I went to the journalism department and said, "I'm married and I need to work," and they gave me the job of opening the newspapers that came in from all over the country and stacking them. It paid me four dollars a week, sixteen dollars a month, which was the rent for the first apartment that Jenell and I lived in. It was in an old army barracks, a walk-up with a hot plate and a kerosene heater. A fifty-five-gallon drum stood outside with a spigot and a lock on it, and we'd go down there and get more kerosene when the heater ran out, invariably on the coldest and wettest nights.

By my second year I had landed the premier newspaper job at Ole Miss—campus stringer for the *Memphis Commercial Appeal,* which Rudy Abramson, now of the *Los Angeles Times*, had willed to me. He recommended me and I held that job for three years. You could make as much as $100 a month working for the *Commercial Appeal.* A classmate, Ed Meek, and I organized our own photography firm, Speakes and Meek, to take pictures of campus events, and that added much-needed income. Jenell and I needed every dollar I could earn. I was working so hard on outside jobs that I had flunked two out of my five subjects my first year. But I added to my newspaper credentials by working in the Memphis bureau of United Press International one summer and for the *State Times* in Jackson another year.

In my junior year I had to turn down the chance to run for editor of the student newspaper, *The Mississippian,* because I couldn't afford to give up my job as a stringer for the Memphis paper. Instead, I became associate editor, which allowed me to write many editorials. In October of that year, 1959, I read in the local paper that Governor Ross Barnett had refused to sign the proclamation designating United Nations Day in Mississippi because he considered the U.N. a Communist organization. Mississippi was the only state that refused to honor the U.N. I wrote an editorial on the front page of *The Mississippian* that week that said, "Mississippi has long had a reputation for being last in everything except in illiteracy. We now have the leadership to keep us there." It was just two paragraphs on the front page, but it was picked up by the Jackson newspapers and reported on the state wires.

That day while I was going back and forth from class to the university news service, where I worked, I kept getting messages that someone was calling me long distance. But whoever it was didn't leave word. That night I was at home in my apartment, and the phone rang at eleven o'clock. A voice said, "Speakes, this is your governor. This is Ross Barnett calling."

He was very courteous, but he said, "You don't understand this organization. It's an evil organization. It's just not right for us to endorse it." I said, "Governor, I disagree with you, and I have the right to do so." "But you don't understand," he said, "I'm so disappointed." He wanted me to retract the editorial, but I stood my ground, and he was genuinely hurt.

During the summer of 1961, after my senior year, I was in summer school trying to get through second-year French so I could earn my degree when I got a call from a fellow I knew named Jesse Phillips. He said, "Some friends of mine and I are buying the *Oxford Eagle*. Would you like to be the news editor?" I took the job at eighty-five dollars a week and never did graduate. On August 1, 1961, I left school for good and went to work for the *Eagle*, a weekly paper with a circulation of about 4,000.

Every Thursday, after we'd get the paper out, the county agricultural agent would come by and pick me up. I'd have a camera and a notebook, and we'd go riding around the county, looking for stories. Oxford was novelist William Faulkner's hometown, as well as where the university was located, and it was full of tales and characters. There were plenty of features for me to write, like one about the farmer who had invented a pea-sheller, which whirred, going round and round, trying to slap the peas out of the hulls.

In November of 1961, the twenty-seventh, to be exact, the first of my three children was born—Sondra LaNell Speakes, or Sandy, as we called her. Bursting with pride, I put a small box on the front page of *The Eagle*, announcing, "We've got a new reporter." My pride has never diminished. Sandy is married now and lives in Dallas with her husband, Raymond Huerta. Justin, my grandson, was born in 1983. In fact, I was so excited about Justin's birth that I announced to the White House press corps that he weighed "fourteen pounds, seven ounces." Just a bit off; it was seven pounds, fourteen ounces. Sandy is completing her master's degree in speech pathology, a rewarding field in which she has a special talent.

My older son, Barry Scott, was born sixteen months later, on March 5, 1963. "They'll either grow up fighting or they'll be devoted to each other," my mother said of the closeness in their age. They had their share of scraps, but, now as young adults, they are very close. Scott has chosen to be a commercial photographer, following in the footsteps of his grandfather, who had a tiny amateur darkroom in the garage, and his dad, who paid some of his college bills by working as a campus photographer. Scott lives in New York, working with a senior photographer who shoots advertising photos for major magazines, and hopes to become a fashion photographer.

I worked for the *Eagle* only from August of 1961 through the following April, when I got an offer to come back to my old home area and be the news editor of the *Bolivar Commercial,* the weekly in Cleveland that I used to string for. I was there for a year, until April of 1963, when I demanded a raise from $95 a week to $125 a week, although I would have settled for $100 a week. The owner refused and I quit on the spot. There I was with a wife and two kids, one of them a month old, and no job. I resumed my stringing for the *Commercial Appeal,* started a twice-daily local news show on WCLD, my old country music station, and was hired to be the county's deputy civil defense director. The civil defense job paid $225 a month, and I added what I could earn from the stringing and the radio show.

I really got fired up for that civil defense job, the most enjoyable job I ever had. I took the training course at Battle Creek, Michigan, at the national civil defense management school. I came back and organized a one-hundred-member volunteer outfit, and taught classes with films and visual aids and booklets.

In Mississippi, those were truly the times that tried men's souls. The U.S. Supreme Court's desegregation decision had been handed down in 1954, but it wasn't implemented in Mississippi until the early 1960s. Then it burst on us with a vengeance, and, as a reporter and later as a newspaper editor, I found myself in the midst of it.

While I was still a student at Ole Miss, Ed Meek and I got a tip that a black man had applied for admission to the university. He would have been the first black student to attend classes at a school whose students formed the famed University Greys during the Civil War and marched off in 1861 to defend the Southern cause. We were still reporting campus events for the state daily newspapers, and we confronted the vice chancellor, Hugh Clegg, who shrewdly took us into his confidence. *"If* I might go off the record," Clegg told Meek and me, "we can lay out the facts." We readily agreed, and got the whole story. But we quickly found out we'd been tricked; we were not exactly experienced investigative reporters, and "off the record" meant we couldn't use it. We had a national story, but there was no way we could break our agreement and get it into print. When we explained our predicament to our journalism professor, Dr. Sam

Talbert, he laughed and gave us a stern lecture: "Never, never take anything off the record."

James Meredith was the student to whom Clegg was referring. He was finally admitted to the university in 1963 after a hard-fought legal battle that fanned the flames of extremism in Mississippi. By then, I was running the *Bolivar Commercial*, and I went back to my alma mater to cover it for the newspaper.

My old nemesis, Ross Barnett, was still governor. He had vowed that Mississippi schools would never be integrated. Barnett went round and round with the Kennedys, Jack and Bobby, who finally sent troops to the Ole Miss campus to protect Meredith and see that he was admitted.

I arrived on campus and slipped past National Guard troops guarding entrances to the school by waving my old student identification card at them—by then two years out of date. I watched a night of hatred and violence unfold. Meredith was already on campus, but, as darkness fell, the crowd—first students, then outsiders from all over the state—grew until it became a mob. By midnight, the campus was aflame, as rioters overturned cars and burned them. Shortly after 1:00 A.M. I heard shots ring out, and after watching the riots turn even uglier, I retreated off campus to spend the night. The next morning I returned to Cleveland and devoted the entire front page of the *Bolivar Commercial* to stories and sidebars about the night of rioting, and the back page to pictures.

I continued to cover the civil rights movement for several years. As a stringer for the Memphis paper in 1964, I was sent to cover the arrest of several Klansmen for the murders of the three civil rights workers in Philadelphia, halfway across the state. I had never felt so alone in my life as I did walking around that town and feeling eyes boring into me, a stranger there, in that atmosphere. I also covered some of the voter registration marches and several Martin Luther King speeches. I heard him speak once in a church, and I can remember the electricity and the sway he held over people, and the way they sang "We Shall Overcome" with such fervor.

I also got a look at civil rights from the law-enforcement side. When I had been with the newspaper in Cleveland in 1962 and 1963, I naturally covered the police, which was the primary source of news in a small town. When I left the paper and went with civil defense, the sheriff, Charlie Capps, Jr., who was a friend of mine, asked me to organize and train an auxiliary police unit. We had uniforms and shotguns and badges, and everyone was deputized. This was during the height of the civil rights movement, and one of our duties was to be a security force during major voter registration marches. We took an old school bus, painted it black, and put bars on the windows for a paddy wagon.

Once we got a call from L. B. Williams, the deputy sheriff in nearby Rosedale, who was under siege. He had arrested some blacks and was holding them in the jail, and the demonstrators were marching on the jail, where the only guards were L.B. and his wife, Velma. We rushed to police headquarters and got our nightsticks and our shotguns and our pistols and drove the fifteen miles or so there at a hundred miles an hour. When we got there the square was filled with 100 or 150 protesters. We formed a skirmish line, where you line up almost shoulder to shoulder across the street and march in formation with your guns at the ready. We dispersed the crowd from around the jail, and then decided to transfer the prisoners from the county jail to the state penitentiary at Parchman, a prudent step to keep the protesters from gathering outside the jail again. About eleven o'clock that night we loaded them into our bus and took them to the prison. We got there about 1:00 A.M. I was in the lead car and there wasn't a sign of life at this maximum-security prison. My partner, highway patrolman John Pressgrove, and I walked up to the gate, saying, "I wonder how you get into this place." All of a sudden a voice from out of nowhere said, "If you take off your guns, we will let you in." The voice came from the guard tower that overlooked the maximum-security unit. So we turned our prisoners, about thirty of them, over to the guards. There was no more trouble after that in Rosedale.

In our auxiliary police unit we found ourselves in the middle, with the tough rednecks on one side and the militant blacks on the other. But we worked closely with the leadership of both groups, and in my section of the state, at least, there was no violence. After a few civil rights marches on the county courthouse, tempers cooled on both sides. The leadership in Bolivar County was successful in conveying the message that violence would do no good, and changes were implemented. I wound up organizing an auxiliary police unit in Leland after I moved there in 1966, and this time there was a new twist: We were integrated. A half-dozen blacks were recruited for our forty-man riot squad, and we were the only organization in town that had a biracial membership.

While there were few incidents in my home area, things were different elsewhere in the state. As governor, Barnett rode the crest of redneck sentiment, and radical elements in the state fanned the flames. A few courageous editors stood up for law and order and were quickly shown how lonely—and dangerous—their stand could be. Hodding Carter, Jr., the father of former State Department spokesman Hodding Carter III, was the most outspoken advocate of civil rights as the editor of the *Delta Democrat-Times*. Carter had come to Mississippi after he was hounded out of Louisiana for his hard-line and heroic stand against Huey Long, and he continued advocating unpopular causes in Mississippi.

My own stint as a newspaper editor came as civil rights violence was winding down. Otherwise, I might have been faced with the choice of taking a stand against the local and state leadership, or keeping quiet and surviving economically. My editorial stands were not courageous, the way Hodding Carter's were, by any means. I mildly campaigned for civic improvements, occasionally chastising the powers that be for failing to keep the potholes filled and the weeds cut on vacant lots. Although I understood the viewpoint of those who battled for their civil rights, I regarded myself primarily as a reporter who covered the news without taking one side or another.

While I performed the usual civil defense duties of training and stockpiling for nuclear war, we also spent a lot of our time doing things like dragging the river for drowning victims. Preparing for nuclear war didn't seem that urgent, and when the *Bolivar Commercial* offered me a raise to $150 a week, I went back there as editor in July 1964. I did everything—reporting, editing, selling ads, sometimes even folding the newspapers and taking them to the post office.

In the fall of 1966 a friend of mine from college, Doug Abraham, called and said he was interested in buying the *Leland Progress,* another weekly in a town about twenty miles from Cleveland. We decided he would buy that paper and I would have an option to buy a half share. I was the editor, making $750 a month, $150 more than I had been earning on my second tour in Cleveland. In addition to putting out a weekly newspaper, we sold office supplies on the side and did job printing, too. Then we bought three more weeklies in that area. We called ourselves Progress Publishers, publishers of the four newspapers.

One of the papers was in a little town called Hollandale, which had one grocery store and a couple of other stores. That town could hardly support even one four-page weekly newspaper. One day a woman called and said she was canceling her subscription, which cost four dollars a year. I asked her why. "I can take your paper, throw it up in the air, and read it before it hits the ground," she said. At that point I decided it was time to think about getting out of the newspaper business.

I never had exercised my option to buy in, because I never had the money. I guess it was just as well. Although we won a number of awards from the Mississippi Press Association, we surely weren't making any money. And, Lord, it was hard work. I'd make pictures and sell what advertising I could on Thursday and Friday, work in the darkroom on Saturday, and go to nearby Greenville and try to sell ads on Monday. Except when it was raining. I had a theory you couldn't sell advertising on a rainy day, because people would be in a bad mood. On Monday night I would start writing copy and finish it on Tuesday. I wrote literally the entire news content of the papers. Then I'd make up the front page. And finally, after the papers were printed, the whole staff, including me, had to fold them by hand, and put address labels on, then seal them and stack them up. It was very primitive and very tedious work.

I had turned down jobs in other places—the daily paper in Pascagoula, Mississippi, offered me its editorship, and there were others—because I knew Jenell would never leave the area. But Jenell and I eventually found that marrying so young had been a mistake, and our marriage broke up. We were divorced in July 1968.

About that time, Noel Workman, who worked for me at Leland, posed a question to me: "Are you interested in going to Washington? I have a friend, Ken Tolliver, who is Senator Eastland's press secretary, and he is moving back here." Eastland hired me as Tolliver's replacement, sight unseen.

I was restless and eager to move on, so this Eastland thing had come out of the blue at the perfect moment. Near the end of July 1968 I loaded my belongings on a U-Haul trailer, attached it to the back of my Pontiac, and headed north.

Talk about a small-town boy! The first thing I did when I moved into the house I had rented in Arlington, Virginia, was plug in my radio, and I was amazed at all the radio stations you could receive in Washington. Then I drove into the city to get myself oriented. I can still remember the feeling of awe I got when I first drove through Arlington, turned by the Iwo Jima Memorial, and looked across the Potomac River to see the Lincoln Memorial, the Washington Monument, and the Capitol laid out in front of me. Even today, I still get that same feeling.

Washington. I had arrived!

3

The Big Leagues

Of all the politicians I have worked for—James Eastland, Richard Nixon, Gerald Ford, Bob Dole, and Ronald Reagan—Eastland was the shrewdest.

No story illustrates his political smarts better than one that occurred during his 1972 campaign for reelection. That year I was press secretary, campaign manager, and, in the aftermath of the assassination attempt in which George Wallace was shot and paralyzed, a bodyguard for Eastland. My old friend back home, Sheriff L. B. Williams, commissioned me a deputy sheriff and gave me a badge and a .38-caliber pistol, which I carried for the rest of the campaign.

Eastland's opponent in the general election was a Republican named Gil Carmichael. Late in the campaign the Republicans sent in a hotshot political adviser from out of state. At an Eastland campaign dinner in upstate Corinth, David Lambert, my press assistant, called me out and told me that this fellow from the Republican National Committee had been beaten up, left bleeding in a ditch near Philadelphia, Mississippi, and then taken to the hospital. Amazingly, he recovered quickly enough to drive to nearby Jackson and appear on statewide television with his head swathed in gauze like a mummy. He may have been attacked, but, obviously, he wasn't badly hurt. Nevertheless, since Eastland was known as an arch segregationist, our immediate thought was, "Oh, God, which one of our Klan supporters did that?"

Eastland and all of his closest advisers were really concerned about what had happened, and we set about figuring out what to do. We thought about calling for an FBI investigation, to demonstrate that we wanted to get to the bottom of this, too. Everyone had an idea.

Eastland sat there without saying a word. Finally he said, "Wait a minute." Everyone stopped talking. And he said, "I've got it. Larry, write this down." And he dictated his statement: "If he were beaten, I am truly sorry."

Everyone looked at each other and it began to sink in that he had done a brilliant thing. He had raised the possibility that it was a hoax and expressed his sympathy, all in eight words. He said, "Larry, go with it." Right away I called the state capital bureaus of AP and UPI in Jackson, and I said, "Fellas, I've got a statement from Senator Eastland on this thing." They got ready to take it. I repeated Eastland's words, "If he were beaten, I am truly sorry." They were still poised, waiting for the rest of the statement. And I said, "That's it." They said, "That's it?" And it dawned on them, too, what a stroke of genius it was. And the issue dissipated overnight.

We never found out who, if anyone, beat up the Republican consultant. By that time, Eastland had mellowed enough to deal realistically with the growing black vote in many Mississippi counties, and he no longer was willing to appeal to racist sentiments on the campaign trail. If it was some of Eastland's racist supporters who attacked the man, their help was definitely unwelcome.

That same year Eastland had had opposition in the Democratic primary in June, which was unusual. His opponent was a lawyer named Taylor Webb. After the campaign we were at a restaurant in Taylor Webb's hometown, Leland, which is where I had run the newspaper. Webb came over to the table and said, "Senator, I'm Taylor Webb." Eastland said, "I know who you are." And Webb said, "You ran a good campaign, Senator, we thought we were going to make some progress against you." Eastland said, "You never knew it, Taylor, but I had a man sitting up in your campaign advising you what to do." And I don't doubt that he did.

Did Eastland know Mississippi! He used to say he could drive through a county and sniff the air, and tell who was going to win that county.

It's hardly an exaggeration to say that Eastland ran Mississippi. One time not long after I went to work for him, Eastland was on his way from the Capitol to National Airport when he got a call to go to the White House and see LBJ. Johnson took him into his private study, and while they talked, some pictures were snapped by a White House photographer.

LBJ was highly unpopular in Mississippi because of his civil rights program, and he tried to put to rest any fears Eastland might have had. "Don't worry," LBJ said to Eastland, "these pictures are not going to get into the Mississippi newspapers." Eastland looked at President Johnson and said, "I'm not worried, Mr. President. Don't you know *I* control what goes into the Mississippi newspapers?"

I had received a personal lesson on how canny Eastland was the very first day I went to work for him in 1968. He had a tradition that after the women on his staff went home, the men would gather either in his office or in what was called the little office, which was his hideaway next door, to partake from his private stock of liquor and talk. The little office was taken up mostly by a desk. He sat behind it with his back to the door, facing the window. We went back about five o'clock or so that first day and everyone was sitting there, and he said to me, "Pour yourself a drink." And I said, "No, thank you," and I sat down. He had a Chivas Regal and water in a fairly small glass. He always poured visitors a larger glass, which upped their alcoholic intake, so he was always in control. About an hour later he told me again to pour myself a drink. I said, "No, thank you." He said, "You don't drink, do you?" And I said, "No, sir, I don't." And he said, "The FBI told me you don't drink." He was chairman of the Senate Judiciary Committee, and he had had the FBI do a full field investigation of me. He was either checking on the bureau's efficiency, or checking on my veracity, or both.

Eastland was a real character, cigar-smoking, round-faced, and bald, and quite a man of the Senate. Impeccably honest, completely trusted by his colleagues, Democrats and Republicans, liberals and conservatives, he was a man of his word, a man I learned a lot from. Outside of my father, he probably had more influence on my life than any other man.

The first thing you learned from Eastland was honesty. Soon after I joined his staff we took a trip to southern Africa, and he insisted on paying his own way, when he could have taken a trip on the government. When we came back he made us declare without fail every single item to Customs; the embarrassment of a story about us bringing in a ten-dollar bottle of booze would have been far worse than paying the duty.

Another thing I learned from Eastland was that you have to understand the other man's politics. You have to understand what is necessary for him to survive in his own political arena. If a Senator had to vote against a bill that meant a lot to Eastland, he understood that and respected it.

A third lesson I learned was that all of Washington revolves not around the White House but Capitol Hill. That's where the ultimate decisions are made. That's where what counts in national life ultimately happens. That's where you put bread on the table, or take it off. The Hill is filled with intrigue, it's filled with tradeoffs, it's more freewheeling than the White House. The White House, on the other hand, is glamorous, it's exciting, it's the top of the pole.

One of my responsibilities when I worked for Eastland was to escort important friends of his from Mississippi on tours of the White House, which is how I made my first visit there not long after I joined his staff. When I arranged one of the tours, Joe Bono, who was in charge of the White House tours, said I should come down and he would show me around. I was absolutely in an unbelievable state, in the White House at last. He took me into the Oval Office, which was hallowed ground for me, and here I was, after just a few months in Washington, actually there. The floor then was cork, and Joe showed me the spike prints from Ike's golf shoes. It struck me both as an historic memento and as kind of uncouth, to scuff up the Oval Office floor like that. Joe also showed me where the helicopter landed and other areas not seen by the public. I gave that tour many times myself after I went to work in the White House.

From the time I first went to work for Eastland, I thought to myself, "This is great being in Washington. It's great working for Eastland, but I'd rather be working in the White House. I'd love to be the press secretary." That idea was in my mind even then. But there was no chance; not only was I new in Washington, but I was a Democrat then, with a Republican, Nixon, about to enter the White House. Still, I felt a tremendous sense of achievement, being one of only one hundred press secretaries in the U.S. Senate, and here I was, not quite twenty-nine years old.

In 1965, while I was at the *Bolivar Commercial,* a young woman named Laura Crawford joined the paper as a proofreader and teletype operator. I was impressed with her hard work and asked her to join my small staff in Leland soon after I moved there the following year. Laura was interested in writing and photography, so I spent a lot of time showing her the ropes. In fact, when my partner and I acquired the *Bolivar County Democrat* in Rosedale, I made her responsible for the editorial content, and she did a great job. When I left Leland for Washington, my alma mater, the *Commercial Appeal,* offered her a job covering a dozen north Mississippi counties, and she left the weekly news business, too.

By the time I moved to Washington, my relationship with Laura had become very special. Three months after I arrived, we decided to get married. On November 3, 1968, we were married at Mount Olivet Methodist Church in Arlington, with a few of my friends from Eastland's staff present. We spent our honeymoon in the Blue Ridge Mountains and watched the election results from a motel in Luray, Virginia, as Richard Nixon defeated Hubert Humphrey.

Soon after our wedding, Edwin Wilson—better known as Big Ed—helped Laura get her first job in Washington. That's the same Ed Wilson who once worked for the CIA, became a renegade agent, supplied arms to Muammar al-Qaddafi, tried to arrange the murder of the prosecutors who nailed him, and is now serving a fifty-two-year sentence in federal prison. Big Ed had wormed his way into Eastland's office and had struck up friendships with Courtney Pace, Eastland's administrative assistant, and Bill Simpson, who was Eastland's legislative assistant.

Wilson was a personable guy, always ready to do a favor for a friend. That was the trait that endeared him to many people in high places and made him particularly effective on Capitol Hill. He was then a maritime consultant, which I believe was a front for his CIA work. Simpson asked Wilson if he could help get Laura a job. "Sure," Ed said. "I've got a friend who needs a receptionist." He took us downtown and introduced Laura to Howard Wickham, an old friend of Wilson's who ran a graphic design firm. As far as I know, Wickham was unaware of Wilson's CIA connections, just as Laura and I and most of Wilson's friends were.

Laura worked for Wickham until shortly before Jeremy Stephen Speakes arrived on October 4, 1970, during halftime of a Washington Redskins game, which Laura and I watched from the labor room. Jeremy is majoring in wildlife conservation in college but is an avid outdoorsman, and he and I often go hunting and fishing. He has talked about being a wildlife conservationist, but lately I have detected a bit of a leaning toward politics. After all, that's been the dinner-table talk in the Speakes household all his life.

Laura and I, meanwhile, settled into a rather normal Washington lifestyle. Always when one comes to the Capital, it's with the idea of "going back home" someday. But we quickly became Washingtonians—or, more accurately, Virginians. As Jeremy reached school age, we moved to suburban Fairfax County and bought our first home. For us, it was small-town living; for Jeremy, it was an opportunity for stability in this modern mobile society. The same kids he went to elementary school with are the kids he graduated from high school with. They've been through it all together: Cub Scouts, Little League, and now the world of proms and weekends at the beach.

Laura and I were never much for Washington's social circuit. Embassy parties weren't our cup of tea. "I can handle the job," I often said, "it's the social life that gets me down." Our idea of a night on the town is to go down to Pepper's Texas Bar-b-que in Fairfax City. If we're really feeling ambitious, we take in a movie too.

We haven't had much of a chance to travel, either. We took a vacation in Bermuda in 1976, when I was working for President Ford and he ordered his staff to take time off after the marathon state-by-state primary struggle. Our next vacation was in 1986, when we spent a week in Nantucket. I kidded Laura, "You can start planning now for our 1996 vacation."

Laura and Jeremy did accompany me to Santa Barbara in 1981, when Reagan took his first summer vacation. They also went with me when the Reagans spent Easter 1982 in Jamaica and Barbados. The White House got holier than thou, however, and wanted to charge first-class ticket prices for family members going along in the government-chartered press plane. So we have made do with an occasional long weekend; one of our favorite spots is a retreat in the Shenandoah National Park in Virginia's Blue Ridge Mountains—seven miles from the nearest telephone.

The Supreme Court during the 1960s and 1970s was really "the Eastland Court," as we pointed out frequently to our constituents in Mississippi. In only the five and one-half years I was with him, he presided over confirmation hearings for four of the nine justices—Warren Burger, Harry Blackmun, Lewis Powell, and William Rehnquist. During those years we also were presented with four other nominees to the Court, all of whom either were rejected or had their nominations withdrawn because of opposition: Abe Fortas, whom Lyndon Johnson wanted to promote from Associate Justice to Chief Justice in place of Earl Warren; and Homer Thornberry, Clement Haynsworth, and Harrold Carswell, three controversial nominees for associate justice.

Fortas's nomination to be Chief Justice was pending when I arrived in Washington. One of the strategies used by the conservatives, led by Eastland, was to pin on Fortas the Warren Court's permissive decisions on pornography, many of which had been handed down even before Fortas joined the Court in 1965. One of my first tasks as a member of Eastland's staff was to take a smut movie downtown and have some eight-by-ten-inch prints made for the Judiciary Committee files. By the time the confirmation hearings got under way, we had the best file of "girlie" pictures in the history of the staid old Senate. One Senator after another—many not even members of the committee—trooped by our office, "just to see the evidence."

On the other hand, Eastland himself practically nominated Rehnquist to the Court. Bill was an obscure young assistant attorney general who had been in private practice in Phoenix for sixteen years before Nixon's attorney general, John Mitchell, offered him a job in 1969. Rehnquist became liaison between the Justice Department and the Senate Judiciary Committee and really impressed Eastland. Eastland used to say he was "smart as a whip."

One day in 1971, while Nixon and his people were trying to decide who to nominate to the Court, Eastland came in at 10:00 A.M. as he always did, picked up the phone, and called John Mitchell. He said, "John, I think Bill Rehnquist is the man for that job." Mitchell said, "I'm going to see the President right now and I will tell him." And, just like that, we had our nominee.

At his confirmation hearings, Rehnquist was the best congressional witness I have ever seen. A brilliant man who was Phi Beta Kappa at Stanford and not only graduated from the law school there but got a graduate degree at Harvard, he spoke in complete sentences with periods and commas, he said no more than he was asked, neither adding nor embellishing anything. Had Robert Bork studied Rehnquist's performance, he might have fared better when Reagan nominated him to the court last year.

In June 1986, when Warren Burger retired and President Reagan nominated Rehnquist to be Chief Justice, I was there when Reagan made the announcement. I stepped up to the podium and Rehnquist leaned over and said to me, "I wish Jim Eastland were here to see this."

Rehnquist and Powell were nominated by Nixon about the same time for vacancies created by the deaths of Justices Hugo Black and John Harlan. Eastland's strategy was to tie them together for their confirmation hearings before the Senate. He knew that if he let Powell go through without Rehnquist, Rehnquist would be blocked by the liberals in the Senate, because he was so conservative and so young that he was likely to be on the court for many years. And he knew this was his chance to place two conservatives on the Court.

At the time Nixon nominated them, Powell was sixty-four, Rehnquist forty-seven. Shortly after Rehnquist and Powell—who was already a federal judge—were nominated, Eastland invited Powell to have lunch with him. Eastland always had a bacon, lettuce, and tomato sandwich and buttermilk. So Powell ordered the same thing. During the course of lunch Eastland said, "Judge, do you know why the liberals will take you and they won't take Rehnquist?" And Powell said, "No, Mr. Chairman, I don't." Eastland said, "Because you're old, and they think you're going to die soon." And Powell choked on his sandwich. No doubt even Eastland would have been surprised to know that Powell lasted fifteen years on the Court before his retirement last year.

While I worked for Eastland, the Senate Judiciary Committee and its staff investigated Republican corruption that served as a preview of Watergate. Richard Kleindienst was nominated for attorney general in early 1972, to replace John Mitchell, who had resigned to become director of the Nixon campaign. The question came up as to whether Kleindienst, while working under Mitchell, had improperly influenced Justice Department lawyers to settle an antitrust suit against International Telephone and Telegraph, in return for a $100,000 contribution from ITT to help underwrite the 1972 Republican National Convention. We called Dita Beard as a witness; she had been an ITT lobbyist and was involved in the convention decision.

Dita Beard had a heart problem and entered a hospital in Denver, forcing the committee to go out there in March 1972 to take her testimony. Normally one would think that a committee chairman would welcome the chance to go out there and be in the spotlight in a hearing of that magnitude. But Eastland was too smart: "I'm not going to be responsible for murdering that woman," he told his Senate colleagues. So he appointed Ted Kennedy and six other members of the Judiciary Committee to be a subcommittee and go to Denver and take Beard's testimony in the hospital. Eastland assigned John Holloman, who was a Mississippian and his chief counsel on Judiciary, and myself to go out there, to keep as much control of it as we could, and report back to him.

Senator Phil Hart was chairman of the subcommittee, and he had a press secretary we didn't trust. Eastland had sent a security man out there named Jack Norphel, a former investigator for the State Department. Hart's press secretary was getting a lot of press calls and answering them. So we raised the problem with Norphel. He said, "I'll take care of that. I'll just have the desk at the hotel tell callers he isn't in and I'll pick the messages up." So he did that for a couple of days while we were out there, and the guy was getting no phone calls and no one was smart enough to figure out why.

The hearings were held at Rocky Mountain Orthopedic Hospital in a room that Dita Beard was going to be wheeled into, wearing a nightgown and still hooked up to I.V.s and a heart monitor. The room had been prepared as a courtroom, and it looked like the set for the court-martial of Captain Queeg. The bed was on one side of the room, with the

American flag and the flag of the state of Colorado, and there were tables arranged on the other side, one for Democrats and one for Republicans. No one was allowed in there but senators, a few staffers, and one news reporter.

During the second session with Beard on the afternoon of March 26, John Holloman and I went downstairs for a soda and all of a sudden someone yelled, "They're breaking up!" The senators were streaming out of that room one after another, and it turned out that Dita Beard had had more chest pains and collapsed while answering a question from Senator Ed Gurney of Florida. The doctors started rushing in, with oxygen and emergency equipment. And Senator Quentin Burdick of North Dakota, who hardly ever said a word, shot out of the room and declared, "Jim Eastland was right!"

Senator Eastland was back in Washington, 1,600 miles from the scene. As usual, he had outsmarted everyone else.

A few months later, when Watergate broke around Nixon with a vengeance and high White House aides were facing jail sentences, Eastland came up with one of his sagest observations: "When people are facing jail, they either get sick or get religion."

Eastland had developed an uncanny political sense in a career dating back to 1928, when he was elected to the Mississippi legislature. He was elected to the U.S. Senate in 1941 and he served until 1978—he literally spanned a half century as a major force in Mississippi politics.

Eastland saw both his country and his state change radically, especially on the subject of civil rights, and he changed with the times, if ever so slowly. He once bragged that no civil rights bill ever became law by going through his committee, and added, "I have a special pocket sewed into my vest just to keep those bills from becoming law." The only way Lyndon Johnson's Great Society legislation could get through the Senate was by using legislative tactics to circumvent the Judiciary Committee. Nevertheless, Eastland was highly regarded by his colleagues for his intellect and his integrity, and by the 1970s he had begun courting the black vote at home. He even hired a black for his Washington staff, and during his last years in office he struck up an odd friendship with Mississippi NAACP president Aaron Henry, who announced his support for Eastland's reelection in 1978, before Eastland decided not to run again.

Eastland was the product of the segregationist South, and he clung to his heritage for many years. Still, in all the years I worked for him, I never heard him speak ill of any man because of his race.

Senator Eastland was a great man in my eyes, a man I will never forget. Before his death in 1986, he directed that the pallbearers at his funeral would be his former aides, whom he called "my boys." I was proud to be one of them. The funeral was a sad but grand occasion, truly an affair of state in Mississippi, and we laid him to rest in his native Scott County.

Not a day goes by—even now—that I don't remember him and tell another Eastland story.

4

Into the

Nixon White House

In politics, as in most other fields, it takes not only skill to get to the top, but luck. You have to be in the right place at the right time. That's how I first got a job at the White House, which is the ultimate dream of almost everyone who works on Capitol Hill, or, for that matter, anywhere in the political arena.

Ken Clawson of the *Washington Post* was one of only a few reporters outside of the Mississippi press who won Senator Eastland's trust and friendship, and Eastland would always take Clawson's calls. So I got to know Clawson very well. Later Clawson left the *Post* and went to work at the White House, as Nixon's director of communications. One day in February 1974 Clawson called me and asked, "How do I get my son a job as a page on Capitol Hill?" "Well, Ken, we can handle that easily, be glad to take care of that," I said, quickly adding, "but when are you going to get me a big job at the White House?" He answered, "I've got a job, are you interested?" Nixon was clearly going down the tubes, but I said to myself, "Having the White House on my résumé will be worth whatever it costs." So when Clawson asked me if I was interested, my answer was, "Absolutely!" And a few weeks later I was a member of Nixon's staff, albeit in the lowest job in the press office, tucked away in the tiniest office in the farthest corner of the Old Executive Office Building, across the street from the White House itself.

To get the job I had to be interviewed by Nixon's press secretary, Ron Ziegler. He canceled several appointments with me, and when I finally got in to see him, I was fascinated to notice that his eyes, like those of an old Mississippi owl, never seemed to blink. He was a very unusual fellow, impossible to read. He asked me a few perfunctory questions and I left his office thinking to myself, "Oh, gosh, I have really missed the boat here." Clawson called the next day and said, "You got the job. You don't even have to talk to Al Haig [Nixon's chief of staff]."

I went in and said to Senator Eastland, "The people at the White House have offered me a job. What do you think I ought to do?" I knew that I was going to take it unless there was a real appeal from him. He looked at me and said, "I want whatever is best for you." It was a lesson I took to heart for people who have worked for me: If they can better themselves, I want what's best for them.

Several months later, in July and August, as the Nixon presidency was collapsing, Eastland called me two or three times and said, "If you want your job back, it's here for you." I said, "Well, Senator, I think I'll stick it out here awhile longer." And the day Nixon resigned, Eastland called me again and said, "Your job is still here if you want it." I told him I thought the Ford people were going to offer me something, and he agreed to wait and see what they did. So another thing I learned from him is loyalty; he certainly taught me that loyalty is returned a thousand times. He once told me, "In politics, loyalty is everything."

I went to work at the White House on March 17, 1974, a date I will never forget. I won't forget my title either: Staff Assistant to the President of the United States.

That first day Ken Clawson introduced me to some people and the very first one was Helen Thomas of United Press International. I said to her, "I used to work for UPI." "Is that right?" she said. "Yep, I worked as summer relief in the UPI bureau in Memphis in 1958 when I was at Ole Miss." And that, from then until my very last day at the White House, January 30, 1987, stood me in good stead with Helen Thomas. By the time I became Reagan's spokesman, she was the senior wire service reporter at the White House, the one who says, "Thank you, Mr. President," to bring press conferences to a close. She and I had our ups and downs during the six years I was with Reagan, but there were more ups than downs. As a matter of fact, the very last interview I did at the White House was with Helen Thomas, and when she was finished, she stood up and hugged me, which was a real surprise. But it meant a lot to me.

Another person I met that first day was Jerry Warren, Ziegler's deputy, who had been doing the daily briefings of the press in place of Ziegler for the past several months. Warren was only about thirty-five or so, but he looked like he was at death's door. He was worn out, he had lost a tremendous amount of weight, his clothes didn't fit, there was about an inch and a half between the collar of his shirt and his neck, and there were lines in his face. After Nixon resigned I really got to know Jerry, and one time he said to me, "You know, there were a lot of times during Watergate when I would drive home after a long day of press briefings, and I would drive up to a red light, and I would say to myself, 'You know, if I run that red light that car coming there will hit me and I'll be injured and I'll go to the hospital, but I won't have to brief tomorrow.'" Even to recall that gives me shivers about what a tough situation Jerry was in.

In circumstances like Watergate you could rise very rapidly. One of my first assignments was to prove that John Dean was lying in his testimony before the Senate Watergate Committee, and thereby destroy his credibility. Ziegler called me in and said, "Get everything—files, newspaper clippings, hearing transcripts—we can nail this guy." It was an important assignment in the first days of my White House career, and I approached it with high hopes. But I had hardly begun checking out Dean, looking for discrepancies between his testimony and the facts, before I reached an unexpected conclusion: John Dean hadn't lied. I had been assigned to work with Diane Sawyer, then Ziegler's executive assistant, on the Dean investigation, and, with trepidation, thinking I had failed in my first important task, I reported what I had found to Diane. But events moved rapidly in the Nixon White House in those days, and we were soon seeking other ways to defend the embattled President.

We had a two-track approach at the White House: Government as Usual, and Watergate. I was soon assigned to the "Government as Usual" team. My first idea was, "I know this is a mess. I know Watergate is bad. I will go down there and keep myself clear of Watergate, not get mixed up in it." So I was delighted to be on the Government as Usual squad. I assigned every public affairs officer in the government to write an Op-Ed piece each week telling how the government was functioning normally, and I would edit them and place them with papers around the country. Placing Op-Eds is not an easy job. But we did remarkably well. If you couldn't get them into the *Washington Post*, or *The New York Times*, or the *Los Angeles Times*, you could always get them into newspapers like the *San Antonio Light* or the *Charleston Gazette* in West Virginia. I also wrote mini-speeches for members of Congress, one-minute items that were usually inserted into the *Congressional Record* by pro-Nixon loyalists like Representative Joe Waggonner of Louisiana.

In May 1974, however, I found myself with the Watergate team. At

Clawson's suggestion, I was assigned to work with James D. St. Clair, a high-powered Boston attorney who had been given the title of Special Counsel to the President. St. Clair had been brought on as Watergate became the top issue on the White House agenda; he was the head of Nixon's legal defense team. Clawson talked me up so highly that Haig agreed to make me press secretary to the special counsel to the President of the United States, even though I was the newest member of the team.

When I signed on with St. Clair, things were pretty far down the line. He had come in only recently, and had plenty of catching up to do. He was surrounded by a bunch of very young lawyers, none of whom was a constitutional expert. They were eager and hard-working, but I guess you'd have to say it was a weak team. St. Clair himself was an exceptionally bright lawyer, but I don't think he really had had the time to immerse himself in the constitutional aspects of the case. Also, it was a political struggle and St. Clair was a legal guy, a big corporate defense attorney. As I wrote Clawson in a memo intended for Haig to see, "This is not a legal matter; that's over and we lost. It's a political fight, pure and simple."

The idea of having a press secretary for St. Clair and his operation was to take a large part of the Watergate response out of the White House briefing room and out of the White House proper and to put it with the lawyers. It was a decision that had been made by Haig and others to try to put distance between Nixon and Watergate.

The press was doing a lot of mood pieces and I would always try to put an upbeat face on the situation, which invariably would not make the papers. Bob Woodward or Carl Bernstein used to call late in the afternoon, when they were on deadline, and say they had another story about declining morale and more defections among the White House staff, but they needed another source to confirm it. Would I confirm it? They were off base and I told them so, but my comments never turned up in the *Post* the next day. This happened more than once. I didn't think they could have found another source that late in the day, so I could only conclude they didn't really have a two-source rule, like they claimed. It was a classic reporter's shell game: if only you'll confirm what we already suspect, we'll go with it. All told to you with the purest motives. They were just fishing.

One of our tasks was to try to disprove the theory that Nixon was responsible for the infamous eighteen-minute gap on one of the tapes. Our campaign was to discredit the sinister implications of the gap. Our position was that it was merely a mechanical failure. We talked about Nixon having no aptitude for mechanics. "He probably wouldn't even know how to work a tape recorder," I told the press. We cited Nixon's visit to the Grand Ole Opry in Nashville during that period. He was on stage with Roy Acuff and tried to work a yo-yo, but he had no conception of how to do it. We were grasping at every straw we could find.

At one point St. Clair and his lawyers brought in a technical "expert" to examine the recorder. He came to a quick conclusion: It was a mechanical "demon" in the machine, not Nixon, that caused the critical gap. Dick Hauser, a member of the legal team, called me and said, "Come down here and let me have your judgment on this guy." Ten minutes later, Hauser and I looked at each other and rolled our eyes. This little bespectacled "expert" would never have gotten to first base with the prosecutors and the congressional investigators, and his explanation would have backfired.

We were always looking for White House people we could send out onto the White House lawn to talk to the press. Someone new, someone to distract them from Watergate. One day Ken Clawson suggested we take John McLaughlin—Father John McLaughlin, the former Jesuit who was a special assistant to Nixon for public relations and became known as the "Watergate Priest"—and send him out to defend Nixon to the press. We took John out and he immediately hit his stride with his theatrics and his overblown gestures, no different then than he is today on his T.V. show, "The McLaughlin Group." He did right well, so we said, "We could use him some more."

About nine the next morning I was walking from my office to Clawson's and I saw a mob of reporters and cameras outside McLaughlin's office. "The good Father is at it again," I told Clawson. He quickly sent for Dick Moore, another aide to the President. Dick was an old Nixon hand, a real pro, but he was the one who had discovered McLaughlin and brought him to the White House. I told Dick that McLaughlin was talking to all these reporters and he jumped up and said, "My God, he's a monster, and I created him!" That was the beginning of John McLaughlin. Ironically, when I resigned as Reagan's spokesman thirteen years later, McLaughlin's wife, Ann Dore McLaughlin, who later became secretary of labor, was one of the candidates rumored as my successor. Ann, John, and I got together at the time and laughed over our recollections of the creation of John McLaughlin.

Wherever St. Clair went, I was with him. It was the old press secretary's rule, you had to be with the man, just as Brady was with Reagan when he was shot. One incident I will never forget occurred on July 18, 1974, when I was riding with St. Clair and another of his staffers, Malcolm

Howard, to Capitol Hill. There St. Clair was going to present his final argument to Peter Rodino's House Judiciary Committee, then in the midst of hearings that were clearly going to end with impeachment proceedings against Nixon. St. Clair had decided to reveal to the committee that Nixon had told Bob Haldeman on March 22, 1973, "I don't mean to be blackmailed by [E. Howard] Hunt. That goes too far." St. Clair believed that that somehow exonerated Nixon; I couldn't understand how. And Nixon's statement came from a tape that Nixon was withholding from the committee, although the committee had subpoenaed it.

I thought St. Clair was making a mistake by offering part of something the committee members had demanded in its entirety, but St. Clair was the kind of man you didn't argue with once he had made up his mind. Also, he had been a $300,000-a-year lawyer in private practice, which was about ten times as much as I was making, so I figured he must have some idea of what he was doing. On our way to the Hill, St. Clair laid out his plan to introduce the March 22 transcript. Twice I started to tell him I thought it was a mistake. "Mr. St. Clair—" was all I got out each time, before Howard elbowed me in the ribs to shut me up. I never had my say. St. Clair went ahead and used the part of the transcript he wanted to—which infuriated the members of the committee, as I had expected it would.

In late July, St. Clair was summoned to meet with Nixon at the Western White House in San Clemente. This was my first visit there. I had a White House phone in my room and my name on the door at the Newporter Inn, and many other amenities that were completely new to me.

St. Clair and I arrived in San Clemente on July 21, a Sunday. Two days earlier, John Doar, counsel to the House Judiciary Committee, had called for the President's impeachment in a blistering statement to the committee:

"My judgment is that . . . the President of the United States authorized a broad, general plan of illegal electronic surveillance, and that that plan was put into operation by his subordinates. . . . Following that, I say . . . the President made the decision to cover up this shortly after the break-in on June seventeenth, and he's been in charge of the cover-up from that day forward. What he decided should be done . . . required perjury, destruction of evidence, obstruction of justice, all crimes. But, most important, it required deliberate, contrived, continued, and continuing deception of the American people."

St. Clair had expected that he would have some quiet strategy talks with Nixon, but otherwise he was looking forward to a relaxing visit to beautiful southern California. But Ron Ziegler had different ideas; he needed someone to distract the press from what Doar had said, so when St. Clair and I reported to Ziegler's office on Monday morning, July 22, Ziegler told St. Clair, "I want you to have a press conference this afternoon." We were taken aback, because that's the last thing we had been prepared for. That gave me a sense of Ziegler's power: he as press secretary could give orders to Nixon's special counsel.

St. Clair and I left Ziegler's office and walked out to a bluff overlooking the Pacific to assess our situation. We took off our jackets, rolled up our sleeves, and walked around out there for about thirty minutes, a lot of it in silence, just listening to the ocean below. It was a strange situation for me. I had been in the White House for only four months, and already I had been catapulted from an obscure, low-level staffer to the spokesman for the Watergate lawyers. I felt like I was in a movie as the drama of the occasion surged up around me. Things were moving very fast, but I was enjoying it. It was almost as if I had been swept away on a magic carpet or was floating on a cloud. But there was also reality: In our hearts St. Clair and I knew that we were being hurtled, almost against our will, toward an inevitable ending, beyond our control; the only thing we didn't know was quite how it would happen, but we knew our backs were to the wall. We weren't thinking in terms of resignation, we were thinking in terms of fighting a big battle in Congress with a very short stick. There was obviously going to be an impeachment vote in the House and a trial in the Senate.

Having St. Clair hold a press conference was another P.R. defense, an attempt to deflect the roller coaster roaring down the track, and Ziegler had selected St. Clair to stand in front of the roller coaster. We went back to Ziegler's office to confer with him, and all of a sudden he stood up and called, "Diane!" Diane Sawyer, then twenty-eight, was one of Ziegler's assistants, hardly as important as she is today. Diane came running in, and Ziegler took off his jacket and tie and dropped them on the floor and kicked off his loafers. Diane had in hand a sweater and his boots. Ziegler threw those on and left without another word. Diane grabbed up his clothes, he jumped on his motorcycle—that was his year for the motorcycle—revved it up, and roared off, with St. Clair and me still standing there in his office, shaking our heads. Diane had to jump in Ziegler's car and speed up to Laguna Beach, where the press conference would be held, to be there with his jacket and tie and shoes when he arrived.

St. Clair and I rode up to Laguna in a White House car and went into Ziegler's office up there and talked a bit more, with Ziegler and me sparring a little over what St. Clair would say. We did the press conference, which was carried live on national television, knowing all the while that St. Clair was being offered up as the sacrificial lamb of the day.

A day later, Al Haig, with whom I was having more contact, called me in and said, "I want you to go back to Washington as quickly as you can and set up an operation to monitor the hearings and provide a quick response." I returned to Washington the next day and set up the "War Room" on the first floor of the Executive Office Building. On the door we hung a sign that was intended to be the cover for the operation: "Office of Communications, Research Division." After Nixon's fall, I took the sign as a souvenir. We had carte blanche to do what had to be done, spend what we had to, get what people we needed. This was to be a rehearsal for the way we would handle the floor debate on impeachment in the House. We were going to test it during the House Judiciary Committee hearings. We would have a press guy, a lawyer, and a speechwriter sit in this room. I explained to Jack McCahill, the lawyer, and Ken Khachigian, the writer, "We will monitor the hearings, and then quickly draft responses as the hearings are taking place and phone them to one of our operatives on the Hill, who will give our response to friends of ours on the committee." The committee member could then challenge his colleagues, based on our background provided on short notice.

Our setup was elaborate. Inside our office, we had three television sets, two radios, and a table. McCahill knew the legalities, and he would say, "That's wrong. Khachigian, go to page 123 of Dean's testimony and you can see." Khachigian would write a response, and then I would polish it up and phone it up to the Hill. But the rules of the committee put us at a tremendous disadvantage. A member of the committee could only question for a few minutes at a time. So if a Democratic congressman made a point and we felt it was wrong, by the time we developed a response the questioning had gone from the Democrat to a Republican, and back to another Democrat, and there was no chance to get our response in. That taught us that we would have to streamline our operation before they began impeachment proceedings on the House floor.

St. Clair stayed in San Clemente for several days after I returned to Washington on July 23, and by the time he came back, he had seen the handwriting on the wall. During his meetings with Nixon, the President at times was irrational, especially on the subject of giving up his tapes, and St. Clair realized that he had a losing cause on his hands. On Friday, July 26, the day St. Clair returned from San Clemente, he and McCahill and I were walking into the federal courthouse for a hearing before Judge John Sirica when Sam Donaldson approached St. Clair and reminded him that he was to appear on ABC's "Issues and Answers" that Sunday. "No way,"

St. Clair barked. I was stunned, since St. Clair had never even mentioned to me, his press guy, that he had decided not to go on the show, but at that point St. Clair had not told me what had happened in San Clemente. However, I read the signs that he had seen Nixon at his worst and didn't like what he saw.

In the next two weeks before Nixon resigned, St. Clair spoke to me several times about quitting himself, feeling that his client had betrayed him by not telling him the truth. From our office in the Executive Office Building next door to the White House we could look over and almost see the Oval Office, but that was about as close as St. Clair was getting to Nixon, and St. Clair was furious that Nixon had both been untruthful with him and cut off his access. Clawson sized it up: "Jim St. Clair has seen the devil and he is us."

Looking ahead to the Senate impeachment trial, I had been after Haig to visit with Eastland, knowing that my old boss would be the last one to abandon ship. Eastland had even told Nixon in June, "I don't care if you're guilty or innocent, I'll vote for you." Not that he thought Nixon was right. But Eastland did believe in the constitutional principle of Executive privilege. The President ought to have the right to receive advice without anybody listening or interfering or overhearing what it was. Eastland told me several times that if he had been the President he would have asked to come up and address the Senate Watergate Committee and would have simply said, "Mr. Chairman, last night I destroyed the tapes."

Haig finally agreed to call on Eastland, and I was told to arrange the appointment. I did, and I also drew up some advice for Haig. The first point was, "Be careful what you drink. If he offers you a drink, he's going to take a small glass and you will have a large one, and yours will be about ninety percent Chivas Regal and his will be about fifty percent Chivas Regal."

On July 31, the day Haig was supposed to go to see Eastland, he kept setting the meeting time back. Haig was at the State Department talking to Henry Kissinger for an hour, then back to confer with Nixon in the President's hideaway in the Executive Office Building. I was left cooling my heels, puzzled, but unaware of what caused the delay. Haig and I finally pulled out of the White House gate at five o'clock. It was not until the following Monday, August 5, that I learned what had happened. The "smoking gun" tape from June 23, 1972, six days after the break-in, had been discovered by White House lawyers painstakingly listening to the tapes. On June 23, Nixon and Haldeman had had discussions in which Nixon admitted he had known about and approved, possibly even instigated, the cover-up from the start. This tape was crucial, because it contradicted Nixon's repeated claims that he had known nothing about the cover-up until John Dean informed him on March 21, 1973.

Most of us mid-level White House staffers did not learn about the "smoking gun" tape until just three days before Nixon announced his resignation. The transcripts of that tape hit me like a ton of bricks; that was one of two or three times in my life where I was handed something of such high drama or awesome importance that I was unable to comprehend it. The words just jumbled and blurred before my eyes, and I couldn't put them in context. On Monday night, August 5, several of us met in the Roosevelt Room to discuss the situation, including Major George Joulwan, one of Haig's aides; White House speechwriters David Gergen and Ken Khachigian; and Cabinet secretary Jerry Jones. Jones, a Nixon loyalist, felt betrayed and made a rather violent speech to us that night in which he declared, "We all ought to resign. We ought to walk out of here en masse." I felt that that really was not an option for me, a firm believer in political loyalty to one's boss. Yet I was neither a Nixon apologist nor a believer, and for me there was no issue of principle involved.

As Nixon prepared to resign, the atmosphere in Washington was a circus, a lynch mob, a near riot, a political convention, and a celebration, all in one. Tremendous crowds surrounded the White House. Across the street Lafayette Park was full. People were shouting and car horns were blaring in response to signs saying, "Honk if you think he's guilty."

About six o'clock on August 8, 1974, the night Nixon announced his resignation, I was on my way from the OEOB over to the White House when a uniformed White House guard closed and locked the gate. At the same time the doors were being locked to the press room and other offices, and no one in the entire White House complex was allowed to move. Nixon had decided to take a last walk. Here was this lone man walking through the White House complex. The press went absolutely berserk at being locked in the press room. They were banging on the doors, shouting, furious, undoubtedly suspecting that Nixon was taking a last walk around the grounds.

After Nixon announced his resignation, there was a real letdown. Clawson's staff had opened the stash of wine from the White House mess. Most of them sat around the OEOB office in silence with glasses of wine in their hands. Down the marble corridor, St. Clair's team had broken the seal on the hard stuff, and an air of boozy frivolity reigned. There was a stark contrast between the two ends of the hall. I thought about Nixon, just across the narrow street on the second floor of the White House— alone, disgraced, the first to resign the highest office in the land.

Around midnight I left to walk to my car, which was parked on the Ellipse, over toward the Washington Monument. Here I was, a lone figure walking out the southwest gate of the White House and through this jubilant mob. I never felt so alone, so dejected, so down. I never had a feeling like that, before or since. I was thinking, "If one of these people asked me who I was or who I worked for, what would I say?" I think in the midst of a mob like that I wouldn't have said that I worked for Nixon.

The next day, when Nixon took his leave, I was there, sitting about three rows behind Haig. I've been to many a southern funeral, and this was much more depressing. Some members of the staff, like Khachigian, were even more broken up than mourners at funerals. The victim had died, but the body was still alive and up there on the podium talking.

Back in the office of the special counsel to the President, St. Clair prepared to make his own departure. He knew where he was going—back to his $300,000-a-year practice in Boston—but many of the young lawyers on his staff would soon be out on the street. St. Clair called them together that last day and told them, "Fellas, I'm sorry, but you're off the payroll as of Monday," which was three days later. Then, I'll never forget, as St. Clair started out the door, he turned back to his young legal staff and added, "By the way, no books. Everything we've done here is privileged attorney-client material, and if any of you try to write a book, I'll have your law license!"

After Nixon resigned, a court placed under seal his personal retreat, an office in the Old Executive Office Building. Nothing could be removed from it. His lawyers finally won a court ruling that he was entitled to his personal possessions, and a month or so after he resigned, I accompanied his secretary, Rose Mary Woods, into his hideaway. Also with us were one of Nixon's lawyers; a Justice Department attorney; and a representative of the Secret Service, which had control over the office.

You've heard stories about the old lady whose husband died and she left his room exactly as it was. That's the way Nixon's office was. It was exactly as it had been on the night of August 8, 1974, when he was last there. We walked in. The shades were pulled and the room had an eerie feeling as if he had been there only moments before and might return at any moment. It was like a tomb. For some reason, the wedding dress that one of his daughters had worn was hanging in the closet. Nixon's horn-rimmed eyeglasses were on the table adjacent to his chair, along with a book he had been reading; it wasn't widely known that Nixon wore glasses, but he did. On the coffee table were pictures of the happy days with Julie,

Tricia, and Pat. Rose Woods removed some of his belongings, and we left, almost afraid to disturb anything.

The five months I worked for Nixon brought home to me the dilemma that every public affairs person in government faces sooner or later: Are you a hired gun, serving the interests of the government official who employs you, or are you a public servant in the true sense of the word, serving the interests of the people?

I greatly admired Nixon as a peerless political theorist. He forged the southern strategy that won him the presidency in 1968 and an overwhelming, if tainted, mandate in 1972. Moreover, his approach to U.S.-Soviet relations was nothing short of brilliant, producing arms control agreements and new understandings between the superpowers. His overture to China was another master stroke, opening up a vast new frontier in U.S. foreign relations and creating an important new element in our dealings with the Soviets.

On the other hand, he had a fatal flaw, the street fighter's hair-trigger overreaction, the below-the-belt instinct that caused him to lash out at his enemies when confronted with the Watergate burglary, instead of admitting his error and apologizing, which almost certainly would have gotten him off the hook.

As a public relations man, you forge a lawyer-like relationship with your client. You are sworn to defend your client to the utmost of your professional abilities. But a public relations man, like an attorney, must be free to pick and choose the clients and the causes he believes in.

On August 9, 1974, as Nixon stood in the doorway of the presidential helicopter, and, for the last time, raised both hands in his famous V-for-victory gesture, I, Larry Speakes, made a vow: I would never again take a client unless I believed wholeheartedly in him.

5

With Gerald Ford

Richard Nixon was out. Gerald Ford was in. Where did that leave Larry Speakes?

In, fortunately. Jerry terHorst, a reporter from Michigan who had covered Ford since his earliest days in Congress and had written a book about him, was named press secretary. TerHorst asked me to stay on and become an assistant press secretary, and I gladly accepted. This time there would be a little security in the job. Ford was not facing impeachment and would be in office a minimum of thirty months, plus another four years if he ran for election and won.

Soon after Ford became President, I made my first flight on Air Force One. We had a trip to Chicago. I grabbed every matchbook, napkin, pencil, and piece of presidential stationery I could get my hands on without being too obvious. Once again, I had this feeling that I had really arrived, and I was literally flying high.

The first thirty days Ford was in office we worked every day, including Saturdays and Sundays, without a day off. Everyone who worked for him was really wiped out. Finally, I got a Saturday off. That was another date I'll never forget: September 7, 1974. I was at home in mid-afternoon when the phone rang and Tom DeCair, another assistant press secretary, called and told me to come in about seven o'clock Sunday morning. He said, "We're going to have an announcement, but I can't tell you what it is now."

My job was to supervise the duplicating of a document and a statement that Ford was issuing, and to guard them with my life to make sure no one saw them before the time was right. Generally, nothing happens on a weekend and to have a Sunday morning press call-out, where you're phoning key reporters all over Washington and telling them to come to the White House, was very unusual. When we called and told them Ford was going to make an announcement, their immediate response was, "Well, what is it?" "I'm sorry, I can't tell you." "Is it foreign or domestic?" "I'm sorry, I can't tell you." "Well, can you give me any hint?" "No, I can't."

The press started trickling in and the reporters were handed a sheet of paper that simply said that the President of the United States would make an announcement later that day and that it would be available for live radio and television coverage. Nobody in the press corps knew whether it was another Pearl Harbor, a foreign trip, if the President was ill, or what.

Nobody had even come close to guessing what it was. We gathered a press pool in the Oval Office, and, thirty seconds before the President walked in, Helen Thomas of UPI said, "I've got it, he's going to pardon Nixon." That's where instinct, experience, smell, touch, feel paid off for her. That was the first of many times I witnessed her do that. Probably the look on my face acknowledged that she was correct, but I did not verbally confirm it.

After Ford finished announcing the pardon, my boss, Jerry terHorst, invited several of us up to his office. We'd gone without lunch, so we ordered some sandwiches from the White House mess. We were sitting around this conference table in the corner that was still there when it was my office years later. We discussed the announcement, analyzing how we did, how it had gone. As we finished eating, terHorst pushed back from the table and said, "Fellows, there's something I want to show you." He reached in his pocket—he was a lovable guy, but sort of a fumbler and a bumbler, and he had trouble finding what he was reaching for—and finally he pulled out a piece of onionskin paper, not the photocopy that everyone was using by then, and he handed it to me to read first. I read it uncomprehendingly, thinking to myself, "What's he doing? I don't quite understand." It was his resignation. I handed it to Jack Hushen, the deputy press secretary, and Jack said, "Jerry, you can't do this"—Jack knowing full well that he had a good shot at being the successor. And I said, "Jerry, I wish you wouldn't do this." But he said, "Fellows, I was misled. I'm going to clean my desk out and fade away. You fellows have a trip tomorrow, and I'll just be gone when you get back. My resignation will be announced." He added, "I gave the President this an hour ago, and he accepted it."

I loved Jerry and I respected him, but I think what he did was wrong. Ford had picked him to be press secretary because he was a friend. And now, in Ford's most difficult moment, terHorst was abandoning him and making a public show of his disagreement with Ford's decision to pardon Nixon.

Moreover, terHorst said he wasn't going to give any interviews, but he quickly turned up on the morning talk shows, and he granted interviews to a number of reporters. I always felt that Jerry let Ford down, not so much by resigning if he felt he had to do that over a matter of principle, but by going out and talking about it. My feeling was if you felt you had been done terribly wrong, you kept your mouth shut and left in your own good time, but you never torpedoed the President.

Ford, of course, was extensively criticized for pardoning Nixon, and his popularity fell like a rock. There's no question that the pardon was a tremendous handicap when Ford ran in 1976. But you have to look at the pardon from Ford's perspective: As he said to me many times, "My first job here is to bring the nation back together." He was spending fifty percent of his time, day after day after day, on what he called "the Nixon thing." He said, "Everytime I looked up, somebody would come into the Oval Office with a Nixon question. I finally just decided the time has come to put this behind us, and we must clean the slate."

Ford did what he thought was right for the country, not what he thought was politically right for himself. I always felt that Ford acted with great courage in putting the good of the nation ahead of his own political interests.

TerHorst's successor was Ron Nessen, and he kept me on as assistant press secretary. He jealously guarded his own power, however, and seldom delegated anything of importance. I would often get such assignments as dealing with the inevitable crank callers to the White House. One man from West Virginia called every afternoon at five o'clock. Finally, Janice Barbieri, who worked in the press office, and I decided to rid ourselves of this pest. We told him that by mistake he had reached Buckingham Palace instead of the White House. "You're talking to Queen Elizabeth and Prince Philip," I said. Before long he sent a telegram to the queen and prince in care of the White House press office, with a message that read, "Let them eat cake." But he never called again. On slow days, we'd miss him. But not much.

Relegated to the background as I was, I welcomed any chance to step into the limelight. One occurred in May 1975 when an American merchant ship, the *Mayaguez,* was seized by the Cambodian navy in the Gulf of Siam, held for two days, and then released. I made an early morning announcement to the press during the crisis, but it fell a little short of my expectations when Tom Brokaw, then NBC's White House correspondent, told a waiting nation that "White House *speaks* man Larry *Spokes* said today . . ." That was the first of many such tongue-twisters from the electronic media.

I genuinely admired Gerald Ford, and in spite of the often dull aspects of working under Nessen, I welcomed the opportunity to be a part of the Ford administration. Like Reagan, Ford was saddled with an image of being not too bright. He was viewed as "once a congressman, always a congressman," rather than being of presidential stature. But I found Ford, by virtue of his congressional experience, to be extraordinarily well-prepared for the presidency. There was no issue that came before him as President that he had not previously dealt with in some way as a member of Congress.

Ford's halting manner of speaking contributed to the general impression that he was not smart, that he was unsure of himself. And of course all the tumbles and spills he took added to that. In reality, Ford was an agile athlete, an excellent golfer and skier, but the press was determined to make him look like a klutz. All this and Lyndon Johnson's famous comment that Ford "played too many football games without his helmet" branded him for life—unfortunately and unfairly.

Hubert Humphrey was the candidate whom Ford had most feared running against in 1976. When Jimmy Carter emerged as the Democratic nominee, we assumed that he would be an easy opponent. His lack of experience, lack of an organization, and lack of national contacts made us highly confident. When Carter picked Walter Mondale as his running mate, there was jubilation in the White House. We thought of Mondale as so dull and liberal that he would be a liability to the ticket, from the standpoint of personality and politics.

I had been chafing under Nessen, feeling that I was not contributing what I was capable of contributing. Not long before the 1976 GOP convention I was standing in the back at a Rose Garden ceremony, and I told Dick Cheney, who had become Ford's chief of staff, that I would like to do something different if the opportunity arose. He said, "Write me a note on that so I won't forget it." So I wrote him a very cryptic memo, saying simply, "Don't forget that thing we discussed in the Rose Garden." I thought nothing more about it until the convention in Kansas City, where Ford was nominated in that bruising delegate fight with Reagan that ended up with my Mississippians tipping the balance to Ford.

The morning after Ford was nominated, he selected Bob Dole as his Vice President. Within a few minutes after Dole's selection was announced, Ron Nessen urgently summoned me to the penthouse level of our hotel, where Ford and the senior staff were staying. Nessen asked if I was interested in being Dole's press secretary during the campaign. I immediately accepted.

Nessen took me into this hotel suite, past a few people in the living room and back into the bedroom, and there was Elizabeth Dole sitting on the bed, with Bob standing next to her. Nessen said, "I'd like you to meet Larry Speakes. He's going to be your press secretary." Dole said, "Fine." Dole later liked to say, "They brought a guy into my hotel room, introduced him as my new press secretary, Larry Speakes, and that's the last I ever heard from the White House." Which was just about true. Sometimes I felt that Dole and I were the mythical "Flying Dutchmen," as we trooped around the political backwaters of America with little or no direction from the White House.

Dole was assigned the job of following Carter around the country and rebutting what he had said everywhere, which helped earn him the hatchetman tag that stuck with him through the campaign and haunts him to this day. He did make a lot of cutting remarks, although more often than not, they were wrapped in his peculiar sense of humor. We were in Jackson, Mississippi, in October for him to address a Republican rally, and I didn't know it, the Secret Service didn't know it, but Dole sent an advance man to buy a hatchet and install it under the podium. Partway through the speech he said, "They're calling me the hatchetman—I'll show 'em what a hatchetman is." He reached under the podium, pulled out the hatchet, and waved it, which got pictures of him in papers all over the country.

The debate between Dole and Mondale on October 15 in Houston was the first time the vice-presidential nominees had been included in the debate format. We didn't particularly care to have it; Dole had not done well in debates in his 1974 senatorial campaign. His mean streak seemed to come through during debates. But we were stuck with the debate, and Dole was wound up tighter than a spring for it. I was worried that he wasn't properly prepared and that instead of projecting the right image he would come across as a wise guy, a mean guy, a shoot-from-the-hip guy.

We had learned from the Ford-Carter debates that he who claimed victory first was the winner. Following that adage, I set up post mortems right after the debate with ABC, CBS, and NBC. We had Elizabeth Dole, John Connally, and Vice President Rockefeller ready to go on T.V. As the debate ended they were to get out of their front-row seats, go straight to an assigned camera, beating the Mondale aides to the airwaves. Each one claimed debate victory for Dole on each of the three networks, so we had nine at-bats. Meanwhile, we had lined up live T.V. coverage of a phone call from President Ford to Dole in a nearby room. We had pulled off literally every P.R. gimmick one could put together to create the image of a victory in this debate; it was my first experience with what came to be known during the Reagan administration as the "Spin Patrol."

I had been so uptight myself about whether Dole would perform well in the debate that when I saw he was not mean-spirited, had used some humor, and had generally scored some respectable debate points, I concluded he had done well overall. The initial polls showed that we had gotten at least a wash, and I went to bed feeling relieved. But it quickly became clear that Dole's "Democratic war statement"—that World Wars I and II, Korea, and Vietnam were "all Democratic wars" that had started when the Democrats were in the White House or in control of Congress—had backfired. The press jumped on Dole for it, reporting that he had accused the Democrats of purposely starting wars, which was not what he had said. Mondale picked it up, too, and within twenty-four hours he was seen as the debate winner.

Early on, Dole and I visited Ronald Reagan at his home in Pacific Palisades. One of Dole's main missions was to reach out to the defeated Reagan forces, who were bitter and demoralized after narrowly losing the nomination to Ford. We hoped to persuade Reagan to campaign for Ford, because we needed solid support from the conservatives to defeat Jimmy Carter. Reagan himself greeted us at the door of his home and introduced us to Nancy, who quickly left us alone to discuss politics. This was my first meeting with the man for whom I would later work in the White House, and the outcome was disappointing. As we sat on the red couches that are now in the West Hall of the White House family quarters, Reagan turned the discussion quickly from the nitty-gritty of how to win the election, and launched into the stump speech he had given across the nation as he had sought the nomination. Dole and I tore ourselves away as quickly as we could. "Mission: failure," Dole observed tartly as we drove off.

Later, I accompanied Dole when he met with George Bush, then the director of the Central Intelligence Agency, for a briefing on U.S.-Soviet military strength. Dole didn't think much of what Bush had to say. "We could have read all that in *The New York Times,*" he quipped. A decade later, these two men would emerge as the leading contenders for the 1988 Republican nomination.

Dole's effectiveness as a campaigner was reduced at times by his stubbornness. Soon after Dole was chosen for the number-two slot on the ticket, *The New York Times* reported that when he was in the Senate he had accepted illegal campaign contributions from the Gulf Oil Corporation. Dole issued a denial, and the White House told me to make sure that he didn't talk about it any more, so that there would be no follow-up stories. But Dole insisted he had nothing to hide, and every time a reporter raised the Gulf issue, Dole would make an angry reply, which led to more and more stories. I finally told Nessen, "The only way I can shut him up is to tape his mouth shut."

Dole was innocent, but like anyone wrongly accused, he seized every opportunity to tell his side of the story forcibly. My goal was for him to tell the truth—tell it once, and then shut up. But Dole would not follow my advice. That experience taught me another lesson about politics: You can't score points as long as you are on the defense. It was true then, and just as true when we struggled under the yoke of the Iran controversy in the Reagan White House ten years later.

By mid-October, as the campaign pace peaked, Dole became hard to live with. He was indecisive; difficult to write speeches for, with speech-writers changing almost daily; and just generally temperamental. The schedulers lived in mortal fear of Dole, because they would work out a very intricate schedule for him and he would reject it. I was ready to say to him, "Senator, if you don't get on the ball, you're going to be making American Express commercials the rest of your life"—a reference to former congressman William E. Miller, who had been Barry Goldwater's running mate and slipped from political view after the 1964 election.

I was so disturbed about Dole and his inability to make a decision that I had asked for a meeting with Dick Cheney to tell him about some of the problems we were having on the campaign trail. I had deep concern, because I had seen Dole fail to respond well under pressure. In the long run, though, Dole profited from his 1976 experience, mellowing with the passage of time, becoming more able to roll with the political punches.

Nonetheless, in 1976 Dole's campaign posture became a moot point when Carter defeated Ford. It was a fairly close election; twenty-nine electoral votes in Ford's column would have won it for him, and there's no doubt in my mind that the pardon did him in. In retrospect, I never felt we had a chance to catch our breath. It was first the resignation, then the pardon, next the 1974 congressional campaign, in which Ford made many appearances on behalf of Republican candidates, and finally, the 1976 presidential campaign, which began almost immediately after the 1974 elections ended. We never had an opportunity to develop a sense of vision, or larger purpose. There was never a moment to think about the long term.

With Nixon's fall and Ford's defeat, I had had my fill of politics for a while. After the election, Dole asked me what I was going to do. I don't know if he intended to offer me a job on his Senate staff or what, but I told him, "I want to get out of politics. I'm tired of getting beat."

After Ford left office he asked me to stay on and handle press relations for him during his transition to private life. On June 1, 1977, I left the political arena after nine years, accepting a job as vice president in the Washington office of Hill & Knowlton, one of the nation's major public relations firms.

Any time Gerald Ford visited Washington during the next few years, I took time off from my job at Hill & Knowlton to do his press work. During one visit in the spring of 1980, he said he was being urged to run for the GOP presidential nomination, but he couldn't decide what to do. By then the New Hampshire primary was over, it was too late to enter Florida and some of the other primaries, and it was getting to be now-or-never time. We were on the eve of the filing deadline for the Ohio primary, one that Ford had to enter if he was going to compete seriously for the nomination.

Bob Barrett, who had been Ford's military aide in the White House and was now his chief of staff, was telling him, "You've got to make the race, Mr. President." I accompanied Ford when he dropped by the White House to pay a call on Jimmy Carter. Afterwards, Ford, Barrett and I were riding in the back of a limousine, with Ford squeezed in the center, me on his left and Barrett on the right. Barrett said, "You have got to sign these papers to get you on the ballot in Ohio." As we drove out of Carter's White House, I sat there holding the papers that would make Ford a challenger to Carter, and Ford signed them with that left hand of his. Before we got out of the car he said, "Now, I want it understood that I've signed these things only on the contingency that I *might* decide to do this." Turning to me, he said, "If I do run, I'm counting on you," and I told him I would be delighted to work for him again.

That weekend Barrett called me from Ford's residence at Palm Springs and said it looked like Ford was going to run. He asked me to come to Palm Springs the following day to make final plans for an announcement. I decided that if I was getting into another campaign, I would do it right. I went out and bought a tape recorder and a new suitcase and started packing. I was to take a five o'clock flight on Saturday afternoon to Palm Springs, and I was practically out my door and on my way to the airport when the phone rang. It was Barrett, saying, "Ford has changed his mind. It's over." By then I had my heart set on returning to the White House, this time as press secretary, and I was really disappointed, but Ford had made up his mind—at least for the time being.

It finally came time for the convention in Detroit. Ford was going to be there—amid rumors of a "dream ticket" of Reagan for President and Ford for Vice President, and I went out to handle Ford's press. Ford arrived at the airport and got into a limousine, with me in a follow-up car. His limousine started up, went a few feet, and stopped. Ford got out and went to one of the other cars. His limousine had had a flat tire, a bad omen right at the start.

Arriving at his hotel, Ford went right into an interview with *Time* magazine, in which he was lukewarm to the idea of joining the Reagan ticket. Later on at a luncheon hosted by *Newsweek* he did express some interest, throwing out the idea that "Reagan could be the chief executive and I could be the chief operating officer," as he characterized his plan. That did it. Detroit was ablaze with speculation about a Reagan-Ford ticket.

Before the convention got under way that night, Ford went over to the convention hall early for a live interview over CBS with Walter Cronkite. Cronkite was interviewing him in his booth, with Bob Barrett and me standing in the back. Cronkite talked up the dream ticket and Ford responded with apparent enthusiasm, but he started setting some very stiff conditions, such as the right to direct the White House staff. As Ford listed more and more demands, Barrett, who knew him very well, nudged me and whispered, "He's backing out." "What do you mean?" I said. And Barrett explained, "One thing I've learned about him, when he wants to back out of something he begins to set the conditions too high. That's what he's doing now."

While the Cronkite interview continued, someone came in and told me that Barbara Walters was waiting outside the booth and wanted to interview Ford on ABC. "We can't do that," I said. "We've promised Cronkite an exclusive." I slipped out of the booth to the walkway. There was Barbara, practically in tears. I told her, "Barbara, I'm sorry, but we can't do it. We're obligated here and we don't have time anyway." She just said, "Please, please, please," almost beating on my chest; I've never had anybody act like that. I went back into the booth, where Ford was saying his good-byes and told him, "Now, Barbara Walters is out there, she's going to ask you to do an interview, and I don't think you ought to do it." He opened the door and there she was, right at the door. As he tried to walk away she just clung to him, saying, "I've got to have an interview, my whole career rides on this." And Ford, kind soul that he was, never demurred: "Sure, I'll do it."

When we got back to Ford's suite the phones were ringing off the hook. All the reporters thought Ford was indicating he would accept the number-two slot on the ticket, and I was taking all the calls and telling them, "Hold up, it's not a done deal." But most of them went with the story anyway.

Ford talked to Henry Kissinger, economist Alan Greenspan, and several others, and after a while he decided once and for all that the "dream ticket" was not for him. It fell as my duty to be the advance man and go to Reagan's suite. I didn't know him or any of his people, and none of them knew me. A Reagan aide named Lanny Wiles was guarding the door. He was a short, roly-poly guy with a thick southern accent. We hit it off right away, and later worked together in the Reagan White House. That night I told Lanny, "The President wants to come by and talk to Governor Reagan." Lanny said, "I understand that. Bring him right through this door and the two of them will meet in here." So I went back and escorted Ford to Reagan's room. He told Reagan, "Ron, I've soul-searched this, and it's not right for me or for you. It wouldn't work." And that was that.

A few months later I ran into Doug Kiker of NBC. He practically hugged me, and he said, "Back at the convention in Detroit, you saved my career. You saved my life." (These T.V. people really take conventions seriously.) I asked him what he meant, and he explained. "That night I was assigned to cover Reagan at the hotel. I was operating from a phone booth in the lobby. Every time I called you, you told me not to go with the Reagan-Ford story, and I told [NBC anchor] John Chancellor not to go with it. We were the only ones to hold back. The other two networks said Reagan and Ford had made a deal. I was sweating because I had steered Chancellor off of it, but you gave me the straight scoop." Kiker said that Chancellor later invited him to dinner at his home in New York, which was highly unusual, and during the evening he gave Kiker a silver cigarette case engraved with the date of the night Ford had turned down Reagan.

What had happened that night had made *someone*, at least, happy. But for me it was not the road back to the White House.

6

Finding My Way

to Ronald Reagan

George Bush. Jack Kemp. Alexander Haig. I thought about signing on with each one of them for the 1980 campaign.

The public relations business was neither as interesting nor as much fun as I had expected it to be. Within six months after I had gone to work for Hill & Knowlton I was figuring out how to get involved in the 1980 presidential election.

In early 1978 I had lunch with Grace-Marie Arnett, a reporter for Copley News Service who had worked for us in Ford's New Hampshire campaign in 1976. "I'd like to be press secretary to the President of the United States," I told her. "I haven't had enough." Grace-Marie asked me how I was going to go about it, and I answered, "I don't know, but I'm going to do it."

My first approach was to Bush. I admired him and he appeared to have a great shot at the nomination. I wrote Bush a letter and told him how much I liked him and would enjoy working for him. He wrote back and said he would like to include me in the group that was planning strategy with him. Then I heard that he and his inner circle had held several meetings in Washington without inviting me, so I said to myself, "So much for that."

Next up was Jack Kemp. I met with Kemp; one of his top aides, Jeffrey Bell; and Jude Wanniski, who was close to Kemp and had been a friend of mine since the days I worked for Senator Eastland and Jude wrote about him for the *National Journal.* I liked Kemp and went with him when he was on "Face the Nation" one Sunday. He was too "hot" for television, too much of a shoot-from-the-hip guy, too quick with every answer. I counseled Jack after the show, "It's no sin to pause after you get the question and appear to be thoughtful." He was then, and is now, a candidate with a base limited to the conservative wing of the party. I felt he had almost no chance of getting to the White House, and I decided to keep looking.

Then I met with Al Haig. I thought seriously about signing on with him because it would have been just him, me, and another aide; I would really have been getting in on the ground floor. Plus, I was really impressed by Haig and his commanding presence. I called Bill Timmons, a longtime Republican activist, and asked him what he thought. Timmons's reply was, "You can do that if you want, but I'll tell you one thing"—he used these very words—"Al Haig ain't going to be President." So I said to myself, "I'm not going to go off and tilt at that windmill."

Toward the end of 1979 it looked like I might even catch on with Reagan. Jim Lake, his campaign press secretary, was an old friend to whom I had directed some work while I was at Hill & Knowlton and he was a Washington lobbyist. He called me and asked, "How would you like to work with me in the Reagan campaign?" "Gosh," I answered, "that really appeals to me, particularly working with you." Lake said we should keep in touch and that he might need me in about a month, to travel with Reagan and handle press for him on the road while Lake supervised things from headquarters in Washington.

In early January, though, Lake called again and said the campaign had budget problems and he couldn't bring me on at a decent salary. That turned out just as well for me, because after the New Hampshire primary they had the massacre within the Reagan campaign. Mike Deaver won out over John Sears and his group, and Lake was among those thrown out of the campaign. If I had been brought aboard by Lake, I would have been out, too.

After the convention in Detroit, I was certain that I would still be out in the cold after Campaign '80. The Reagan campaign was in full swing, and, although I had become more and more impressed with Reagan as the race wore on, I was across town, still at Hill & Knowlton, a million miles away from the action.

Once the election was over in November, I tried to find some way to hook up with Reagan. I spoke to another old friend, Bill Greener, Jr., who had worked with me in the Ford White House and was still plugged in to Republican politics. He said I should call Jim Brady, whom he called "the East Coast distributor." That meant that Brady ran the press operation in Washington, while Lyn Nofziger, a longtime Reagan insider, ran the California end of it. But I couldn't get through to Brady. The lines were always busy. The transition headquarters was the biggest zoo you've ever seen. One day a person I knew named Meg Duke, who had worked for the lawyers in the Nixon and Ford White House, called and said, "I need your help. I'm working at the transition headquarters and we've got so many press calls we need someone to tell us who to call back."

I went over there the next afternoon and helped get Meg and press relations back on track. While I was there, I went by and said hello to Brady. I had known him for five years or so, since I worked for Ford and Brady was at the Office of Management and Budget. In 1979, when Brady was leaving his job as press secretary to Senator William Roth of Delaware to join the presidential campaign of John Connally, he and Dennis Thomas, then Roth's administrative assistant and later an aide to Don Regan in the Reagan White House, approached me about replacing him at Roth's office. Now I went in and I said, "You need any help?" Brady said, "We start at seven in the morning, can you be here?" I went back to Hill & Knowlton walking on air.

Initially, I was spending a few hours a day at both Hill & Knowlton and the transition office, and I more or less fell into the role of Brady's deputy. He had this long conference table and from one end to the other about eighteen inches high was this pile of résumés from people who wanted jobs in the new administration. Brady was never the most organized person in the world, and the place was just not functioning. Phone calls would come in and be placed on hold until they died on the vine. All I could do was try to help straighten things out.

We were buffeted with rumors of who the press secretary would be. Brady wanted to be the press secretary, but Lyn Nofziger was thought to have the inside track. That was bad news for me, because of the bad blood that had developed between Nofziger and me during the Reagan-Ford battle in 1976. I was always wary of him because I felt he held the Ford connection against me, and there was lingering bitterness between the two sides.

But Nancy Reagan finally put her foot down and ruled that Nofziger would not be the White House press secretary. It was one thing when Reagan was only a governor, but now that he was going to be President, Nofziger did not fit her image of what a press spokesman should be. He was rambunctious, profane, and rumpled, almost always wearing a Mickey Mouse tie pulled way down and with the top button of his shirt open. The story was that she wanted someone young and handsome. Later on she started kidding Brady, especially after he got shot, by calling him "Y and H," for young and handsome, just as Reagan was known within the White House as "O and W," the oldest and wisest.

Even with Nofziger out of the running, Brady was no cinch for the job. Finally, shortly after the first of the year, we got the word—from a news reporter, of all places. Jerry O'Leary from the *Washington Star* was a friend of Nancy Reynolds, who was close to the Reagans, and, just three weeks before the inauguration, O'Leary called Brady and said, "I'm not going to write this yet, but you've got it."

Reagan had scheduled a meeting with Mexican President José Lopez Portillo in El Paso to get our south-of-the-border relations off to a good start. Brady and I flew out with the press from Washington to be on hand for the meeting. During the flight Brady leaned over to me in the seat next to him and said, "I want you to be my deputy." In El Paso, I met Mike Deaver, who said, "I heard you were on board. Welcome." "My God," I thought to myself, "I'm really on my way back to the White House."

We obviously had a lot to do, and a short time to do it. I drew a sketch of the White House press office and even listed who would take which office. I was Brady's detail man, his manager. I figured out the description of each job, and who would hold it. Brady never thought about details. People like Jim Baker, who was going to be chief of staff, kept telling him to "get your staff structure together, tell us who you want, who does what, give us a plan." Brady kept saying, "Just wait, I'll get to it," but time was running out, so I took it over.

Another problem for Brady and me was Karna Small, who was dumped in our laps as a deputy press secretary. Karna had known the Reaganites since she was a T.V. weather girl in California years earlier. There was apparently a thought that a visible woman was important, and what more visible woman than a ranking one in the press office? Brady had no choice. She was just handed to him by Mike Deaver.

The day before the inauguration Karna asked me, "Where is the inauguration held, at the White House or the Capitol?" I thought to myself, "Uh-oh, we've got trouble here." My son Jeremy was ten at the time, and I went home and asked him, "Jeremy, where is the inauguration held?" He looked at me like I was crazy, and said, "At the Capitol, of course."

Brady and Karna had been announced in their jobs with a grand show on the steps of Blair House, with the President-elect doing the honors, but I had never been officially anointed. Finally, on January 19, 1981, the day before Reagan took office, it fell to me to read a statement to the press: "The President-elect today announced that he will appoint Larry Speakes to be deputy press secretary to the President." Somebody said that not since Napoleon had crowned himself emperor had someone been able to announce himself.

That day Brady took me across Lafayette Park to Blair House and I met Reagan for the first time since the 1976 campaign. Brady introduced me, saying, "I'd like you to meet my new deputy, Larry Speakes. I hope you'll treat him just like you treat me." And Reagan said, "I'll treat him better than I'll treat you."

Among my transition duties was to help prepare Al Haig for his confirmation hearings for Secretary of State. His were clearly going to be the most controversial, because of his role as chief of staff in the Nixon White House. One day a group of us were in a conference room waiting for Haig when the door sprang open and practically slammed back against the wall and in walked two of Haig's people—John Lehman, wearing an ascot, and Richard Perle. The two of them announced, "Gentlemen, General Haig." And Haig strode in, ever the commander-in-chief. He pounded the table and shouted, "All right, we're going to go up on the Hill and win this thing. We're going to show those sons of bitches how the game is played." That was General Haig.

During the transition I also got a call from a reporter inquiring about Raymond Donovan, Reagan's choice to be secretary of labor. The caller said, "This guy Donovan is trouble. He has some unsavory connections." I went to Fred Fielding, who was counsel to Reagan. Fielding had heard similar rumors but had reviewed Donovan's FBI file and found no hint of the trouble that was to hit us four years later, in the heat of the '84 election campaign, when Donovan and several others were indicted in New York, accused of stealing $7 million on a New York subway project during his days in the construction business. He was forced to resign from the Cabinet in 1985, but was acquitted a year later.

Before Reagan took office, transition director Ed Meese met with all the Cabinet members and talked to them like schoolchildren: "You are the cream of the crop. We believe you're the best." Then I gave them my own pep talk: "I don't want you to talk to the press until you are confirmed by the Senate," and we sent them out to meet the press and say nothing.

We introduced the new Cabinet to the press with great fanfare in the ballroom of Washington's Mayflower Hotel. Brady and I felt that Reagan himself should make the announcement, with the Cabinet members on stage. But Reagan was in California, and we had to do it ourselves. "This is ridiculous," I said to Jim. "After all, it's *his* Cabinet." Jim just rolled his eyes. This was to be our pattern throughout the Reagan presidency. A big announcement, no President, so *heeeere's* the press secretary.

Mark Weinberg, an aide on our press team who was all of twenty-three years old, wrote out the Cabinet announcement. Brady, Weinberg, and I got on the phone and read it to the President-elect in California. "Fine with me," he said. I told Weinberg, "This will be the easiest approval you'll ever get for a presidential statement. After we get to the White House, there'll be a lot of cooks in the kitchen."

As the time approached for the Reagan team to move into the White House, I remembered from my own experience with Ford when we left in 1977 and the Carter crew came in what a rude shock it was, leaving and not knowing what you were going to do. With Jim Brady occupied by other business, I was the one who had to inform the press three days before Reagan took office that more than two dozen accountants, secretaries, mail openers, and others in low-level White House jobs were being fired. Most of those employees had been hired under Jimmy Carter to replace staffers from the Ford days, and I pointedly remarked, "We're striving to treat the employees of the Carter administration with the same dignity and courtesy that President Carter accorded the staff of President Ford in 1977."

To add to the chaos of moving into the White House, there was the Iranian hostage situation, which was coming to a head on January 20, 1981, at the moment Reagan was sworn in as President. The fifty-two Americans who had been seized at the U.S. Embassy in Teheran in 1979 had now been captives for 444 days. They were on the runway at Teheran, but they hadn't been allowed to take off.

We would take over from the Carter people precisely at noon, and about eleven I set out for the White House, along with Karna Small, Mark Weinberg, and Kim Hoggard of our press team, and two hundred copies of Reagan's Inaugural Address. But by then it was so late that most of the streets in downtown Washington had been blocked off for the inaugural parade. I showed the police my identification and told them, "I'm Larry Speakes, Reagan press office." Through a half dozen checkpoints, the response was always the same: "I'm sorry, I can't let you through." As we maneuvered through the streets of downtown Washington, we were getting farther away from the White House, not closer. By about eleven-thirty I was near the Lincoln Memorial and I saw a U.S. Park Policeman on a motorcycle and told him my story. Pay dirt. "Follow me," he said. He had his sirens blaring, the whole works, and we went flying behind him, right to the Ellipse across from the White House. We had to park near the Washington Monument, run across the Ellipse with the boxes of speeches, and as we got to the White House gate, the guard said, "Where have you been? They want you in the press office. Get up there right away."

Jody Powell had gone up to the Capitol with Carter, and Brady was on the inaugural platform with Reagan. Rex Granum, Jody's assistant, and an aide from the White House Situation Room, who was monitoring events in Teheran, briefed me. The Carter and Reagan teams had agreed that none of us would say anything until the hostages cleared Iranian airspace. About twenty reporters had gathered in Rex's office, and they were firing questions at me about the hostages. I looked at the clock on the wall and it was ten till twelve. I said, "It's still Rex's watch." Rex told them what he could, which was nothing. Ten minutes later I gave the first, and perhaps least informative, of my dozens of White House briefings on Iran. At this first briefing my response to all questions was, "I'm sorry, we can't answer that at this time."

And with that, the Reagan years began.

7

All of

President Reagan's Men

If you worked for Ronald Reagan, you had better be good at your job. Reagan's operating style, delegating many of his oversight duties to his subordinates, gave his aides more power, for better or worse, than they would have had under any other President in memory. Some of Reagan's appointees—like Don Regan, George Shultz, and Jim Baker—were superb. But too many, such as Ed Meese, Caspar Weinberger, and Jim Watt, were ill-advised choices who caused problems for the President and his administration.

From the day he became President—for that matter, going back to his two terms as governor of California—Reagan consistently expressed his philosophy of governing by saying, "The Cabinet is like a board of directors and I'm the chief executive officer, except that I'm the only one who has a vote at the end."

Reagan really did have little interest in details, whether they concerned arms control or who was using the White House tennis court (which was an issue of some importance to Jimmy Carter). Nor did he choose to involve himself in many points of substance on a day-to-day basis. However, until the Iranian crisis of 1986, his style of management did work reasonably well, producing a string of legislative victories on tax and spending cuts that put the Reagan Revolution into motion.

Who were the key players, and what were they like?

*   *   *

During Reagan's first term, the innermost circle consisted of a troika: White House chief of staff James Baker; presidential counselor Edwin Meese; and deputy chief of staff Michael Deaver, who functioned as a personal aide to Reagan and his wife.

After the troika was replaced by one man, Don Regan, in early 1985, Regan, the new chief of staff, was often referred to as "the Prime Minister." But Meese was actually the first prime minister, a role of virtually absolute authority he had carved out for himself during the transition. I saw what Meese was up to during the weeks before Reagan's inauguration and warned Baker. My acquaintance with Baker went back to my years with Gerald Ford; I did not know Meese at all; and I certainly felt sympathetic to Baker as I saw the brewing infighting that was to dominate the first years of the Reagan administration. Baker appreciated my concern, but he didn't seem too worried himself, and, as it turned out, his self-confidence was borne out.

Meese and Baker actually had worked out a carefully worded written agreement that defined what duties each would have and even which office. From there, it was each man for himself. Baker eventually won out in part because Mike Deaver sided with him. Deaver had worked with Meese when Reagan was governor of California, and was familiar with Meese's shortcomings—his propensity for manipulating the President along dogmatic ideological lines and his lack of organizational skills. The joke in the White House during the first term was that once Meese put a document in his briefcase it was gone forever. Whenever something was missing, people used to say, "Where is such and such?" And the answer always was, "Probably in Meese's briefcase." So Deaver engineered Baker's emergence as first among equals, suggesting it to the President and Mrs. Reagan, who relied heavily on him for advice.

Deaver, meanwhile, carved out for himself the role of control of the President's body—the personal role, the scheduling of the President. As a confidant of the First Lady, he was destined to spend hours on the phone with her. He sometimes talked to her as many as a dozen times a day, as she checked and rechecked the most minute details.

In my view, Mike Deaver got more credit for being a public relations genius than he deserved. He wasn't so much a brilliant public relations practitioner as he was a genius at knowing instinctively which stories and events would present Reagan at his best. When we talked about going to London for the economic summit in 1984 and knew we would be in Europe on the fortieth anniversary of D-Day, Mike instantly grasped how dramatic it would be to have Reagan go to Normandy and make a speech at Pointe du Hoc, one of the landing sites, with the old Rangers who had invaded the French coast on June 6, 1944, standing around him. It turned out to be one of Reagan's best news events.

One Deaver idea that didn't turn out so well was President Reagan's 1985 visit to the cemetery in Bitburg, where Nazi soldiers from World War II were buried. Deaver had toured the cemetery while doing advance work for this trip. On the first draft of the President's schedule, which included the visit to a German army cemetery, I red-flagged it immediately. On every trip we had made to Europe, the press had always raised the question, will the President visit a concentration camp? The President did not want to visit a concentration camp, mainly because of his own personal feelings about it; he did not want to be reminded of the horror of it all. He meant no disrespect toward those who had died during the Holocaust. It was simply that if you had a choice of places to go, a concentration camp to him was too horrible even to be reminded of.

I told Deaver we were going to run into trouble if this was a German military cemetery since we hadn't been to a concentration camp. His response was, "No, no, the whole theme of this trip is reconciliation." So I let the point pass. But as soon as we announced it to the press, they seized on it, which Deaver should have anticipated.

Deaver also functioned as the conscience of the White House. I was quite surprised when Deaver got into trouble less than a year after he left the White House. He was accused of lying to Congress and to a federal grand jury over allegations that he improperly lobbied Reagan aides after he set up a Washington public relations business in 1985, and was eventually convicted of three counts of perjury in December 1987. Looking back, I guess one tipoff was that he really enjoyed the trappings of power. His office contained dozens of photographs, framed in silver, of Deaver with kings, queens, and prime ministers, many of whom he had prevailed on for autographs. There was a lot of the small-town kid from Bakersfield, California, in him, and I suppose he just got carried away by his own importance.

As a member of the troika, Deaver was the one who argued within the White House for women's issues and minority issues. I think he was sincere, but he was also finely attuned to the political importance of those groups. Reagan was often accused of being insensitive to blacks, because of his budget cuts or some remark that seemed prejudicial. Deaver said more than once that "Ronald Reagan does not have a bone of prejudice in his body." There was absolutely no anti-black feeling whatsoever; however, Deaver would say, Reagan had had almost no experience with blacks. Not that he was against them, but that he did not understand their problems, their hopes, their dreams, and could get no feel for what an inner-city black must experience. The only exposure to blacks Reagan's midwestern upbringing had provided was during his days as a football player at Eureka College, when one of his teammates was black and Reagan took him into his own house after the player was denied a hotel room. Baker shared Deaver's concern that the President not appear insensitive to women and minorities, while Meese showed little understanding of the problems of the disadvantaged; in December of 1983, for example, Meese declared that he saw no evidence that there were hungry children in the United States, and added that some people go to soup kitchens "voluntarily, . . . because the food is free." Meese's insensitivity helped bring Baker and Deaver even closer together, at Meese's expense.

Aside from Deaver's support, another advantage Baker had going for him was his top aide, Richard Darman, who had worked with Baker previously at the Commerce Department. Although Darman and I were occasionally at odds, I think Baker's choice of Darman was very wise, the most important one he made. Darman was exceptionally bright, well-organized, and added a strategic dimension to Baker's staff, all of whom were extremely capable, while Meese's aides were not so savvy.

Because Baker was responsible for White House relations with Congress, he and Darman created what was known as the Legislative Strategy Group very early in Reagan's first term. The membership was limited to only as many as could sit around Baker's conference table, six or seven, the elite of the White House decision makers. That meeting became the engine that ran the White House. Meese had the policy apparatus, but it was slow and creaky. Baker's legislative strategy group had to react immediately to legislative developments. His group quickly became a policy group as well as a legislative group; the fast-breaking give-and-take of the legislative process required that policy decisions be made on the fly. What happened around Baker's conference table was the key as Baker seized control of the White House from Meese.

Meese was more conservative than Baker or Deaver, much less pragmatic, much more California-oriented. Unlike Baker, who had not joined Reagan until the 1980 campaign, Meese was old-line Reagan, tuned in, knew all the players. He also knew how to work Reagan by playing to the President's conservative leanings. Meese's initial influence quickly waned, because he was so disorganized and because he lacked a crackerjack staff like Baker's. Moreover, Meese was responsible for one of the biggest blunders during the early part of the Reagan administration; it was Meese's decision not to awaken the President, who was in California, after two U.S. Navy jets shot down two Libyan fighter planes off the coast of Libya on August 19, 1981. The aerial dogfight took place during the middle of the night, California time, and Meese's failure to awaken Reagan made the President look foolish and lazy, and became a cause célèbre in the press.

It was a good move for Meese when William French Smith resigned as attorney general in 1984 and Meese replaced him. The President continued to rely on Meese for advice periodically, as he did when the Iran-Contra affair broke in November 1986, but Meese was no longer in the inner circle. A member of the Cabinet may have rank, but it's proximity that counts.

Baker often referred to Meese as "Poppin' fresh, the doughboy." The name spread among the press, many of whom had little use for Meese. Nothing could sink someone in the White House faster than a derogatory nickname, which I put to use myself in my battles with David Gergen, the director of communications. I started calling Gergen "the Tall Man," and before long, top White House staffers and the press began referring to him as "Tall," which was a source of ridicule at Gergen's expense that helped give me the upper hand in our rivalry.

Baker thought Meese was too dogmatic, and not politically astute, while Meese thought Baker was too pragmatic, too willing to compromise on what Meese considered nonnegotiable conservative positions. Baker played the President differently than Meese did, and Baker's methods soon proved more effective. Baker would maneuver the President toward compromise, showing him how he could get half a loaf now and the other half later on, instead of insisting on the whole loaf now and getting nothing. I always watched closely to see how Baker handled the President, and I got a kick out of how Baker could bring the President around to his point of view. Baker also cultivated the press, sometimes spending as much as fifty percent of his time with reporters and editors; this gave him considerable influence on how policies were treated in the press. But Meese usually played only to the California press or the right-wing reporters.

In spite of the differences among them, and considering that you had a three-headed monster running the White House, Baker, Deaver, and Meese often worked surprisingly well together. The Big Three would set aside differences whenever it became crucial. One thing they had in common was an appreciation for the perks of office. That's not to fault them; the privileges that go with the White House—the limousines, the parking spaces inside the White House gates, the deference with which people treat you, the lunches in the Executive mess at the White House—

are all very seductive. I remember that after reports surfaced that Libyan terrorists were stalking U.S. government officials in 1981, Baker, Deaver, and Meese used it as an excuse to get Secret Service protection. They quietly ordered guard details for themselves, probably at Deaver's instigation, then dropped them after a few months when it threatened to become a public issue. The day the Big Three got their Secret Service details, New York Mets baseball player Rusty Staub, a hulk of a man, was visiting the White House and walked into the press room with me for the noon briefing. I introduced him as "my one-man Secret Service detail."

Being chief of staff is an extremely wearing job; you never have a moment to reflect as you move from one issue to the next, and it just takes a toll on you. Jim Baker wisely felt that Reagan's final four years could in no way match the first four years, and that one term in that job would be enough for him. So Baker was always looking for a place to go when he left his job as chief of staff. He was always interested in attorney general, but Meese took that job. Baker also thought of being secretary of state or secretary of defense or head of the CIA, but all of those jobs were filled, too. The thing that really surprised me was that Baker was ready to accept the job of baseball commissioner when Bowie Kuhn was forced out by the Major League owners after the 1984 baseball season. And Baker wasn't even an avid baseball fan. Baker was intrigued by the baseball job, but because the opportunity arose during the 1984 campaign, and Baker was committed to seeing the President through to reelection, he didn't pursue it.

By the spring of 1985, the troika had been dissolved, with Deaver leaving to establish a public relations firm, Meese moving over to head the Department of Justice as attorney general, and Baker swapping jobs with Treasury Secretary Donald Regan.

Once Don Regan took over as chief of staff, there was only one man in charge—no more Big Three—and there was no question who it was. As secretary of the treasury, Regan had clearly been one of the stars of the first Cabinet; one of two take-charge guys, along with Secretary of State Alexander Haig. Regan was the guy with the most polish and self-assurance, the one who had accomplished the most on his own by rising to the top of Merrill Lynch. Regan had caught my eye from the very first meeting of Reagan's cabinet designees during the transition; he was clearly head and shoulders above the others.

Regan was known for having a bad temper, but his bark was worse than his bite. I only saw him lose his temper twice during the two years we worked closely together. Once was when National Security Director Bud McFarlane tried to usurp his authority. It happened while King Hussein of Jordan was visiting the President in 1985. Hussein had recently held negotiations with Israel, and he was planning to make a statement about the talks while he was in Washington. But Hussein was not willing to discuss his meetings with the Israelis in a formal, written statement, or a departure statement as we called it. He would only agree to make the statement if asked a question by the press. Bob Sims, my foreign policy deputy, came in to my office and said that Bud McFarlane had arranged for President Reagan and King Hussein to take questions, and Sims had also arranged for the question on the talks between Hussein and the Israelis to be asked by ABC's notoriously unruly Sam Donaldson, of all people.

Within minutes, the private line between Regan's office and mine rang. The chief of staff ordered me to come to his office right away. "Why did you arrange this press conference?" he asked me. I told him, "I didn't arrange any press conference. It's a Bud McFarlane deal. In fact, he used my man Bob Sims to arrange it without my knowing it." Regan was furious. Pounding the desk, he exploded, "Damn it, I'm in charge of scheduling around here, and anybody that's going to do anything like that has to get *my* approval." His face reddening, he sprang from behind his desk and went charging off down the hall to the Oval Office to try to head off the meeting between the President and Hussein and the press, but it was too late.

McFarlane also used to make Regan mad by sneaking things for the President's approval into the daily briefing, the leather-bound compilation of top-secret intelligence data that the National Security Council provided the President.

Regan was insistent on being kept abreast of everything that was going on in the White House, and the other time I saw him lose his temper was when someone failed to keep him informed. He and I were on our way back from visiting the President at Bethesda Naval Hospital during one of the President's illnesses. The driver told Regan he had heard on the radio that there had been a small fire at the White House. Regan exploded. He picked up the phone and shouted, "Get me Tom Dawson!" He reached Dawson, one of his aides, on the car phone and said, "What is this about a fire in the White House?" Dawson meekly explained, "I didn't know about it either until after it was over." Some repairmen working in the White House had started a fire of minimal proportions, but the D.C. Fire Department sent about a dozen fire trucks roaring down Pennsylvania Avenue, as they did, justifiably, whenever anything happened at the White House. Regan wasn't satisfied with Dawson's explanation. "Dammit! I'm the chief of staff! I've got to know when these things happen!" he roared. "Suppose the President called me and asked me, 'What about the fire?' And I didn't know anything about it? You guys have got to keep me posted on these things and I don't want this ever to happen again." When we drove up to the White House a few minutes later, the lanky Dawson was waiting outside, and before we could even get out of the car, he began giving Regan the most minute details of the fire.

Regan was a victim of bad press. The *Washington Post* reported last August that he liked to be addressed as "Chief," and that he liked to have people rise when he walked into an office. Neither story was true. People used to ask him, "What would you like me to call you: 'Mr. Secretary,' 'Mr. Chief of Staff?' And he would say, "Why don't you call me 'Don'?" It was Pat Buchanan who started calling him "Chief," and that must have been the grist for the *Post* story. But no one else called Regan that, nor did he ask them to. Regan would even make light of his own ego. When I was helping him prepare to testify before the congressional hearings on Iran in the summer of 1987, after he had left the White House, I said to him, "Two things: Leave your ego at home and leave your temper at home." And he just laughed.

But, like his predecessors, Regan did enjoy the perks of his office, which may have contributed to his downfall. During the nine days the President was at Bethesda Naval Hospital for his cancer surgery in the summer of 1985, Regan and I rode out there together about ten o'clock every morning. That's when I really got to know Regan and became friendly with him. One thing I noticed was that he would always make a strategic pause just outside the hospital to confer with me or one of the advance men in full view of the photographers, which helped create the "I'm in charge" image for Regan that many people—not least Nancy Reagan—resented.

While the President was recovering from his cancer surgery, Regan really got on Mrs. Reagan's bad side by ordering a helicopter to pick him up each morning and fly him to the hospital. I happened to be sitting with Mrs. Reagan at the hospital when her chief of staff, Jim Rosebush, who had little use for Regan, called and gleefully informed her about the helicopter. She asked me about it, and I told her that nobody had ever used a helicopter unless the President was on board. She got very upset; she wasn't using a helicopter, and her attitude was why should anybody else? Regan had already left the hospital for the day, and with me still sitting there, she called him at home. She began with a little cordial chitchat and then asked innocently, "You're not going to use a helicopter, are you?" They talked for a few minutes more, and she was steaming when she got off the phone. I sat in awkward silence, waiting for her to speak. "He intends to fly out here," she said with exasperation. But Regan was smart enough to read the tone of her remarks quite well. He canceled the helicopter, but the damage had already been done.

Aside from the flap over the helicopter, someone posted signs all over the hospital directing people to "Chief of Staff Regan's Office." Moreover, Regan's aides handed out sheets with typewritten directions to his office at the hospital. I don't think Regan ordered anyone to post the signs or pass out the directions, but his aides probably thought he would enjoy what they had done, and I have no doubt that he did. I also have no doubt that Mrs. Reagan thought it was all a little too much.

I don't think Regan was ever given enough credit for being as much on top of things as Jim Baker was. I found that out firsthand, being one of a small group who prepared Baker, and later Regan, for television interviews. It would take only a few minutes to brief Regan. But the Baker briefings were quite different, lasting for hours on end. He would invite so many people to sit in, and everybody wanted to offer their view of what he might say. Then there would be great debate around the table, with Baker writing down every word that he planned to say on a yellow legal pad. He would say, "That's a good answer on that, now let me get that down. 'The President will hang tough on Democratic efforts to block his budget cuts.' " And then someone, most likely Darman, would say, "Wait a minute, maybe you ought to couch that in a different way." And Baker would say, "Well, let's see how this sounds now." It was a tortured process that took hours longer than it should have, tying up Baker, me, and several other top-level White House staffers. I began making excuses, like "My son is playing Little League baseball," to avoid as many of those sessions as I could. Baker was just painfully cautious about what he was going to say on the air.

Their staff meetings were just the opposite: Baker's too short, and Regan's about the right length. Baker ran brisk staff meetings that lasted only ten or fifteen minutes and provided for little interplay between the chief of staff and his aides. Regan's staff meetings ran for forty-five minutes or so and were much more productive than Baker's because Regan encouraged open give and take with his staff. Moreover, Regan, unlike Baker, always relayed our deliberations to the President.

On the other hand, Baker's aides were much more capable than Regan's. Someone dubbed Regan's three top aides—Dennis Thomas, David Chew, and Tom Dawson—"the Mice." And Regan was not nearly as effective as the troika had been in planning the President's schedule. Mike Deaver not only had a feel for which events would be best for the President and the pace that should be set for Reagan, he held scheduling meetings once a week. Regan would go for weeks without holding a meeting on scheduling the President, and things would just end up haphazardly on the President's schedule. Without as much input from other staffers, the planning of the President's schedule under Regan lacked the spark for using it as a tool for communication, legislative efforts, foreign policy, and the whole range of issues.

First among equals in the Cabinet was the secretary of state. But after Al Haig's performance the day Reagan got shot, early in the first term, Haig's star quickly began to fall. His abrasive personality and his outspokenness made him a constant thorn in the side for Baker, Deaver, and others, who began looking for a way to get rid of him. "What an ego!" Baker would comment as he hung up after a phone call from Haig.

The beginning of the end for Haig came in early 1982. On February 19, based on a leak from a member of Haig's inner circle, Bob Woodward reported in the *Washington Post* that notes of Haig's meetings at the State Department revealed that a few months earlier Haig had called Lord Carrington, the British Foreign Secretary, a "duplicitous bastard." Carrington had enraged Haig by stating that Saudi Arabia had put some kind of pressure on the British over the Multinational Force and Observers (MFO) that helped keep peace between Israel and Egypt in the Sinai Desert. According to Woodward, Haig added, "European friends—just plain cowardly. British lying through their teeth on MFO. Saudis never pressured British and Europeans on MFO." It was hardly a diplomatic choice of language. When a reporter asked me what the President thought of Haig's remarks, I made it clear that Reagan was displeased: "He didn't have any reaction that I wish to convey to you."

Haig had been pushing El Salvador to the forefront ever since Day One, and in early March of 1982, he announced that he had evidence that El Salvador's rebels were controlled by outsiders. As proof of his position, Haig reported that Salvadoran troops had captured a Nicaraguan, Orlando José Tardencillas, who admitted that he had helped the rebels in El Salvador. One week later, however, Tardencillas recanted his statement. He was Haig's boy, and that left Haig with egg all over his face.

It had been my instinct that touting our role in El Salvador was a mistake from a public relations standpoint for Haig or anyone else, because the majority of the American people are not concerned about

Central America and don't want to see us get involved there. The American public is wrong, in my opinion; Central America is on our doorstep and we should do our best to help put friendly governments in power, but it's a losing proposition from a public relations standpoint. We should just have done what we had to do and tried to work quietly with Congress behind the scenes instead of trying to mobilize public opinion, which was impossible to do.

A few weeks after the Tardencillas debacle, the Falkland Islands war broke out between Great Britain and Argentina, and Haig—shades of Henry Kissinger—launched his shuttle diplomacy between London and Buenos Aires. Meanwhile, Baker, Deaver, and Bill Clark, a longtime Reaganite who by then had succeeded Dick Allen as national security adviser, really had the knives out for him. They had had enough of Haig and were just trying to irritate him enough to make him quit. They conspired to assign him a plane without windows in the cabin for his trips between England and Argentina. Haig refused to fly on it—he didn't know it, but they had one with windows available and just gave him the windowless one out of spite. They finally assigned him one with windows, but not before showing Haig who was in fact "in control here."

Then in early June of 1982, we went to Europe for the economic summit in Versailles. From there we went to England, and Deaver, who controlled assignments for our helicopters, put Haig and his wife, Patricia, on the number-four helicopter for a flight from the airport in London to Windsor Castle. Protocol dictated that Haig and his wife should ride aboard Marine One, the President's helicopter, or at least on Helo Three, where the senior staff ordinarily would fly. Now, Helo Four opens down the back like the ones the troops used in Vietnam, and you sit on a bench instead of in a comfortable airplane chair, and there's no soundproofing, so it's extremely noisy. There were Haig and his poor wife—a very delicate and proper lady who had once been a concert pianist—on number four, taking off in a cloud of dust and noise. It was all part of the hazing of Al Haig.

On the way back from London to Washington, on Air Force One, Haig said to me, "I'm just going to march into the Oval Office and tell the President that I cannot do this job under these circumstances. If he wants me to be secretary of state, I'll be secretary of state. But I'm not going to be treated like this." He fully expected that Reagan would side with him and tell Baker, Deaver, and the rest to treat Haig with the respect to which Haig believed he was entitled.

Another thing that Haig told me annoyed him was that Baker and Deaver passed notes in Cabinet meetings and NSC meetings, "like schoolboys," as Haig put it. I, too, thought that practice was rather strange. They would write quips or make fun of somebody, and pass notes to each other there at the table. I have never seen that happen at corporate board meetings or any other high-level meetings like those at the White House.

On June 25, a couple of weeks after our conversation en route from London to Washington, Haig did offer his resignation. Baker, Deaver, and Meese spent a lot of time in the Oval Office, urging the President to accept the resignation, and to Haig's surprise, the President did so without trying to talk him out of it.

George Shultz, who replaced Haig, was a buddha, hard to read—and he looked like one. He would speak to you one day and ignore you the next. He never did that with me, but many people of lesser rank commented on it. He had a way of treating underlings badly. Jim Kuhn, the President's aide who sat outside his door, was once singled out by Shultz. The first session at the Geneva summit in 1985 where Reagan and Soviet leader Mikhail Gorbachev met alone with interpreters ran way overtime, and we were all left drinking coffee with the rest of the Russians for well over an hour. After a while, Don Regan called Kuhn over and said, "This is running on and on. Do you think we should break it up? Why don't you ask Shultz?" So Kuhn went over to Shultz and said, "Mr. Secretary, should I go in and try to break this up?" And Shultz said, "If you don't have any more sense than that, you ought to be fired." Shultz repeated that story more than once without identifying Kuhn, but it was terribly embarrassing to Jim, because everyone knew who Shultz was referring to—and the question actually had come from Regan. I once told Kuhn that he should have said, "Well, if you want me to go tell Don Regan he ought to be fired, I'll be glad to." But a staff man gets paid to take that kind of guff.

Shultz was beyond fatigue. Although he is in his late sixties, he would spend longer hours than President Reagan at a summit in Europe, and then take off in a whirlwind for Australia and New Zealand. He is very effective at articulating his points, both publicly and privately. Publicly, he's a calming influence, giving the appearance of being thoughtful. Also, he's not a yes man, like so many of the people you find around Presidents. He insisted on having two thirty-minute private meetings each week with the President, where he laid out our foreign policy in detail. I think those sessions were good for Shultz and good for Reagan.

By the time I left the Reagan administration in January 1987, the only one of the key Reagan aides who had been on the job for as long as I had was Secretary of Defense Caspar Weinberger. Cap was chosen to head the Pentagon because of his reputation for cutting fat out of government programs: Cap the Knife. He was going to pare down the military budget and get us 100 cents on the dollar. But he quickly became a captive of his generals and admirals, and it was while Weinberger was in charge that we had all the stories about $640 toilet seats for the navy and $7,400 coffee brewers for air force planes. Cap turned out to be a hardliner, a small man, a whiny type of guy. With a green eyeshade, he would have looked just like an accountant instead of the head of our largest governmental department.

Cap more than once cut his nose off to spite his face when he got before Congress. He would argue for seven percent real growth in the defense budget, Congress would come back with five, and Cap would say, "Absolutely not, we will not take that," and then Congress would slap us with a total increase of three percent. Cap was responsible for a lot of his own problems because he wouldn't compromise.

Let me hasten to say that I had my own problems with Cap, because he was the only one in the administration who consistently refused to follow our game plan for dealing with the press, which originated in my office. It was up to me, in consultation with Jim Baker, and later with Don Regan, to decide who would give which interviews and make television appearances.

But Cap was always getting out of line. He was the worst. When he traveled, you'd wake up one morning and there would be Cap from London or Karachi or wherever on the "Today" show. I'd call Bob Sims, after he left my staff to become Cap's press guy, and I'd say, "Sims, you've got your man on T.V. and he's talking out of line." In 1986 a reporter asked me about something Cap had said in London, and I tartly replied, "Well, I'll find out exactly what he said before I cut him off at the knees." I was losing my patience with his off-handed statements.

Cap was just the loosest of the cannons, the baddest boy. I used to imitate Sims's reports: "Well, Cap was just walking down this hallway and looked into this room, and there was this podium and cameras and a microphone and Cap said, 'I wonder what this is?' and all of a sudden he's in a press conference." I was always waiting for Sims to call and say, "Cap met with a group of reporters this morning and told them that we were going to bomb Moscow, but I don't think he made any news."

Guys like Weinberger shouldn't screw up. They're grown men, they've been around, they've got some smarts. But Cap was always putting his foot in his mouth. One of his major screwups came at the 1984 meeting between Reagan and Canadian prime minister Brian Mulroney in Quebec City. That was the meeting where Deaver made his Canadian contacts and set the stage for the trouble he got into over lobbying for Canada after he left the White House. Anyway, Cap started talking about who would control the U.S. military aircraft based in Canada. We had always left that fuzzy—saying it would be a joint decision of both governments. But Cap said the U.S. would decide. His statement irked the Canadians and spoiled the Reagan-Mulroney meetings.

David Stockman, the director of the Office of Management and Budget, was in a class by himself. He was talented, hard-working, and brilliant, but unreliable.

He and Cap Weinberger had a continuing battle. Stockman felt that Cap the Knife had become a mouthpiece for the military brass and wanted to spend willy-nilly with no constraint whatsoever. Cap, on the other hand, felt that Stockman lacked an understanding of what was needed at Defense, and that Reagan's promise to the people was to restore our national security, but Stockman stood in the way of that. Cap also felt that Stockman had a lack of philosophical understanding of what we were trying to accomplish, to negotiate with the Soviets from a position of strength, which was the only thing they understood. And so Stockman and Weinberger fought over the budget, year after year. Stockman would take two or three days arguing against Cap's expenditures, and then there would be a Cap rebuttal, which was generally shorter, but would play on the President's sympathies about negotiating with the Soviets from a position of strength. And then the two would be sent off to work it out. Over a period of days they would come back with a compromise. The President would rarely make a hard choice between the two, leaving them to settle it; sometimes Jim Baker would have to take a hand in it.

My most vivid recollection of David Stockman is from November 1981, when the infamous Bill Greider article broke in *The Atlantic*, the one where Stockman disclosed that he didn't really believe in the Reagan administration programs he had been pushing to Congress and the public. Stockman was quoted as saying that he reprogrammed his computers after discovering that Reagan's tax cuts would produce "absolutely shocking" budget deficits; that "none of us really understands what's going on with all these numbers"; and that Reagan's beloved supply-side economic theory was nothing more than a "Trojan horse" and a sugar-coated way to sell the Republicans' notorious "trickle-down" policy under which you cut taxes for the rich and the benefits trickle down to everyone else. Stockman was in Darman's office the night before the story was coming out and they called me down there. Stockman looked just like the kid who had been caught with his hand in the cookie jar. He was really in a panic. "What should I do?" he asked. My advice was to step up and make a straightforward, open statement that he had made a mistake.

I regarded Stockman as the brightest guy in the Cabinet. He was the most effective member of the Cabinet at arguing his position to the President, using simplistic charts and graphs to illustrate his points. He once snowed Cap Weinberger with a chart comparing U.S. and Soviet troop strength. He had drawings of outsized American soldiers and Russians half their size to help him make his point, although, in fact, Soviet numbers far outstripped ours. He seemed to have an encyclopedic grasp of the budget and economic figures, maybe too good a grasp. It has since come out that he was using a lot of hocus-pocus. You talk about voodoo economics—he practiced it on paper. You gradually learned that he could produce the figures to prove his point, although none of us, including the President, knew if what he was saying was right or wrong.

Stockman's resignation in July 1985 was a good move on his part, because by then his credibility had eroded, both with Capitol Hill and within the administration. One interesting thing about his departure was that he consulted with Don Regan about the offer he had received from Salomon Brothers, drawing on Regan's Wall Street background—even though Stockman and Regan had been enemies from the start, when Regan was Secretary of the Treasury and Stockman was director of OMB. At the outset, each one wanted to be the administration's economic spokesman, and Stockman won out initially, even though he was barely half Regan's age and had little experience in finance. When Stockman asked if Wall Street was the place for him, Regan urged him to take the job. Despite their differences, I believe Regan was sincere, and his advice was proper. Stockman was so good with the figures and had such an effective staff that his resignation was a loss to the administration, in spite of all the problems he had created.

As Stockman's book about his White House days, *The Triumph of Politics: Why the Reagan Revolution Failed*, worked its way toward publication in the spring of 1986, we got a general idea of how critical it was going to be. Our strategy was to no-comment it and we steadfastly did that throughout the administration, from the President on down. We knew that the unkindest thing we could do was to refuse to comment, rather than give him any publicity that would just help sell books. The book turned out to be more of an indictment of Stockman than it was of the President, because Stockman was telling how *he* cooked the figures in order to make things work. His book also bombed, leaving the publishers holding the bag on much of the $3 million advance they had paid him.

Now that Stockman and I are both in New York, we have no contact. But I hear within Wall Street circles that when his book came out, the management of Salomon Brothers became concerned that he might do the same thing to them, so everyone is careful what they say around him. Other than that, I never even hear his name mentioned on Wall Street.

After Stockman announced his decision to resign, Don Regan asked me if I thought it would be a good idea to appoint Jim Miller, the head of the Federal Trade Commission, as Stockman's replacement. I really had nothing strong to say for or against Miller, although as it turned out he sometimes got his mouth in gear too quickly, which led to unfortunate statements when he testified on Capitol Hill or gave interviews to the press. And then I would have to clean up the damage he had done. In staff meetings, Miller was so loud that he also had the habit of beginning every comment with an explosion of volume that would blow your wig off. I wish now I had been able to give Regan a good reason for picking someone else.

Two men have served as attorney general under Reagan. The best I can say for the first, William French Smith, is that he was adequate. There is no rule that you have to have an advocate like Bobby Kennedy or Ramsey Clark to head the Justice Department. Smith certainly was a low-key attorney general. Most of the controversial issues that the Justice Department got involved in, such as the Bob Jones University case, a 1982 decision to revoke a twelve-year-old government policy denying tax exemptions to schools that discriminate against blacks, came from Meese over at the White House. Smith was close to the President, but did not use his friendship to press for any specific issues.

To be honest, Smith was kind of a quiet, unassuming man, surprisingly low-key for a job as important as attorney general. My most vivid memory of him is when Laura and I shared the presidential box at the Kennedy Center with Smith and his wife one time. We were served wine, but part of the cork had disintegrated into the bottle, and Smith just sat there while his wife made a big fuss and refused to drink it. Smith did seem inordinately interested in participating in the Washington social scene. Instead of buying a home or renting an apartment, Smith even lived for the four years he was in Washington at the Jefferson Hotel, where Reagan insiders from out of town usually stayed when they visited Washington, thus enabling him to maintain his social contacts. I know that one Washington big shot observed that Smith was so wrapped up in attending the right parties and the right opening nights and the right art gallery exhibits that he "would go to the opening of a door." But his performance as attorney general was competent if not spectacular.

Smith's successor as attorney general was Ed Meese, whose appointment turned out to be a bad choice. But Meese had always had his eye on the Justice Department and leaped at the job when Smith decided to leave. Meese was an ideologue and he pushed issues that were not popular on Capitol Hill or with the American public. Many were flag-waving, beat-your-head-against-the-wall issues that gained us nothing. Meese packed the Justice ranks with right-wingers, and I often found myself putting distance between the White House and some of their ideas. An example was the commission on pornography in 1986, which came to a hilarious conclusion when Meese delivered the group's final report while standing near an eight-foot-high-Classical statue of a woman with undraped breasts. If Meese had nothing better to do, let him do it over at the Justice Department and leave us out of it. When Meese became the subject of more than one investigation by an independent counsel, the ever-loyal Reagan stuck by him, believing the probes were politically inspired and aimed not at Meese but at the President himself.

Drew Lewis, Reagan's first secretary of transportation, was clearly the best of the rest. He was an activist with a good solid business-like, take-charge approach and good political instincts. A lot of people didn't like him, considering him abrasive, hard-charging, and overly ambitious, but I got along with him fine. I think he was one of the most able people who worked for Reagan. I remember in the summer of 1981 during the trouble with the air traffic controllers, Drew and I were in the Oval Office with the President, and Drew was very insistent. He declared, "Mr. President, I recommend that we fire these people. We can't tolerate this," and he assured Reagan that the system would be able to function without the striking controllers. Reagan was just as decisive in his action as Drew Lewis had been in his recommendation: He immediately said he would fire any of the controllers who went on strike. I think that was a very bold move that reinforced the public's perception of the President's strong leadership.

Ambassador to the United Nations Jeane Kirkpatrick was cantankerous, ideological, and difficult to work with. She was clearly an important appointment because she was a woman, a Democrat, and yet a conservative, so she represented a lot of constituencies. But she was always a problem, for Haig, for Shultz, for everyone. Every year or so, when we needed a new national security adviser, Baker and others always made sure to head off quickly any possibility that she would get the job.

My only run-in with her came when she announced her resignation in November 1984. She didn't like the way I worded her departure announcement. She called me and without so much as a hello, said, "I just want you to know that I don't know why you would say a thing like that." And I replied, "Well, let me assure you that I never said anything in that briefing room that did not reflect the attitude of the President and in this case the secretary of state." But she was in no mood to listen, she just wanted to have her say and get off the phone.

Then there was the first secretary of interior, James Watt. His record speaks for itself. He did coin one catchy phrase: "Let Reagan be Reagan." Otherwise, he was a constant embarrassment. He withdrew an invitation for the Beach Boys to play at a Fourth of July concert on the Mall near the Washington Monument, lashing out at the "evils of rock music." Nancy Reagan registered her disdain for Watt's action by promptly inviting the Beach Boys to play at a site across the street from the Washington Monument—the South Lawn of the White House. Watt's blunders continued throughout his almost three years in the Cabinet:

- In July 1982 we had to disavow publicly a letter Watt had sent a month earlier to Israel's ambassador to the U.S., Moshe Arens, stating that our support for Israel might be hurt if Jewish liberals here opposed the President's energy resource development program.
- Six months later, Watt further embarrassed Reagan by telling a reporter that Indian reservations were "an example of the failures of socialism."
- Finally, in September 1983, Watt remarked that he had "a black, a woman, two Jews, and a cripple" on an advisory commission of his—which resulted in his very welcome "resignation."

We spent a lot of time cleaning up after Watt; Dave Gergen once produced a mock-up of a foot and then shoved Watt out before the press with the "Foot in the Mouth Award," aimed at having Watt eat a little crow and turning the spotlight on himself instead of his staff. But Watt's behavior was not funny, and he was a real liability for President Reagan.

When Watt resigned, Bill Clark was tapped to replace him. It was another Baker-Deaver engineered deal to get rid of Clark, who was then in the White House as national security director. Baker and Deaver thought that Clark's direct access to the President and his old friendship with Reagan were enabling him to put a lot of ideas in the President's head, which was a mistake because of Clark's inexperience in both foreign policy and in politics. I always felt that Nancy Reagan played a behind-the-scenes role in forcing Clark out of the White House, in order to solve the problem at Interior and to solve the perceived problem at the White House.

Clark resigned and went back to California after less than two years at Interior. He was succeeded in 1985 by Energy Secretary Don Hodel, who implemented many of Watt's policies without all the controversy. I once got into trouble with Hodel over a statement I made when I was asked at a briefing how we decided whether the White House issued an important announcement or a department head did it. "What's good news, we announce at the White House; bad news comes from Interior or Education," I said, mostly tongue-in-cheek.

Speaking of the Education Department, Terrel Bell, the secretary of education during the first term, presided over a department the President had promised to abolish. But Bell's heart wasn't in it. Bell may not have believed in his mission, but he always tried to butter up the President by telling him how good a job they were doing with budget reductions over at the Education Department. I would always joke with whomever I was seated next to at the Cabinet meetings that no matter what the subject, Ted Bell would quickly come in and say, "Now, Mr. President, we over at the Education Department have cut *our* budget, we've done *our* part."

We certainly had our share of lightning rods, like Watt, who drew constant fire from the environmentalists; Ray Donovan, who could never establish rapport with the labor unions; and Ted Bell over at Education. All three were decent gentlemen who were unsuited for their posts.

Then there were the two special cases, George Bush and Pat Buchanan. One tried to avoid taking a portfolio, and the other was always after a portfolio that wasn't his.

George Bush is one of the best qualified men who ever held the office of Vice President. He has been a successful businessman, as well as congressman, ambassador to China and to the United Nations, and director of the Central Intelligence Agency. But he never seemed to give Reagan the benefit of that experience. Seldom did I hear him speak up, either in Cabinet meetings or in private sessions like our issues luncheons on Monday. Almost never did he weigh in except to say that he had heard something from the Texas oilmen or he would say he had just been in Iowa and he had heard such and such. I never heard him say, "Mr. President, my advice to you would be, this is the wrong thing to do." Or, for that matter, "This is the right thing to do." In a way that's the ideal Vice President, but in a much bigger way it was a waste of Bush's talent and his office. The bottom line is he was the perfect team player, the perfect yes man. Bush explained that he provided his advice to the President in private—and the Vice President refused to tell even his staff what he told Reagan.

One of Bush's contributions to the administration was his vice-presidential "joke of the day" for Reagan, which helped to keep the President in a good mood.

With Bush the popular image may be accurate: that he does not have a strong philosophical base, that he is not decisive, that he is not willing to take stands on the big issues. I know he agonizes endlessly over the public positions he does take, and he is a bit wishy-washy when he takes a stand.

A Vice President is torn between whether to exert influence and leadership or walk in the President's shadow. It's difficult to do both. I found Nelson Rockefeller, Ford's Vice President, a surprisingly good team player for a man who had outranked Ford in the Republican Party. Rockefeller was a strong Vice President, too; the ideal mix.

When I would suggest to Bush that he make an appearance on the "Today" show or that he make a statement or that he appear on "Meet the Press," he would often be very reluctant and would say, "Well, is this really what the President wants me to do? I don't want to do anything that he doesn't want me to do." I would say, "Yes, it's a part of our plan," but more often than not he would worm out of T.V. appearances. I never knew if Bush was avoiding appearances because of his own political interest, or if he preferred to remain in the background.

But perhaps Bush will come through when the chips are down, as he did in the biggest crisis of his career in public office—the day Reagan was shot.

From my point of view, Pat Buchanan caused more trouble in only two years than anyone else who worked closely with Reagan during the first six years. Don Regan had seen the energy a fellow moderate like Jim Baker had had to waste dealing with the right wing. A pragmatist like Regan or Jim Baker had to be forever on guard in the Reagan White House, because if somebody unleashed the right wing on you they could really do a job on you, fair or unfair. It was much more dangerous to be a moderate than a right-winger; if you were a right-winger, the moderates weren't going to come after you, but if you were a moderate, the right-wingers definitely were out to whip you into line. Baker agonized over and was victimized by Evans and Novak, Richard Viguerie, and that bunch.

In order to avoid those pitfalls, Regan decided to appoint Pat Buchanan communications director in early 1985—not so much because he wanted him in that job but because he needed Buchanan to cover his flanks with the right. Regan very quickly came to regret his decision, because Buchanan immediately became a problem. We wasted more time and energy in meetings trying to pacify Buchanan on every conceivable subject than we did making decisions. In dealing with Congress, Pat lived to veto. He was always looking to pick a major fight with Congress, although every poll we did showed that the American people wanted the President to get along with Congress, not be confrontational. Don Regan went well out of his way time after time to make sure that Pat was satisfied with his decisions so that Pat wouldn't turn Jesse Helms and the rest of the right loose on him.

I genuinely liked Pat. He's honest, up-front, and there's nothing devious about him, but I had forgotten that people like him existed. I hadn't encountered anyone like Pat since I had to deal with the White Citizens' Councils in my days as a Mississippi newspaper editor. That's not to say that Pat was at all a racist, just that he was so blindly reactionary.

At my suggestion, Dennis Thomas from Regan's staff, Buchanan, one or two others, and I met around five-thirty each afternoon in Dennis's office. My idea was that we would spend fifteen minutes or so making sure that everything was in order for the next day, particularly when the President had a public appearance scheduled. Instead, these meetings deteriorated into "Pacify Pat" sessions, where Buchanan said, "Gosh, the President needs to do more of this," and then we'd spend a half hour trying to talk Pat out of his position. Generally he was pushing for meetings between the President and Jerry Falwell or Pat Robertson, or for Reagan to go to New York for the celebration of *The National Review*'s thirtieth anniversary in 1985 (which Reagan did), and other things on Buchanan's agenda.

Regan and Buchanan also had a long-running controversy over speechwriters. Buchanan was always pushing right-wing ideologues to assume more and more of the speechwriting duties, which Regan resisted. Regan refused to appoint Buchanan's protégée, Peggy Noonan, as head speechwriter when an opening occurred. Aside from being dogmatic, she insisted on taking credit in public for many of the speeches she had written. She was always saying, "I wrote this" and "I wrote that." The best speechwriters are heard and never seen. Also, we occupied a lot of time cutting hardline stuff written by Buchanan's people out of speeches, things that it just would not do at all for the President to say. Pat should have learned some lessons from Tony Dolan, who was extremely right-wing, but a very effective speechwriter. Reagan's best speechwriter was Ken Khachigian, who wasn't even on the White House staff. He was often called in to write the major speeches. Khachigian would produce a balanced, well-reasoned speech and had a good working relationship with the President.

Buchanan was just a constant pain in the neck. His Op-Ed piece for the *Washington Post* in March 1986 advocating aid to the Contras was completely unauthorized, vicious, and had the opposite effect he had intended. Instead of getting Congress in line behind us, he antagonized them, writing that a vote in Congress on Contra aid would show whether the Democratic Party stood "with Ronald Reagan and the resistance—or Daniel Ortega and the Communists." Buchanan impugned the patriotism of Congress, and you can never do that. Don Regan had never seen Buchanan's article until it showed up in the *Post*, and he was incensed too. When the press asked about what Buchanan had written, I carefully cut the ground out from under him and disavowed his piece in the *Post*, but a few days later Congress voted not to provide aid to the Contras. We felt that Pat's attack on Congress had cost us votes, perhaps enough to make the difference.

Pat kept writing these unauthorized Op-Ed pieces and running around after the Iranian story broke and calling Ollie North a hero. And then finally, in early 1987, he started talking about running for President. That's when Regan told me, "I'm going to call Pat in and tell him either to run for President or work in the White House, he can't do both." Pat decided not to run for President, but he left anyway in March 1987, one month after I did.

I have often wondered if there is a different standard of morality in California. Mike Deaver's public relations business after he left the White House led to his being found guilty of perjury; Lyn Nofziger was charged with six counts of violating federal ethics laws; and Ed Meese has been under investigation for alleged conflicts of interest virtually since Reagan took office. Another Californian was Environmental Protection Agency aide Rita Lavelle, who wound up being convicted of perjury. Talking to Meese in particular, you would feel that he was totally above board, totally honest, totally of the highest moral character. That's the impression he gives you. But he was always on the hotseat for questionable activity, dating back to his loan to buy a house in 1981, and it did make you wonder. Questions about Meese's character also made members of the Senate wonder; the investigation of his qualifications and the confirmation process took more than a year after Reagan nominated him to be attorney general in January 1984.

Something else I often thought about was whom I would have placed in the most sensitive jobs in the administration. This is not to second-guess; I think that in general, President Reagan assembled an outstanding team. Based on six years of hindsight, however, I have presumptuously put together my choices for some of the key jobs in the administration. Call it the Super Cabinet, my "dream team."

Don Regan would be my chief of staff. By all rights he should have been a success in that job. But he was a victim of the image he created for himself. He was a big target and the press took glee in shooting him down. The bigger they are, the more they like to see them fall.

I would have definitely had a place for Jim Baker as the chief political and legislative operative. Nobody was ever better at dealing with Congress. He earned the utmost respect as a straight shooter, as a guy who would deal with the lowest-ranking congressman as quickly as he would the most powerful senator. He was a good tactician and he had a good political feel.

I would certainly have found a spot for Mike Deaver, who knew the Reagans better than anyone else. Deaver's knack for spotting a story or an event that would play well for President Reagan was a talent no one else had. I would have picked him as my presidential scheduler.

Instead of Al Haig, George Shultz would have been my secretary of state from the beginning. He was solid, cool, and calm, and could have served equally well as secretary of defense, treasury (a job he had held previously), commerce, or many others. Had he been a bit more friendly and cultivated a politician's way with people, he would have had the makings of a President.

Cap Weinberger did have one plus as secretary of defense. He carried out a presidential mandate to restore pride in the military, right down to the lowest soldier in the field, but overall, he would not be my choice as Pentagon chief. In my fantasies, I have what I think would have been the perfect choice for this job. The secretary of defense presides over the military-industrial complex, and many of our top civilian officials at the Pentagon were once captains of industry, such as Charles Wilson, who coined the famous saying, "What's good for General Motors is good for the country"; Robert McNamara; David Packard; and Cap himself. Since General Motors has had a shot with Wilson and Ford with McNamara, why not try a Chrysler? Yes, the secretary of defense of my dreams would have been Lee Iacocca. Iacocca, by the way, was quietly approached by Deaver when Ray Donovan got into trouble to see if he would be interested in being labor secretary, but he quickly turned it down.

The perfect attorney general—or the closest we could have come to it—was Bill Rehnquist. And I have a hunch he would have been interested. Remember, when Reagan took office, Rehnquist had already served on the Supreme Court for nine years, and he was still only fifty-seven. Moreover, there was no hint that he would someday become Chief Justice. Being attorney general would have been a new challenge for him, and if he had been willing to leave the Court and move over to the Justice Department, he still would have been the likely nominee for Chief Justice when Warren Burger resigned in 1986.

At OMB, David Stockman had a fatal character flaw, which you couldn't see initially. He was sharp with the numbers, he knew his budget from top to bottom, he had a good rapport with Congress, having been a congressman. But under the surface he had that problem: "I am advocating an economic program that I don't believe in." Jim Miller was not an adequate replacement; he just doesn't have the stature and the credibility. A better selection would have been Steve Bell, the chief staffer on Senator Pete Domenici's Budget Committee. He understood the nuts and bolts of the budget process, and also knew the members of Congress. It has to be both, because that's the guy who sells your budget. And it is the budget that develops the character and tone of the administration, the policy of the administration. All policy is set by dollars.

At the CIA, Bill Casey did what Reagan wanted him to. His job was to restore the morale and the capability of our intelligence operation after Jimmy Carter emasculated it, and he did so. But Casey became a target for Congress and the press because of his obsession with secrecy; at one point, in May 1986, Casey went so far as to threaten to prosecute the *Washington Post, The New York Times*, the *Washington Times, Time*, and *Newsweek* over stories that had been leaked to them.

Casey's fixation on leaks was especially curious, considering that he was talking extensively to Bob Woodward, as we now know for sure. Starting in 1982, Casey sent numerous "zingers"—notes with wire stories or newspaper clippings attached—to Jim Baker, admonishing Baker to "stop these leaks . . . they are coming from the White House." Baker always showed Casey's memos to me, and I would tell him, "We should turn this right back around and send it back to the CIA. That is where the leaks are coming from." By 1984, I was convinced that Casey himself was a source of the Woodward stories that were appearing more and more frequently in the *Washington Post*—most of which went straight to the heart of our most sensitive intelligence and the methods that were used to gather it. Casey, I believe, was charmed by Woodward, who convinced him he could have a hand in shaping the history of his CIA reign in Woodward's forthcoming book. During regular Thursday foreign affairs luncheons, I often put my suspicions directly to George Lauder, the veteran CIA official who was then the agency's public affairs officer. Lauder, who was close to Casey, always professed to be dumbfounded by Woodward's revealing stories and always denied that Casey was the source.

In spite of my suspicions that Casey was a secret source for Woodward, I liked and respected the CIA director. His image was that of a bumbling old man who was not very articulate. The classic example was that he could not pronounce Nicaragua: He would say, "Nicawawa." He didn't apologize for it. When Casey would discuss Nicaragua, he would just say "Nicawawa," and everyone present would know what he meant. Casey might have been overzealous in some situations, and he certainly made some public relations mistakes, such as threatening to prosecute leakers as well as the members of the news media who reported those leaks, but I never thought Casey got his due. I thought he was made a laughingstock, when in reality he did a solid job. The President appreciated Casey's performance as CIA director, and of course the President was very loyal to him because Casey had straightened out his 1980 campaign when it was floundering and low on money.

Jim Watt, no way. You need someone with more environmental expertise and political skills. We finally got it right at Interior on the third try. Don Hodel took the post and has handled it quietly and well.

And, finally, for Vice President, George Bush. But only with the promise that it would be the real George Bush, one who would speak his mind and give the President the benefit of his experience and his intelligence.

8

Ronald Reagan

Behind the Scenes

What kind of man is Ronald Reagan? Above all, he is an actor, and we never apologized for his Hollywood background. Communicating is a key ingredient of leadership, I always maintained, and if being an actor made him a better communicator, then so be it. One of the most revealing reminders of his days as an actor is his habit of ending almost every speech and almost every public appearance with a quip. The actor in Reagan dictates that he must have an exit line.

On a more personal level, there is a big difference between the public Ronald Reagan, an outgoing, friendly, personable man, and the private Reagan, who is still charming and affable, but in an impersonal way. Privately, he tends to be a loner, content to spend most of his time with his wife and no one else. He almost never reveals his personal emotions to anyone but Nancy. Perhaps it's because he was an actor and his every move was closely scrutinized, so now he feels that his emotions should be private. Two examples stand out in my mind:

- After his cancer surgery the doctors went into Reagan's hospital room, where the President was reading a book about Calvin Coolidge, *Return to These Hills.* He looked up and asked, "Did you get it all?" The doctors said they had, and he went back to his reading without another word.

• In November 1981, it fell to me to inform him after the news came over the wire that actor William Holden, once Reagan's closest friend, had died. Reagan started reminiscing about how he and Nancy had gotten married at Holden's house in 1952 and how Holden was his best man, but he didn't show any real emotion over Holden's death while I was with him.

The most emotional I saw Reagan was when he received word that the space shuttle *Challenger* had exploded on January 28, 1986. It occurred at 11:39 A.M.; a few of us were in the Oval Office preparing the President for a lunch he was scheduled to have with several columnists on the State of the Union Address, which was to have been that night, but was postponed because of the *Challenger* disaster. I had just posed a mock question to the President when Kathy Osborne, his secretary, cracked the door open and motioned for me to come outside. Before I could rise from my chair, George Bush, Pat Buchanan, and John Poindexter, who had been watching a live telecast of the launch, rushed into the Oval Office. Bush started to speak, but Buchanan blurted out, "The *Challenger* just blew up." Everyone was stunned. All the President could say was, "Oh, no," and he cradled his face in his right hand. He had very closely followed the selection of the first civilian astronaut to ride on the *Challenger,* and had announced the selection of New Hampshire schoolteacher Christa McAuliffe months earlier, with all the finalists present in the Roosevelt Room of the White House. A White House photographer rushed in to record the moment that we learned of the *Challenger* explosion, and the President had the saddest look on his face I have ever seen. He also looked extremely old. That photograph was so unflattering that I refused to release it to the press.

Somebody said, "Let's turn on the television," and we adjourned to the next room. While we were watching, the President said, "I hope everything is done to track the remains, to track down what happened." There was no question that all seven astronauts had been killed, as the space shuttle had burst into pieces. I said I thought I had better get down to the briefing room, and he said, "Tell them [the press] what we will do is we will fix it [the space program] and we will keep on going. These people were dedicated to this program. We couldn't do more to honor them than to go forward." He had tremendous instincts for saying the right thing at the right time.

Although they are loners, the Reagans have a number of good friends, such as U.S. Information Agency head Charles Z. Wick, and his wife,

Mary Jane, with whom they usually spend Christmas Eve; publishing tycoon Walter Annenberg and his wife, Lee, whose Palm Springs home is where the Reagans spend New Year's; Washington consultant Nancy Reynolds, an old friend of theirs from California, and a few others. But the Reagans aren't that close to anyone, not buddy-buddy close, and they don't see that much of the Wicks, the Annenbergs, or anyone else; the President and his wife just aren't the kind of people who pick up the phone and say, "Why don't you come on over for dinner?" or "Why don't you come spend the weekend with us at Camp David?" In part, of course, that's because of the restrictions of living in the White House. Moreover, the Annenbergs and many of the Reagan's other friends live in California, where the Reagans do socialize more than they do in Washington.

The main point, though, is that Ronald and Nancy Reagan are never alone as long as they have each other. They spend most evenings by themselves, whether they're at the White House, their ranch near Santa Barbara, or Camp David. When they're in Washington, they change very early into their pajamas and robes and sit in front of the television, eating their dinner from silver television trays while they watch the news or a favorite program.

The Reagans have one of the great love affairs I have ever seen, in or out of politics. They truly are best friends, as well as husband and wife. After thirty-five years of marriage, they frequently hold hands, and, especially when he is giving a speech, she fixes those big eyes of hers on him with an adoring look that some of us in the White House began calling "The Gaze."

The Reagans' affection for each other even overrode protocol during one of our visits to England. We were calling on Queen Elizabeth at Windsor Castle in 1982. When the ceremony was over the President and the Queen walked out together, and he motioned for Mrs. Reagan to come up beside him. Members of the socially conscious British press contingent rushed up to me and said, "This is a breach of protocol." I shot back some good ole American protocol, pulling one out of my hip pocket: "It's an old American custom that's predominant in the Reagan family that husbands and wives walk side by side." The British press accepted that and dismissed it; otherwise, it might have been a full-blown British tabloid flap.

Ironically, considering how much in love the Reagans are, it was Mark Weinberg of the press office who usually sneaked out and bought the President's Valentine candy for Mrs. Reagan. The President said, "After all, I can't just walk out of the White House and drop by the candy store." Mark not only bought the candy, he generally paid for it out of his pocket as well, along with the candy that was offered to the Reagans and any guests—usually White House aides—who watched movies with them during weekends at Camp David.

At times the loss of privacy gets to the Reagans. The President, tired of so many questions about his personal life, especially his medical problems, decided to get even with the press in the summer of 1986. "We'll go where we want to, we don't have to tell these people where we're going," he declared, and he and Mrs. Reagan slipped away to the Jockey Club in downtown Washington for dinner. They told the head of the Secret Service detail, Don Regan, and Jim Kuhn, but they didn't tell me or anybody in my office. I didn't find out about it until after they had left the White House. That was the only time they left the White House without announcing it in advance to the press. I knew that meant trouble, so I convinced Don Regan and he convinced the President that it was the wrong thing to do. I told him it would be just like Carter at Plains or Carter at Camp David. Carter wouldn't take a press pool and wouldn't announce forays outside the camp, so the press staked every possible route. I said, "That's what we're leading to here. You're going to have people watching every gate of the White House every weekend, every night. It'll be chaos."

As in love as he is with Nancy, I'm certain that Reagan would never consider having an affair, but he does get a twinkle in his eye for an attractive woman. He would call a woman who worked for him by her name long before he would remember a man's name. One woman who caught his eye was named Cece Kramer, a flight attendant on the United Airlines charter that flew Reagan's 1980 campaign. She came on the White House staff afterwards and worked in the advance office. Elizabeth Dole is another favorite. And he's enamored of Margaret Thatcher. Not only is she attractive and dynamic, but the two of them see eye to eye on politics and economics, and they're personally fond of each other. He always looks forward to meeting with her and talks about her quite a bit.

Nancy's power is most evident in personnel matters. If she becomes convinced that someone's presence is making the President look bad and hurting his ability to do his job, she starts a sometimes not so subtle campaign to get rid of that person, and she won't give up until he or she is gone. It made no difference to her whether or not a person like Dick Allen, Reagan's first foreign policy adviser, or Don Regan was being treated unfairly by the press. They embarrassed the President and, in large part thanks to Nancy Reagan, they were gone. She was also the one who recognized, often before the President, that an issue like Iran was building up and had to be defused. Another area where Nancy's influence is noticeable is in the scheduling of the President; she insists that Reagan not be overscheduled.

Nobody has ever been as good at working with Mrs. Reagan over the schedule as Mike Deaver, but even he would get tired of all her calls. One day I was in Deaver's office and the phone rang twice with calls from Mrs. Reagan. "That's seven calls so far today," Deaver sighed. It was noon. I, too, received a lot of calls from her, and I always experienced a bit of discomfort when the White House operator would say, "The First Lady is calling." I remember once, shortly before Reagan was inaugurated, Mrs. Reagan called Jim Brady. "Tell her I'm out," Brady quickly said. I was appalled, but I soon learned that was a necessary tactic at times. One of my staff people summed up his relationship with the First Family: "The only thing worse than being *in* is being *out.*"

One thing to remember about Nancy is that she was once an actress herself, and she has a bit of the prima donna in her. Just before Election Day in 1984 the Reagans were staying at the Red Lion Inn in Sacramento. Their bed was on a platform, and during the night Mrs. Reagan got out of bed, stepped off that platform in the dark, and fell and hit her head. White House physician Daniel Ruge examined her and felt she wasn't badly hurt, but she skipped a campaign appearance the next day. On Election Day, a day or two later, we flew in a helicopter from Los Angeles up to the Reagans' voting precinct near Santa Barbara. Mrs. Reagan made herself a bed across a bench seat and spent the entire flight stretched out there. I kept trying to signal cryptically to Dr. Ruge to check her out, but he just waved me off. Later on he cornered me and said, "There's absolutely nothing wrong with her, she just wants a little attention." Ruge said she was acting, and she really was playing it with a dramatic flair and enjoying it. As she and the President walked out of the polling place she continued her act, clinging to his arm for dear life, as if she was terrified of falling. It was like she was making a statement for the benefit of all of us: "The show must go on, and I'll make out."

The press joked about her age—her records from Smith College indicated that she was a year or two older than she admitted to being. But you had to be careful that the banter didn't get back to her, because it was a sensitive matter to her. The big question was whether she had at some point lied, whether she was a female Gary Hart on the age issue. Not to mention that her real name is Anne Frances Robbins Davis Reagan—there's no Nancy in there at all. Anyway, whenever I was asked a question about her age, I would always tell the press, "She's as old as she says she is." It soon became a laughing matter to the press. But for Nancy Reagan, it was no joke.

Another thing about Mrs. Reagan: There is room in the White House for only one star-type lady. When her new press secretary, Jennefer Hirshberg, said in 1985 that she had been mistaken a number of times for Farrah Fawcett, I knew she was not long for the job. Sheila Tate, Mrs. Reagan's former press secretary, had the same reaction; she called me and said, "Jennefer had better learn and learn quickly. There isn't room for but one female lead in this White House, and it ain't Farrah Fawcett." In fact, while Mrs. Reagan and I were waiting together to find out if the President had cancer that summer, one of the things we discussed was changes she was planning to make in her press operation. While I had worked extremely well with Sheila Tate, Hirshberg was difficult to work with, and she lasted only six months with Mrs. Reagan. I must confess I was not sorry to see her go. No one in the White House, by the way, had any trouble telling the difference between Hirshberg and Farrah Fawcett.

Aside from Reagan's tendency to isolate himself with his wife, another peculiarity is his relationship with his children. There always seemed to be a controversy about when the Reagans had last seen the kids, whether they had ever seen Michael's daughter, the President's granddaughter, and who was coming for the holidays, if anybody. But where you really ran into a problem was when there was some serious presidential illness. This is the father of these four children, but most of the time the children didn't call to see how he was, and he and Mrs. Reagan didn't call them. It was very strange. Over the years the Reagans became more sensitive to it and made more of an effort to call the children, even if it was just for P.R. reasons. But sometimes after surgery it would be twenty-four hours or thirty-six hours before they would have any phone contact with the kids.

Another complication is the situation with Jane Wyman, Reagan's first wife and the mother of Reagan's two oldest children, Maureen and Michael. She is an unmentionable to both the President and Mrs. Reagan. One time George Skelton of the *Los Angeles Times*, who had covered Reagan when he was governor of California and had a way of asking the most foolish and embarrassing questions, was being transferred back to California, and he had his farewell interview with the President. During the interview, George said, "There's one thing I want to ask you, Mr. President, ho, ho, ho." And the President said, "Oh, sure, George, go ahead, ho, ho, ho." And George said, "Do you watch 'Falcon Crest'?" The President obviously didn't because he didn't quite get the connection and asked Skelton what he meant. And George said, "Jane Wyman is the star," and the President said, no, he didn't watch the program. There was a bit of a chill in the air for a moment, and I quickly ushered Skelton out of the Oval Office.

Another classic George Skelton question on a personal matter came when he was interviewing the President aboard Air Force One en route to California. Reagan told some great tales about wrestling black snakes out of a pond near the ranchhouse with his hands, and stepping on rattlesnakes with his boots and shooting them. As the interview wound down, Skelton asked, "Mr. President, do you still enjoy sex—" and, while the President fumbled for an answer, George continued, "—on a regular basis?" That was one question that went unanswered.

It is interesting that the child born to Reagan and Jane Wyman—Maureen—has become very close to Nancy. Of course, Maureen put the President in an embarrassing position when she ran for the Senate from California in 1982. He couldn't endorse her in the Republican primary, but he wanted her to win, although he was somewhat worried about some of her stands; she is the one who is really to the right of Attila the Hun. Reagan passed off some of Maureen's statements by quipping, "Disagreements with my daughter are nothing new. I just can't take her over my knee for a good spanking any more." Maureen lives in the White House much of the time because her work for the Republican National Committee requires her to be in Washington. She and Mrs. Reagan would embrace when they greeted, they would exchange stories, and on a number of occasions when I went up to the family quarters to speak to the President, Maureen and Mrs. Reagan would both be there in their robes, chatting like schoolgirls and enjoying themselves.

The President's aides, even George Shultz, are all afraid of Maureen. She can be as much of a problem for a staff guy or a Cabinet guy as Mrs. Reagan. You didn't want to stir her up. You would avoid her if possible, and agree with her if you had to deal with her. She pushed hard to get rid of Don Regan, even before Nancy did. Maureen is much more of a straightforward blusterer, punch-you-in-the-nose type. Mrs. Reagan is more circumspect, more likely to stab you in the back. Reagan's aides aren't the only ones who are terrified of Maureen; her husband, Dennis Revell, seems to live in mortal fear of her. I've seen her cut him down one side and up the other, and he just stands there and takes it.

Before the 1984 convention Maureen came up with the idea of selling china cups made by Royal Doulton with the President's bust on them. They were a limited edition, numbered, with part of the proceeds going to the Republican National Committee and part to a fund for the benefit of Jim Brady. But the cups were hideous, and not even the most loyal Republican would fork over any money for them. Dennis, her husband, was retained by the Republican National Committee to be a consultant in charge of marketing these things when they were stuck with a huge number of them after the convention. Then Maureen got the idea that she should go on television hawking them, and she wanted to go on "Good Morning, America." They turned her down, saying they weren't going to accept a fund-raising gimmick for the RNC on that show, and she got after me to call the show's host, David Hartman. So I did, and I said, "David, here's the story, and if it can be done, great, and if it can't, I will understand." He talked it over with the brass at ABC and came back and said no. I told that to Maureen—it was one of those deals where I was getting calls every fifteen minutes from her: "What's being done?" "Why isn't this being done?" When I gave her Hartman's answer, she said, "What do you mean, you can't get us on T.V. about this? This benefits the Brady fund." I said, "Yes, Maureen, but they're aware it's also a partisan thing." She said, "You just tell them you're the White House. Just tell them who you are. Tell them we want to be on that show." But I told her it didn't work that way. She definitely wasn't pleased.

Michael Reagan always had schemes for making money from his father's position, and Fred Fielding, who had to deal with potential conflict-of-interest problems as the President's counsel, would come around and say, "Well, Sonny Boy's at it again." Michael's latest deal is as host of a syndicated television game show called "Lingo," and I have a feeling the "Lingo" people wouldn't have been too interested in him if his name were, say, Michael Smith.

At times Michael was on the outs with the President and Mrs. Reagan, and they wouldn't have any contact for months. Finally, they were to have a big peacemaking meeting during one of our New Year's visits to California, while the President and Mrs. Reagan were staying at the Century Plaza Hotel in Los Angeles. The press got wind of the impending pow-wow and built it into nothing less than a repeat of the signing of the Treaty of Paris.

This was one time when I really experienced Mrs. Reagan's methods. I made the mistake of calling her in her suite right after she had returned from shopping; she had noticed that reporters were staked out everywhere, and she started complaining. "They're just waiting for Michael and his family to arrive so they can mob him." There was a presidential entrance at the rear of the hotel that the President used, and the plan was for Michael and his family to enter there. But there was a five-story parking garage next door, and the press was up in that garage, shooting down from overhead with their cameras. I said, "I know they're out there, Mrs. Reagan, but we can't run them off, that's public property." "Well," she said, "they've just got to go. I want you to do something about it." I quickly turned to Mark Weinberg, my assistant who specialized in matters pertaining to the Reagan family, and had him call the Secret Service. But they said they couldn't do anything about the press; the role of the Secret Service is strictly to protect the President and his family from danger, not to keep the press corps away. We talked to the Century Plaza people, and they said there was nothing they could do. Meanwhile, Mrs. Reagan was calling me about every five minutes: "Well, what's happened? What have you done?" "We're working on it, Mrs. Reagan." I tried to duck her calls, but there was no escaping the White House operators. Finally, the Secret Service asked the press to move, and they agreed to move around to the lobby of the hotel. So when Michael arrived for the big peacemaking, what did he do? He came in the front door of the hotel into the lobby, right to where we had moved the press corps. Fortunately, he was such an unfamiliar face to the White House reporters that they missed his entrance.

Patti, the youngest daughter, who used Davis, her mother's maiden name, as her last name, has been the problem child for years. She is the rebellious one who lived openly with her boyfriend, a member of the Eagles rock group, and she's the one who wrote the unflattering novel, *Home Front,* about the politician that was obviously based on her father. The President read it when it came out in February 1986; "It's fiction," he observed. Mrs. Reagan never admitted to having read it, but I'm sure she heard enough about it. Shortly after the book was published, we did an interview with Barbara Walters on the top floor of the White House. One of the stipulations to Barbara was, don't ask about that book. So Barbara waited until the end of the interview and brought it up. The President characterized it as "very good fiction." She turned to Mrs. Reagan, and Nancy really tightened up. Afterwards they said good-bye cordially, but Mrs. Reagan was furious that Barbara had brought it up. There were long periods of estrangement between Patti and her parents, stretches of no contact at all.

One day in April 1984 Mrs. Reagan called me and asked me to come over to the family quarters at two o'clock. She revealed to me what she hadn't even told her own press secretary, Sheila Tate, that Patti was going to marry Paul Grilley, her yoga instructor. Mrs. Reagan and I discussed when she should send out the invitations for the August wedding, who was on the guest list, and where the wedding was going to be (the Hotel Bel Air in Los Angeles). Mrs. Reagan wanted to be sure that it would be depicted as a family wedding with Patti's friends, instead of a grand state occasion with the princess getting married, which is what happened when Johnson and Nixon had daughters get married while they were in the White House. Patti didn't fit the image of a princess at all. The wedding went off without a hitch, although the press wasn't too happy about being banned from the hotel, at the Reagans' insistence. I doubt if Mrs. Reagan and I would have had that discussion if Patti had gotten married a few years later; by 1987, Patti was completely estranged from the Reagans, and she neither attended the funeral nor sent flowers after Mrs. Reagan's mother, Edith Davis, died in October 1987.

Young Ron has always been *the favorite*, particularly Mrs. Reagan's. He's more attentive to his parents than any of the others are. The President and Mrs. Reagan had gone through the trauma of his choosing to be a ballet dancer, although they professed to be proud of his career. They felt he had achieved a lot in the ballet, going as far as he did, making the second company of the Joffrey Ballet, but they were proud of his decision to leave ballet when he said he didn't see a future in it. They think he has real talent as a writer, although they aren't too pleased about some of his stories appearing in *Playboy*. The President himself often said, "I think we could have picked a better place to put his stories." It was always a must for me to read his articles, because I knew Mrs. Reagan was going to ask my opinion. When Ron appeared in his underwear as guest host of "Saturday Night Live," the Reagans didn't really understand what was going on. They had not seen *Risky Business*, and Mark Weinberg had to explain to them that Ron was doing a takeoff on the movie.

The President often talked about his Hollywood days, which, of course, were long before the age of permissiveness. Skin magazines like *Playboy* and the idea of an actor performing in his underwear on national television were completely foreign to him. He used to talk about how one of an actor's best tools is the audience's imagination, especially when he was discussing the subject of sex scenes in today's movies. He talked about a director who dismissed the leading lady and the leading man just before a bedroom scene between newlyweds. The director said everyone could go except the leading lady's stand-in, the President recalled, and then he had the camera focus on the door of their hotel room. The door closed, then it opened, and the stand-in reached out—only her bare arm and bare hand were visible—and she put a "Do Not Disturb" sign on the doorknob and closed the door. Reagan strongly believed that that was sexier to the audience than the explicit sex they show nowadays.

Unlike many parents, the Reagans have a definite order of preference for their children. Ron is first in the pecking order, Maureen second, Michael third, and Patti last.

President Reagan is usually a dapper dresser, but when he went to Iceland for the second summit meeting with Mikhail Gorbachev in 1986, he wore a scruffy camel-colored overcoat with a fur collar. It was too big and even the sleeves were too long, and it appeared old-fashioned, moth-eaten, and just generally ratty. Laura saw us on television and said it looked like something from the wrong era. Reagan had worn it to a governors' conference at Lake Tahoe many years earlier when he was governor of California, but not too many times since then. For some reason, he was really excited about taking that coat to Iceland. My assumption was that the only reason he got away with it was because Mrs. Reagan wasn't going with us, and she called him while we were there and told him not to wear it anymore.

Reagan has his suits custom-made at Mariani in Beverly Hills, and he wears them for ten or twelve years. They all have the date they were made sewn on the inside pocket, so you knew how old they were. He would have them refitted and restyled to fit the current trend. A couple of them were altered so they would fit over the bullet-proof vest ("My iron corset," the President calls it) he often wears since John Hinckley shot him. Then there was a plaid suit, an awful-looking suit, that we referred to as his Mutt-and-Jeff suit. It was a big, bold, loud plaid. He would invariably wear it on press conference days. I would send word over to the residence to make sure he didn't wear it to the press conference—until I learned that it was Nancy Reagan who had selected the material at Mariani's. Another outfit you wouldn't soon forget was the red-and-green-plaid pants, the Reagan clan plaid, and the green blazer, which he wore on Christmas.

Both of the Reagans prefer to dress casually whenever possible; at their ranch they usually wear jeans, and on Air Force One, the President would always take his suit pants off and change into sweatpants, but leave on his tie and shirt and his wingtip shoes, while Mrs. Reagan would change into a maroon velour running suit that looked very stylish on her. Andrea Mitchell once directed her NBC camera crew to film the President aboard the plane. After that I assigned the President's military aide to close the door that led to the press section of Air Force One. I doubt if the aide considered that job quite as important as his usual task, which was to carry the codes that would be used to signal our nuclear forces to retaliate if the Russians attacked us.

The President was always amused by stories saying that he dyed his hair. Occasionally I would show him a feature story where they would say that his chestnut hair was flecked with gray. He would say, "Thank goodness. Maybe people will believe me when I say I don't dye my hair."

Reagan is out of the old school where they wash their hair once a week. And he would often comment with a lisping voice, "I washed my hair last night and I just can't do a thing with it," and then give a flick of his wrist. He does a very good gay imitation. He would pretend to be annoyed at someone and say, "If those fellows don't leave me alone, I'll just slap them on the wrist."

The President seldom uses any curse words stronger than "hell" or "damn," but he can be earthy at times. Mrs. Reagan, of course, shares the President's distaste for vulgar language, as well as a dislike for something else: the smell of fresh paint. The Reagans always stayed at the Waldorf when they were in New York, but the Plaza Hotel was very eager to get the Reagans to stay there, and they finally agreed to give it a try. The Plaza saw them as clearly the most prestigious guests they could have, not to mention the business that an overnight stay of several hundred White House staff and Secret Service agents would bring. The Plaza's management spent a considerable amount of money redesigning the presidential suite and making improvements. The suite was repainted shortly before we arrived, and the smell of paint was very strong. The Reagans wanted to open the window to get some fresh air, but the paint had stuck the windows together, and the Reagans spent a very uncomfortable night. The hotel management had also gone out of its way to pamper the rest of the White House staff in every way possible, but the Reagans never stayed there again. All because of a stuck window.

There was a residue of rivalry between Reagan and Gerald Ford left over from their campaign against each other for the Republican nomination in 1980. From time to time, Reagan would make fun of Ford. He would say, "I bumped my head, I'm getting like Jerry Ford." I believe that down deep Reagan thinks Ford is not very smart.

Not only did he not have a lot of respect for Ford, he didn't like it that Ford palled it up with Jimmy Carter after Reagan was inaugurated. Ford and Carter, who had been enemies since they ran against each other in 1976, developed sort of a home-and-home series where Carter would go up to the Ford Library in Grand Rapids and Ford would go down to the Carter Library in Atlanta. They would do seminars on the presidency together, and Reagan quipped, "There go the Bobbsey Twins, again."

I don't think Reagan truly dislikes Carter, but he resented Carter's criticism and would joke about him, too. There's no room for doubt about Mrs. Reagan's feelings for Rosalynn Carter. Nancy never forgave her for saying over and over that Carter should have been reelected and making disparaging remarks about the Reagans after the Carters went back to Plains.

When Carter's presidential museum in Atlanta opened in October 1986, the Reagans flew there for the dedication. The President had gotten mousetrapped into doing it. Somehow it got onto his schedule and then it got bigger and bigger and bigger, from a brief visit to the museum to a speech at the dedication. Every time we looked around there would be another event that the President would have to participate in. I was surprised that Carter wanted Reagan for that, that Carter initiated it. During the flight to Atlanta, the Reagans called me to their cabin and told me, "We have made up our minds that no matter what happens, we're going to be gracious."

President Carter could not have been nicer, and Reagan's speech was one that picked Carter's best traits and praised them, as Reagan addressed Carter directly and declared, "Your countrymen have vivid memories of your time in the White House still. They see you working in the Oval Office at your desk with an air of intense concentration, repairing to a quiet place to receive the latest word on the hostages you did so much to free, or studying in your hideaway office for the meeting at Camp David that would mark such a breakthrough for peace in the Middle East." Carter himself got up afterwards and responded in kind: "I think I now understand more clearly than I ever had before why you won in November 1980, and I lost." Which for a man of Carter's pride took a great deal of humility. But Rosalynn never gave an inch during that day. Her jaw was clenched tight from the time we arrived until the time we left. Flying back to Washington on Air Force One, Mrs. Reagan just went, "*Whewww*, I'm glad that's over." Both of the Reagans mentioned how rigid Rosalynn had been.

Although Reagan didn't have that much contact with either Ford or Carter, he had more and more with Richard Nixon as time wore on—and not only contact that was initiated by Nixon. Reagan would reach out to him for advice on arms control, Soviet relations, and other foreign matters. In addition, Nixon often wrote memos to Jim Baker while Baker was chief of staff, and White House emissaries would travel up to Saddle River, New Jersey, where Nixon lived, to seek his advice in person. We usually tried to keep these communications secret, but the fact is, Nixon was very helpful to Reagan.

Just before the 1984 election, we were in New York at the Waldorf-

Astoria. I became suspicious of an unexplained opening on the President's schedule and a bustle of activity around his suite. With a bit of detective work I discovered that the President was having lunch with Nixon, former senator Edmund Muskie (whose 1972 challenge to Nixon had been destroyed by White House dirty tricks), and Senate majority leader Howard Baker to talk about U.S.-Soviet relations. Mike Deaver swore me to secrecy, and I never broke the silence, to avoid embarrassment for Muskie, a Democrat. Two months later, a picture of the Waldorf luncheon appeared in *Life* magazine—courtesy of Mike Deaver.

Ronald Reagan also had strong opinions, which he kept within the White House, about the leaders of Congress with whom he met regularly. I wasn't at all surprised when he picked Howard Baker to replace Don Regan in February 1986, after the Iranian crisis came to a head; Baker and the President developed a mutual respect during the first four years of Reagan's term when Baker was Senate Republican leader. Baker was the most effective majority leader that I had ever seen. He walked a tightrope as a good majority leader has to do. You have to be your own man and vote your conscience, be honest about legislative realities, and still support the President as much as you can, when he's from your party. Above all, tell the President the realities—and Baker did that.

Reagan and the rest of us in the White House were apprehensive when Baker retired from the Senate in early 1985 and Bob Dole succeeded him, but Dole did not turn out to be quite as confrontational or as erratic as we had expected. Still, it was never quite the same, and Dole was never as effective as Baker in presenting the Hill viewpoint to the President. Moreover, when Dole opposed the President, he often did so with quips that had a cutting edge to them.

House Republican leader Bob Michel never had as much clout with Reagan as Baker or Dole and never was as effective a leader as either Baker or Dole. But Michel was in a difficult position because Democrats always far outnumbered Republicans in the House. We had all the confidence in the world when we presented Howard Baker to the press in the briefing room after leadership meetings, but we stopped doing that with Dole and Michel because they would constantly go in there and put both feet in their mouth or deliberately undercut something the President was doing. The whole goal of the press when you took a Republican leader in there was to develop a split between the leadership and the President, and Dole and Michel often played right into their hands.

The President used to like Tip O'Neill personally, but grew tired of

Tip's repeated attacks on him. Reagan would have respected Tip more if Tip had not been so two-faced, acting like his friend while he was at the White House, and then saying vicious things about the President as soon as he got back to Capitol Hill. When Reagan was doing something that Tip knew better than to oppose politically, the Speaker was always favorable, but when it was something he could attack Reagan on, he would come armed to the teeth, so that he could go out and say, "I told the President such and such." He got more and more confrontational with the President as it came time for him to retire from Congress in 1986.

I had seen Tip treat President Ford the same way, giving him the buddy-buddy act and even playing a friendly round of golf with him—and then turning on him whenever it suited Tip. And some of the things Tip said about Reagan in his book, *Man of the House,* are just outrageously false. At one point Tip recalls how George Shultz phoned him on September 1, 1983, at 7:00 A.M. Eastern time—Tip was at Cape Cod—to inform him about the Russians shooting down Korean Air Lines Flight 007. Tip claims that he and Shultz had the following conversation:

O'NEILL: What does the President think about this?
SHULTZ: He's still asleep. He doesn't know about it yet.
O'NEILL: You've got to be kidding. You mean you're calling me before you've even notified the President?
SHULTZ: We'll tell him when he wakes up.

Tip didn't want to spoil his story by pointing out that Reagan was in California, where it was 4:00 A.M., or that the President had been kept abreast of the situation until 10:30 P.M. Pacific time, when Reagan went to sleep. That would be 1:30 A.M. Eastern time, only five and a half hours before Shultz called Tip.

Tip also calls Reagan "the worst" of all the Presidents Tip has known, dating back to Harry Truman, and says it was "sinful that Ronald Reagan ever became President." Tip's account of the Shultz anecdote and his assessment of President Reagan must be weighed against his standards of accuracy and fairness. According to columnists Rowland Evans and Robert Novak, for example, Tip's assertion that he "kicked them right out of my office" after they allegedly offered him "great press notices" when he became House majority leader in 1973 if Tip "kept them informed as to what was happening in Congress and the White House" was "outrageous, wretched libel"; Evans and Novak insist they never offered O'Neill such a deal. Evans and Novak also note that Tip once told them that another congressman, Bruce Caputo of New York, "has two employees on his payroll who check the sex life of his colleagues, who check to see if they are out cheating on their wives, who check if they go on corporate planes"—but that when Caputo challenged Tip to identify those staffers, Tip was unable to do so and had to apologize in a speech before the House.

Reagan found Tip's successor, Jim Wright, easier to get along with and more willing to compromise on legislation. One thing that helped us with Wright was that even though he's a Democrat, he was sympathetic to our Central American policy. But pressure from House liberals after Wright became Speaker caused him to split with the President on Contra aid. On the other hand, he's extremely sanctimonious. When Wright began in that Texas drawl, "Now, Mistah Pre-si-dent, Ah wanna hep you on this matter," Reagan would roll his eyes. Afterwards, the President would say, "That's when I check to see if my wallet is still there."

Senate Majority Leader Robert Byrd is also sanctimonious and always overly verbose. He would preface everything by saying, "I want to be cooperative with you, Mr. President," but he would always have a reason for opposing Reagan. His relationship with the President is virtually nonexistent. Everybody else could be bipartisan, but Byrd would pompously mouth phrases about bipartisanship and then rip into the President.

Wyoming, one of the least populated states in the U.S., has only three representatives in Washington—two Senators and one member of the House—but two of those three, Senator Alan Simpson and Congressman Dick Cheney, are among the President's favorites. Simpson is generally supportive of Reagan without being a yes man, so he has tremendous credibility within the White House. He gave the President some real straight talk on Iran and its effect on public opinion in late 1986 and early 1987, and for the first time the extent of the problem began to sink in on Reagan. The President also likes Simpson for his easygoing, rugged western style, and his lively humor, which unlike Dole's, does not have a nasty edge. Simpson's quips, coming at strategic moments, broke the tension during many a congressional leadership meeting.

Dick Cheney is probably the most effective supporter the President has in the House of Representatives, because he's intelligent and he can support the President without appearing to be following the President blindly. Having been White House chief of staff under Gerald Ford, Cheney has seen both ends of the street and knows what the score is within the White House. He understood when we had screwed up because he knew the inner workings of the White House. On the other hand, he knew what a tough job it was to be President or chief of staff.

In contrast to Dick Cheney there is Jack Kemp, who often drove the

President and the rest of us up the wall. During White House meetings you could just sit there and wait for him to explode over some economic issue. We used to have bets on how quickly he was going to erupt. I would nudge whoever was sitting next to me and say, "I'll give Kemp ten minutes before he pops off." He would come on strong and loud, in his high-pitched voice, in rapid-fire machine-gun language—and sometimes his tirades bore no relationship to the topic of discussion. This is the trait I first noticed in my meetings with Kemp in 1980 when I was shopping around for a presidential candidate to support that year. He's just a hair-trigger guy, always ready to leap in and say, "Here's the answer." Ask him a question, press a button, and you get an answer. And it's done with such a passion, not a false passion, but not an attractive passion either. In leadership meetings he would broadside one of his colleagues in the Congress or a member of the Cabinet with something off the wall, like a return to the gold standard. Shultz and Regan, when he was treasury secretary, often were the targets of Kemp's attacks, but the President himself never was.

And then there are some of the crosses the President has to bear, like Strom Thurmond, Jesse Helms, and Alphonse D'Amato. Strom speaks in an almost incomprehensible drawl that is unmatched, and even I, a southerner, was amused by it. He used to get hung up on textiles, which is a major industry in South Carolina. For a solid year, at every legislative meeting, as a textile bill was winding its way through the process, he would speak up, no matter what the subject was, and put his two bits in. "Mr. President, Ah want to let you know I oppose yo' textile bill. How can we fight a wah without unefahms and pare-shoots?"

Jesse Helms is a longtime friend of Reagan's and had supported him for President as far back as 1976, so the President feels a sense of loyalty toward him. Nevertheless, Jesse is a thorn in his side, holding nominations hostage and making constant demands that the President follow the conservative line. Although, as the saying goes, at least he's our thorn, our guy, instead of being from the left wing.

Al D'Amato is also a strong supporter of the President, but he's a motormouth and whenever we went to New York, instead of having a presidential trip that was totally structured the way we liked it, we had to be prepared for D'Amato to impose on the President and say, "Well, I'd like you to meet these five other people." He once assembled his wife and all their children so that the President could pose with them for a picture on the D'Amatos' wedding anniversary—a photo that found its way into one of the senator's home-state newspapers, the *New York Daily News*.

*   *   *

One of the few people that Reagan genuinely disliked was former Israeli prime minister Menachem Begin. Reagan was furious after Israeli warplanes bombed and destroyed an atomic reactor in Iraq in June 1981—with no advance word to us. It wasn't just Begin's policies Reagan disliked, it was also his personality; Begin is very prickly, very hard to deal with. Reagan often observed that "That fellow Begin makes it very difficult for us to support Israel," and he was delighted when Begin, to the surprise of almost everyone here and in Israel, announced in August 1983 that he was resigning.

The only other living creature for whom Reagan expressed a strong animosity was his former co-star Bonzo the chimpanzee, who shared billing with Reagan in the 1951 classic, *Bedtime for Bonzo.* The President used to talk about how Bonzo didn't like him and once pulled his tie so tight that it had to be cut off with scissors. You could say that there was a hearty mutual dislike between Reagan and Bonzo.

Not only did the President have few real enemies, he seldom lost his temper. One of the few times I did see him angry was after one of the early press conferences, when the President closed the door almost entirely on a tax increase. The next day it was obvious that was going to be the first question in the press briefing, and Baker, Meese, and I asked him if he wanted to foreclose forever a tax increase of any type. First Baker said, "Mr. President, we really ought to leave ourselves an opening," and the President said no, and then Meese went at it, and the President said no, and then I said, "Mr. President, I have written out something here. Maybe this will suit you." My statement left some room for a tax increase, and he looked at it and no more than got halfway through it, before he reached to the front of his desk, where there was a stand with two pens in it. He grabbed one of the pens with such force that the base of the stand flew across the room, and he wrote "NO TAX INCREASE" across the piece of paper and said, *"This* is what I want to say!" He paused a minute and said, "Strong message follows," and we all laughed and we said, "We think we know what you mean."

I have seen him go after Jim Wright or Tip O'Neill at congressional leadership conferences in the White House. Tip would say, "Mr. President, you're always quoting these welfare stories to us, but you get your facts wrong and I don't believe them," and the President would say angrily, "Now wait a minute, Tip, let me set the facts straight," and he would light into Tip with a barrage of figures that surprised his staff.

* * *

The President is happiest at Rancho del Cielo, the Ranch in the Sky, his 688-acre retreat in the mountains above Santa Barbara. There were times when the President would look like an old man when he arrived, and would appear twenty years younger after a week or two at the ranch. From atop the mountain trails were breathtaking vistas of the blue Pacific far below, once the morning fog burned off. Gentle winds would ruffle the live oaks and part the ranch grass. It was truly a beautiful setting, and Reagan often said, "Up here, you feel like you are on top of the world and the problems and cares are far, far below."

The President once told me how he and Mrs. Reagan found the ranch after deciding they needed a larger one than their place in Malibu. He recalled how you drive up Highway 101 north of Santa Barbara toward San Francisco for about thirty miles. Then you turn and go through lemon orchards to the base of the mountain. The higher up the mountain you go, the more hairpin turns there are and the more steep cliffs off the side. The road up to the ranch is little more than a single lane. He said on his first trip up, the higher they went, the more they thought, " 'This can't be much.' But when we topped the ridge and looked down to the little 100-year-old adobe that was to be our ranchhouse, then looked up to the mountains on each side, we both said, 'This is it.' " There was no doubt that that was the place; the moment he saw it, he wanted it.

The tiny adobe house has no heating except for the fireplace, which is why they don't go in the coldest part of the winter and why he's always chopping wood for the fireplace. The living room, where they spend most of their time, is very, very western with Indian blankets and a hatrack by the door with a dozen hats and caps of various types that he wears.

The communications setup is so elaborate up there that the President can talk from horseback to anywhere in the world. A four-wheel-drive White House communications truck follows him wherever he rides, and he can stop on one of the trails and be connected instantly to anyone he wants to talk to, no matter where. Such a system obviously costs money, but Reagan has always been mindful of the furor over the millions Nixon spent on his homes at Key Biscayne and San Clemente. From day one, Reagan issued a hard and fast rule to the Secret Service about improvements at the ranch: "Put nothing in that you can't take out when I come back here for good."

The President used to go into the lake where the black snakes were, grab them by hand, put them in a garbage sack, and take them to another part of the ranch and turn them loose. The Secret Service, of course, was nervous about it, but he did it. There were also rattlesnakes all over the place. Reagan usually wears boots at the ranch, but one time he was out in sneakers instead, encountered a rattlesnake, and stomped it with his sneakers before he realized he didn't have his boots on.

The Reagans resent the T.V. networks shooting them at the ranch from "Privacy Point," as the T.V. people call it, which is off the Reagans' property and several hundred yards away from the ranchhouse, but there isn't anything they can do about it. CBS even brought in the lens and camera that were used for the space launches and they could actually zoom in on the window of the ranchhouse and see the Reagans through the window or see the President on the porch. He often joked, "I'm going to fake a heart attack and tumble off this horse to see how quickly they get down the mountain with the news." When the Reagans were in a good mood they would wave to the cameras, and Mrs. Reagan had a sign made with her theme on drugs, "Just Say No," that she would hold up.

At the White House, President Reagan's day begins at seven or seven-thirty in the morning when the White House communications operator calls to wake him up. He turns on the television, takes his shower, and has breakfast. On his breakfast tray each day is the news summary that is prepared overnight. The news summary, which goes to all White House senior staff and members of the Cabinet, has the world's most exclusive circulation. I hired only journalism school graduates to prepare it. Only twenty-two or twenty-three years old, they were entrusted with preparing the President's total diet of national and international news each day. I wanted people who not only could write, but could recognize the news. The zinger in a story might be in the first paragraph, but it could also be down in paragraph six.

Reagan does not read many newspapers thoroughly. He glances at the *Washington Post*, *The New York Times*, the *Washington Times*, the *Los Angeles Times*, and *USA Today*. They all come into his office each morning, but he doesn't have much time to read newspapers. When he does look at a newspaper, the President's habit is to read the comics first. Contrary to his public image, Reagan is not that much of a sports buff. He would generally talk baseball at World Series time and football at Super Bowl time, but he does not follow those sports regularly, and he knows next to nothing about sports other than baseball and football. Reagan does love to meet sports figures, especially old-timers. The President would always tell about the time he was recreating a baseball game on the radio from wire reports and the ticker broke down. "I had the guy foul off a dozen pitches before the wire came up. We set a world record for foul balls. Just then the teletype came back on and the operator handed me the note: 'The batter struck out on the next pitch.' "

The President's newspaper reading tends toward conservative columnists. William F. Buckley is an in-house favorite. George Will has always been sort of the crown prince, although he keeps turning on Reagan and criticizing him, which has always irritated me. Reagan also likes Hugh Sidey of *Time* magazine and columnist James J. Kilpatrick. Reagan would usually agree to grant Sidey or Kilpatrick an interview, and he would even call them at home on Saturday night after seeing them on a weekend talk show to discuss what they had said and thank them for representing our position.

Pete Roussel, my deputy press secretary who left the White House when I did, is a close friend of Sidey's. After the Iran affair broke in November 1986, Hugh called Pete and said he would like to talk to the President by phone before Reagan left to spend Thanksgiving in California. Pete sent a memo to Don Regan, and I gave my approval. When Sidey called, Don said, "Sure, he's a personal friend, let him through." Disaster was lurking. Hugh thought he had a press-office-approved interview, while the President thought he was talking to an old friend with whom he could let his hair down, so Reagan made his famous remark to Sidey that "Ollie North is a national hero." I didn't find out about it until Sunday night, when I heard on television that *Time* magazine was reporting that the President called North "a national hero." As North's shenanigans became known, I had to develop a response to the question, "Does the President still think Ollie North is a national hero?" And I would say, "I haven't heard him call him that lately. Period."

Always precisely at nine Reagan enters the Oval Office. Kathy Osborne, the President's personal secretary, rings the chief of staff and the Vice President and says, "The President is in," and they hoof it down the hallway. They go over the daily schedule with the President, the issues facing the Senate and the House, and press matters.

During the Baker-Meese-Deaver days no one was allowed in the Oval Office unless one of them was present. I don't know what they were afraid of, but it was just not done. I felt in the first year or two of the administration that we in the press office were not getting enough regular access to the President, and he was in the dark about what was happening in the press. He should have been more abreast of issues that were of interest to the press, and more honed on his answers. Instead, when there was a lapse of much time between press interviews or news conferences, he would be totally out of the swim on what was in the press and what had happened two weeks ago, and it would be like reinventing the wheel to get him prepared. After Don Regan replaced Baker, I had "walk in" privileges to the Oval Office. I would always pop in on the President before a photo opportunity or any other meeting with the press and brief him on the current hot topic.

At nine-thirty every day Reagan meets with the national security adviser to receive a briefing on foreign policy. The NSC director is usually accompanied by his deputies, and sometimes if a U.S. ambassador from a hot spot is in town, he will be there as well.

The President's nine-thirty meeting with the NSC director is one of the few times that an Ollie North would have gotten into the Oval Office, if there was something breaking in the hostage area, or if the President was seeing a hostage family that day. Bud McFarlane would bring Ollie with him, and Ollie would tell the President what happened. We researched the records, and there was never a time when Ollie was alone with the President in the Oval Office. North was clearly exaggerating about the amount of time he spent with the President. And North's claim that he was watching television with the President when our medical students arrived back in the U.S. from Grenada in 1983 was an outright lie.

An effort is made to reserve personal time for the President in the ten-to-eleven slot in the morning or from two to three in the afternoon. It's always at least an hour where he can have a chance to look at his paperwork, to read whatever he wants, or to catch up on his correspondence. There's going to be a larger body of presidential handwriting when Reagan's papers are released than there has been since the invention of the typewriter. He likes to write notes and personal letters in longhand, and he often sends checks to people in need, like a child who might need a kidney transplant or someone who is down on his luck. There are a lot of stories about his generosity that we don't know and probably never will know.

At noon the President eats in his office unless he has a luncheon scheduled. The stewards, who have a small kitchen just off the Oval Office, bring the food up from the mess and prepare it—usually a bowl of soup and a big bowl of fruit. Reagan has gained a few inches around his stomach during the White House years, although he attributes it to his weight-lifting program. In diet, as in many other things, the Reagans are very much creatures of habit. What they had been doing all their lives is what they still do. That's why macaroni and meat loaf are the mainstays of the White House menu.

Throughout the day the President constantly checks his personal copy of his schedule, which is printed on green stationery with the gold-embossed presidential seal on it. His copy of the schedule contains many meetings that are never revealed to the public, just meeting after meeting after meeting. At the conclusion of each meeting, Reagan draws a vertical line downward and puts an arrow pointing to the next meeting. By the end of the day his schedule would be filled with lines and arrows. "It gives me a feeling that I am accomplishing something," he said, as he went through those meetings and marked them off.

Around five o'clock Reagan cleans out his desk and leaves for the residence, usually with a pile of things to read. In the evenings he spends an hour working out with weights in the mini-gym they had set up in his private quarters, and then he and Mrs. Reagan slip into their pajamas and robes and eat, watch television, and read. The President does work almost every evening, and several packets of material are delivered to him during the night, so, contrary to popular belief, he is by no means off duty when he leaves his office.

The President usually goes to sleep at ten or eleven o'clock, and, despite what people think, he *never* takes naps during the day. He is a sound sleeper, and he often said that when he woke up at night and could not go back to sleep, he would fall asleep by reciting "The Cremation of Sam McGee," which he would sometimes break into during meetings. "Last night," he once said after a particularly difficult day, "I went through it three times." He once recited it for England's Queen Mother when he was seated next to her at a huge state dinner in England. The Queen Mother was also fond of Robert Service, and she matched the President by reciting "Sam McGee" in its entirety, right at the dinner table.

Much has been made of Reagan's sleeping habits, particularly about the incident when he dozed off during his meeting with the Pope at the Vatican on June 7, 1982. I would like to set the record straight on that. Our itinerary on that trip was brutal. We left Washington on June 3 and flew to Paris, arriving there on the morning of June 4 by European time. After meeting with Margaret Thatcher and French President François Mitterand that day, the President helicoptered out to Versailles the next day for economic summit talks with the leaders of Japan, West Germany, Canada, and Italy, as well as Thatcher and Mitterand.

On the final night of the summit, June 6, there was a banquet at Versailles that lasted until 1:00 A.M. or so. Afterwards, the President and several of his advisers, including Secretary of State Alexander Haig, had to review the situation in Lebanon, which had been invaded that day by the Israelis. Early the next morning, after the President had gotten less than six hours of sleep, we departed for Rome. To add to his fatigue, the President has never learned how to sleep on airplanes, which is one reason he hates foreign travel.

After landing in Rome, we went straight from the airport to the Vatican and into the meeting with the Pope. Reagan and the Pope sat at the end of the papal library, which was uncomfortably warm. Arrayed in a straight line before them on either side were the officials of the U.S. government and the hierarchy of the Vatican. Mrs. Reagan was seated slightly behind the President. As the Pope droned on, Reagan's eyes began to close slightly and then open. Then he nodded a bit and his eyes began to close again. It was agony for me, because I knew he was playing straight into the hands of those who said that Reagan was not up to the job, that he was lazy, that he takes naps, that he's not with it, all of those problems that we faced through the years. I was standing at the opposite end of the room, totally in a panic. All I could do was shift back and forth, hoping to catch the President's eye and keep him from nodding off again. I wanted to shout, but I had a feeling that wouldn't go over too well. Mrs. Reagan was clearing her throat and shuffling her feet and the President would pop to, and then he would nod off again. Mort Allin, my foreign policy deputy, was watching the ceremony on live television in the press office across town, and he told me later he was cheering, "Come on, Dutch, you can do it, you can do it, come on, Dutch, you can stay awake."

Mike Deaver later made a bad situation worse by giving an interview to NBC's Chris Wallace and foolishly trying to excuse the President by saying that Reagan occasionally nodded off at Cabinet meetings—as everyone did. And Deaver was the one who had overscheduled him on that European trip in the first place.

I'm nearly thirty years younger than the President, and no one has ever accused me of sleeping on the job, but I found myself exhausted on many a foreign trip. Once in Bonn for the economic summit, I discovered that my suit jacket and trousers did not match. I had two dark suits, one was a pin-stripe and one wasn't, and I was so tired that I didn't even realize what I was putting on. I had been up until midnight or 1:00 A.M. the night before for a post-dinner press briefing, and then I had to roll out of bed at six-thirty the next morning to get in the motorcade. Finally about noon I went to my room to lie down for a few minutes and then go back over to the press center. When I took off my coat I discovered that I was wearing one coat and another pair of pants. Nobody else had noticed it, either.

That visit with the Pope, by the way, wasn't the only time that Reagan was wiped out during an important international meeting. One night during the 1983 economic summit in Williamsburg, he stayed up into the wee hours watching *The Sound of Music,* and he wasn't quite on top of his game the next day.

The tiredness business was always a standard story in the press: "President Reagan today, appearing tired . . ." I finally got to where I'd say to the press corps, "Sure, he's tired. We're all tired. Look at you, you're all half asleep out there." So we quit making excuses for it.

Also, we stopped making excuses for him making mistakes on small facts or stumbling over words. Finally, it just dawned on us that we were just beating our head against the wall and making second-day stories. So we finally said, "To heck with it. He's human, and he makes mistakes." And they went away a lot faster after that.

To be sure, some of the mistakes the President made were hilarious. When he signed the 1981 tax-cut bill into law—the major triumph of his first year in office—we were in Santa Barbara, and for one of the few times during his presidency, we invited the entire press corps up to the ranch to witness the signing. This was one of those deals where he used a different pen for each letter of his name, so that he could give away the pens as souvenirs. After using several different pens, the President quipped, "It's times like these I wish I had a middle name." I guess he meant that he wished he included his middle name when he signed something. But at that moment, Sam Donaldson piped up and said, "You do, Mr. President. It's Wilson." And that brought down the house.

Many times I heard Reagan say, "I long for the days when the President never left the continental United States, when it was traditional that he never traveled abroad." The farther away he had to go, the less he cared about going. He likes to be at home in the White House, or at Camp David, or, most of all, at the ranch.

Much as he dislikes traveling abroad, President Reagan loves to fly around the United States, viewing this great land of ours from above and then landing and meeting the people. Once, as we were flying over southern Illinois just before the President was to meet with Soviet Foreign Minister Andrei Gromyko with hopes that it might lead to a summit with Mikhail Gorbachev, Reagan turned to me and observed, "What I would like to do is bring him up here and fly him across the country and say to him, 'Mr. General Secretary, this is where the American people live,' and show him the rows of houses and white fences and the cars in the driveways, and tell him, 'Mr. General Secretary, they own those houses.' That way we could show him what America really is."

When we were traveling aboard Air Force One, Reagan often wrote speeches, particularly the major ones; the less important ones he would leave to his speechwriters, subject to his editing. One speech I will never forget because of my role in it was Reagan's first inaugural address, which he wrote aboard the plane as he flew from California to Washington just before he became President. He wrote it in longhand on a yellow legal pad, and we made a big point about it as part of the hoopla leading up to the inaugural. *Time* magazine wanted to photograph the pages, so I set it up in my little office in the transition headquarters. After the photo session, I put his handwritten speech in my desk overnight. The next morning when I came in I could not find it. I was in sheer panic, thinking I had lost the handwritten copy of Ronald Reagan's first inaugural. But after searching frantically for a few hours, I finally found it somewhere in my desk.

Ronald Reagan certainly finds his job frustrating at times. Obviously, he would spend most of his time at his ranch if he could; I think if he could move the White House to his ranch, he would be the happiest man in the world. Still, there's not a day he gets up, no matter where he is, that he doesn't want to come to work. He never second-guesses himself; he makes a decision, and then it's behind him and he's off to the next case. I suspect a lot of chief executives would enjoy their jobs more and do them better if they had his approach toward their work.

The one thing to remember about Reagan as President is that he's a man in love with his job. And that's no act.

9

Eyeball to Eyeball

with the Evil Empire

THE END OF KOREAN AIR LINES FLIGHT 007

The word begin trickling in on the evening of August 31, 1983, in Santa Barbara, where President Reagan was vacationing: Halfway around the world, and even on a different date—September 1 by Russian time—a Korean Air Lines flight from Anchorage, Alaska, to Seoul, South Korea, was apparently missing off the coast of the Soviet Union.

During the two and a half years since I had replaced Jim Brady as White House spokesman, there had been major stories to deal with, such as the economy, which dominated our attention throughout 1981; the air traffic controllers' strike which led to Reagan's firing thousands of striking controllers and breaking their union in the summer of 1981; a presidential illness—Reagan's bout with urinary tract problems in the spring of 1982; the Falkland Islands war between England and Argentina at about the same time; and the sudden resignation of Alexander Haig as Secretary of State in June 1982.

But there had been nothing of the magnitude of the October 1983 invasion of Grenada, the 1985 and 1986 summit meetings between Reagan and Soviet leader Mikhail Gorbachev, and the delicate White House moves that resulted in the ouster of Filipino dictator Ferdinand Marcos in 1986—until September 1, 1983, when the Russians shot down Korean

Air Lines Flight 007, killing 269 innocent people. At the time, the downing of the KAL 747 jumbo jet was the fifth-worst aviation disaster in history. The KAL tragedy was a crisis for the U.S. because South Korea is one of our allies; because the flight had originated in New York and refueled in Anchorage, before taking off for its final destination, Seoul; and because among the 240 passengers and twenty-nine crew members were sixty-one Americans, including Representative Larry McDonald of Georgia.

National Security Director William Clark informed the President at seven-thirty Pacific time on the evening of August 31 that there were reports indicating that the plane might be missing. At 10:30 P.M., just before the President went to sleep, Clark gave him further details, but it was still very sketchy. Information continued to pour in through the night, as Clark, White House counselor Edwin Meese, Secretary of State George Shultz, and Secretary of Defense Caspar Weinberger kept in touch with each other by telephone.

By mid-morning Santa Barbara time on Thursday, September 1, it was obvious that the KAL plane had somehow strayed into Soviet airspace and that the Russians had shot it down. I prepared to brief a frantic press corps about the incident. This was one occasion when you could tell how serious the crisis was by what the presidential spokesman was wearing. I made three appearances before the press that day, and in each one my attire was a signal that the situation was escalating.

In the first one, at 10:05 A.M. Pacific time, I was wearing jeans and a western shirt, which is what I normally wore in Santa Barbara, and I delivered a statement on live television that I had written out in longhand, declaring that "the President is very concerned and deeply disturbed about the loss of life aboard the Korean Airlines flight. . . . The Soviet Union owes an explanation to the world about how and why this tragedy has occurred."

Fifteen minutes later, having changed into a blue blazer, an oxford shirt, and a tie, but still wearing jeans, I held a regular, nontelevised press briefing that was devoted primarily to KAL and lasted forty-five minutes. CBS had their camera pan up and down, showing that I was wearing jeans, and played it on the evening news, which I thought was a little unfair. It was one thing to have showed me in my jeans a few minutes earlier when I was on live television in the midst of a crisis, but there was no need to record below-the-belt pictures for the much larger audience that would view the evening news.

Having changed into a full-fledged business suit, I held another brief-ing, this one live on national television, at two-thirty-three in the afternoon Pacific time. This time I delivered a very strong statement from President Reagan, who declared, "Words can scarcely express our revulsion at this horrifying act of violence. The United States joins with other members of the international community in demanding a full explanation for this appalling and wanton misdeed. . . . The whole incident appears to be inexplicable to civilized people everywhere."

Understandably, the press had hundreds of questions about the destruction of Flight 007—and I had to provide the answers, because I was speaking for the White House and the entire U.S. government, and the Soviets were stonewalling the whole affair. At first they denied that the plane had crashed; then they denied shooting it down; then they accused the United States of having sent it over Russian territory on a spy mission; and finally, nearly a week later, they acknowledged shooting down the plane, but claimed that poor visibility that night prevented them from determining that it was a civilian plane. (In fact, I told the press, there was a half moon, and the Soviet jet fighter that shot down the KAL plane circled it and had ample opportunity to see what kind of plane it was; the KAL plane was fully lit and clearly marked as a Korean Air Lines aircraft.) As late as a month after the attack, Soviet leader Yuri Andropov, in his first public comments about the attack, was still blaming the U.S. for causing his pilot to fire on the KAL plane by sending it on a spy mission.

I was very much restricted, however, in what I could say, at least initially, because we had received the bulk of our information from intercepts of Soviet radio transmissions by Japanese air traffic controllers and military sources, and revealing what we knew would also reveal how we knew it.

I did disclose, aboard Air Force One as we flew back to Washington on September 2, that there was "unmistakable evidence in radio transmissions that the Soviet pilot locked on, armed and fired his missile, and went on to say, 'Target destroyed.' "

At the suggestion of Mike Deaver, who told the President it would look bad for him to remain in Santa Barbara under the circumstances, Reagan had cut short his vacation to return to the White House and meet with his national security advisers about the crisis. Immediately after returning to the White House, President Reagan held a two-hour meeting on the night of September 2 with about twenty top advisers, including Clark, Meese, Shultz, Weinberger, Chief of Staff Jim Baker, Deputy Chief of Staff Mike Deaver; Vice President Bush; and CIA director William Casey. The most dramatic presentation came from General John

W. Vessey, Jr., chairman of the Joint Chiefs of Staff, who reported that on the tapes of intercepted Soviet radio transmissions, you could hear the excitement in the voice of the pilot of the Soviet fighter as he pulled within a mile and three-quarters of the KAL plane, inspected it, fired, and reported his success.

During a subsequent meeting with leaders of Congress, Clark pointed out that the Soviets did not initially make any claim that it was a case of mistaken identity, which would have been their best alibi. They did use that defense later, and it was probably true, but their failure to claim mistaken identity at first made them look guilty. Shultz told the congressional leaders that this was not a U.S.-Soviet problem, but "a Soviet versus the world problem"; nearly every nation had joined the United States in condemning the Soviet action—not that the Russians had as yet accepted blame. Shultz added that the image of the Soviet Union as a peace-loving country "is pretty well shot in the rear end by this incident." During that discussion, Strom Thurmond, the ultimate hawk, suggested returning 269 KGB agents to the Soviet Union, "dead or alive, either way."

As that meeting continued, Bill Clark handed me a note that said, "Get back to the need for an explanation from the Soviets. If it was a mistake, they should tell the world." He said they might have initially confused the KAL plane with a U.S. reconnaissance plane that had flown near the Korean aircraft long before the attack, but by the time they shot it down "they should have known irrefutably what it was."

I did as Clark said, but as my confidence grew during my first major crisis since the 1981 assassination attempt, I also did a little improvising on my own: Since the President had had almost nothing to say during the national security and congressional leadership meetings, I made presidential quotes out of Shultz's comment about the incident pitting the whole world against the Soviet Union, as well as some of Shultz's suggestions about what retaliatory steps we should take. My decision to put Shultz's words in Reagan's mouth played well, and neither of them complained.

At the insistence of National Security director William Clark and CIA director William Casey, we in the Reagan administration made a serious mistake by not immediately releasing the tapes or the transcripts of the conversations between the Soviet fighter pilots and their ground controllers. The tapes were extremely damning, especially the excited claim, "The target is destroyed," by the pilot who actually fired the missile that downed the KAL plane.

I was not yet enough of an insider to make my case to the President, who was persuaded by Clark and Casey not to release the tapes or the transcripts for several days. Clark and Casey feared the release would reveal sensitive methods we used for eavesdropping on the Russians, which was certainly a valid concern. Moreover, they didn't want the tapes to become public until our ambassador to the U.N., Jeane Kirkpatrick, could play them in the General Assembly. The inner circle wanted a dramatic replay of Adlai Stevenson's presenting photos of Russian missiles in Cuba during the 1962 crisis. Nevertheless, the delay hurt us from a public relations standpoint, in particular because House Democratic leader Jim Wright very foolishly went out twice during the meeting of congressional leaders at the White House and told reporters that we had information that the Soviets had misidentified the Korean airliner as a U.S. spy plane—which was untrue. The press immediately jumped on Wright's "scoop" and ran with it. We wanted Wright to correct his mistake, but before we could get hold of him I found that he had left on an American Airlines flight for Dallas–Fort Worth and would be out of touch for three hours. I did reach him after his plane landed, but by then the story had been on the air for those three hours.

Clark and Casey failed to take into account that we were in an international battle for public opinion. What they should have done was let me go on background or deep background, providing the information as "a senior administration official," and, without allowing reporters to identify me by name as their source, give the facts about how the intelligence was gathered and what evidence we had. And, of course, we should have released the tapes on the spot. In spite of that mistake, the Soviet attack on an unarmed civilian plane was so monstrous that we won the public relations battle anyway, although we could have won it earlier and more decisively.

As for the destruction of Flight 007, my own theory, later confirmed by exhaustive government and private fact-gathering, was that it was simply an incredible mistake by the Russians, who confused the Korean plane with the U.S. reconnaissance plane that had flown near it but veered off much earlier. They saw this plane flying over restricted territory where they had secret military installations, and their pilot, who was probably young and inexperienced, misidentified the KAL plane as a military plane. Then, I believe, the local ground commander, relying on what the pilot was reporting, gave him permission to shoot it down. It was a case of shoot first and ask questions later that backfired on the Russians. But I don't believe they meant to shoot down a civilian plane; the proof of the pudding is that afterwards they purged several senior military officials, including Marshal Nikolai V. Ogarkov, their military chief of staff.

The KAL incident was an indication of the myth of Soviet military supremacy. That myth was further eroded last year when a West German teenager managed to fly a small plane all the way from the Russian-Finnish border to Moscow and land it in Red Square without being detected or stopped. In the case of KAL, the vaunted Russian air force apparently couldn't even tell the difference between a 747 and one of our RC-135 spy planes, which is about the size and shape of a 707.

In the aftermath of the Russian attack, we barred Soviet delegates to the United Nations from flying into the U.S. on Aeroflot and from landing at civilian airports in the New York area—which forced Soviet Foreign Minister Andrei Gromyko to cancel his plans to attend the U.N. General Assembly meeting in New York a few weeks later. This episode certainly marked the low point in U.S.-Soviet relations during the Reagan administration, and colored our views of the Russians for the next eighteen months, until Mikhail Gorbachev took over and began liberalizing his country's policies, both domestically and internationally.

THE 1985 SUMMIT IN GENEVA

The world viewed the November 1985 summit meeting between President Reagan and Soviet leader Mikhail Gorbachev with great anticipation. The November 19–21 talks in Geneva would be Ronald Reagan's first chance to meet face-to-face with his Soviet counterpart, in part because Gorbachev's three predecessors, Leonid Brezhnev, Yuri Andropov, and Konstantin Chernenko, had all died during Reagan's first four years in office. Whenever Reagan was asked why he waited so long for a summit with the Soviets, his answer was, "They kept dying on me."

As a matter of fact, Bud McFarlane and George Shultz had wanted the President to go to Chernenko's funeral in March 1985 and meet Gorbachev. McFarlane went so far as to tell Bob Sims, who then worked for me, to "pack your bags" early one morning. Sims went down, and, without authorization from me, told the same thing to AP and UPI: "Pack your bags. We're going." As soon as that moved on the wire I knew it was wrong. I knew the President well enough to be sure that he wasn't going to go; I had heard him say many times, "I have no desire to go to Moscow, and a funeral is not a good time to try to do business with these people." McFarlane and Shultz were lurking in the Oval Office, waiting for the President to come over that morning, in order to convince him to go. Mike Deaver, the one who knew the President best, outwitted them by meeting Reagan in the residence as he came down by elevator, walking over with him, and urging him not to attend the funeral. By the time the President had reached the Oval Office, he had made up his mind not to go.

Now Reagan and Gorbachev, who had only been general secretary of the Soviet Communist Party for eight months, would have a chance to size each other up. In addition to being Reagan's first encounter with the top Russian official, it was the first U.S.-U.S.S.R. summit in six and a half years and only the eleventh in the forty years since World War II.

Within the White House we had little expectation of reaching a substantive agreement with the Russians at this first Reagan summit; the best we could hope for was to better define the issues and establish points of common ground. There was no way we were going to bargain away our position on four key issues: We wanted deep cuts in nuclear weapons; no first-strike advantage for either side; a continuation of defense-oriented research, notably the Strategic Defense Initiative, our space-based "Star Wars" missile defense system; and an assurance that there would be no cheating on either side. The Russians were demanding that we abandon Star Wars, which Reagan would never do, creating the likelihood of an impasse. The President told those of us on the senior staff, "We're going to stick by our points. This is what we want." Shultz underscored that by declaring, "We are prepared to say to the Russians, 'If you don't want an agreement, that's fine, we can go home without one.' " Shultz's staff had even drafted in advance a statement to be issued at the end of the summit, in the event talks collapsed over Star Wars. Nevertheless, Reagan and his top advisers had high hopes that the summit would allow the President to work some of his famous personal charm on Gorbachev and establish groundwork for future meetings that might prove more fruitful.

Reagan, who had broken the ice at his first economic summit in Canada in 1981 by suggesting that all of the leaders be on a first-name basis, raised the same question during preparation sessions for Geneva: "Should I call him Mikhail?" Before anyone could answer, he continued, "Or better, still, Mik, my ole buddy!" Everyone laughed, but our Soviet experts steered the boss off, saying such familiarity was not the Russian way at the first meeting. Reagan finally got on a first-name basis when the two met in Washington in 1987.

As part of his preparation for the summit, the President held a working luncheon on Thursday, November 7, with a group of Soviet experts. The most useful advice came from Bill Hyland, editor of *Foreign Affairs*, who told Reagan the timing was good for us because "our own economy is resurgent, while the Soviet economy is in shambles." Hyland also advised the President that large meetings might not be successful because the Soviet leader would have to perform and posture before his colleagues, who could criticize and second-guess later in private, but one-on-one sessions between him and Gorbachev could be constructive.

During the meeting, someone brought up the question of human rights, and the President, just as he would three months later while trying to ease Filipino President Ferdinand Marcos out of his job, observed, "We can't back them into a corner." Once again, he showed his belief in quiet diplomacy in order to achieve his goal. This advice had come from Richard Nixon, who told Reagan, "You have to leave them maneuvering room. They have to save face back home." Reagan went on to tell a story about when he was negotiating on behalf of the Screen Actors Guild. "Negotiations would sometimes go on for days, and finally my opposite number would give a little signal. Then we would go to the men's room for a short break. There we would make a deal without any of our aides to second-guess us."

By the same token, as Reagan told a White House gathering of congressional leaders that I attended the next day, he was going to remain firm on arms control: "I intend to make the point that we are the only two countries that can guarantee there will be no world war. Everything we do is for our national security, and we understand that everything he [Gorbachev] does is for his national security. But we're not going to let them acquire a margin of superiority. We will do whatever we have to do to be certain of that. We will do whatever the hell has to be done. As far as verification is concerned, if they won't agree to that, we'll look 'em in the eye and say, 'That means you want to cheat!' " It was vintage Reagan.

As the summit approached, a series of unusual events helped set the stage:

- Tass, the Soviet news agency, made an unusual request for an interview with the President. The Tass-White House correspondent, Alexander Shelnev, was a new breed of cat as Russian journalists go. The press room staff had dubbed his predecessor "The Colonel," a not-so-veiled reference to our belief that all Tass correspondents assigned to the White House were crack KGB agents. "The Colonel" had the shifty-eyed look of the spy about him and seemed to be straight from central casting. Shelnev, on the other hand, was dapper, articulate in English, and had a great sense of humor. Not that we had any illusions about who his true masters were, but due to his relative youth, he was known as "The Major." Shelnev got so much publicity out of this episode that the press corps gave him a promotion, to "Little Colonel."

After somewhat delicate negotiations involving Shelnev, myself, Ed Djerejian, and Pete Roussel—negotiations that would have done justice to those for the Treaty of Versailles—four journalists from Tass showed up to interview the President in the Oval Office on October 31. Afterwards, they hung around the President as if he were a rock star, asking for autographs and making small talk with him. Although the Russians had promised to publish Reagan's remarks in full, they deleted some of his tougher statements on Afghanistan and the Soviet threat in Europe when they printed a transcript of the interview in *Izvestia* four days later. Unable to resist a little posturing on behalf of freedom of the press, I zinged the Russians for "censorship." Still, it was an historic interview, the first one by the Russians with an American President since Aleksey Adzhubei, chief editor of *Izvestia* and son-in-law of Soviet Premier Nikita Khrushchev, had interviewed President Kennedy in 1961.

- The Soviets allowed President Reagan to address Russian listeners on November 9 via the Voice of America without jamming the broadcast. The Russians had jammed every Voice of America broadcast since 1980, and resumed jamming after Reagan's address. The President told his Russian audience that Americans are "a peace-loving people" with no hostile intentions against the Soviet Union.
- The Russians permitted human rights activist Andrei Sakharov, who was in internal exile in Gorky, to speak by telephone with his relatives in the United States for the first time in six years, and gave permission for his wife, Yelena Bonner, to travel to the U.S. for medical treatment.
- The Russians also announced that ten Soviet citizens who had married American citizens were free to leave.
- Revelations continued to surface in the spy case of former navy man John Walker and members of his family and in the unrelated case of former FBI agent Richard Miller. Miller and the Walkers were accused of providing sensitive information to the Russians.
- Vitaly Yurchenko, a high-ranking KGB officer who had defected to our side in Rome three months earlier and disclosed extensive information about Soviet intelligence operations under debriefing in the Washington area, walked away from his CIA keeper during dinner at a restaurant in Georgetown, went to the Russian embassy, and announced that he was returning to his homeland. U.S. intelligence experts have been arguing ever since whether Yurchenko was a bona fide defector who simply changed his mind, perhaps because his Russian mistress refused to join him in exile, or was a KGB plant designed to embarrass us on the eve of the summit.

- A Russian merchant seaman twice jumped ship while his vessel was anchored near New Orleans, but U.S. Customs officials, believing he wanted to go home, returned him to his ship and the custody of his captain.
- And *Playboy* magazine hired the First Son, Ron Reagan, to cover the summit, creating a furor in the American press corps, where it was felt that Ron had a conflict of interest as both the President's son and a journalist.

The President cracked that there was so much going on that the blitz of news events reminded him of "a fire in a zoo."

The circus continued as we flew from Washington to Geneva on Saturday, November 16. We arranged to have a mounting of the American and Soviet flags passed out as a gift to the 175 journalists on the press plane. However, the American flags contained only forty-eight stars. Historic it was.

Much more serious, word came to me on Air Force One that *The New York Times* was reporting that Cap Weinberger, ever the loose cannon, had written a letter to the President, advising Reagan not to give in to the Soviets on arms control. From over the Atlantic I talked by phone with the Pentagon spokesman, my old deputy Bob Sims. He denied any knowledge of the letter and said they were issuing a quick statement to play down the controversy. Sims was quoted in press reports as saying, "The Department of Defense had nothing to do with the release of Secretary Weinberger's letter to the President to any publications." However, in my opinion, the letter was specifically written by Weinberger or other hardliners in the Defense Department to be handed out to the press. I suspected that either Weinberger or Pentagon arms control expert Richard Perle, at Weinberger's suggestion, had leaked the letter to the *Times.* Aboard the President's plane, I openly expressed irritation about the letter, saying, "The President would have preferred to read it in the privacy of the Oval Office rather than in *The New York Times.*" Bud McFarlane was asked by reporters in the press pool on Air Force One if the Weinberger letter constituted sabotage. He paused grimly, then, with the understanding that the press could not identify him by name, said, "Sure it was."

Everyone from the President on down was steaming. I felt that the leak of the Weinberger letter was almost treasonous, since it was designed to ruin the summit talks. In my opinion, the leaker should have been locked up. The Weinberger letter certainly dominated the evening news, pushing aside much of the planning we had laid out. Bill Moyers on CBS cited it as proof that "The administration's act is not together. Torn by factions and poorly prepared for these talks, it can't agree on what it wants." Connie Chung on NBC led by saying, "[Reagan's] arrival is tainted by the leak of a Pentagon letter making public internal dissension on how to deal with the Soviets."

Another controversy developed on Monday, November 18, the day before the summit opened, as the *Washington Post* quoted Don Regan as saying that most women were more interested in what Nancy Reagan and Raisa Gorbachev had planned in Geneva than they were in the substantive issues at stake: "They're not going to understand throw-weights or what is happening in Afghanistan or what is happening in human rights. Some women will, but most women . . . would rather read the human interest stuff of what happened." The reaction was predictably furious; for example, Eleanor Smeal, head of the National Organization for Women, commented that she was glad to learn that "the President took Bonzo to Geneva with him." Regan, of course, had to apologize, but his screwup was another one that the press would remember a year later when the Iran-contra arms scandal broke.

We in the press office had prepared as detailed a communications plan for getting our points across as I had ever seen, dating back to my earliest experience with the 1976 debates between Ford and Dole on the Republican ticket and Carter and Mondale on the Democratic side. Before the summit we blitzed all the morning and evening talk shows with guests, and made administration spokesmen available to any media outlet that wanted to interview them.

We knew that we were up against a communications juggernaut in the Soviet press operation. This was the Soviets' first attempt in the Gorbachev era of *glasnost* at a Western-style media campaign, and they provided unprecedented access to senior officials, who had heretofore been unavailable to the press corps in Moscow. The Soviets stole the march by putting a team of generals, scientists, and arms control experts in Geneva a week ahead of the conference. For several nights U.S. television gave extensive play to the Russians without anyone from our side to reply. The President, McFarlane, and Regan were getting nervous, fearing that we were getting whipped and should have someone over in Geneva right away. I got the brunt of the criticism as the Soviets dominated U.S. television, but I counseled people to bide their time and not to panic, that we would be fine.

The Soviets gradually found that their openness was more trouble than it was worth because it attracted demonstrators to protest against them in Geneva. They had no experience to teach them that free speech and freedom of the press can be a two-edged sword; you can't simply state your position openly with any guarantee that there won't be criticism.

Problems arose in one of the Russians' first all-out encounters with a free press. A cable to me from the State Department reported that the Soviets' November 16 morning press conference, which lasted fifty minutes, was characterized by persistent questioning on Afghanistan and Soviet-Israeli relations. Leonid Zamyatin, the main spokesman for the Soviets for many years, was conducting the briefing, and he kept sidestepping questions. Finally, a dissident who had been allowed to leave the Soviet Union just two weeks earlier began harrassing Zamyatin on the subject of human rights. The dissident, Irina Grivnina, who had obtained press accreditation from the Dutch magazine *Elseviers,* interrupted by shouting questions about political prisoners and the use of psychiatry as a punitive measure. She had been jailed for thirteen months in Lefortovo Prison in Moscow and exiled for another twenty months in the Central Asian republic of Kazakhstan for her protests. Zamyatin quoted Gorbachev as saying, "Within the Soviet Union political prisoners do not exist." When Grivnina tried to continue, Zamyatin asked, "Do we have to call the militia to remove this lady?" and then literally stalked off the stage and canceled the remainder of his press conference. The cable informed me that the Russians also canceled an afternoon press conference that day. When I showed the cable to Bud McFarlane, he laughed, let down his guard for once, and said, "We're back in the ball game."

My first task in Geneva was to meet with Leonid Zamyatin, to discuss how we would handle the press. He was a former editor of *Tass* who had served as spokesman for Brezhnev, Andropov, and Chernenko, as well as Gorbachev. Zamyatin had a formidable reputation, having once run rings around Ron Ziegler in a joint press briefing in Moscow, and Ziegler had warned me to be on guard with him. So I decided the best approach, as it often is, was humor. When I first met him in Geneva, with only an interpreter and my deputy, Ed Djerejian, present, I said to Zamyatin, "Some of my predecessors gave me one piece of advice." "What's that?" he responded. "Beware of Zamyatin." He laughed, and then I presented him with a gift, a White House paperweight, and told him, "I just want to assure you that that's not a listening device." He laughed again, and from then on we seemed to be on good terms. At that first meeting he proposed that each side talk only about what its leader had said; in other words, I wouldn't comment on Gorbachev's statements, and Zamyatin would not comment on Reagan's, to which I readily agreed. In spite of the warnings I had received about Zamyatin, I found him easy to deal with in what turned out to be his last summit before Gorbachev promoted him up and out, naming him ambassador to Great Britain.

At the same time, I had no illusions about what all of us on the American side were faced with. Gorbachev arrived in Geneva on Monday, November 18, and that evening a Secret Service agent took me aside and quietly informed me that Swiss authorities had identified half a dozen members of the Soviet party on Gorbachev's plane as the same Russian "diplomats" who had been kicked out of Great Britain several months earlier for espionage activities. Although sorely tempted, we never publicized the Soviets' second try.

Not that every moment was tense. That same day President Reagan made a trial run to inspect Fleur d'Eau, the nineteenth-century chateau overlooking Lake Geneva, where Reagan would host the opening talks the next day. He sat in the chair in the corner of a tiny room where he would sit when he and Gorbachev met the following day, and Nancy Reagan sat down in Gorbachev's chair. "My, my, you're much prettier than I expected, Mr. General Secretary," the President quipped.

And then there was the weighty matter of state when the goldfish died. Let me explain: During the summit conference, the Reagans moved into Maison de Saussure, a magnificent eighteenth-century chateau that was leased from its owner and occupied by Prince Karim Aga Khan. The Prince agreed to loan it to the President and Mrs. Reagan while they were in Geneva. The Prince's young son had left the President a note asking him to take care of his goldfish, along with instructions which the President followed. Presidential aide Jim Kuhn came in one evening and saw that one of the fish had gone belly up in the tank. Jim was in a panic and was hesitant to tell the President. When he finally did, Reagan was horrified. No one knew what to do. Finally, we decided to freeze the fish in the refrigerator, and when advance man Andy Littlefair finally had a free moment, he took the dead fish and went downtown and bought a duplicate. The President, not wanting to fool the boy, left him a note saying one of the fish had died but they had replaced it and he hoped all the fish would do well. "And we'd come to Geneva thinking our toughest job would be to handle the Russians," Kuhn cracked.

Not long after we arrived in Geneva, George Shultz took me aside and asked me, "What do you think of imposing a news blackout until the conclusion of the summit?" I was adamantly opposed. I told him, "I don't think we can control our people and if there is a leak in the *Washington Post*, then we will have a press riot on our hands, led by *The New York Times* and the *Los Angeles Times.* Mr. Secretary," I continued, "everybody else who paid good money to come on this trip will tar and feather us." Shultz said it had worked for him previously in his meetings with Soviet foreign minister Eduard Shevardnadze in Helsinki.

I hoped the idea of a news blackout would be forgotten and Shultz wouldn't bring it up again, but he presented it to the President at our 9:00 A.M. senior staff meeting before we went over to the Fleur d'Eau for Reagan's first meeting with Gorbachev on Tuesday, November 19. Don Regan was ambivalent about a blackout and Bud McFarlane wasn't even consulted. The President asked me what I thought and I repeated my argument of the day before, but Reagan went for the blackout, saying, "I like the idea, let's do it."

Then Shultz said to me, "You've had your meeting with the Russians, why don't you negotiate this?" So it fell my duty to negotiate something I didn't believe in. I met Zamyatin a little later at the Fleur d'Eau and used a variation on President Kennedy's old tactic from the Cuban missile crisis, when the Russians sent one offer and then a second much tougher one, and Kennedy decided to accept the first one and ignore the second. I told Zamyatin I would like to take him up on a suggestion he had made the day before about controlling the content of our briefings. "All we would release would be the time of the meetings, the participants, and the general subject matters covered." Then, without giving him a chance to answer, I quickly added, "What we're proposing is a total news blackout. No television, no details of the meetings, until the summit ends."

"That is a decision I cannot make," he replied. "I would like to talk with my foreign minister." With the time approaching for my first press briefing of the day, I needed an immediate answer, and I said to Zamyatin, "Let's do it right now." We went into the adjoining room where Shultz and Shevardnadze were in an animated conversation with their interpreters at their elbows and other officials gathered around, including Bud McFarlane, U.S. Ambassador to the Soviet Union Arthur Hartman, and others. Shultz, knowing what was going on, stopped his conversation with Shevardnadze and I explained, "My colleague and I have discussed a news blackout and would like to present it to you." Shevardnadze paused but a second and said, "That's a decision I cannot make. We will have to take it to the general secretary."

The Reagan-Gorbachev meeting had begun at 10:14 A.M. It was now after eleven, and I was due to begin my briefing at the Intercontinental Hotel, a few blocks away, at eleven-thirty. Several hundred of the 3,000 journalists who had descended on Geneva were waiting for me in the briefing room, and I still didn't know whether or not there was a blackout. I assumed it would take a long time for the Soviets to decide how to respond—a period during which they would continue issuing their propaganda—while I would be left exposed before the entire press corps, just swinging in the breeze. I was afraid that I might have to go to the first briefing of the Geneva summit without anything to say or without even being able to explain why I could not say anything. I grabbed Zamyatin and pleaded, "I've got to have an answer," and he said through his interpreter, "I will see to it that it is resolved at once."

The meeting between Reagan and Gorbachev finally broke up at eleven-eighteen. The two leaders posed for pictures, standing together before a fireplace at the end of the rectangular table instead of at their usual places across the table from each other. As the first group of cameramen left and we waited for wave number two to come in, Zamyatin was standing to Gorbachev's left, and I worked my way to Zamyatin's side and whispered desperately to him and his interpreter, "I've got to know." Zamyatin said in Russian to Gorbachev, "They would like a news blackout." As the photographers began snapping pictures, Gorbachev continued smiling for the photographers, and, without even looking over to the side at Zamyatin, never hesitating a moment, simply said, "Do it." I turned to Zamyatin and said, "What did he say?" Through his interpreter he said, "It is approved."

I had my marching orders, and I scribbled out a statement in my car as it wound its way through the Geneva traffic. I reached the Intercontinental ten minutes late, rushed in, and announced the first agreement of the summit—neither side would provide any substantive details until the talks had concluded. There would be no background briefings, no television appearances by either side, I told the press corps. Zamyatin and I would be the only spokesmen. "Those who talk don't know what's going on," I warned the press corps. "And those who know what's going on won't talk." To my surprise, the press didn't object to the blackout. Reporters understood that the summit talks had more chance for success if they weren't subjected to a daily public relations battle in the press. The blackout also relieved the reporters of the burden of having to scramble twenty-four hours a day to protect themselves against leaks to competitors.

Gorbachev's handling of the blackout proposal taught us a lot about him. As the President, Shultz, and I rehashed what had happened, Shultz said that the blackout episode showed that "Gorbachev is clearly a man in charge. He didn't ask for option papers. He didn't ask for time to think about it. And a lot was at stake. But he was willing to make a decision in the blink of an eye." The President said with a wink, "Maybe he's our kind of a guy."

At lunch after the first morning meeting, back at the President's residence, Reagan said that at whatever point he felt comfortable he was going to ask Gorbachev to break off and go talk in private. We had very carefully arranged to have a fire burning in the Fleur d'Eau's poolhouse, which was located about one hundred yards down a winding gravel walkway toward Lake Geneva. Not only was the fireplace set up, but White House stewards were in place with coffee and tea, and a White House photographer was stationed there. But it was supposed to be an impromptu gesture on the part of the President.

The afternoon session started at two-thirty-five, and at ten of four the President suggested that he and Gorbachev walk outside the residence toward Lake Geneva. The two of them walked down to the poolhouse and sat in easy chairs that offered a spectacular view of the lake through plate-glass windows. They met there from three-fifty-five to four-forty-four with only interpreters present—later, during a briefing, I spontaneously dubbed their meeting "the Fireside Summit." Reagan, Shultz, and I later discussed it and decided to use the term "Fireside Summit" in all of Reagan's subsequent statements. Our aim was to convey a sense of warmth, congeniality, and mutual understanding that the general public could identify with. David Hoffman of the *Washington Post* asked me at a briefing that evening if the fact that we had a fire burning there didn't prove that the whole thing had been staged. I replied, "No, I would judge it's probably one of those poolhouses that has a twenty-four-hour-a-day fire burning in it," amidst a great deal of laughter.

The poolhouse setting had the desired effect: As the two leaders stood in the driveway of the chateau after their fireside chat in the poolhouse, the President, in the friendly, informal spirit of their poolhouse talk, invited Gorbachev to come to the U.S. and Gorbachev accepted without hesitation.

The next morning at the Soviet Embassy the private session was on human rights and the President came out in a fairly foul mood because Gorbachev hadn't budged at all. Instead, Gorbachev had shot back for the first time some of the standard Soviet rhetoric about the U.S. military-industrial complex. Reagan was surprised that Gorbachev was still putting out these old worn-out phrases that went back to the Eisenhower administration. "I can't believe a man as savvy as Gorbachev is using those terms," Reagan said to several of us during a private moment. "I suspect he really believes what he's saying. Maybe we can educate him otherwise when he comes to see us."

The afternoon session on the second day quickly bogged down in disagreement over a proposed statement on arms control. Shultz and Shevardnadze suggested that the two delegations continue their discussions without the leaders, so Reagan and Gorbachev and their translators adjourned to a parlor, where they drank tea and coffee, nibbled on pastries, and made small talk. Reagan, finding his material running thin, reported to me later that he had turned to jokes. "You ever hear the one about—" he began. I'm sure Gorbachev must have sat bolt upright at that. But Reagan continued, "The old Russian woman went into the Kremlin and demanded to see Gorbachev. When admitted to the inner sanctum, she said, 'In America, one can go into the White House, walk up to Reagan's desk, and say, "I don't like the way you are running the country." ' Gorbachev answered, 'Why, my dear, you can do the same thing in the Soviet Union. You can go into the Kremlin, come up to my office *anytime*, and say, "I don't like the way Reagan's running his country." ' " Reagan said that Gorbachev listened intently, and, as the translator continued to relay Reagan's joke, his smile widened, and, when he heard the punchline, he broke into loud laughter.

Reagan actually confirmed something with his jokemaking—that Gorbachev understood little, if any, English. "He never laughed until he heard the punchline interpreted," Reagan said later.

As the two whiled away the time, Reagan later recounted to us, he was sorely tempted to tell what we called "the potato joke," which was the President's favorite. It seems that a commissar was visiting a collective farm, and he asked one farmer about his success in meeting the quotas of the latest five-year plan. The farmer said, "Comrade, the potato crop is magnificent. You can stack the potatoes so high they will reach to the feet of God." The commissar, taken aback, said, "Shame on you, Comrade, you know in Russia there is no God." And the farmer shot back, "And there are no potatoes, either." I always wondered how Gorbachev would have reacted. Had the bargaining session not broken, I feel certain the President would soon have tried the potato joke.

It was during this private chat that Reagan did get a hint that Gorbachev might believe in God. We had seen published statements that Gorbachev had referred to God. For the leader of an atheist country, that was indeed startling. Reagan told us the next morning, "Gorbachev told me that Raisa was an atheist, but he himself had had the Bible read to him as a child by his Christian grandmother." Although Reagan never pushed the Soviet leader to explain his religious views, the President was convinced the childhood exposure to the Bible had had an influence.

The two delegations finally ended their discussions and filed in to report to their leaders. Shultz reported, "Gentlemen, we have failed to agree on key language instructing our arms control negotiators. I am afraid we are at an impasse." Gorbachev seized a copy of the disputed text, paused only briefly, and then spoke rapidly, as his subordinates struggled to get down his words. "That should do it," he commented when the English translation was relayed to us. Shultz could not contain a rare smile. Gorbachev, demonstrating once again his decisiveness, had laid out very explicit instructions to the negotiators to get moving.

Gorbachev was not only showing that he was in charge of his delegation, he was proving himself a master at dealing with the press—whom, in private asides to me, he delighted in referring to as "the animals" or "the villains."

I felt that Gorbachev was really getting the advantage over us in his give and take with reporters, while Reagan was very tentative and stilted. For example, when a member of the press pool questioned the two leaders on the morning of the nineteenth, after the first session, Gorbachev said, "The fact that the meeting has taken place and is going on in a very careful way [with him and Reagan] looking at all of the problems that are of concern to both the Soviet people and the American people, that fact [shows] that this is a responsible discussion." The President was asked, "Are you encouraged?" But all he would say was, "Yes. As I say, we have agreed that we won't do any reporting until the meeting is over. . . . We're not going to comment on anything." Then Gorbachev said, "We had a lively discussion of everything. You may be sure that the discussion is lively."

And when asked about Don Regan's comment about women not being interested in throw-weights, Gorbachev, who probably never had heard about the remark or the flap, had a brilliant answer: "My view is that both men and women in the United States and the Soviet Union, all over the world, are interested in having peace for themselves and being sure that peace will be kept stable and lasting for the future, and for that they're interested in the reduction of countless weapons that we have and they're interested in having this reduction. Therefore, these matters are in the center of my discussions with the President." So, a man who wasn't prepared, and knew nothing about the Don Regan interview, took that question and literally blasted it out of the ballpark and broke the windows across the street. That comment showed his ability, his agility, his way of operating in a good give-and-take atmosphere and accomplishing what he set out to accomplish. The U.S. delegation was extremely impressed by our first encounter with the new Soviet leader, to say the least.

Fearing that Reagan was losing the media version of Star Wars, I instructed Mark Weinberg to draft some quotes for the President. I polished the quotes and told the press that while the two leaders stood together at the end of one session, the President said to Gorbachev, "There is much that divides us, but I believe the world breathes easier because we are talking here together." CBS had me on the news Wednesday evening giving that quote. And Chris Wallace said, "The talks were frank. The President's best statement came off-camera, aides quoting him as saying, 'The world breathes easier because we are talking together.' " Another Reagan quote which we manufactured that received extensive play in the press was, "Our differences are serious, but so is our commitment to improving understanding."

In retrospect, it was clearly wrong to take such liberties. Certainly, Reagan would not have disavowed the words, but the Soviets could have said they never heard anything like that. Luckily, the Russians didn't dispute the quotes, and I had been able to spruce up the President's image by taking a bit of liberty with my P.R. man's license.

President Reagan was feeling very upbeat about the discussions he had had with Gorbachev as several of us, including him and Mrs. Reagan and me, stood warming ourselves in front of the fireplace in the library of Maison de Saussure, on the evening of November 20. We were awaiting the arrival of the Gorbachevs for the final dinner of the summit.

Nancy Reagan perhaps felt less enthusiastic about the impending arrival of Raisa Gorbachev; the two First Ladies had hosted each other at reciprocal teas during the summit, and Mrs. Reagan had privately come to dislike Mrs. Gorbachev. Mrs. Reagan regarded her Soviet counterpart as a dogmatic Marxist who simply spouted Communist philosophy and shared little of Mrs. Reagan's interest in fighting drug abuse, or other issues of substance. Considering that both First Ladies boasted huge wardrobes and were regarded as international fashion plates, perhaps they would have gotten along better if we had held Strategic Dress Limitation Talks in advance of the summit. Mrs. Reagan found Mrs. Gorbachev even more to her distaste the following year as a result of the second summit meeting between their husbands in Iceland. Mrs. Gorbachev initially said she wasn't going to accompany her husband, so Nancy Reagan made other commitments for the weekend of the summit. Mrs. Gorbachev changed her mind at the last minute and did go to Reykjavik, but Mrs. Reagan could not alter her plans and was unable to be there—which left her with the feeling that Mrs. Gorbachev had tricked her.

While the Reagan were waiting for the Gorbachevs it began to snow, and the snowflakes were illuminated by the television lights that flashed on as the Gorbachevs arrived and the Reagans greeted them at the door and posed for pictures in honor of the festive occasion. Drinks were offered to the two First Couples, and the other guests: Shultz, Regan, McFarlane, Ambassador Arthur Hartman, Shevardnadze, Soviet ambassador to Washington Anatoly Dobrynin, and two other members of the Russian delegation. But I noticed that the Soviets, in view of Gorbachev's campaign to reduce alcoholism at home, steadfastly refused to have any hard liquor, particularly vodka. Secretary Shultz, in an aside, said, however, that Georgi Korniyenko, the Soviet deputy foreign minister, eagerly gulped down glass after glass of vodka when he attended preliminary planning sessions where Gorbachev wasn't present. The Reagans and their ten guests finally sat down to a five-course dinner at a table set with a special version of the "Nancy Reagan china," a red-bordered pattern made by Lenox with a gold image of the White House and the signatures of the President and Mrs. Reagan in the center.

Across town, aides to Reagan and Gorbachev were trying to hammer out a joint statement to be issued to the press the next day. Our strategy, formulated by George Shultz, continued to be never to look like we really wanted a joint statement. "We never want to appear to be overly eager for any type of concession, even something as minor as how, when, or if we would give a joint statement to the public, much less the substance of any arms control agreement," Shultz said repeatedly. "The President has given us the authority to walk away from a bad agreement."

After dinner the two leaders and their top aides adjourned to the library to receive a report of the discussions that had been held across town. There had been little progress made, and Shultz was steaming. In probably the most dramatic moment of the summit, he staged a diplomatic temper tantrum. The Secretary of State shook his finger in the face of Georgi Korniyenko. Turning abruptly to Gorbachev, Shultz declared, "Mr. General Secretary, *this man* is holding up progress. *This man* will not allow the delegations to agree." It was Shultz at his finest. Gorbachev glanced at his minister, who looked like a kid who had broken his mother's best china, and said, "I will speak to our delegates."

As I scribbled notes of what I knew was a momentous encounter, I watched a little scene unfold within this drama. Reagan and Gorbachev sat side by side on the red silk couch in the wood-paneled library, as their aides hovered anxiously over the two of them. Don Regan was in a chair facing them when the after-dinner talks began, but, as the conversation turned tense, Regan began to maneuver across the room until he was behind the couch where the two leaders sat. En route, he practically elbowed Korniyenko aside. Just as the White House photographer began to record this historic moment, the chief of staff leaned over the couch, his head perfectly positioned between the two. It was front-page material, but three was a crowd. The photo came back to haunt Don Regan, serving only to reinforce his image as a man with a monstrous ego.

In the end, the two leaders agreed to issue a joint statement calling for accelerated arms control negotiations. They also agreed to exchange visits to each other, with Gorbachev to tour the United States in 1986 and Reagan to travel to Russia the following year, a schedule that, of course, was later postponed by one year. As the two of them prepared to sign the statements on the final day of the summit, Reagan leaned over to Gorbachev and whispered, "I bet the hardliners in both our countries are squirming." Gorbachev nodded in agreement.

The Geneva summit was one of the highpoints of the administration. As *The New York Times* reported in its aftermath, both American and Soviet officials viewed it as a triumph for Reagan, who simply wanted to meet and take the measure of Gorbachev and perhaps lay the groundwork for a future arms agreement, and a defeat for Gorbachev, who had hoped for a breakthrough on arms control that Reagan never intended to occur in Geneva.

Flying home triumphantly, Reagan told us, "We've seen what the new Russian looks like. Now maybe we can figure out how to deal with him." It was my impression that the two had decided they could do business. I believe they genuinely liked each other. And their first meeting set the stage for the agreement on arms control that would follow in Washington in December 1987.

A few days after we got back to Washington, Reagan gave me his impressions from the fifteen hours he spent talking to Gorbachev, about five of those hours one-on-one. "We sat in a room," the President recalled, "and I told him, 'Here we are, between us we could decide things that could probably bring peace for years and generations to come. And if we could erase these things that have made us suspicious of each other, it would be very worthwhile." He added, "I think I'm some judge of acting, and

I don't think Gorbachev was acting. He, I believe, is sincere, as we are, in wanting an agreement. But he feels we have no right to lecture him about human rights in the Soviet Union; he sincerely believes that human rights are being violated in our country as well."

THE ARREST OF NICHOLAS DANILOFF

It didn't compare to the destruction of KAL Flight 007, but the arrest of American journalist Nicholas Daniloff in Moscow on August 30, 1986, nonetheless threatened to put U.S.-Soviet relations in the deep freeze. Daniloff, a correspondent for *U.S. News & World Report*, was charged with espionage—an accusation that was patently false. Daniloff's arrest obviously was in retaliation for the FBI's arrest several days earlier of Russian spy Gennadi Zakharov, a Soviet employee at the United Nations, who we believed was a KGB ringleader.

Zakharov and Daniloff were arrested in the midst of major arms control talks between the U.S. and the Soviet Union, which were already even more sensitive than usual because many details about negotiations were being leaked to Michael Gordon of *The New York Times*. Gordon's stories were accurate and all too often laid out our bottom-line position on arms control well before we had presented it to the Soviets. This gave the Russians the advantage of knowing just how far we would go before they had to give in. My State Department friends told me they suspected Ken Adelman, director of the U.S. Arms Control and Disarmament Agency, of being the source, but we never could prove it. In addition to the arms control talks, we were holding discussions with the Russians that both sides hoped would result in a second summit meeting within a year between President Reagan and Mikhail Gorbachev.

The arrests of Daniloff and Zakharov added a new, threatening controversy to the mix. Our aim in the Daniloff affair was twofold: to win the journalist's release, and to do it without letting it appear to be a trade for Zakharov. Reagan's public stance, especially in negotiations with the captors of U.S. hostages in the Middle East, was clear. "We must never permit those who held American citizens to think they are getting something in return for releasing them," he would say privately. "Otherwise, they will be encouraged to kidnap more Americans. It would be open season." His observations would soon prove correct—especially as they applied to the Middle East—to Reagan's chagrin.

Behind the scenes, however, a Daniloff-Zakharov trade was always a possibility, and is, in fact, the usual way to bring these things to a conclusion. When a State Department source said immediately after Daniloff's arrest that Daniloff would never be traded for Zakharov, I responded that that statement had been made by "a fool at the State Department," and that "we do leave our options open." The State Department spokesman also said that the arrest of Daniloff might preclude a summit meeting, but I also pointedly denied that, commenting that "a summit is a potentially important event, and we continue to pursue our discussions." Certainly, the Daniloff arrest might have torpedoed the summit, but, again, all I wanted to do was keep our options open and leave us room to bargain. At that point, I'd had enough of the striped-pants brigade who too often pursued their own agenda and left the President dangling. I knew, too, that my statements from the White House—often made without bureaucratic approval—gave them fits in Foggy Bottom. That pleased me enormously. I was lucky, though, that George Shultz didn't come down on me with a vengeance. Al Haig would have.

Try as we might, there was no way of avoiding the fact that the situations of Daniloff and Zakharov—whom FBI agents in New York had inexplicably arrested without full consultations with top administration officials, thereby setting the crisis in motion—were almost identical and were linked one to the other. We finally proposed that the two men be released from jail into the custody of their respective ambassadors, and the Soviets agreed on September 12, although George Shultz tried to put the best face on it by declaring that it was the Russians who had originally suggested the dual release and we who had reluctantly accepted it.

A week later, on the morning of September 19, Soviet foreign minister Eduard Shevardnadze was in Washington for talks with Shultz, when Shultz called the White House out of the blue and said Shevardnadze would like to meet directly with the President on the Daniloff affair. The President quickly canceled his appointments, and Shultz escorted Shevardnadze into the Oval Office, where Don Regan and John Poindexter were also waiting. During a forty-five-minute noontime meeting, Reagan forcefully told Shevardnadze that he was very concerned about the arrest of Daniloff and its effect on any summit talks between him and Gorbachev. On the other hand, if the Soviets released Daniloff, Reagan told Shevardnadze, "I will be happy to meet with the General Secretary."

It was that meeting that really broke the ice, as the Soviets finally decided to free Daniloff and we agreed that Reagan would meet Gorbachev in Reykjavik, Iceland, in October. Daniloff was released and allowed to fly home on September 29. The Russians also agreed to let two dissidents, Yuri Orlov and his wife, Irina Valitova, emigrate. The day after Daniloff's release—still denying that we had traded Daniloff for Zakharov—we let Zakharov plead no contest to espionage charges and leave the United States, and we also announced that Reagan and Gorbachev would meet in Iceland on October 11 and 12. Several days after his release, a very emotional Nick Daniloff visited the Oval Office to thank Reagan for his intercession, telling the President that "the government turned itself inside out for me. This is proof that this is a country of individuals. Every life is precious."

No matter what we said at the time about the virtually simultaneous release of Daniloff and Zakharov, it obviously was a trade. If that makes the Reagan administration look bad, so be it, but the episode had a very positive side: We used the capture of Daniloff as an excuse to accelerate the reduction of the number of Soviets at the United Nations. While denying it all along, of course, we kicked them out in retaliation for Daniloff's arrest. And the twenty-five Russians on our list had been carefully selected; they were the key KGB operatives at the U.N. We felt we had knocked out a hornet's nest of Russia's top spies, setting back Soviet espionage in the U.S. for years, if not decades.

I had thought about trying to do my bit during the crisis by lifting the press credentials of Tass correspondent Alexander Shelnev and two or three other Soviet journalists, in retaliation for Daniloff's arrest. I finally decided, however, that it wouldn't work, because the Russians simply would have expelled an equal number of U.S. reporters from Moscow.

There were two interesting sidebars to the Daniloff-Zakharov incident. First, complicating matters for me, Daniloff's boss, the editor of *U.S. News,* was none other than David Gergen, who had been White House communications director and my antagonist from the time I succeeded Jim Brady on March 30, 1981, until December 1983, when Gergen resigned.

Gergen kept calling me throughout the Daniloff affair, but I didn't return his calls. If he was calling as a journalist, I was not going to answer questions from him or any other news person, and if he was calling as an executive of a media company with a reporter in trouble somewhere, it was a diplomatic matter that was reserved for the State Department. I suspected that Gergen was wearing two hats, the worried news executive and the reporter. Knowing of his reputation as a world-class leaker, I didn't trust him to keep confidential any conversations we might have had. Of course, if Gergen and I had been on better terms, I might have made Daniloff my business, but as another White House antagonist of mine, Dick Darman, wrote to me, "The wheel turns 'round and 'round in this town," and people do remember things and get even for them.

Moreover, Gergen called one of my aides and said Daniloff might want to ask Reagan a few questions when he visited the Oval Office. My response, which was relayed to Gergen, was "absolutely not." We would allow Daniloff to see the President only in order to thank him, not to conduct an interview.

The other distraction was George Will, who pretended to be a friend of the administration in order to gain access to the President and Mrs. Reagan, and then turned on Reagan in his column whenever it suited him. Will wrote on September 18 under the headline, "Reagan Botched the Daniloff Affair," that "When an administration collapses, quickly and completely, like a punctured balloon, as the Reagan administration has done in the Daniloff debacle, a reasonable surmise is that the administration, like a balloon, has nothing in it but air."

Will wrote a similar column a week later, and the President invited Will to the Oval Office on September 26 to tell him that he was hurt by his criticism. I think Reagan made a mistake by dignifying Will's comments with a response, let alone a private audience; he simply should have ignored Will, who, in one of his rare instances of being a true conservative, wanted us to bash our heads against the wall on this one, to throw down the gauntlet and tell the Russians to keep Daniloff until hell froze over. Will didn't have the benefit of knowing that the arrest of Daniloff turned into a big plus because we were able to accelerate our plan to expel the KGB people from the Soviet mission to the U.N. and really cripple their spy apparatus.

THE 1986 ICELAND SUMMIT

When I saw President Reagan emerge from his final meeting with Soviet leader Mikhail Gorbachev on the afternoon of October 12, 1986, at Reykjavik, Iceland, I knew instantly that agreement on a landmark arms control treaty—which had appeared to be within their grasp a few hours earlier—had eluded them.

The President was so grim and downcast as he and Gorbachev stalked out of Hofdi House, where they had been holding their summit talks for the past two days, that I was worried about his health. Reagan's teeth were clenched, his lips were drawn tight, his face had lost much of its color except for being flushed around his cheek bones, and his eyes were almost glazed because of the heavy burden on his mind. Jim Kuhn went up to the President and asked if there was going to be a joint statement, and the President snapped, "There is going to be NO statement!"

I watched as the President escorted Gorbachev to his waiting limousine. Gorbachev said, "I'm sorry it didn't work out," and the President looked at him coldly and replied, "It could have worked out if you had wanted it to." Gorbachev continued, "I hope to see you in the United States," but the President answered, "I don't know that there's going to be a meeting in the United States." The cold wind that cut through our overcoats felt appropriate.

We would later be accused of turning the Iceland summit into a classic example of "spin patrol," where we took what was supposedly a disaster—the reported collapse of talks between Reagan and Gorbachev—and presented it publicly as a triumph. Furthermore, it was said that we did so for crass political purposes, the summit having taken place as it did three weeks before the 1986 congressional elections. Those allegations overlook the fact that public opinion polls showed the American people were very solidly behind the President virtually from the time the summit ended—long before our so-called spin patrol could have had any appreciable effect.

There will be those who will now charge me with presenting a revisionist account of Reykjavik. However, after thinking over what happened in Iceland for more than a year, I am comfortable in saying that the Iceland summit truly was a success for both sides. Like Geneva, it laid the groundwork for the historic arms control agreement eliminating intermediate-range nuclear weapons that Reagan and Gorbachev signed when the Soviet leader visited the United States in December 1987. But Reykjavik was viewed as a failure because we raised the media's expectations too high and because of some unfortunate circumstances, namely the fatigue of President Reagan and George Shultz by the end of the summit, which made them appear disappointed when they had nothing to be disappointed about.

Overall, in my judgment, these talks were a giant step toward reaching an arms control agreement because the Soviets showed us what their bottom line was and we showed the Russians what ours was. Without Reykjavik, the 1987 agreement never would have been achieved.

If mistakes were made in our handling of the Reykjavik summit, it may be partly because the whole trip was a rush job. A mere nine days passed between the time we formally agreed to hold the summit talks and President Reagan's flight from Washington to Iceland.

Because of the lack of time, Reagan's preparations for this summit were not as extensive as they had been for previous summits. Ordinarily, we would gather in the Cabinet Room and one of the State Department officials would sit across the table and act out the role of the President's counterpart, just as I and others played the role of reporters posing questions during rehearsals for Reagan's press conferences. Before an economic summit, for example, one of us would say to the President, "If I were President Mitterand, I would probably confront you with something like, 'Why do you criticize me for my position on agriculture subsidies?' " and Reagan would rehearse his answer. But we were unable to do that before Reykjavik.

We arrived in Iceland in violation of Henry Kissinger's cardinal rule: "Never go into a summit unless you know the outcome." Our lack of preparation backfired on us during the final day. The two leaders, sitting in a room overlooking the Bay of Reykjavik, came to the crucial issue of whether each would do away with *all* nuclear weapons. Reagan said he would. It was potentially a tremendous blunder that could have put the U.S. at a disadvantage against the Soviets' overwhelming conventional forces. Yet Reagan said, "Yes," and Shultz sat next to him in silence. It was only Gorbachev's insistence that we virtually scrap SDI that caused the summit to break down and saved the President from disaster.

Shultz also permitted Reagan and Gorbachev to wander into topics that the President wasn't expecting to discuss. President Reagan even asked Shultz at one point during the summit why Shultz, who had established the ground rules with the Russians, was allowing them to go into full-scale negotiations, when the President had anticipated only preliminary talks in Iceland that he hoped would lead to further discussion in the U.S. in the near future. "George let the President down," National Security Director John Poindexter later confided to me.

There were also logistical problems. Because of limited housing in Iceland, we took a much smaller support contingent with us than usual. The U.S. delegation to a summit ordinarily numbered 1,000 or more, but at Reykjavik we had only 267: seventy-five Secret Service agents; seventy-two military personnel; sixty-two from the State Department; thirty-four White House staffers (including nine from the press office); fourteen from the National Security Council; eight from the Arms Control and Disarmament Agency; and two from the Pentagon.

And because Nancy Reagan wasn't able to accompany her husband, the President was deprived of his one indispensable adviser. That isn't to say that Nancy Reagan didn't keep a keen eye on things. Jim Kuhn spent hours on the phone with her, hearing admonitions like, "Make certain he doesn't have to have George and Don over every night. They'll keep him up too late."

*   *   *

Just as we had in Geneva a year earlier, we agreed with the Soviets to impose a news blackout in Reykjavik. At one point I had to reprimand John Poindexter publicly for violating the blackout by answering a question, even though his answer was only one word. As Poindexter, Don Regan, and White House communications director Pat Buchanan left a meeting on October 11, the first day that Reagan and Gorbachev met, reporters shouted questions about how the talks had gone. Regan and Buchanan ignored the questions, but Poindexter answered, "Businesslike." When I was asked later if I agreed with what Poindexter had said, I answered, "I will not do that, and Poindexter should not have."

With a blackout in place, the press corps had little to report, which left them scrambling for news. I decided that one story, by Niles Latham of the *New York Post*, was so good it deserved an award, namely "the Niles Latham Award for Enterprising Reporting." Under the headline, "Big Flush a Success After Iceland Toilet Crisis Comes to a Head," the *Post*, with its way of getting right to the heart of the matter, revealed that "After a two-day argument the world's two superpowers finally reached agreement on a major issue: which bathrooms would be used by President Reagan and Soviet leader Gorbachev."

Reuters earned another commendation, the coveted *Washington Post–New York Times* Consistency in Foreign Policy Award. The *Times* and *Post* always tried to one-up each other. Every time one wrote a story, the other would come back with an entirely different interpretation of the same event. Shortly after one bargaining session ended, Reuters sent two separate stories over the wire. One said, "Reagan looked relaxed and smiling." The other said, "Reagan appeared stiff and impassive, but Soviet leader Gorbachev was relaxed and chatty." "It's like the weather here in Iceland," I told the press in reference to the two conflicting Reuters leads. "It changes every few minutes."

Reykjavik was to have been just another opportunity for Reagan and Gorbachev to meet in person; we embarked on the trip to Iceland without any great expectation of actually concluding an arms control agreement. Given the hostility over the Daniloff-Zakharov affair, the mere fact that the two leaders were meeting so soon afterwards was enough of an accomplishment.

As talks went on for four hours on Saturday, October 11, and six more hours on Sunday, October 12, however, the two sides made so much progress that at least for a while on Sunday it looked as if we were on the verge of a dramatic breakthrough. Gorbachev unexpectedly appeared to be willing to eliminate all medium-range nuclear missiles from Europe, and to accept Reagan's proposal that all offensive missiles belonging to us or the Russians should be eliminated worldwide over the next decade.

Sunday was to have ended with a short midday session between Reagan and Gorbachev, and then we were to go directly to the airport for the flight home. But their talks went so well that an agreement seemed imminent and the talks continued long into the afternoon.

As the talks grew tense and the President and Shultz realized that a far-reaching agreement was within our grasp, Reagan asked for a break, so that he could confer with our arms control experts who were waiting in a tiny room on the floor above the conference room. Those of us in the U.S. delegation huddled together and pored excitedly over a proposed statement that clearly was a giant step forward. In our mind's eye, we could see the President and Gorbachev announcing an historic, lasting agreement under which both superpowers would eliminate all nuclear weapons.

During all my White House years, I had seldom let my emotions come to the surface, except for that warm spring day nearly six years earlier when I sat in the Rose Garden and slowly realized the burden that had been thrust on me by the wounding of Jim Brady. But now, as the darkness descended around us in Reykjavik, I felt a shudder go down my back and tears well in my eyes. We were on the verge of something momentous.

At the same time the thought occurred to me, what if we don't understand what we are doing and we are in the process of making a grave mistake here in agreeing to something we don't understand? Things were moving so quickly that it was difficult to grasp what we were doing.

As we grew more and more optimistic on Sunday, the delay made it obvious to the press that we might be on the verge of agreement. As a result, the television networks started reporting Sunday afternoon that a breakthrough might occur. Hopes grew higher and higher, but in the end the talks fell apart over the same old sticking-point: Gorbachev demanded that we stop our Star Wars research—which was still nonnegotiable for President Reagan.

Two days later, back in Washington, the President replayed for me the final bitter moments:

GORBACHEV: It isn't too late.
REAGAN: It is for me.

GORBACHEV: I think we can still deal. There is still time.
REAGAN: I don't think you wanted a deal.
GORBACHEV: I don't know what else I could have done.
REAGAN: You could have said, "Yes."

It was a crushing blow for Reagan, who had high hopes for an arms control agreement as the crowning achievement of his presidency. Now he saw time running out. I believe when he told Gorbachev "It's too late," he was—for once—confronting his own mortality.

After the meeting broke up we rushed back to the U.S. Embassy to get our wits together and figure out exactly what had happened. We gathered in the dining room of the embassy and Shultz outlined what we were to say to the press. "First, we made good progress on regional and bilateral matters and on human rights. We were successful in getting something in writing on human rights, which was a breakthrough." Then the punch-line: "Gorbachev is to blame for the end to the talks. He insisted we give up SDI." It was important to emphasize that Reagan and Gorbachev made dramatic progress, Shultz continued. "The President will hang in there and will not abandon his efforts." But, Shultz hammered home, "The President will not compromise on what is essential to our security."

Shultz left to brief the press, while the rest of us went to the airport to fly home. Shultz himself was flying to Europe to give NATO ministers a report on the summit before he returned to Washington. Shultz had given us a very upbeat analysis, and he tried to sound upbeat before the press, using words like "magnificent" to describe the President's perform-ance and stating that important agreements had been achieved. But Shultz's body language and words were two entirely different things—and his talk was transmitted live to a huge audience back home, as CBS and NBC interrupted their Sunday afternoon pro-football games to put Shultz on. He was somber, downbeat, very deliberate, slow of speech, and tired. As Sam Donaldson said, Shultz "look[ed] like his dog had just been run over by a truck." And in the end Shultz admitted that we were "deeply disappointed" with the outcome, for which he placed all the blame on the Russians.

Aboard Air Force One shortly after takeoff from Reykjavik, Dan Howard and Pete Roussel, coping with press reaction back at the Iceland press center, radioed that the wire leads were downbeat. I told Regan and

Poindexter, "We've got to go all out to brief the press on this one. There's too much at stake to leave one stone unturned."

They agreed, and Poindexter himself walked to the rear of the plane where the pool reporters were sitting and gave the first and only detailed on-the-record briefing of his nine months as national security director, which would founder on the shoals of Iran and end abruptly in six weeks. Exhausted and with a stubble of beard on his face, he got down on his knees so that his arms and elbows could rest on the press table, and, puffing away on his pipe, talked for an hour and twenty minutes without referring to notes. It was an extraordinary performance. "Soviet rhetoric was far out in front of what they were actually willing to do," he explained. At the end of Poindexter's brilliant talk to the press, I walked back up to the staff lounge, where I gave an account of Poindexter's briefing. "A star is born," Don Regan observed.

As the homeward trip continued I took a piece of Air Force One stationery and began to outline an unprecedented news blitz that would begin when we got back to Washington. We'd send Secretary Shultz to New York to meet with the editorial boards of *The New York Times* and the *Wall Street Journal,* as well as with key people at the three networks. Shultz agreed to do that when he got back from Europe. We would also brief the three news weeklies, the *Washington Post, Washington Times*, *USA Today*, and the *Los Angeles Times* and *Wall Street Journal* bureaus in Washington. The President would do an Op-Ed article for *The New York Times*, Shultz would do one for the *Post*, Buchanan would do the *Washington Times*, and we would do them also for newspapers in Atlanta, Chicago, Los Angeles, and Dallas—all within the next two or three days. In addition, we put Buchanan on ABC's "Good Morning, America," Kenneth Adelman on NBC's "Today," arms control negotiator Paul Nitze on the CBS morning program from Brussels, and another negotiator, Max Kampelman, the head of the permanent U.S. arms control delegation in Geneva, on PBS's MacNeil-Lehrer show. The highlights came on Monday, the day after we returned home, when we had Poindexter in the White House briefing room, and that night the President addressed the nation at eight o'-clock, declaring that he had offered the Russians the "most sweeping and generous arms control proposal in history." We also dispatched a "truth squad" of Nitze and others to London, Paris, Rome, and Bonn, and scheduled all key Cabinet members for speeches and interviews wherever they traveled over the next two months.

This was the biggest effort we ever made to get out the White House side of a story, and we did something like ninety press appearances over the first three days.* The extent of our blitz drew as much press attention as the message itself, and we were criticized for it. That puzzled me. What we said was true; we never said that night was day or black was white. We told the story as it happened, and let the blame fall where it may. And we did it on the record; there were no "administration sources" this time. How could it be wrong for those of us in the Reagan administration to do our best to give our side of the story?

By week's end, Don Regan had made so many press appearances that he finally gave his famous remark to *The New York Times:* "Some of us are like a shovel brigade that follows a parade down Main Street, cleaning up." Regan was not suggesting that the President or anyone else had made mistakes that needed correcting; the point he was making was badly misinterpreted. The context was that a reporter asked him if was worn out and he was saying he was, from the strain of doing several dozen press engagements in three days, on the heels of the four-day whirlwind trip to Iceland. It was a joke and everyone laughed, including the reporters, and then the *Times* turned it totally around. Another day, another nail in Regan's coffin.

*Helen Thomas of UPI paid grudging tribute to us in a dispatch on October 17:

"A rampaging administration public relations campaign has turned the first somber impressions of defeat and failure of the Iceland summit into triumph and success, White House aides say.

"The credit goes to spokesman Larry Speakes, who, with the help of his deputy Peter Roussel, devised a master plan to reverse the perception that President Reagan had struck out in extraordinary nuclear arms negotiations with Soviet leader Mikhail Gorbachev."

10 *The Grenada Fiasco*

Rear Admiral John Poindexter had hung me out to dry, and I didn't even know it.

This was on October 24, 1983, more than three years before Poindexter became a household name. That afternoon, Bill Plante of CBS came to me very privately and said he had the makings of a big scoop: that U.S. forces were assembling in the Caribbean for an invasion of the tiny island nation of Grenada, which had been flirting with Communism and with Cuban leader Fidel Castro. "I've got to know," Plante told me. "It looks like something's coming down as early as tomorrow."

Grenada had been in an uproar since October 13, when a military coup occurred and the prime minister, Maurice Bishop, was placed under house arrest. Bishop was a Communist, but relatively moderate by Grenadian standards. Several thousand of Bishop's followers staged a protest of his arrest on October 19 and freed him from captivity. As Bishop led a demonstration through the streets, he somehow was recaptured by soldiers, and he and several of his supporters were executed. Grenada was of special interest to the United States because of its proximity, because several hundred Americans were students at St. George's University School of Medicine on the island, and, more so, because the Cubans were building an airport there with a 10,000-foot-long runway.

A day after Bishop's execution, the prime minister of Jamaica, Edward

Seaga, warned that the new rulers were Cuban-trained Marxists, and on the following day, October 21, a ten-ship U.S. Navy convoy that had set sail for Lebanon was secretly diverted to Grenada, as President Reagan, Secretary of State George Shultz, and National Security Council director Bud McFarlane learned that the Organization of Eastern Caribbean States, a group of small island nations, was considering asking us to intervene.

I was blissfully unaware that we were about to invade Grenada. Two and a half years on the job, and I was still out of the loop, not completely trusted by Jim Baker, Mike Deaver, and Dick Darman, Baker's assistant.

Instead, I was looking forward to my first weekend off in several months. President Reagan was one of the guests in the annual four-man "George Shultz Invitational Golf Tournament" at the Augusta National Golf Course in Georgia, the scene of the somewhat more famous Masters Golf Tournament each spring. It appeared that the weekend was going to be so routine that for one of the rare times in my six years with Reagan, I decided not to accompany him on an out-of-town trip, and planned a quiet weekend at home with my family.

Reagan and Shultz flew to Augusta on Friday, October 21. Although I didn't know it, the two of them and Bud McFarlane were already deeply involved in planning the invasion of Grenada, and the President was awakened at 5:15 A.M. on Saturday, October 22, and told that Grenada's neighbors were interested in having the U.S. provide military assistance against Grenada's rulers. For me, the promise of a quiet weekend ended later on Saturday, but it was not the impending invasion of Grenada that caused the problem. An armed man raided the heavily guarded country club and seized five hostages, including Reagan's personal aide, David Fischer, and White House advance man Lanny Wiles, my old friend from Detroit in 1980, while the President and Shultz were out on the golf course. Secret Service agents, not knowing the extent of the incident and fearing that others might be involved, quickly pulled the President off the golf course and into his armored limousine, then issued the chilling command, "Launch Nighthawk Two," the order for emergency helicopter evacuation. The gunman, Charles Harris, demanded to talk to the President, who broke his long-standing rule against negotiating directly with terrorists because the lives of two of his aides were at stake. Reagan tried to call Harris on a radio phone, but didn't make connections; Harris was captured without anyone being hurt. I monitored the situation by telephone from my home in Annandale while Deputy Press Secretary Pete Roussel did a superb job of briefing the press in a touch-and-go situation.

The hostage-taking incident at the country club was bad enough, but the next day, Sunday, October 23, turned out to be perhaps the worst day of the entire Reagan administration, when terrorists bombed U.S. Marine headquarters in Beirut, killing 241 Americans.

When Bill Plante came to me on Monday with his question, I was preoccupied by the bombing in Lebanon. I had suspected we might send troops into Grenada at some point to rescue the American medical students, but I had no inkling that that was imminent, nor did I have any idea that we might launch a full-scale invasion of the island. In retrospect, I might have sensed that something big was afoot because a preview of the President's schedule for the following day, October 25, said that he would meet at 9:30 A.M. for a maximum of one hour with congressional leaders. Ordinarily, the subject matter of that meeting would have been listed on the schedule and background papers would have been attached, but there was no mention of the subject and there was a notation that briefing papers would be "available later." Before I would have guessed that Grenada would be the topic of discussion at that meeting, however, I would have guessed Lebanon.

I relayed Plante's question about a U.S. invasion of Grenada to Admiral Poindexter through Bob Sims, then the press officer for the NSC. Poindexter had been named deputy director of the National Security Council the previous week, when Bud McFarlane was promoted from the number-two job on the NSC to replace Bill Clark as NSC director. Poindexter's response was, "Preposterous!" He added that I should "knock it down hard." I, in turn, used Poindexter's exact word when I spoke to Plante: "Preposterous!" Twelve hours later, as dawn was breaking on October 25, 1,900 U.S. Marines and Army Rangers—accompanied by three hundred troops from Antigua, Barbados, Dominica, Jamaica, St. Kitts-Nevis, St. Lucia, and St. Vincent's, which gave us an excuse for being involved—launched "Operation Urgent Fury," the invasion of Grenada.

In spite of efforts by Poindexter and others in the administration to mislead the American press corps, the invasion was not exactly a well-kept secret; newspapers and radio stations throughout the Caribbean, with information provided by other island nations involved in the attack, reported it in advance. But those of us in Washington, both in the White House and in the press corps, either were unaware of the obscure Caribbean press reports or discounted them as rumor. Someone from CBS, however, had noticed U.S. helicopters and other signs of military activity on Barbados, which is near Grenada, and had guessed that an invasion was imminent.

That Bill Plante was the one who raised the question made the whole episode doubly uncomfortable for me; two years earlier the *Washington Post* had quoted him as saying about me, "I've never known him to lie." That *Post* story, and Plante's comment about me in it, were near and dear to my heart, because the article was published in September 1981, six months after I succeeded Jim Brady as the principal White House spokesman, and was one of the first news profiles of me. In the furor over Grenada, the casual observer might have thought I had lied about the invasion, although Plante and other savvy journalists understood that I had been lied to, not the one who had been the liar.

At eight o'clock on Monday night, just hours before the invasion, President Reagan convened a meeting in the family quarters of the White House to make final plans. Among those present for the two-hour session were Shultz; Cap Weinberger; McFarlane; Jim Baker; Ed Meese; Deaver; Darman; General John W. Vessey, Jr., chairman of the Joint Chiefs of Staff; and several congressional leaders, including Tip O'Neill, Howard Baker, Robert Byrd, Bob Michel, and Jim Wright. The members of the congressional delegation were brought from Capitol Hill in White House limousines and were told the meeting was so secret that they couldn't even call their wives and let them know they wouldn't be home for dinner.

I knew something was going on, and when I found out that the meeting had started with the congressional leadership and a half-dozen White House staffers, but not their own press spokesman, I got disgusted and went home.

Not long after I got home, Bill Plante called me again and said he was hearing more rumors about an invasion. I got hold of Jim Baker, who was at a dinner party by then. Baker still wouldn't come clean, but he did caution me, "Larry, be careful what you say. There is something going on." Baker told me to come in early the next morning, and we met at 5:45 A.M. in the White House mess, where Baker told me about the invasion, handed me a packet of documents on Grenada that was about an inch thick—and told me to announce it to the press at seven o'clock. That was when I first learned not only that the U.S. was going into Grenada, but also that our troops had already been ashore for a couple of hours.

Not only was I furious about having been deceived, but I had been given just an hour or so to go through dozens of pages of material and prepare myself to present it to the press and to the world in some coherent fashion. That was treatment about as unfair as I had ever received. I had never been so mad in my life, but I knew there was nothing I could do except to choke it down and head out there in front of the press and try to do my job.

John Poindexter later told me that he had wanted to let me know about the invasion even before I had asked, and had talked to Baker and Darman about it. Poindexter said that when he raised the question, before Baker could even speak up, Darman said, "No, absolutely not." Baker didn't disagree with Darman, which meant that in reality Poindexter was under orders from the chief of staff not to reveal to the press office what was going on. That mitigates what Poindexter did to some extent, but a lie is still a lie.

The Grenada affair did teach me one valuable lesson about dealing with people like Poindexter: In the future, if I asked a question like, "Are you invading Grenada today?" and the answer came back, "Preposterous!" I would have to follow up with, "Then are you invading Grenada tomorrow?" Once, during the Iran mess in 1986, Poindexter gave me some information for the press that smelled a little fishy to me. I told him, "John, I'll do it, but only in your name." Poindexter smiled and said, "You don't trust me, do you?" "John," I replied, "you know why I don't trust you."

I never forgave Poindexter or Darman for the spot they put me in over Grenada. Darman's attitude toward my office was, "We will give them just enough to do these foolish daily briefings." After Grenada, I started telling people that Baker would give me two lines to say, and Darman would take one of them away. Two years later I told a writer from the *National Journal* that Darman—who had moved over to the Treasury Department along with Baker by then—was "the ultimate second-guesser." I added that although Darman was an all-pro Monday morning quarterback, his response had always been "No way" whenever I asked him to brief the press on subjects he knew about. Before long I received Darman's handwritten response—complete with a threat—addressed to me as "PERSONAL AND CONFIDENTIAL," on the stationery of "The Deputy Secretary of the Treasury." It read:

I was disappointed to read your comments about me in the latest *National Journal.* You may feel I "second-guessed" a lot. I guess you do not much appreciate that I helped and defended you a very great deal—at times when your position was at serious risk.

It has been my experience that the wheel turns 'round and 'round in this town. Please be assured that the next time I am in a position to influence the prospects of your success, failure, or capacity to serve, I shall remember your thoughts.

Ironically, both of us ended up on Wall Street with firms whose headquarters are in the World Financial Center, right next to each other. We do *not* have lunch together.

Grenada definitely marked my low point as Ronald Reagan's press spokesman. It was not just Baker and Darman, but Shultz and Weinberger—and the President himself—who wanted to keep the truth from me, the press, and the public. I later discussed with Reagan the decision to keep the press in the dark about the invasion, and to prohibit reporters from accompanying U.S. troops, as they have in every war dating back at least to the Civil War. "It was a commando raid, it had to be a surprise, lives were at stake, and the media might have jeopardized the success of the invasion," he explained. His attitude was that the press could not be entrusted with the secret, which may have been true. But his own press staff should have been brought in at some point; Reagan and the rest of the Grenada planning group could have had the benefit of our advice, and we could have done a better job of explaining Reagan's reasons for the invasion.

I always preached to members of the White House staff, "Tell me everything, so I'll know not only what to say, but what not to say." Still, after preaching that for six years, my reaction when I found out about the Iran-Contra scandal in 1986 was, "Thank God that Ollie North and John Poindexter didn't tell me about Iran."

Reagan was really adamant about secrecy. He felt we were getting a raw deal from the press and from people who leaked things to the press. In spite of his twenty years in the political limelight and his eleven years as governor and President, Reagan still had no real understanding of how a press secretary worked and what the value of a press secretary was. In fairness to him, ninety percent of the politicians deal with press secretaries in the same fashion. Two exceptions were Jimmy Carter, who gave extraordinary access to Jody Powell, and Dwight Eisenhower, who did the same with Jim Hagerty. It's no accident that Hagerty and Powell were two of the best press secretaries of all time.

At one briefing after Grenada a reporter told me that the inner circle had kept me in the dark because "They want to give you deniability." My response was, "I want the truth. I don't want deniability." Deniability was a word I would not hear again until the Iran-Contra hearings in 1987, when Poindexter claimed he kept the President in the dark to give him deniability. It was a lousy way to do business.

During my six years with Reagan, I never was asked to lie to the press.

But there are times when lying may be unavoidable for a presidential spokesman. That happened to Jody when he was confronted directly in April 1980 with the question, "Are we attempting a rescue mission in Iran?" He knew that a "no comment" would reveal the deal. So he lied, and as soon as it was over he revealed that he had lied, and the press didn't hold it against him.

If I had been told the truth about Grenada I would have tried to avoid giving an answer. There are 10,000 ways of saying "no comment." For six years I was successful at avoiding making mistakes or lying when I talked to the press about things I did know about. I was involved in many things just as secret as Grenada and was never backed into a corner—arms control negotiations, the *Achille Lauro*, the TWA rescue mission, the whole attack plan on Libya. Day in and day out I dealt with top-secret information and avoided spilling the beans.

Furthermore, there are a variety of tactics a press secretary can use in avoiding a direct answer, such as saying, "I'll get back to you," and ducking the press for as long as necessary. If I had known about the Grenada invasion, I would simply have gone underground. I would have kept my door shut and told my staff I just cannot take any calls today, because there's no way I can discuss this issue without blowing the cover on something. And there were times when I wanted to duck the press, and I would close myself in my office and even have to buzz my secretary, Connie Gerrard, and ask, "Can I come out to go to the men's room?"

Moreover, if I had been involved in the planning of the invasion, I would have raised the question, "How are you going to have the press cover this thing?" I could have made some suggestions that would have at least allowed a pool to operate from the ships and be briefed by the military commanders there—and prevented the firestorm of criticism that followed the administration's decision to bar the press from Grenada until the military escorted a pool of twelve reporters around the island two days after the invasion. As it was, I wrote Baker in a memo the day after our troops landed that "the credibility of the Reagan administration is at stake," and, after David Gergen and I told Baker that we were running the risk of turning public opinion against us if we didn't allow the press to cover the events in Grenada, Baker agreed to tell the Pentagon to let reporters onto the island.

I had been lied to, I had been given only an hour to prepare to brief the press, and then I had to go out and defend the administration against accusations from reporters that I had deceived them.

At a raucous press briefing that began at 12:43 P.M. on October 25, the day of the invasion, and lasted more than an hour, I fielded questions like, "Are you going to resign?" "You ever hear of Jerry terHorst?" "Were you misguided?" "You're not angry?" and "You don't believe anybody in this government made a conscious decision to deliberately mislead the press on this?" My answer to the last question—and it wasn't easy for me—was, "No, I honestly do not," and I tried to ignore the other ones.

Afterwards, I went back into my office, feeling, as we say in the South, as low as a snake's belly in a wagon rut. "This stinks!" I shouted to my staff, as I slammed my briefing notes down on my desk.

So why didn't I quit? Because I enjoyed the job, I thought I was doing something important, and I wanted to stay until I could prove that I could do the job as well as anyone had ever done it. And if I had resigned, I would not have done it right after the invasion. I would have waited until the whole thing had blown over, and then left without telling anyone why.

The idea that I might resign then just wouldn't go away. Lou Cannon and David Hoffman of the *Washington Post* reported in the paper's October 27 editions that I was "furious," which was true, and that Les Janka, my deputy press secretary for foreign affairs; Bob Sims, the press officer for the NSC who had relayed my question from Bill Plante to Poindexter and received the "preposterous" answer; and I had discussed resigning. Janka had considered quitting, and I can't speak for Sims, but the *Post*'s claim that I had talked to anyone about quitting was untrue.

I first received word of my impending "resignation" when Robin Gray, a member of my staff, called me at home late on the evening of October 26, just after the early edition of the *Post* had hit the streets. "The AP is quoting the *Post* as reporting that you plan to quit," he said. I told Robin, "Deny it!" Then, just before midnight, standing in my kitchen, I called Lou Cannon at home and we had the following conversation:

"Lou, where did you get that story?"

"I got it from a good source."

"Well, Lou, it's absolutely untrue. You have been sadly misled on that because I don't operate that way. If I'm going to make objections to a policy I'll make them within. But I don't offer to resign because that would only harm the President. Somebody has got to pay for this. They've done a terrible disservice to me and a terrible disservice to you. You've got a bad story in your paper. Who told you?"

"I can't reveal my sources."

"Lou, you've got to tell me!"

"Well, it was Les Janka," he finally sputtered out.

Much as I respect Lou, he made two unpardonable mistakes in this case: first, he failed to check with me before writing his story, and second, he let me badger him into revealing a confidential source.

After fuming most of the night, I went in the next morning and told my deputy, Pete Roussel, whom I often bounced ideas off of, "I'm going to fire Les." Pete said, "You're the boss. You have to do what you think is right." Moreover, Les had not been getting along with the NSC staff. My thought in hiring him was that he was a Middle East expert, a former NSC staff guy under Henry Kissinger, and someone who was exceptionally bright and articulate and knew how to handle the press. But he had been a disappointment.

After my conversation with Pete, I went to Jim Baker and Darman, who were seated in their usual spot at a corner table in the Executive mess. I slid into a chair and told them that the *Post* story was untrue, and that I had no intention of resigning. "I'm going to fire Janka because of it," I added. They raised no objection.

Back in my office, I called Les in and gave him the news: "Les, I'm going to have to ask you to leave. I don't have confidence in you anymore. The story is incorrect, you've leaked something about me, and if you leak about me there's no telling what else you might leak." He reacted with shock, but understood that he had no choice. I asked him to be gone by the end of the day, promised to carry him on the payroll as long as I could, and told him we would picture it as a resignation, which is how it was reported in the press. Thus, I became the first person in the Reagan administration to fire someone for leaking. Through the years, I thought that was the best solution to the continuing problem of news leaks.

Using me to deceive the media and preventing the American press corps from accompanying our invasion force were the worst public relations mistakes the Reagan administration made in Grenada. But there were several other blunders:

- Several American journalists, including reporters from the *Washington Post*, the *Miami Herald*, and *Newsday*, were actually held incommunicado after they attempted to land on Grenada and file stories without official approval, and Vice Admiral Joseph Metcalf III, the commander of the American task force in Grenada, said he had ordered his ships to fire at any boats that attempted to take reporters to the island.

- The State Department incorrectly reported two weeks after the invasion that a mass grave containing the bodies of one hundred victims of the military government that had overthrown Maurice Bishop were found on the island. The department had to retract that assertion a day later.

- U.S. Information Agency director Charles Z. Wick, who had a penchant for speaking his mind, said that British prime minister Margaret Thatcher had opposed our action against Grenada and refused to lend support because she was a woman. No sooner were the words out of Wick's mouth than he asked those journalists who were present not to report what he had said. They, of course, quickly reported it, and his remarks, naturally, created a furor.

Grenada could have been as big a public relations disaster for the Reagan administration as the Iran-Contra arms deal became three years later. Having the United States take on Grenada, a country with a population of 111,000 and a land area of 133 square miles, twice the size of Washington, D.C., was the equivalent of the Washington Redskins scheduling my old high school team, the Merigold Wildcats. A win meant very little and if we had lost, there would have been hell to pay.

Those who were involved in planning the operation—McFarlane, Shultz, Weinberger, and Vessey, to name a few key strategists—lacked both a feel for public relations and the sense to include me or David Gergen or anyone from the press operation. Typical of their attitude toward the press was a remark by Shultz several weeks after the invasion that reporters "are always against us and so they're always seeking to report something that's going to screw things up." Nor did the invasion strategists provide the press office with adequate information once they did decide to let us in on the secret; the facts were sketchy and those who knew the details were scattered all over the State Department, the Pentagon, and the NSC. If the invasion had not been a success, we were so poorly prepared to deal with the press that we might have been nailed by Congress and the American people, as well as by the news media.

Grenada did turn out well, to some extent through blind luck. First, we won. This time, David did not upset Goliath. We ousted the leaders who had taken over in the coup against Bishop, suffered minimal casualties—eighteen killed and 116 wounded—and rescued the American medical students.

Second, the medical students were grateful for the rescue. In fact, they were almost delirious with joy. When that first planeload returned to the air force base at Charleston, South Carolina, on October 26 and the first student off the plane knelt and kissed the ground and they all cheered their country and thanked the U.S. military for rescuing them from a dangerous and chaotic situation, the public relations problem was solved right there. There was no way that all the negative reporting and complaining by the press about being kept off the island could overcome the power of that television picture. My staff and I were watching when the first students arrived in Charleston, and when we saw how happy they were to be home, we started cheering and pounding the table. "That's it! We won!" I shouted.

Finally, we found what we were looking for, including hundreds of Cuban "workers" who were armed to the teeth; large stores of military equipment; and a March 1983 document in which Soviet Chief of Staff Marshal Nikolai V. Ogarkov told Major Einstein Louison, then the Grenadian chief of staff, that twenty years ago, "there was only Cuba in Latin America, [but] today there are Nicaragua, Grenada, and a serious battle is going on in El Salvador." Moreover, the airstrip the Cubans were building in Grenada was alarming. It was a second base in Central America after Cuba, and a third, counting Nicaragua, that could have been used to recover Soviet bombers and reconnaissance planes that fly up and down the U.S. coast.

Soon after the invasion, an NSC staffer named Oliver North reported in a secret memo to NSC director Bud McFarlane that the Salinas airfield being built on Grenada was a major airbase exclusively under Cuban control, that the airfield contained barracks, a communications center, and a warehouse with weapons and ammunition stacked to the ceiling, and that there were 1,100 well-trained, professional Cuban soldiers on the island.

This time, at least, North and McFarlane were on the right track. Obviously, we did not need another Cuba in the Caribbean.

The question remains, did we need to invade Grenada? I'm not so sure we did.

The administration justified the invasion with two major points:

• First, I read a State Department–prepared statement to the press at 7:00 A.M. on October 25, the day of the invasion: "The United States government has decided to accede to an urgent plea from the Organization of Eastern Caribbean States . . . to support and participate in a collective security effort to restore peace and order in Grenada."

The President himself used similar language when he appeared in the briefing room two hours later: "The United States received an urgent, formal request from the five member nations of the Organization of Eastern Caribbean States to assist in a joint effort to restore order and democracy on the island of Grenada."

What we were claiming was that the OECS had invited us to participate in the invasion. The truth of the matter is that on Sunday, October 23, the day the "invitation" was issued, a representative of President Reagan, former U.S. Ambassador to Costa Rica Frank McNeil, was on hand at the OECS meeting in Bridgetown, Barbados—just to make sure that when the invitation was issued, it was sent to the right address. You might also say that we RSVP'ed in advance.

We were tremendously alarmed by the aerial photography of the airport that was under construction in Grenada, and the fact that the Cubans were involved there. Did we nudge the OECS nations into asking for U.S. help? U.S. forces were already in place before we were asked to participate. Before the request for help was received, the President, Shultz, and Bud McFarlane were down in Augusta, working on plans in the late hours of Saturday and the early hours of Sunday morning, more than forty-eight hours before the invasion. So it's clear that we had set in motion and taken this opportunity to move against Grenada and clean it out before our allies could change their minds.

- Second, Reagan told the press that an "overriding" reason for the invasion was "to protect innocent lives, including up to 1,000 Americans whose personal safety is, of course, my paramount concern."

Although the leaders of the coup in Grenada had warned that anyone who went outdoors would be shot, there really was no hard proof that they intended to harm the American medical students. To do so, in fact, would have been disastrous from an economic standpoint, since the medical school was a major source of income on the island, which was also heavily dependent on the tourist trade.

Moreover, the leaders of the coup sent us an urgent message the night before the invasion that any American citizen who wished to leave was free to do so. Nevertheless, at ten-fifteen Monday night, less than eight hours before the invasion, Shultz ordered the U.S. Embassy in Barbados to notify the Grenadian military leaders that their message was being rejected because we questioned whether they constituted a legitimate government. Shultz also sent along a veiled warning to the leaders of the coup: "We will be in touch with neighboring states and give substantial weight to their assessment." That was long after the "neighboring states" had "invited" us to lead the invasion and we had accepted, and also more than four hours after President Reagan had signed off on final authorization for the invasion.

And President Reagan himself admitted to the press that the Americans on the island "were in no danger in the sense of that, right now, anything was being done to them. . . . This was a case of not waiting until something actually happened to them." Still, he said, he was concerned about their well-being because "the airports were closed. There was no way of leaving." But that was twelve hours after Grenada had notified us that the Americans were free to leave on either regular or charter flights—and no less an authority than Lieutenant Colonel Oliver North appeared in the briefing room and told the press that the main airport in Grenada had been open for two hours the day before the invasion.

Probably the most bizarre analysis of the Grenada invasion has been provided by Tip O'Neill. In his book, *Man of the House*, published in 1987, Tip wrote:

"We should not have invaded Grenada. . . . As far as I can see, it was all because the White House wanted the country to forget about the tragedy in Beirut.

"It was bad enough that Grenada was really about Lebanon. Unfortunately, that's not all it was about. My greatest fear about Reagan's foreign policy is that ten years from now we'll look back on the Grenada incident as a dress-rehearsal for our invasion of Nicaragua."

There are only two overwhelming problems with Tip's reasoning:

- Grenada had nothing to do with the bombing of the Marine barracks in Lebanon. The Beirut disaster occurred on Sunday, two days before we invaded Grenada, but the invasion of Grenada had been under consideration within the Reagan administration for at least a week. Furthermore, the OECS members first raised the idea of us joining them in an invasion on Friday, two days before the bombing in Lebanon.
- If Grenada does turn out to be a dress rehearsal for an invasion of Nicaragua a decade from now, a 1997 invasion of Nicaragua will be ordered by some future President—maybe even a Democrat—unless, that is, Tip believes that President Reagan intends to somehow circumvent the Constitution, serve for at least eight years past the expiration of his second term, and still be calling the shots at the age of eighty-six.

I'm not sure how long Tip will feel this way. Consider some of his previous remarks:

October 25, 1983 (the day of the invasion): "It is no time for the press of America or we [*sic*] in public life to be critical of our government when the U.S. Marines and Rangers are down there."

October 28, 1983 (with the U.S. Marines and Rangers still down there): The Reagan administration's foreign policy, as illustrated by Grenada, is "frightening."

November 8, 1983 (after public opinion polls showed that the American people were solidly behind the President): The invasion was "justified" because it saved American lives.

When he wrote this portion of his book, Tip was not going to let a full recitation of the facts ruin a good story.

11

America

Held Hostage

What was to have been a peaceful weekend of golf with some friends in the fall of 1983 quickly turned into the beginning of three major crises which occurred in the space of four days. The President, George Shultz, Secretary of the Treasury Donald Regan, and former U.S. Senator Nicholas Brady of New Jersey had flown from Washington to Augusta, Georgia, on Friday, October 21, for their golf outing. Reagan went to sleep before midnight, but was awakened at 5:15 A.M. Saturday by a phone call from National Security Director Bud McFarlane, who had accompanied the President to Augusta. "George [Shultz] and I must see you immediately," McFarlane informed the President. "What is it, Bud?" Reagan asked, with a hint of irritation in his voice. "I'll explain when we get there, Mr. President," McFarlane insisted. When McFarlane and Shultz arrived a few minutes later, Reagan immediately understood that they had come about a subject that was too sensitive to discuss on the telephone: Word had been received that chaos reigned on the island of Grenada and its neighbors were asking the U.S. for help. Reagan, realizing that he was about to send American servicemen into direct combat for the first time during his administration, readily agreed to authorize U.S. troops to invade the island three days later.

The planning of the Grenada invasion had cast a pall over the vacation weekend, but much more was to come. It was while Reagan and his

164

golfing partners were out on the course Saturday afternoon that a gunman seized several hostages, including White House aides David Fischer and Lanny Wiles. The captives were released unharmed, but the incident brought an early end to the golf match. The President did try to make light of the situation by quipping, "Well, the golf game is shot. And I was on my way to my best game of the year." Which was true, since it was his *only* golf game of the year.

After a quiet dinner with Shultz, Regan, and Brady, the President went to sleep early Saturday night. He didn't sleep for long. McFarlane awakened him again at 2:27 A.M. Sunday, this time to inform him that two hours earlier a suicidal Islamic radical bent on martyrdom had driven a truck carrying 12,000 pounds of dynamite into the lobby of the U.S. Marine barracks in Beirut, Lebanon. All hell literally broke loose. The four-story building collapsed, killing 241 of the approximately 300 American troops who lay asleep inside. Most of the victims, who had come to Lebanon to try to bring peace to that war-torn nation, never knew what hit them. Two minutes later a similar attack occurred at French military headquarters two miles away, killing fifty-eight French soldiers.

Marine officers responsible for our peacekeeping force in Beirut had violated every rule in the book. Their men were huddled together, asleep in their lightly guarded headquarters—sitting ducks in the most volatile and dangerous part of the world, an area overrun with fanatics sponsored by the likes of Iran's Ayatollah Khomeini and Libya's Muammar al-Qaddafi. I never could understand why the marines had no roadblocks or other fortifications to prevent terrorists from driving into their compound, and why there was only one sentry on duty in front of the building—with his rifle, under our rules of engagement, unloaded. Moreover, we had intelligence information that such an attack was probable. It was a case of almost criminal negligence, to my way of thinking.

The President was stunned and sickened when McFarlane and Shultz gave him the initial word about the Beirut bombing in his cozy cottage on the edge of the Augusta National Golf Course. Shultz suggested an immediate return to Washington, and Reagan agreed. It was left to Pete Roussel to round up the travelers. Before daybreak a few hours later, Reagan and his staff were aloft, headed back to the capital. A somber President Reagan arrived at the White House around dawn, his face etched with every one of his seventy-two years.

Back in the White House, there was little the President could do except express his outrage at the "despicable" bombings. For a short time after the murder of our marines, it appeared we might be able to get even. Our intelligence agents thought they had pinpointed the terrorists responsible for the bombings at a training camp in Lebanon's Bekaa Valley. McFarlane urged action, but Shultz and Cap Weinberger preached caution, and before we could strike, the French beat us to the punch with an attack on the camp.

Twelve days after the bombing, a grim President and Mrs. Reagan flew to Camp Lejeune, North Carolina, the home base of many of the dead, to attend a memorial service and greet dozens of grieving relatives of the marines in a cold downpour. It was the most somber, heartwrenching hour of his presidency. The bombing of the marine barracks was the worst instance to date of Middle East terrorism involving Americans during the Reagan administration, and it was far from the last.

Like his predecessors, Reagan faced the cauldron of the Middle East believing he would be the American President to solve the nasty riddle that had eluded Nixon, Ford, and Carter. President Carter had come closest with his Camp David accord between Menachem Begin and Anwar Sadat five years earlier, but even that had had little lasting effect, except on relations between Egypt and Israel and between Egypt and its allies, who had spurned their Arab ally as a result.

Although Reagan had entered office with the highest hopes in the Middle East, he, his secretaries of state—Alexander Haig and Shultz—and their advisers had stumbled through minefields and booby traps, meandering from Sadat to his successor, Hosni Mubarak, to King Hussein of Jordan, to President Hafez al-Assad of Syria in a fruitless search for lasting peace. Four months after the Beirut bombing, Reagan was forced to admit that our attempts to keep the peace in Lebanon were a failure and order the marines home.

Nevertheless, always in the forefront of our nightmares, dating from even before the marine headquarters bombing until the present, has been Lebanon.

THE HIJACKING OF TWA FLIGHT 847

Lebanon was a place none of us in the Reagan administration ever wanted to hear about again after October 23, 1983. But all too soon, in June 1985, we had another nightmare there.

TWA Flight 847 took off from Athens, bound for Rome, at around 3:00 A.M. Eastern Daylight Time (10:00 A.M. in Athens) on June 14, 1985. There were 153 people aboard, including 135 Americans. Minutes after takeoff, two gunmen, soon identified as members of the Islamic Jihad (Holy War) terrorist organization, commandeered the Boeing 727 and ordered pilot John Testrake to fly to Beirut, where he landed at 5:00 A.M. our time, in spite of protests from Lebanese air traffic controllers. After arriving in Beirut the hijackers demanded that Israel release over 700 Lebanese prisoners who had been captured during Israeli raids on Lebanon in return for freeing the TWA hostages. During the next two days the hijackers forced the TWA crew to fly the 1,800 miles from Beirut to Algiers, back to Beirut, back to Algiers, and finally, to Beirut again on June 16. During the plane's second stay in Beirut, the hijackers demanded that Amal militiamen join them aboard the plane, and, when none did, the terrorists brutally beat U.S. Navy diver Robert Stethem, shot him in the head, and dumped his body on the tarmac. After five days of tense negotiations, forty Americans remained as hostages—divided between competing terrorist factions and hidden in the warrens of war-torn Beirut.

The hijacking, which dragged on for more than two weeks, was the longest and most frustrating crisis of the Reagan administration before the Iran-Contra arms scandal. The TWA hijacking quickly became a worldwide media event as the terrorists turned it into a made-for-TV drama. Amal leader Nabib Berri, who claimed control over the terrorists who held the plane and most of the hostages, appeared on "Meet the Press." Captain Testrake was interviewed live, a gun held to his head, while sitting in the cockpit of his plane. The terrorists, by far the most news-savvy we had ever encountered, produced other hostages for live television interviews; they even knew enough to capitalize on the seven-hour time difference between Beirut and Washington and make the hostages available for the morning news shows on the three American television networks. Moreover, on June 28, while President Reagan was visiting with relatives of some of the hostages in Chicago, the hijackers arranged for those same hostages to be interviewed live.

The terrorists' sense of playing to the news media manifested itself in other ways. Instead of showing the hostages holed up in an embassy as our foreign service officers had been in Teheran from 1979 to 1981 or in uniform with several days' growth of beard the way the Vietnamese displayed captured U.S. troops, these kidnappers were shrewd enough to display the hostages at seaside resorts, wearing clean clothes and freshly shaved. The kidnappers treated their captives so well that one of the hostages who was selected to be the spokesman for all of the captives, Allyn Conwell, went on television and said he and many of the other victims had come to feel "profound sympathy" with the Shiite cause. That gesture may have scored points for Conwell with the hijackers, but it certainly earned him an icy welcome from both the President and Mrs. Reagan when the hostages finally returned to the United States and the

Reagans met them at Andrews Air Force Base on July 2; the Reagans felt Conwell's remarks bordered on treason.

The hijacking dominated the news until the end; television audiences watched in record numbers for the whole seventeen days, and Cable News Network had record ratings the weekend the hostages were finally released. One observer with firsthand experience, a hostage named James Dell Palmer, said the hijacking was intended to attract the attention of the world press to the Shiite cause and that the hostages were released after they had served that purpose. The media circus went from the absurd to the ridiculous at the end, when NBC flew relatives of several of the hostages to Frankfurt, West Germany, for an "exclusive," a reunion on the "Today" show, and the family members refused to give interviews to ABC or CBS.

Even as the terrorists were communicating with us through the media, the podium of the White House press briefing room became an instrument of U.S. foreign policy. That was underscored for me as I took a call from Dan Rather just before airtime one day during the hijacking. Dan told me that he had just spoken to Amal leader Nabib Berri, and Berri's first question was, "What did Speakes say today?"

The seven-member crisis management group was meeting daily in the super-secret White House Situation Room: President Reagan, Vice President Bush, George Shultz, Cap Weinberger, Bill Casey, Don Regan, and Bud McFarlane assembled with maps and intelligence cables spread before them. By the fourth day, Monday, June 17, I was so frustrated over being excluded from the strategy sessions that I went to Don Regan and said, "I cannot brief anymore." "What do you mean?" he asked. I answered, "There's too much at stake here. U.S. policy is being made from my podium. Every word I say is heard instantly in Beirut. I am negotiating for the release of those hostages from that podium out there. I'm negotiating for their lives. Anything I say could cost the hostages their lives, and I'm not going to brief any more unless I'm in the know."

Regan agreed, telling me I was "exactly right," and promised to see what he could do. He fingered Shultz as the one who didn't want me in the meetings. I argued back: "They say Shultz objects. I don't believe that, because Shultz lets his own press secretary into almost every meeting he has over at the State Department. It's imperative that I be over there or I just won't be able to brief."

Although Don Regan urged that I be allowed to attend the meetings, Shultz insisted that no press people be present. Instead, they worked out a compromise: Bud McFarlane would leave the Situation Room after each meeting, come straight to my office, and give me virtually a verbatim account of what happened. That was the best Regan could get for me, and I had to live with it.

McFarlane, Shultz, and I did work together to devise a three-stage communications strategy that was intended to bring increasing pressure to bear on Nabib Berri:

1. Berri, in a turf battle with his rivals, had claimed responsibility for the hostages' well-being. We took him at his word. "Our idea is to make the press focus not on what the U.S. is going to do, not on what we are going to give to get the hostages back, but on what Berri is going to do," McFarlane told me. "He claims responsibility for the hostages' safety, so we are going to hold him to his word." On June 17 I told the press that McFarlane had spoken to Berri that day, and "we have made it plain what we want Berri to do, and that is to use his influence to resolve this situation. . . . We believe he is the key to the solution there and if he wishes to step forward and take that leadership role and use his influence, then we think it could go a long way toward resolving the problems involved."

2. Near the end of the second week, McFarlane cryptically told the press, "We will increase the pressure on the terrorists." On his orders, I announced on the twelfth day, June 25, that President Reagan was considering various options to secure the release of the hostages. "This includes an embargo on shipment of goods to Lebanon and a shutdown of the Beirut airport," I said. Either course would have required the use of U.S. military forces, and the press quickly jumped on that as a possibility, even a necessity. That was the stick; now for the carrot. "President Reagan will let diplomacy run its full course before taking further steps, but he is prepared to take whatever actions are necessary," I said. We left the door open for Berri and his cohorts—but only slightly.

3. The next day, at Shultz's suggestion, we imposed a total news blackout. Since the terrorists were relying on my briefings to tell them what the U.S. position was, I would say nothing, leaving them completely in the dark.

We imposed the blackout on June 26 and the next day I repeated that my policy was, "I have nothing to add to anything on the hostage situation and won't answer any questions. So if you wish to ask them you may." I was asked about half a dozen questions but said in response to all of them, "I'm just not going to answer any questions." "How long are you intending to no-comment questions about this?" "Until I quit no-commenting questions about this." Press reports that day said that "Speakes flatly refused to answer any questions dealing with the hostage crisis, maintaining a blackout of the news in Washington imposed by the administration."

That afternoon I called a meeting of the key public affairs officers from the State Department, the CIA, the office of Vice President Bush, the Federal Aviation Administration, and the Departments of Transportation, Defense, and Justice, to discuss how we would handle the media. This was an effort to completely silence the entire administration, and it worked; we were able to impose a virtually unprecedented government-wide press blackout on a front-page news story. My instructions to the public affairs people were that they were to say, "The proper solution is the prompt release of all hostages, and no comment beyond that." I emphasized that it was "essential, with no slip-ups." No leaks, not even to family members or close friends.

Shultz's blackout gambit paid off immediately. We started picking up intelligence right away that Berri, unable to learn from news reports what we were planning, was talking about how to get the hostages off his hands. "He has a hot potato and he doesn't know which way to turn," Shultz told the President. Berri was considering passing them off to the French or some other Western nation, or even to the Syrians, who played an ever more important role as the hijacking wore on and eventually persuaded Berri to release the hostages. No more news event, no reward to Berri and his men for guarding, feeding, and being responsible for thirty-nine innocent Americans (the fortieth, James Dell Palmer, was released on June 26 because of a life-threatening heart condition).

This show belonged to McFarlane and to Shultz from beginning to end. Although Bud spoke several times on the telephone to Nabib Berri, he was the hardliner throughout, the one who was ready to take military action against the hijackers or against the sources of terrorism in Iran and Libya. But Shultz and Weinberger—as they had in the aftermath of the attack on the U.S. Marine barracks nearly two years earlier—always came up with a reason for holding back: namely, that we weren't sure exactly where the hostages were being held, and any use of the U.S. military was likely to result in the death of some or all of the captives. President Reagan followed this line in his press conference on June 18, which was dominated by questions about the hijacking. Reagan declared, "I'm as frustrated as anyone. I've pounded a few walls myself when I'm alone about this. . . . [But] you can't just start shooting without having someone in your gunsights."

I don't know if it was because the strain finally got to Bud after sixteen days of masterminding our response to the hijacking, but on the day the hostages were released, Sunday, June 30, he staged one of his patented bizarre acts. Previously Bud had always entered the White House through the West Basement, down by the SitRoom, but when this crisis began, he started coming up the steps to the front door around 6:30 A.M., which the T.V. people recognized was good footage for the morning news. So they would nab him out there and he would make a statement; then I would have to find out what it was and live with it. After a few days I went to Don Regan and told him, "Bud has got to stop talking. We must speak to the world with one voice." Regan passed it on to Bud, and Bud made a testy crack in front of one of my aides: "Speakes thinks I'm talking too much. He only wants the spotlight on himself." But he did shut up—until the final day of the ordeal.

On that last day, though, Bud drove his own car to the West Lobby door, forsaking the government's chauffeur-driven Chrysler, and started to walk in. It was a Sunday, however, and he had forgotten that the door was locked. So he had to stand there with egg all over his face, obviously locked out of the White House, with his hand on the doorknob, looking back over his shoulder, and field questions from reporters.

The TWA hijacking was part of an epidemic of terrorist incidents that unnerved those of us involved in trying to cope with it. Three days before the TWA plane was seized, some other Shiite Moslem gunmen hijacked a Jordanian airliner in Beirut that had four Americans aboard and blew it up after releasing the passengers and crew. As the TWA hijacking wore on, four additional acts of terrorism added to the pressure on everyone in the administration:

- Four U.S. Marines who were taking a break from their guard duty at our embassy, as well as two American businessmen and seven other people, were murdered and fifteen people were wounded on June 19 in El Salvador by leftist guerrillas who opened fire on sidewalk cafés in San Salvador, the capital.
- A bomb exploded in the international departure lounge at the Frankfurt Airport that same day, killing three people and wounding forty-two. An Arab radical group, our nemesis, claimed credit.
- An Air India 747 jumbo jet en route from Toronto to Bombay, with stops in Montreal and London, crashed into the Atlantic Ocean off the Irish coast on June 23, killing all 329 passengers and crew. Sikh

extremists were suspected of putting a bomb aboard the plane before it left Canada.

- Less than an hour before the Air India crash, two baggage handlers at New Tokyo International Airport were killed when a bomb exploded in luggage that was being unloaded from a Canadian Pacific Airlines 747 that had just arrived from Vancouver. The Sikhs were suspected of planting that bomb as well.

One key element of our strategy, as it was whenever Americans were taken hostage—up to and including the John Poindexter–Ollie North plan to ship U.S. arms to Iran in 1986 in hopes of freeing several Americans held by Lebanese terrorists under Iranian control—was to deny that there was any quid pro quo. Thus, on Monday, June 24, when the Israelis released thirty-one Shiite prisoners, we claimed that there was no linkage between that and the fate of the TWA hostages—although there obviously was.

Meanwhile, there was considerable discussion among White House senior staffers on what pose to take while the passengers and crew from the TWA flight remained prisoners. Hardliners like political director Ed Rollins and communications director Pat Buchanan argued for a more dramatic response. They wanted Reagan to really rattle the sabers, and they pressed him to go out to Andrews to receive Stethem's body, but McFarlane said that the more the President got involved, the more it would tempt the hijackers to harm other Americans. When Stethem's body arrived at Andrews on June 18, Vice President Bush joined Stethem's family at the airport. Reagan did not go, but later paid his respects by visiting Stethem's grave in Arlington Cemetery.

In contrast to Rollins and Buchanan, McFarlane and Don Regan insisted that we avoid making strong statements and try to conduct business as usual, in order to bypass the Carter syndrome of bringing the entire U.S. government to a halt because of a hostage crisis. On June 24 I announced that the President would remain in Washington over the Fourth of July weekend because of the hijacking, instead of going to California, and the press used that to say that the President was being consumed by the crisis. Had the President taken the national holiday off and gone to California, the press would have turned the tables, saying the President was paying too little attention to the crisis. They wanted to know what percentage of his time he was spending on it. I told them it was "exactly eight percent" of his day, a figure I picked out of the air to demonstrate the absurdity of it.

The question of whether or not the Reagan administration considered this crisis a crisis seemed to be an obsession with some reporters. I don't mean to sound unduly hard on the press. Obviously, the reporters had a job to do, and I thought they usually did it well. Still, some of them could be unbelievably stupid at times, and this was one of them. At one point Lesley Stahl and others started badgering me about whether or not the administration considered the hijacking a "crisis," in a puzzling attempt to force me to state the obvious. One exchange went like this:

STAHL: Do you consider this a crisis?
ANSWER: That's a foolish, elementary, and simplistic question.
STAHL: Do you consider it a crisis? What do you call it—an incident? A diversion? Entertainment?
ANSWER: It is certainly an incident, but—
STAHL: Not a crisis. Is it a crisis?
ANSWER: Well, now, come on. I mean, who—let's have a vote on the foolishness of that question. . . . Do I call it a crisis? That is a foolish, simplistic, and elementary question.
STAHL: You were the one who brought it up.
ANSWER: No I didn't.
STAHL: Yes, you did.
ANSWER: I did not. You—
STAHL: You did.
ANSWER: You said, will you consider a crisis at end, and I said, we haven't called it a crisis. That's the fact.
STAHL: Well, will you?
ANSWER: I ain't going to fool with you, Lesley. . . . You've gone beyond your bounds, or below your standards or something.

The strain on me and members of my staff was so intense that Rusty Brashear, who had gone to work for me as my deputy for domestic affairs just before the hijacking, developed a tic in his left eye during the period the Americans were held captive. Rusty's tic lasted for three months and it was so bad that he had trouble reading.

Near the end of the first week, the President did become more involved publicly when he met for the first time with the family of a hostage during a trip to Indianapolis on June 19. Those of us who were advising him were torn about having him meet with the families, because it would show the kidnappers that they were reaching the highest levels of government and getting results; the terrorists knew that through the families they could bring pressure on Reagan to give in to their demands. But Reagan did meet with the family and fiancée of James Hoskins, twenty-two, who had just graduated from college and had been given the trip as a graduation present. With tears in her eyes, Hoskins's mother begged the President, "Don't do anything that would give rise to hostile acts against the hostages." She was apparently concerned about a rescue attempt. He told her, "We are doing everything we can to bring them home safely. You can be assured we have their best interest at heart." He hugged her and she shook visibly as her tears flowed. The President later held similar meetings with the families of hostages in Dallas and Chicago, always seeking to reassure them that he had no intention of endangering the captives. In public, meanwhile, Reagan presented a harder line, which his audiences loved. He opened a speech at the National Jaycee Convention in Indianapolis by declaring, "We must not yield to the terrorist demands that invite more terrorism. We cannot reward their grisly deeds. We will not cave in." His remarks were greeted with applause and chants of "U-S-A, U-S-A!"

By week's end, we knew from our unbelievably good intelligence sources in Beirut that a break in the siege was at hand. The U.S. ambassador to Syria, William Eagleton, put pressure on Syrian president Assad, and, for the first time, Assad cooperated. Berri's power play had backfired and the Syrians felt he had bitten off more than he could chew. "We believe Assad will intervene," Ambassador Eagleton cabled Washington.

Friday night, June 28, was one of the longest nights of my life. There were unmistakable signs that the hostages' release was near. At seven o'clock that night press reports from the Middle East said the release was imminent, and we were getting the same feedback from our intelligence sources. I went home early that evening for a short break, returning to the White House around midnight, in anticipation that something would happen early Saturday. Sitting in my office during the pre-dawn hours I had the eerie feeling that daylight had already broken; the television lights burned outside all night, as the camera crews shot through the windows of the White House, showing the press office staff waiting nervously. We were glued to the T.V. as CNN broke in to carry a raw, unedited tape, only minutes old, showing our hostages gathered in a dusty East Beirut schoolyard.

At four-eighteen Saturday morning I gave the press a background briefing, one where reporters could attribute their information to "an administration source" but not quote me by name, and said that the hostages were on their way from Beirut to Damascus, Syria, where they would catch a U.S. military plane for a flight to one of our bases in West

Germany, where George Bush would meet them. Our sources in Beirut had seen the hostages get on a bus outside of the schoolhouse, and we had U.S. Embassy people at the border between Lebanon and Syria to notify us when they crossed into Syrian territory, but we lost track of the captives after their bus left the school. George Bush also jumped the gun, announcing to reporters upon his arrival at Orly Airport in Paris that "the hostages are released."

By 7:00 A.M. our time, word came in that the hostages were still in Beirut, because Nabib Berri was now demanding that the U.S. promise not to retaliate against Lebanon for the hijacking before he would approve the release. Our hopes had been dashed temporarily, and at one-twenty-eight Saturday afternoon I announced that "My staff and I are going home. We will get back to the press by telephone if anything happens."

The ultra-militant Hezbollah faction, which had separated four of the hostages from the other thirty-five, was behind the demand that we not retaliate. This clearly broke our rule of "no promises to terrorists," but we were too close to a solution to quibble. The President conferred with McFarlane and Shultz at nine-fifteen Saturday night and gave approval for the State Department to issue a carefully worded restatement of our policy forty-five minutes later: "The United States reaffirms its long-standing support for the preservation of Lebanon, its government, its stability and security, and for the mitigation of the suffering of its people."

That statement had its desired effect, as the Syrian government notified the U.S. Embassy in Damascus at three-thirty Sunday morning our time that Syria had "solved" the problem delaying the hostages' release. The motorcade containing the hostages began to roll a few hours later. Finally, at one-thirty Sunday afternoon, the good news came from a U.S. Embassy officer stationed at the southern Syrian border. He spoke from a roadside phone booth to the embassy, and his message was relayed instantly to Washington: "They're free." We whooped it up, and a half hour later I told the press that Bud McFarlane had informed the President, who responded, "That's very welcome news. Let me know when they are wheels up." I emphasized that "We made no concessions. We made no deals, no guarantees."

Delighted as we were by the hostages' release, the mood was dampened by the murder of Robert Stethem and by the knowledge that we had failed to obtain the freedom of the seven other Americans who had been kidnapped in Lebanon during the previous year or so. Still, we were a group of happy campers in the White House.

Late Sunday afternoon I sat in the Oval Office with the President when he placed a phone call to the U.S. Air Force plane that was carrying the freed hostages from Damascus to Frankfurt. As the plane cleared the runway at Damascus, Reagan's words to the passengers and crew from TWA Flight 847 were "Happy landings." A few minutes later, President and Mrs. Reagan left the White House for a dinner party at George Shultz's home, a party where there truly was something to celebrate.

THE ACHILLE LAURO

The *Achille Lauro* incident in October 1985 proved to be John Poindexter's shining moment—and may have been a disaster for the Reagan administration in the long run for that reason, since it firmly established the credentials that led to Poindexter's appointment as national security director less than two months later.

The episode began on October 7 when four heavily armed Palestinians seized the *Achille Lauro,* an Italian cruise ship, as it approached the Egyptian harbor of Port Said. When the terrorists hijacked the ship there were about four hundred people aboard, most of them crew members; most of the passengers had left the ship in Alexandria, Egypt, for an overland tour and were planning to reboard it in Port Said. The hijackers declared that unless Israel released fifty Palestianian prisoners, they would murder the passengers and crew aboard the ship, starting with the Americans. One complicating factor early on was that Maureen Reagan was a passenger on another Mediterranean cruise ship when the *Achille Lauro* was seized. We were tight-lipped about Maureen's whereabouts, refusing at first to even acknowledge she was abroad. We quickly determined that she was not the object of the hijacking, nor ever in any danger, but we declined comment on her until she was out of the region.

After holding the ship and those aboard for two days, the hijackers surrendered on October 9 to a representative of the Palestine Liberation Organization in Egypt. During those two days, however, they murdered passenger Leon Klinghoffer, sixty-nine, of New York, who was confined to a wheelchair. After shooting and killing Klinghoffer, the terrorists cold-bloodedly dumped him off the ship; his body, partially devoured by sharks, washed ashore in Syria a few days later.

During the two days that the gunmen held the ship, U.S. and Israeli intelligence agencies monitored the situation closely, but there was little that those of us in the White House could do except watch the drama unfold and hope for the best. On the morning of October 9, just before the hijackers surrendered, I was asked to restate our policy on terrorism. I responded, "Our policy of not negotiating with terrorists or asking other countries to do so is well-known." But in the sensitive time during a hijacking, when terrorists were holding Americans, conceivably at gunpoint, it didn't serve any purpose to hammer out that hardline policy again. To do so, I told the press, might simply serve to agitate and infuriate a terrorist with a gun in his hand. But the press persisted in trying to get me to restate it anyway, even though there clearly was no news in repeating what we had said so often. In reality, there was danger that repeating it would have sent a trigger-happy gunman off the deep end.

The morning after the hijackers gave up, we went through with a previously scheduled trip to Chicago, where the President visited the headquarters of Sara Lee, the food conglomerate, and a high school. It was raining when we landed, but he decided to field a few questions from reporters huddled under the wing of Air Force One. Reagan got off to a terrible start, implying that a request by PLO leader Yasir Arafat to take custody of the hijackers and punish them was acceptable to the United States: "Well, I think that if he believes their organization has enough of a national setup like a nation they can bring them to justice, then all right. Just so they're brought to justice."

I cringed when he said that, because it clearly contradicted our long-standing policy that the PLO had no standing as a nation. The press pounced on it right away; UPI moved a story within moments of the President's statement, saying, "President Reagan said today justice might be served if the PLO tried and punished the hijackers. Reagan's statement in the rain beneath the wing of Air Force One appeared at odds with other administration spokesmen, who had expressed doubt that PLO justice would be acceptable." Bud McFarlane, who was with us on the Chicago trip, tried to smooth it over while we were en route to Sara Lee by saying the President meant that he wanted the PLO to turn the hijackers over to competent authority for trial.

The uproar mounted as the President spoke to assembled Sara Lee employees and toured their baking kitchens. But he corrected himself while he was there, saying the PLO should turn the hijackers over to a sovereign state instead of bringing them to justice themselves.

While we were in Chicago, Poindexter, then number two to McFarlane at the NSC, was in charge of handling the situation back in Washington. He and McFarlane were in constant communication, and we huddled just off stage at Sara Lee, out of sight of the audience, as Bud briefed the President. Early that morning Reagan had approved a plan to intercept the hijackers if possible, force them down, and spirit them away to the United States to stand trial. Throughout the day information flowed in from U.S., Israeli, and Tunisian intelligence. Egyptian President Hosni

Mubarak had arranged for the hijackers to have safe passage from Egypt, and he refused to hand them over to us, but our intelligence sources told us exactly when they boarded a plane to leave Egypt, what kind of plane it was (a Boeing 737), and even what the tail number was. As the President left the stage, Bud told him everything was in place for the interception, and Reagan replied without hesitation, "Go with it. Let's see if we can't get 'em." He winked and licked his lips, hungry to even up the score with the terrorists.

An Egyptian plane carrying the terrorists left Cairo at 4:15 P.M. Eastern time, ten minutes before we landed at Andrews Air Force Base on our return from Chicago. It was headed for Tunisia, where the PLO headquarters were located, but Tunisian authorities, in cooperation with us, closed their airport and denied the plane permission to land. Meanwhile, four F-14 attack jets launched from the U.S. aircraft carrier *Saratoga*, which was in the Mediterranean, intercepted the Egyptian plane south of Crete at 5:30 P.M. Washington time, the middle of the night over there. The Egyptian pilot was cruising along in the dark and suddenly he saw on either side of him two U.S. F-14 fighter planes armed to the teeth, with our pilots instructing him to follow them and land at Sigonella, a joint U.S.-Italian military airbase on Sicily. He had no choice.

Our plan was that when the plane landed we would have Navy SEALs surround the plane and send the terrorists right to the U.S. before we announced anything. But the Italian forces insisted on taking control of the hijackers, and an ugly confrontation occurred between our men and the Italians. As the standoff continued, Reagan, at the urging of McFarlane and Poindexter, placed an urgent phone call to Italian Prime Minister Bettino Craxi. But Craxi, fearful that terrorist elements would retaliate against Italy if he appeared to play along with the United States, refused to hand over the terrorists. The President then ordered our troops to let the Italians have them.

Andrea Mitchell later asked the President if we had been prepared to shoot down the plane, and he replied, "That's one of the questions I'm not going to answer. That's for them to go to bed every night wondering." In fact, we would have made threatening motions, trying to make the pilot think we would shoot him down if he didn't obey, but in the end we would have broken off without attacking them.

Needless to say, we were jubilant over the terrorists' capture after all the frustration we had endured in the last few years at the hands of Middle Eastern terrorists, and President Reagan told the nation that "these young Americans [the F-14 pilots] sent a message to terrorists everywhere. The message: You can run, but you can't hide." *Newsday*, Long Island's

Larry Speakes and his girlfriend Jenell Robinson, who later became his first wife, with Elvis Presley in 1956. *Photograph by Harry E. Speakes.*

Senator James O. Eastland meets reporters as the Judiciary Committee announces the defeat of Supreme Court nominee Judge Clement Haynsworth in 1969. *United Press International photograph.*

A lowly assistant press secretary reports to the President, as President Ford and
key aides listen to information on congressional statements.
White House photograph by David Hume Kennerly.

Impromptu briefing for reporters outside George Washington University
Hospital after the attempt on President Ronald Reagan's life on March 30, 1981.
Photograph by James Thresher, The Washington Post.

Conference with Secretary of State Alexander M. Haig in the White House Situation Room moments after Haig made his controversial "I am in control…" statement. *White House photograph by Karl Schumacher.*

The White House press corps at the press secretary's office for an early-morning briefing, November 24, 1981. *White House photograph by Bill Fitz-Patrick.*

With President Reagan as he reviews a draft of the 1984 reelection announcement in the Oval Office. *White House photograph by Jack Kightlinger.*

Fielding questions in the Rose Garden with Vice President George Bush and President Reagan. *White House photograph by Bill Fitz-Patrick.*

Election Night, November 6, 1984—with Ed Meese and Mike Deaver, joining the Reagans in their Los Angeles hotel room for TV coverage of President Reagan's victory over Walter Mondale. *White House photograph by Pete Souza.*

A favorite trick: catching a weary staff member as he takes a nap aboard Air Force One. *White House photograph by Terry Arthur.*

Speakes *(background, left)* taking notes at a tense moment during the first
summit meeting of President Reagan and Premier Mikhail S. Gorbachev in
Geneva, Switzerland, November 2, 1985. *White House photograph
by Mary Anne Fackelman-Miner.*

Conference with President
Reagan and then–Treasury
Secretary Donald Regan at
the Williamsburg Economic
Summit, May 29, 1983.
*White House photograph
by Jack Kightlinger.*

A friendly greeting from the
Gorbachevs during the
Geneva Summit, 1985.
*White House photograph
by Pete Souza.*

Conferring with Secretary of Defense Caspar W. Weinberger and the President
on December 15, 1985. *White House photograph by Michael Evans.*

At his 2,000th press briefing, offering cake to friend and foe alike in the White House briefing room. *White House photograph by Terry Arthur.*

The Speakes family bidding farewell to the President on their final day at the White House. Sons Jeremy, 16 (*extreme left*), and Scott, 24 (*extreme right*), join Larry and Laura Speakes in the Oval Office, January 30, 1987. Daughter Sandy, 25, is married and lives in Dallas. *White House photograph by Mary Anne Fackelman-Miner.*

tabloid newspaper, headlined "Got 'em!"—and pictured a very stern White House spokesman at the podium, shaking his finger.

Our only regrets were that the Italians refused to ship the Palestinians to the United States so they could stand trial here, and that the Italians didn't arrest the mastermind of the *Achille Lauro* hijacking, Mohammed Abbas, who had directed the hijackers by radio from land and was aboard the Egyptian plane with the four hijackers. Happy as we were with the outcome, it would have been even better if I had been able to announce to the press, as I had planned to, "Ladies and gentlemen, the terrorists who took over the *Achille Lauro* and murdered Leon Klinghoffer are now aboard a U.S. aircraft bound for the United States, where they will face trial for terrorism and murder."

Immediately after our return to Washington from Chicago I went to the NSC offices, where Poindexter and his assistant, Oliver North, were running a tight, hands-on command post, directing virtually every move our people in the Middle East made. They told me we had to be very careful in what we said because the Italians and the Egyptians were scared to death of the PLO. "The only peole who have any guts are the Tunisians," North said.

That night at eleven o'clock I provided the press with details on the capture of the terrorists. Asked a tricky question about U.S.-Italian extradition laws, I replied, "First of all, I am not an Italian lawyer. . . . But the United States will seek extradition on the grounds that an American citizen was murdered, that American citizens were victims of a terrorist attack. Now, what Italian law is, I don't know."

Afterwards, someone handed me a note on a yellow legal pad. It read, "Speakes, you may not be an Italian lawyer . . . but you ought to be." Signed "North."

THE RAID ON LIBYA

We had intercepted the hijackers of the *Achille Lauro* and obtained the safe release of everyone aboard TWA flight 847 except for Robert Stethem, but in view of the 1983 bombing of the marine barracks in Beirut and numerous other attacks on U.S. interests, we still had a tremendous score to settle with the people behind the acts of terrorism.

Outsiders were always saying, "Why don't you do something about it? Why don't you bomb Iran or Libya? Why don't you attack the Shiites who were responsible for the kidnappings, the murders, and the bombings in Lebanon?"

Getting even was much easier said than done. These terrorist incidents were not a case of one nation starting a war against another, where we could retaliate against the country that had attacked us. The terrorists in Lebanon lived in small roving bands among the civilian population. There was no way to punish them without slaughtering innocent bystanders, which would have made us as bad as those who had wronged us. Similarly, although Iran was probably behind the Marine Corps bombing, there was no target in Iran that we could strike and know for sure that we had hit the radicals who directed the terrorists. We could obtain no direct proof linking any person or group within reach to any specific attack.

Then, in April 1986, we finally got an opportunity for some payback. April 4 was a Friday, and the LaBelle discotheque in West Berlin, a favorite hangout of U.S. military personnel stationed in the area, was packed that night. At one-forty-nine Saturday morning, April 5, a bomb exploded inside the LaBelle, killing an American sergeant and a Turkish woman, and injuring more than two hundred others, including about sixty Americans.

Ten minutes before the LaBelle bombing, someone at the Libyan People's Bureau in East Berlin, Libya's version of an embassy, had called home to Tripoli, reporting that an operation was "happening now." A few minutes after the bombing, the Libyans in East Berlin wired their headquarters in Tripoli: "Operation a success. Cannot be traced to Libya." Unbelievably, the Libyans communicated on an open phone, without any code or attempt to scramble their messages, and the CIA intercepted them. That gave us the evidence we needed, at last enabling us to place responsibility for a terrorist attack directly on Libyan leader Muammar al-Qaddafi.

By the time of the disco bombing, President Reagan was way past being fed up with the terrorists' attacks. Another one had occurred less than three days before, when a bomb exploded aboard a TWA airliner over Athens, Greece, killing four American passengers. There was no evidence to link Libya directly to the TWA bomb, but a radical Arab group claimed credit, and it was one more episode of terrorism that might very well have been connected to Libya. And Libya was also a prime suspect in terrorist attacks the previous December 27 at airports in Rome and Vienna in which twenty civilians, including an eleven-year-old girl and four other Americans, were murdered.

Rhetorically signaling what was about to come, President Reagan described Qaddafi during the next few days as both "the mad dog of the Middle East" and as someone who was "not only a barbarian, but he's flaky." These lines were off-the-cuff-Reagan tough talk. He has had a knack throughout his political career for cutting through the standard rhetoric of State Department diplomats and other bureaucrats, and coming up with something that the average person could understand and relate to. You could see people in pool halls and barber shops and gas stations saying, "Did you hear what Reagan said about Qaddafi? He's flaky."

Retribution came at 7:00 P.M. Washington time on April 14 (2:00 A.M. on April 15 in Libya). Thirty-two U.S. bombers, some of which were launched from aircraft carriers in the Mediterranean and some that flew all the way from England, swooped in low, beneath Libyan radar. Our targets included Libya's intelligence center, the military portion of Tripoli's airport, a port that Qaddafi's terrorists used as a training base, and two other military posts. All of our planes except one returned safely, after dealing extensive damage to some of Qaddafi's military planes and the airbase from which he launched his worldwide terrorist operations.

Our British-based F-111s had been forced to fly an extra 1,200 miles down the Atlantic Coast and into the Mediterranean via the Strait of Gibraltar because the government of France denied us permission to overfly French territory; by chance, the French Embassy in Tripoli was badly damaged during our ten-minute raid. That was a mistake, but it was not an accident that Qaddafi's residence compound at the intelligence center in Tripoli was hit during the bombing. The Libyans asserted that Qaddafi's infant daughter was killed and two of his sons were wounded during our attack. If that was true, it was unfortunate. But the Libyans' intelligence center was our primary target, not Qaddafi's tent. I wondered if there might have been an unspoken wish among National Security Director John Poindexter and some of his aides that we could get Qaddafi. They were uncertain of Qaddafi's whereabouts, but North said, "If we get him, that's a bonus." We did have intelligence that Qaddafi was there some of the time, but we did not know whether he would be there when we bombed them. He was paranoid about being attacked, and seldom slept in the same place two nights in a row, our intelligence said.

Two hours before the bombing, my hands full of press Q's and A's, I headed across the street to a secure room in the Executive Office Building, where President Reagan was explaining the action to the congressional leadership. "We have convincing evidence of Qaddafi's involvement in terrorism. There is clear evidence in intercepts of messages from Tripoli to East Germany that the Libyans were responsible for the disco bombing," he said. He revealed that right after the bombing a cable went from Tripoli to East Berlin congratulating the Libyans there on the successful assignment that had been carried out, and gave the exact time of the cable. He added that we had earlier foiled a plot in Paris where

Libyan terrorists were going to scale the wall of the U.S. Embassy and launch an attack. "We got the goods on him," the President said.

All of the congressional leaders, including Tip O'Neill, were totally supportive, except for Robert Byrd, who, as usual, tried to have it both ways. He spoke in favor of the bombing, but he also raised the point that we might be getting into a tit-for-tat retaliatory exchange with the terrorists. He went on that we had violated the spirit if not the letter of the War Powers Resolution by having the bombers leave for the mission before Congress was informed.

Our silence on Libya throughout the day gave the press a hint that something big was afoot. To maintain the secrecy of the mission, the press office had to stage an elaborate hoax. The President was scheduled to attend Senator Paul Laxalt's annual black-tie lamb fry, one of the city's biggest political-social events. He was due to leave the White House at 7:00 P.M., and we would have to assemble the press in the waiting motorcade long before that. An announced delay would have been a sure tipoff. I instructed Dale Petroskey, my assistant press secretary, to don his black tie and move the press pool to the motorcade. It got more complicated. We had to bring the press back inside in time to cover my announcement of the bombing, still without giving away our plans. I kept Petroskey on an open line from the White House guard station on the South Lawn to Pete Roussel inside my office—and we summoned the press back in the nick of time.

I waited to report the bombing to the press until seven-twenty, twenty minutes after the attack, in order to give our planes time to clear the target areas. On my way to the briefing room, I stopped by Poindexter's office to see if there was any last-minute information. George Shultz was there, sitting in a wing-back chair with his feet propped on Poindexter's coffee table. He and a weary Poindexter were in a mood of quiet satisfaction because our planes had made it to the site and carried out their mission, and, except for the plane that had been shot down, killing the two men aboard, were en route to their bases. I wouldn't say there was jubiliation in the air, but there was definitely a feeling of "We've finally been able to do it."

From Poindexter's office I made my way to the briefing room, where I had the pleasure of announcing: "U.S. military forces have executed a series of carefully planned air strikes against terrorist-related targets in Libya."

A short while later, Reagan addressed the nation from the Oval Office. "Today we have done what we had to do," he announced. "If necessary we shall do it again. . . . Self-defense is not only our right, it's our duty, and that's the purpose of tonight's mission."

The raid on Libya was overwhelmingly popular. In the eleven hours after the President's speech, we received by far the highest volume of phone calls that we ever had in a similar time span during the Reagan administration. The deluge of calls was so great that it jammed the White House switchboard. There was a total of 5,836 calls, with 4,672, or eighty percent, favorable, and only 1,164 against.

The President had to pass up Laxalt's lamb fry, but Marine Corps commandant P. X. Kelley announced there that we had bombed Libya. The news was received with wild cheering from the audience, which included much of official Washington.

One of the few dissenters was Helen Thomas of UPI. During a press briefing, Thomas, a fiercely proud woman of Lebanese descent, had a short and heated exchange with Cap Weinberger. "How many people do you think you killed?" she inquired. "We have no idea that we killed anybody," he answered. But Helen pressed on: "Do you care?" Cap ignored her last question. Helen had antagonized the President during the TWA hijacking ten months earlier, raising questions like, "Mr. President, people wonder why you don't lean on Israel a bit, since the U.S. says that their holding of Shiite prisoners is against international law." Helen had strong anti-Israeli feelings, and she would even call the Israelis "murderers" in her questions.

Helen Thomas and Bob Timburg of the *Baltimore Sun* shared the foolish question award in the aftermath of the Libyan raid. They kept trying to pin me down on the exact time the President had reached a final decision to bomb Libya. I kept trying to explain to them that that wasn't how government worked, that it was an evolving, ongoing process as you gathered intelligence, assembled forces, and inched forward over a period of days. You couldn't say that a decision was made at a particular minute or second, but they persisted. Finally, in exasperation, I told them, "The decision to bomb Libya was made at 6:59 P.M. and fifty-nine seconds."

The best quote of the entire Libyan affair, however, belonged to the venerable Texan, Sarah McClendon, who has kept Presidents on their toes since FDR. When I subsequently announced the damage assessment from the raids, Sarah remarked, "Bad as war is, it's better than a lamb fry"—where, in the Basque tradition, Reagan was always presented with cooked lamb's testicles, which sheep herders regarded as a delicacy.

The bombing of Libya's intelligence headquarters, military airport, and terrorist training center was part of a three-phase secret plan for destabilizing Qaddafi's grip on the country. The other two stages included:

- A raid on missile batteries located near Syrte, Libya. That segment was carried out three weeks before the April 14–15 bombing, and again was in retaliation for Qaddafi's aggression. Qaddafi had claimed sovereignty over the entire Gulf of Sidra off Libya's coast, not just the portion within twelve miles of shore, and had warned us not to cross what he called "the line of death" at the north end of the gulf. To prove that we did not honor his claim, we sent thirty warships, including three aircraft carriers, to conduct maneuvers in the Gulf of Sidra starting on March 23. The Libyans launched several missiles against our ships from the Syrte battery the day after our exercises began, and we responded by knocking out the radar at the missile site and sinking at least two Libyan missile boats.
- The third phase, which was never carried out, was to bomb the key junction sites and pumping stations on the Libyans' main oil pipeline, which would immobilize their oil supply and ruin their economy. The pipeline bombing was a contingency to bring Qaddafi to his knees economically in the event of a prolonged fight. For now it remains simply prudent military planning that has never been needed.

Much has been made of the so-called disinformation campaign against Libya that was disclosed in the fall of 1986—much too much, in my opinion.

President Reagan did approve a memo from John Poindexter on August 14, 1986, which simply updated our previous contingency plans for retaliating against Libya. But that plan had been in existence throughout the Reagan administration and had been implemented as early as 1981, when U.S. fighter jets shot down two Libyan planes that attacked our planes over the Gulf of Sidra.

The whole disinformation controversy grew out of Poindexter's poorly worded memo, which said that the strategy against Libya "combines real and illusionary events—through a disinformation program—with the basic goal of making Qaddafi *think* that there is a high degree of internal opposition to him within Libya, that his key trusted aides are disloyal, that the United States is about to move against him militarily." Ollie North once summed up our goal in a one-line remark to me: "We've got to keep Qaddafi in his box."

Disinformation was an explosive word to the press, akin to waving a red cape in front of a bull. There was nothing wrong with trying to deceive Qaddafi, but the use of the word "disinformation" in a paper signed by the President, with the risk that the memo might someday become public, was simply bad staff work on the part of Poindexter and his aides. It was another example of Poindexter's mismanagement, which would soon lead to the Iran-Contra debacle. Poindexter and his staff should have had the savvy to eliminate such inflammatory language from the document before it went to the President for his signature.

What would become the smoking gun in the disinformation scandal was a front-page story by John Walcott in the *Wall Street Journal* on August 25. Walcott reported that the Reagan administration was making contingency plans for "a new and larger bombing of Libya" based on evidence that Qaddafi had "begun plotting new terrorist attacks." That story was correct, but blew the whole thing decidedly out of proportion. When asked about it by reporters, I said it was "authoritative." I have always suspected, by the way, that Ollie North was the one who leaked that story to the *Journal.*

The disinformation scandal blew up a little over a month after Walcott's article, when Bob Woodward disclosed in the *Washington Post* that the Reagan administration had launched "a secret and unusual campaign of deception" against Libya. Woodward wrote that the *Journal* had been had. I assume that Woodward's source was Bill Casey; the whole affair was a power struggle between the CIA and the NSC. After Woodward's story appeared on October 2, Walcott came to me very sheepishly, feeling that he had been embarrassed professionally, but I told him he had no cause to feel humiliated. His story was correct, and the Woodward story simply made a mountain of a molehill. There was never any intention to plant disinformation in the U.S. media; the aim was to confuse Qaddafi by movement of the U.S. fleet in the Mediterranean and by quietly influencing Qaddafi's rivals within Libya to overthrow him. As Reagan said, he wanted Qaddafi to "go to bed every night wondering what we might do."

The episode took on even larger proportions six days after Woodward broke his story, when Bernard Kalb resigned as State Department spokesman, in protest over the alleged campaign of deception. He resigned on principle, when in reality there was no principle involved, because there was no attempt to mislead the American press. Although I respected his decision, I strongly disagreed with it. Kalb never sought an explanation from Shultz or Reagan on the alleged disinformation campaign. He just up and bowed out one morning. Kalb's action reminded me of Jerry terHorst's resignation as Ford's press secretary over the Nixon pardon in 1974: I think they both wanted out of their jobs; each found a convenient excuse; and each managed to present himself as a martyr.

12

A Cancer

on the Presidency

"It's cancer. It's big, it's black, it's ugly," Dr. John Hutton whispered to me on Friday, July 12, 1985, as we met in the corridor just outside the examining room at Bethesda Naval Medical Center. Down the hallway, President Reagan, still groggy from the anesthesia required for a forty-three-minute proctoscopic examination, was being wheeled into a recovery room. Behind me, in a tiny, cluttered doctor's office that had been made available for her use, sat Nancy Reagan, awaiting the outcome of her husband's examination.

The news confirmed what we had feared most. The cancer, growing on the President's large intestine, had just been diagnosed by a team of doctors who had thoroughly examined Reagan after removing a small benign polyp from his lower intestine; that growth had been discovered four months earlier when doctors performed a routine follow-up examination on Reagan, who had had another small polyp removed from his intestine in May 1984.

The discovery of Reagan's cancer was to be one of the major stories of the Reagan presidency. I had already made it my business to study presidential illnesses, dating back more than a hundred years. President Garfield had lingered on for eighty days from the time he was shot in 1881 until he died; several years later, President Grover Cleveland had gone out on a houseboat on the Hudson River between New York City and Albany and had a malignant tumor removed from his mouth (the White House reported at the time that Cleveland was on vacation, and it wasn't revealed until a year later that he had undergone surgery for a malignancy); President Wilson was incapacitated by a stroke in 1919 and served for two more years, with his wife virtually functioning as President; President Eisenhower was unconscious three different times, after a heart attack and a stroke, and during surgery for ileitis; and President Johnson underwent surgery twice, on his gall bladder in 1965, and to have a polyp removed from his throat a year later.

Knowing that the press corps would expect thorough briefings from me on any presidential health problem, I had borrowed a copy of *Physician's Desk Reference* from the White House doctors, and I had done my best to keep myself informed about Reagan's health. By the time of the cancer surgery, I had developed a file an inch thick with every detail of his medical track record.

Nevertheless, I was hardly a medical expert. I used to joke with the White House physicians each time a medical problem arose: "Just give me five medical terms, tell me how to pronounce them, and I'll make it."

The morning the cancer was discovered, the ever-jaunty Ronald Reagan had waved vigorously to the shouting reporters as he walked out of the White House and prepared to board the presidential helicopter for the trip to Bethesda. Carrying the President and Mrs. Reagan, his personal aide Jim Kuhn, a military aide, and me, the chopper flew past the Washington Monument, turned right, and headed up the Potomac River. The rest of us respected the silence the Reagans obviously wanted. Mrs. Reagan sat across from the President, facing him, their knees almost touching. He avoided her glance during the ten-minute trip, looking down on the tree-lined Maryland shore instead. Had he looked at her, he would have seen an enormously concerned wife, with a bit of a smile etched on her lips.

As we landed at the hospital and the whine of the engines slowly died, Nancy Reagan reached over and touched her husband's hand. "Let's go," she said, and he gave her a wink. Inside the hospital, the President gave Mrs. Reagan a lingering embrace and a kiss, said, "I'll see you soon, honey," and headed for the examining room.

Mrs. Reagan was a bit adrift as the busy hospital staff concentrated on her husband. In the waiting room that had been prepared for her she was alone for the first time under these circumstances—no family, no friends, no Mike Deaver, who had been a family confidant for so many years.

Assistant press secretary Mark Weinberg, Jim Kuhn, and I moved quickly into a sitting room that had been reserved for the staff. I had just settled in when the military aide stuck his head in. "The First Lady would like to see you," he said. Both Kuhn and Weinberg looked up, knowing that I had drawn the short straw.

I had worked for the Reagans for four and a half years and we'd been through a lot together, but I still wasn't close to either of them personally. I dreaded this duty because Mrs. Reagan had never developed her husband's ability to put people at ease in her presence. There were often long, awkward periods of silence when you were with her. As much as I felt out of place at that moment, though, there was no one else.

She and I sat together during the entire procedure, just over an hour, all told. She obviously wanted someone there with her, so I stayed. I steered the conversation to everything except what was going on down the hall in Bethesda's Examination Room Number One. We discussed her travel plans, my love of California and its lifestyle, even their retirement plans. After thirty minutes of small talk, Mrs. Reagan glanced at her watch; we'd been told the procedure would last about a half hour. Again, fifteen minutes later, she looked at her watch with increasing anxiety. I finally asked her, "Would you like for me to go and see?" She nodded yes, and I readily got up to leave.

I moved quickly up the hall, knowing she would follow behind, and I ran into the doctors coming our way. "What have we got?" I asked Hutton, a slim, bald army colonel who was the assistant White House physician. Hutton had a way of cutting through complex medical terms and stating the problem in plain English, and this time he did not fail: "It's cancer, it's big, it's black, it's ugly." With my limited knowledge of medicine, my first impression was that Dr. Hutton was talking about a massive cancer, perhaps one that was life-threatening.

The First Lady looked at Hutton apprehensively, but never spoke. "Let's go inside," Hutton quietly told Mrs. Reagan, steering her back to her little office. The others on the medical team followed. She sat down and said, "I want you to tell me everything." She was unflinching, solid as a rock. They told her that they had found a malignant tumor in the President's colon and that they thought surgery was essential as soon as possible. "You and the President could go on to Camp David and come back on Monday," Hutton said. "But since he is already in the hospital and already prepped, this is the best time to do it." She looked at me questioningly, and I said, "Mrs. Reagan, as far as I'm concerned, it's best to go ahead and do it right now. From a public point of view, it will keep speculation to a minimum." "Let's ask him," she said.

She and I went into the President's recovery room. She gave it to him very straight: "You've got something that needs surgery. What do you want to do?" He didn't hesitate a minute. "Let's get it done," he said, almost matter-of-factly. Although tragedies like the deaths of U.S. military troops in Lebanon or Grenada could make President Reagan get very emotional, he never betrayed his feelings about himself. Oftentimes he made jokes to deflect personal emotions, the way he had after John Hinckley shot him. Then he had looked up at the doctors as he was about to undergo surgery at George Washington University Hospital and quipped, "I hope you are all Republicans." This time, though, there were no quips, no tears, nothing but those words, "Let's get it done."

Mark Weinberg had become quite a medical expert himself, and had made a list of a dozen questions that would need answers if we got this kind of report. As soon as the Reagans decided to go ahead with the surgery immediately, I questioned the members of the examining team and jotted down all the details of the President's problem.

It was after five o'clock when Mark and I sprinted down the hospital hallway and into a waiting White House car. We both knew it was imperative that we report to the press before the network news shows went on the air at six-thirty; otherwise, without authoritative information, speculation would run wild as reporters filled air time. We cajoled the White House driver mercilessly as we neared downtown in the height of the evening rush hour. About four blocks from the White House, we encountered gridlock, and I ordered the driver to edge out into K Street, shift into the oncoming lane of traffic, and push ahead. As we reached Lafayette Park, we directed him the wrong way up a one-way street and into the northwest gate of the White House.

After a dash into Don Regan's office to outline my statement, I entered the briefing room at six o'clock to announce, "The President will undergo surgery tomorrow for removal of a polyp." At Mrs. Reagan's behest, there was no mention of the words "cancer" or "malignant."

By six o'clock the next morning, I was back at the hospital, where Weinberg gave me a tour. We concluded our once-over by donning operating room sterile suits, complete with shoe covers and caps, and, clad from head to toe in green, we inspected the actual operating theater where the President would undergo surgery.

Five hours later, the President was wheeled toward the operating room, with Mrs. Reagan walking alongside him, holding his hand. Even at that moment, he sought to reassure her, saying, "After all they did to me yesterday, this should be a breeze." And with that he was off.

By noon the doctors had removed the tumor, as well as two feet of the President's bowel. By an amazing coincidence, Reagan's older brother, Neil, had undergone virtually the exact same operation ten days earlier, also for the removal of a malignant tumor from his colon.

The previous week, as soon as it became apparent that the President would have to undergo major surgery, the question arose on whether to invoke the Twenty-fifth Amendment, transferring his powers temporarily to Vice President Bush. Since the President would receive a sedative that would make him drowsy, the press began to ask if he would be alert enough to exercise the duties of his office.

I went to Fred Fielding, counsel to the President, who said he had talked to the doctors and didn't feel it was necessary for the President to relinquish his powers. But I was very concerned, because I couldn't get a clear-cut answer from Dr. Burton Smith, the physician to the President. I had always had reservations about Dr. Smith's guidance; he was a urologist who couldn't articulate much about medicine outside of his specialty. During the President's previous illnesses, Smith—while always trying to be helpful—gave answers to my questions that were ambiguous and confusing. My staff and I often referred to him as "a celebrity doctor." Moreover, Smith was semi-retired. As press questions persisted, we quietly raised the question with Dr. Hutton, who indicated that the President would be a little more heavily sedated than Smith had led us to believe.

I asked Fielding to convene another session with the doctors to find out exactly what the story was. Fielding agreed, and we set up a meeting in his office on the second floor of the White House. We had Hutton and Smith on one side of the table, Weinberg on the other, with Fielding and me at either end of the table. We went right at the doctors in courtroom style: "Would he be capable of signing his name?" "Would he be capable of making a statement?" Dr. Smith was ambivalent, saying, "The anesthetic will have no more effect on the President than drinking a couple of martinis."

Following our discussion, Fielding decided that the President should transfer power temporarily to George Bush. However, Reagan felt strongly that he did not want to set a precedent that would bind a future President, forcing him to relinquish his duties for some minor incapacitation. As Fielding said, "What's the threshold? Do we invoke the Twenty-fifth Amendment when a President has a tooth pulled and is given gas in the dentist's chair?"

In the end, the President did sign a historic letter transferring to Bush the "constitutional duties and powers of the office of the President of the United States" during the time Reagan would be under anesthesia. The transfer actually took place when the President was given anesthesia at 11:30 A.M. on July 13. Even without invoking the Twenty-fifth Amendment for the first time—it had been passed in 1967, after Lyndon Johnson was without a Vice President for the fourteen months between the time he succeeded President Kennedy and Hubert Humphrey was elected Vice President on Johnson's ticket in 1964 and inaugurated in January 1965—Reagan had set a precedent by giving Bush the first temporary transfer of presidential authority.

As soon as Reagan signed the letters, they were delivered to Speaker of the House Tip O'Neill and President Pro Tempore of the Senate Strom Thurmond by Dick Hauser, Fielding's deputy. Hauser found O'Neill in his office, but arrived at the Senate Office Building as Thurmond drove up in his car. Thurmond took the letter without reading it and invited Hauser to sit alongside him in the car. "Come on, git in," Thurmond drawled. "Enjoy some of these heah good South Carolina peaches." Hauser chomped down on the succulent fruit while Thurmond read the historic document, dismissed Hauser, and drove off, leaving the White House lawyer at curbside—still holding the peach.

The transfer of power ended early that evening. Don Regan, Fielding, and I visited the President in the recovery room shortly after 7:00 P.M., with a letter reclaiming his authority. Reagan was awake but still a little drowsy when we entered the darkened recovery room. His cubicle was surrounded by heavy white drapes and a Secret Service agent stood by his bed.

Reagan looked up and saw us standing at the foot of his bed. "Don't tell me. The Russians have fired a missile," were his first words. The Reagan humor was intact, which was a good sign.

"Boss, how do you feel?" Regan quizzed the President.

"Fine. Fit as a fiddle," the President replied.

At 7:22 P.M., as the chief of staff held the paper, Ronald Reagan became President again, signing his name in a good, steady hand. This time even Lesley Stahl would have recognized his signature.

I was with Nancy Reagan again that afternoon when the doctors came in to tell her the results of the operation. This time, we were not alone; her step-brother, Philadelphia neurosurgeon Richard Davis, had come down to be with her. The doctors, still in their surgical greens, gave it to her straight: "It is almost certainly cancer"—although they wouldn't know for sure until they performed a biopsy. She took the news without flinching, just as she had the day before.

After giving the medical report to the press, I returned to see how Mrs. Reagan was bearing up. Once again, I found her alone, sitting outside the President's empty room; he was still in the recovery room. Bethesda's Presidential Suite was designed to accommodate a President who was running the country from his hospital bed. There was a very large bedroom, a sitting room, a conference room half as large as the White House Cabinet Room, several examining rooms, two bedrooms for top aides, and elaborate communications equipment. As I tiptoed into the suite, Mrs. Reagan was using some of that equipment. She was speaking on the phone to Don Regan, laying down the law for the President's recuperation. The President was to have no visitors for several days, after which Regan himself could visit, and later Bush and National Security Director Bud McFarlane, she told Regan.

I was also present two days later, when two grim physicians—Dale Oller, the head of the surgical department at Bethesda, and Steven Rosenberg, chief of surgery at the National Cancer Institute—walked into the sitting room next to the President's bedroom to give Mrs. Reagan the pathology report. It was what we had expected: The tumor was malignant, but its spread had been minimal. "Prospects are for a full recovery and a normal life," Dr. Rosenberg told her.

All four of us went to inform the President. He took the news in stride, looking up and commenting, "I'm glad it's all out," before returning to his reading.

Sometime later, when Lou Cannon asked him about his bout with cancer, the President replied, "I didn't have cancer. I had something inside of me that had cancer in it and it was removed." I feared the press would go after him for his unrealistic—and, of course, incorrect—rendition of his medical history, and I discussed it with Hutton and Rosenberg. "Ignore it," Rosenberg said. "It's simply the President's way of dealing with cancer." I followed the doctor's orders, but often recalled this incident when the Iran arms scandal broke the following year and Reagan kept insisting that he hadn't sent arms to Iran in exchange for the freedom of American hostages in Lebanon. He believed that, just as he believed he hadn't had cancer, but he was wrong each time.

During the President's hospital stay, Mrs. Reagan relied heavily on her brother, a calm, orderly man, who provided reassuring interpretations of the array of medical information she was receiving. The two were very close, and we were to see him at the White House frequently in the coming months, at state dinners, important presidential addresses, and other special occasions.

It hadn't always been that way, however. Several years earlier, when Dr. Loyal Davis, Richard Davis's father and Mrs. Reagan's step-father, died in Phoenix, she and Dick had a family tiff that threatened to rupture their relationship permanently. On the evening before Dr. Davis's memorial service, the two got into a loud argument at the family home. Dick Davis left on the next plane back East, missing his father's service. Although we heard of the spat between the two, we never knew what caused it.

While the President was in the hospital for his cancer surgery we took every precaution to prevent the press from obtaining any more information about his condition than we wanted to disclose. After our experience when Reagan was shot, with reporters obtaining the emergency room records, we were always concerned about leaks. I was even suspicious that the press would pay lower-echelon staff at the hospital for information.

"Even a President has some right to privacy," I had often argued to the press. Mrs. Reagan was particularly upset by the sight of a detailed diagram of the President's intestines on national television, and was appalled when CBS ran an actual medical school videotape of a proctoscopic instrument probing the inside of a colon.

Aside from the need to protect the President's privacy, there was great concern about the effect news of his condition would have on the nation and the world. All in all, the cancer surgery was the most serious personal crisis during the Reagan presidency, except for the assassination attempt. Obviously, there was no chance to make plans in advance of the assassination attempt, but this time I wanted to be certain that everything would go off without a hitch. I wanted to be able to satisfy the demands of the press, which would need accurate updates on the President's condition as frequently as possible. We literally picked up the press office and moved it to Bethesda Medical Center. And, irony of ironies, the hospital officials set up the press office in the hospital's psychiatric unit, which was complete with signs reading "Psychiatric patients only."

I conducted my fourth and final briefing of the day the operation took place at 7:40 P.M. By then I was relaxed and laid back, which was fortunate, because Lyndon Johnson's precedent of displaying his scar to the press after an operation on his gall bladder quickly became a topic of discussion.

"Can we see the scar?" I was asked.

"No," I replied. "He wants to show you the point of entry of yesterday's examination."

The press had no trouble recalling the proctoscopic exam twenty-four hours earlier. They roared with laughter—and, I hope, went home happy.

We carefully controlled the release of pictures, as well as information. The first photograph of the President after surgery was artfully arranged to conceal the nasogastric tube that had been inserted in Reagan's nose and was held in place by tape. The photo showed Mrs. Reagan leaning over to kiss her husband. Her face strategically covered the tube.

The whole episode was one of mutual dissatisfaction between me and the press: Acting on instructions from the Reagans, I was to reveal only what they felt the news media and the public absolutely had to know, while the reporters wanted to know everything. None of the press corps seemed to have much regard for the President's privacy or to appreciate how forthcoming we were compared to previous administrations. Nor was the Reagan press corps confronted with a situation where the President disappears for weeks or months amidst rumors that he is seriously ill or even dead—as has happened several times recently with leaders of the Soviet Union. Nevertheless, no matter how much information we gave out, it never satisfied the press.

President Reagan left Bethesda Medical Center and returned to the White House on July 20, one week after his operation. He was up, dressed, and ready when I arrived with Mrs. Reagan and several other members of the White House staff to escort him home. I had called Mrs. Reagan the night before, suggesting she bring another shirt and pair of pants for the President to wear home. I worried that the inevitable weight loss, although it was under five pounds, might make his collar look loose and take the edge off what we were presenting as his miraculous recovery. "He'll already be dressed when we get there and won't want to change," she said. I knew she was right, but I persuaded her to take some different clothes, and she was able to prevail over his grumbling protest and talk him into changing before we left the hospital.

The President recovered so rapidly that reporters suspected we were doctoring the doctors' reports to make him look healthier than he was.

Not so. We told the whole truth—no varnish, no hype. He was indeed Superman.

During and after the colon cancer surgery we made every effort to show that the President was conducting business as usual from his hospital room, then rushing home in almost record time. As we settled back into the White House routine, we congratulated ourselves on having provided a truthful, detailed account of the President's hospital stay.

And so we put the issue of cancer and the President behind us—for all of ten days. Once again, though, cancer cropped up, and, thanks to Nancy Reagan, my credibility was placed in greater jeopardy than at any other time during my tenure as White House spokesman.

The President had developed a pimple on the right side of his nose, which he thought was caused by irritation from the tape that had attached a tube to his nose after his surgery. Dr. Burton Smith examined him at the White House on July 30 and decided that the scab on his nose looked serious enough to warrant having it removed and biopsied to determine whether it was malignant. Mrs. Reagan immediately panicked, with some justification; just having successfully handled a serious illness, she was afraid that the public would now think her husband was cancer-prone. Of course, his colon cancer and the spot on his nose—if in fact it turned out to be malignant—were completely unrelated. The public understood that. Perhaps if the President had not just undergone major cancer surgery a few weeks earlier, Mrs. Reagan would have taken a more rational approach to the problem on his nose. After all, skin cancer caused by too much exposure to the sun is a common and minor form of cancer, and Mrs. Reagan herself had had a skin cancer removed from her upper lip in December 1982.

When Reagan returned to Bethesda to have the spot on his nose biopsied, I sent Mark Weinberg with him, as usual. Before long, Mark called me and said, "Don't dare breathe a word, but there is a problem. This thing on the nose, they've taken a biopsy from it." He had overheard that from Smith and other doctors who had been called in. So Mark had information that he wasn't supposed to have and information that Mrs. Reagan intended to withhold from us.

I alerted Don Regan, and Mark pressed Dr. Smith, who at first denied that anything had been removed from the President's nose. When Mark insisted that he knew something, Smith finally acknowledged that the tissue was being biopsied, but said that results wouldn't be known for a week or two. But Smith said Mrs. Reagan was insistent that the scab was merely an irritation caused by the nasal tube the President had had after his colon surgery. She had told Smith that no other information was to be disclosed to the press. And everyone knew that you didn't cross Nancy Reagan if you expected to continue working for her husband.

After hearing Mark's report, I went over to Don Regan and told him that we had a problem. Mrs. Reagan had dictated a statement declaring that the President was in excellent health and not mentioning the possibility of skin cancer. She was going to be calling Regan, and he knew what he had to do: He had to get her to admit that they were doing a biopsy and that there was a distinct possibility that the President had skin cancer. The hitch was that Don couldn't let her know that he knew.

In a few minutes she did call him and said the tape they had used to apply the tubes had irritated the President's nose, and a patch of his skin was being tested for infection. Which was at the least very misleading. When she got to the end of her statement, Regan said, "Nancy, have you told me everything?" She said, "What do you mean?" He said, "Is there any other problem with the nose? Are you sure that it isn't cancer?"

For the rest of that afternoon we went back and forth, with Regan talking on the phone several times to Mrs. Reagan, and me back and forth to Regan's office. As the afternoon wore on, Regan would wash his hands of it and tell me to handle it. I would take a go at Mrs. Reagan without getting anywhere; at one point she told me, "Dammit, Larry, the President does not have cancer!" I said to her, "Just tell me what you want me to say. Let me advise you that if you mislead the public, you'll make more problems for yourself than is necessary."

We finally decided to say nothing for the time being. The next day, Wednesday, July 31, the President and Maureen Reagan posed for pictures in the Oval Office, but the President had his head turned so that only the left side of his face was visible to the photographers. At that point, however, the President was not trying to mislead the press; he was merely presenting his "good side," or, more to the point, keeping his bad side, the one with an incision, away from the cameras, as any actor might do. The President himself did not know that a biopsy was being checked for cancer until Friday, August 2, when the First Lady informed him while they were at Camp David.

Mrs. Reagan and Dr. Smith had gone to extraordinary lengths to prevent the press, not to mention the President, from learning the full story. Both Mrs. Reagan and Smith denied to reporters that a biopsy was being performed, and the tissue sample to be biopsied was sent to the lab under a false name. The name on the pathology report was Tracy Malone, who was identified as a white *female*, age sixty-two. Tracy Malone actually was a military nurse assigned to the White House medical unit, and, to put her in the same age bracket as the President, they added nearly forty years to her true age.

It was on Thursday, August 1, that all hell broke loose. That day the President addressed a group of evangelical broadcasters and writers at the White House, and despite Mrs. Reagan's attempts to suppress news of another presidential bout with cancer, members of the regular White House press corps who were present noticed the small scar on his nose.

What followed was a chaotic press briefing. One reporter opened up by asking me, "What's the scab on the President's face?" and I, under orders from Nancy Reagan, responded. "The scab on the President's face is an irritation from the tape that . . . held the . . . nasogastric tube in place." The reporters sensed that something was up, and the questions came fast and furious:

QUESTION: He had a surgical procedure?
MY ANSWER: Yes.
QUESTION: And what was it that was removed?
MY ANSWER: I don't know exactly what it was. It was a skin irritation . . . caused by the tube.
QUESTION: Was it a growth?
MY ANSWER: I don't know. I wouldn't characterize it as a growth. I'd characterize it more as a skin irritation or a gathering of the skin, piling up of the skin or something like that.
QUESTION: You say there will be a biopsy on it?
MY ANSWER: There'll be a routine check of it, yes.
QUESTION: Larry, is the test for cancer? What kind of test is it?
MY ANSWER: I don't know. Just a routine examination, as you would if you had a piece removed from your face.

In the end, after dozens of questions from the press, I finally acknowledged that what was being done was a biopsy, although I described the President's health as "excellent, A-1."

Wrung out from my grilling by the reporters, I went back to my office and wrote a somewhat defiant note to Mrs. Reagan. My reputation was definitely at stake, and if she didn't like my tone, she could demand my resignation. I told her, "The press questions will not go away and will only become worse if we seek to avoid the obvious question. Our credibility is on the line and we should do everything we can to preserve it."

I also attached a proposed statement that I believed was honest and forthright:

"On Tuesday, July 30, a small area of irritated skin on the right side of the President's nose was removed. The irritation was one which had recently become inflamed and was aggravated by the adhesive tape used to secure the nasogastric suction tube the President had in the hospital. It was submitted for routine studies, determined to be an early skin cancer, and no further treatment is necessary. It is not related in any way to the cancer removed from the President's colon. The President is not cancer prone."

Mrs. Reagan was not at all satisfied by my proposed announcement. In her unique handwriting, almost a little girl's print, she wrote back to me:

"Larry—I think the other [my statement] sounds too medical & serious & right now could make people jump to conclusions we don't need. I *know* we don't need right now. Who has never picked at a pimple!!

"Why can't we just say—You asked about the Band-Aid on the Pres. nose. He had had a pimple on his nose which he picked at & irritated it. After surgery adhesive tape was used to secure the tube that went down his nose. This further irritated the area so when the tape was removed the doctors, to avoid infection, treated it. Routine examination was done and nothing further is necessary. It was exactly what they thought—an irritation of the skin."

On August 1, at her direction, we released a fifty-five-word statement that pointedly omitted the magic words "cancer" and "biopsy." It simply said:

"On Tuesday, July 30, a small area of irritated skin on the right side of the President's nose was removed. The irritation had recently been aggravated by the adhesive tape used while the President was in the hospital. It was submitted for routine studies for infection, and it was determined no further treatment is necessary."

But there was something about the statement that should have been a red flag to any alert reporter. Instead of issuing the statement under my name as we usually did, it appeared without attribution to me—a clear signal, although a subtle one, that I was not staking my credibility on these words. For the first time, I refused to put my name on a statement. This announcement was attributed instead to "The White House, Office of the Press Secretary." However, none of the White House press corps noticed my signal.

By Monday, August 5, after the Reagans returned from Camp David, it was obvious that the controversy was not going to die down and that the President was going to have to own up to the truth. Reagan held a press conference in the Oval Office, inviting six reporters in to question him, with the session available for live television coverage. When a reporter asked about his nose, the President replied, "Well, I'm glad that you finally got around to that subject and asked that question. I was worrying [that no one would ask it]." And at last he admitted that he had

had a "basal cell carcinoma" removed from his nose. (The President has since had two more skin cancers removed from his nose without threatening his health, in October 1985 and July 1987.)

The press by and large understood why I had not been able to lay out all the facts for them. But the next day in the briefing room, Sam Donaldson and Helen Thomas raised questions about my credibility, without directly accusing me of lying. For a half hour at my morning press briefing on August 6, I had to let Helen and Sam grill me, while I did my best to defend myself and to give them hints, which they did not seem to understand, that I had been acting at Mrs. Reagan's direction. Sam, who hadn't even been in town the previous Friday and had to catch up on the controversy over the weekend, led the charge.

DONALDSON: You know that your credibility now is severely damaged by this.

SPEAKES: My credibility is not damaged at all, Sam. . . . My credibility is not damaged. You look very closely, and before you raise anything like that in a briefing, or privately, or publicly, you look very carefully . . . at that briefing transcript.

DONALDSON: So you think you've been fully candid with . . . the American people?

SPEAKES: Wait a minute. You look very carefully at that briefing transcript and see if I told anything that was not true. Can you allege that? Do you want to answer that question? Did I tell anything that was not true? Did I?

DONALDSON: Yes, I looked at the briefing transcripts.

SPEAKES: All right, cite it to me.

THOMAS: Okay. On Thursday, when you issued a statement, you said that it was checked for an infection. You would not answer any questions on it.

SPEAKES: That's right. . . . Helen, is that a lie? Do you want to say that's a lie?

THOMAS: I want to say that by omission you left a big hole in the truth.

SPEAKES: I did not tell a lie. There is no lie there.

DONALDSON: Wait a moment. . . . When you were asked whether a biopsy would be performed and you said, "Sure," well, then you were saying one was going to be performed.

THOMAS: And on Friday, you refused to say one was performed.

SPEAKES: That's right. But refusal to say . . . does not constitute a lie, Helen.

THOMAS: But we are questioning your candor.

SPEAKES: No, no.

THOMAS: You were not candid.

SPEAKES: I was. I told the truth. And I told the truth from the first. . . . Do you want to say that I did not tell the truth?

THOMAS: Oh, come on. Get off of that.

SPEAKES: No, you come on.

THOMAS: Larry, you pulled an iron curtain . . . down on the truth last Thursday.

SPEAKES: But I did not lie. And I told the truth.

DONALDSON: Well, what's the difference between pulling down an iron curtain on the truth and being completely credible or not being completely credible?

SPEAKES: I told the truth from top to bottom. And if you'll look at it, you will see. Now, I think you ought to clarify the record as to what you said here. Would you like to do that?

DONALDSON: I'm not withdrawing a thing about questions being raised about your credibility.

SPEAKES: Did I mislead you, Sam? No. Did I lie to you? No. Did I fail to tell the truth? No. . . . Sam, . . . you're totally off base. And you've questioned me about something and you have not backed up what you said. And I think you owe it [to me] to back it up. If you're going to question my credibility, that is the only . . . thing a government spokesman has, is his credibility and his ability to tell the truth.

DONALDSON: You're right.

SPEAKES: I have never, ever lied in this job, and will not lie in this job.

THOMAS: Why did you handle it that way? That's all we're asking.

SPEAKES: I think if you had two grains of salt for sense, you could figure it out.

It was Grenada all over again. There was no lie, but they were right; there was a glaring omission, and I had to take the heat. Both Sam and Helen knew the dilemma I was facing, and they weren't really after me. They were zeroing in on Mrs. Reagan, and I was between them and their target. I often teased, "That's what I get this high government salary for." But this was no joking matter to me.

I spent a restless night and slipped out of bed at 5:00 A.M. to go downstairs to the kitchen table and write out a statement in longhand. At my morning briefing I delivered my last word on the subject, borrowing from Jerry Ford's inaugural statement: "It's time for some straight talk among friends." Then I gave my defense:

"When you look at an individual and remove everything—money, position, power—you only have your reputation to stand on. And I have spent my lifetime building a reputation, and I've spent eighteen years as a press spokesman in Washington building a reputation. That's all I have, is a reputation.

"Government salaries aren't very high. And I have a reputation for telling the truth, for dealing fairly with people and for hard work and a professional approach to my job. This is a long-term investment. It goes back to Capitol Hill, it goes to the P.R. business, and it goes to the White House under three Presidents."

That same day, Sam wrote me a somewhat apologetic letter, which he also posted on the bulletin board in the press room. Written on ABC stationery and addressed "Dear Larry," his letter said in part:

Not once yesterday, or at any other time in this matter, did I call you a liar. I said I believed you had lost some of your credibility as a result of your handling of this skin cancer story. I made it clear I believe there is more to the question of a presidential spokesman's credibility than the narrow issue of whether a direct lie is told. . . .

There are reports that you privately argued against this policy obfuscation and that others ordered you to carry it out, but I think on the question of your credibility, that is beside the point. . . .

I regret this incident. I know that walking that tightrope between Presidents and the press is a very tough job. By and large, I think you have done it well.

But Frank Borman is right. Each of us had to earn our wings every day—or risk losing them.

It was a gutsy thing for Sam to do—and I should have extended the olive branch right then. But my back was up and stubbornness prevailed. Sam later made several other peace overtures through my deputy, Pete Roussel, but I never came off my high horse. A challenge to my credibility was too serious for me to soon forgive and forget.

Last year, in his book, *Hold On, Mr. President*, Sam wrote that he likes me and that he understood my job was a "very tough one." Nevertheless, at least from my side, things were never the same between us after his attack on me on August 6. And I'm sorry his charges against me damaged our relationship, because I have always liked him personally and I still respect him as a first-class reporter.

Perhaps John Madigan, a commentator on WBBM radio in Chicago, had the best perspective on the whole incident:

I never thought I'd see the day when the credibility of a White House news secretary would be put in jeopardy because of a pimple on a President's nose! . . . Speakes obviously was operating under some restrictive guidelines. What could the poor man do! What with Mrs. Reagan conferring with him both before and after he briefed reporters! . . . The problem with the President's nose apparently is that Speakes didn't go far enough in volunteering information or left too much out in his replies. I can't evaluate the nuances involved. I wasn't there. But it's a little gross for ABC's Sam Donaldson to say that Speakes's "credibility is severely damaged." Who does Sam think he is . . . Dan Rather?

When all was said and done, the controversy over the President's nose cancer made my last year and a half on the job a lot easier. The President went out of his way to defend me and praise my handling of a difficult situation. Moreover, he sent me a message via Don Regan that I would never again be asked to withhold information about his health.

And I even made a little more White House history in August 1986, when the President developed a minor infection of the bladder and had an examination under local anesthesia. Pressed by reporters about details of the procedure, I replied, "It's an instrument that's inserted in the penis and goes up the urinary tract and it has a viewing apparatus where the doctor is able to examine the interior of the urinary tract."

Looking over at Pete Roussel, I remarked, "I bet that's the first time this word's ever been mentioned in the briefing room." Public discussion of the President's penis? Yes, it happened in the Reagan White House, on my watch. Take that, all of you who claim I wasn't candid with the press!

13

Giving Ferdinand

Marcos the Bad News

In the early morning hours of February 26, 1986, Filipino officials in Manila entered the Malacanang Palace office of former president Ferdinand E. Marcos, only hours after he had fled into exile. A single light burned over Marcos's desk in the ornate presidential office, revealing neatly arranged stacks of paper and books. In the center of his desk was a copy of a wire-service story containing a statement that I had hastily dictated to the media from my bedroom less than thirty-six hours earlier. Don Regan and John Poindexter, after awakening President Reagan and confirming our course of action with him, had called me at home at 5:00 A.M. on Monday, February 24 (Monday night in the Philippines), and directed me to issue a statement immediately, in hopes that it would make the evening newscasts in Manila and avert bloodshed during the last hours of the Marcos regime. Our statement read:

"President Marcos has pledged to refrain from initiating violence and we appeal to him and those loyal to him and all other Filipino people to continue to do so. Attempts to prolong the present regime by violence are futile. A solution to this crisis can only be achieved through a peaceful transition to a new government."

For President Reagan and the government of the United States, cutting our ties to Marcos was a difficult and painful decision that ended the most turbulent period in U.S.-Filipino relations since World War II.

For me, it had been another critical week of walking a political and diplomatic tightrope during my twice-daily press briefings.

Just as we had done when the lives of forty American hostages were at stake for seventeen days after the hijacking of a TWA plane in Lebanon eight months earlier, we again were compelled to use the White House news podium as the major instrument of foreign policy.

Marcos had held power in the Philippines for twenty years, functioning for most of those two decades as a virtual dictator. He was an important asset for us primarily because he had always been a loyal ally of the United States, much like the Shah of Iran. His country was strategically located in the vast southwest Pacific Ocean, and was the linchpin in U.S. defense planning, providing a launching pad for our naval and air power in the event of a confrontation with the Soviets. The U.S. Navy base at Subic Bay and nearby Clark Air Force Base are the largest American military installations outside the United States and are essential for us to maintain our military presence in the Pacific.

But Marcos was clearly on the ropes. Between a faltering economy and a growing Communist insurgency, his authority had been steadily eroding for several years. His downfall became almost inevitable on August 21, 1983, when his most formidable political opponent, Benigno Aquino, was assassinated as Aquino returned to the Philippines from exile in the United States. Marcos claimed that Aquino had been shot by a Communist hitman as he left his airplane at the airport in Manila, but the evidence strongly suggested that Aquino had been murdered by Marcos's own troops, who had also slain the alleged hitman at the scene.

Aquino's widow, Corazon, quickly transformed herself from housewife to opposition political leader. She took up her husband's cause, and in November 1985 Marcos agreed to hold an election on February 7, 1986, more than a year before his latest six-year term as president was due to expire. President Reagan had sent Senator Paul Laxalt of Nevada, his best friend in Congress, to the Philippines as Reagan's special emissary in October 1985, and Laxalt, after establishing a rapport with Marcos, persuaded him to call the early election. Mrs. Aquino became the leading opposition candidate for president.

As the campaign wore on, Marcos's position grew weaker and weaker. He had played to Filipino nationalism by presenting himself as a World War II hero who had led Filipino guerrillas against the Japanese occupying forces and had been highly decorated by the U.S. military for his efforts. But on January 23, 1986, two weeks before the election, *The New York Times* reported that American military records showed that Marcos's claims were "fraudulent" and "absurd," and that the unit he supposedly led had never existed. As the U.S. media focused its attention on Marcos, his life continued to unravel. The press, sparked by rumors that Marcos and his wife, Imelda, had stolen a fortune from their country, revealed that the Marcoses owned Manhattan real estate worth $350 million. The Roman Catholic Church, a powerful force in the Philippines, became increasingly disenchanted with Marcos. The clergy used the pulpit to help turn public opinion against him. And the U.S. Congress, increasingly worried about growing violence and the heavy-handed martial law imposed by Marcos, threatened to halt the $900 million in foreign aid we had promised the Philippine government over a five-year period, unless Marcos defeated Aquino in a fair election or accepted the result if he was defeated.

President Reagan, also under pressure from Congress and fearful that Marcos might try to steal the election, sent a twenty-member delegation, headed by Senate Foreign Relations Chairman Richard Lugar of Indiana, to observe the balloting. Returning to the U.S. several days later, Lugar's delegation reported to the President that, as we had feared, Marcos was trying to steal the election.

As the election results were counted, both Marcos and Mrs. Aquino claimed victory. The mounting evidence made it clear that Mrs. Aquino was correct. But Marcos refused to back down, and a standoff punctuated by violence followed.

On February 11 President Reagan suggested during a press conference that fraud had occurred on both sides and proposed that Marcos and Aquino "work together to form a viable government." That touched off a firestorm of reaction from political leaders both here and in the Philippines who said that all the fraud had been committed by Marcos and that the President's statement appeared to condone what Marcos had done. Reagan started attempting to salvage the situation the next day by beginning to back away from his statement and sending veteran U.S. diplomat Philip Habib to Manila to assess the election outcome.

Marcos was no stranger to President Reagan. Reagan had visited the Philippines twice on missions for President Nixon and had had a personal relationship with Marcos since his first trip to Manila in 1969. Reagan had also played host to Marcos during the Filipino president's state visit to the United States early in the Reagan administration. Reagan valued Marcos as both a friend and as a U.S. ally, and it was extremely difficult for Reagan to turn his back on Marcos. Reagan's loyalty to Marcos had caused us problems, both with Congress and with Marcos, who continued to hope it would enable him to cling to power. Not until February 22, long after it had become obvious that Marcos's rule was doomed, was I finally allowed to take an official government position declaring that the elections were "marred by fraud perpetuated by the ruling [Marcos] party, so extreme as to undermine the credibility and legitimacy of the election." It was a clear message intended to let Marcos know the end was near.

Meanwhile, Marcos's grip on the Philippines had continued to weaken. On February 19 the U.S. Senate voted 85 to 9 in favor of a resolution calling the Filipino election fraudulent. And on February 22, the day I issued the statement accusing Marcos of claiming a fraudulent victory, two Marcos stalwarts, Defense Minister Juan Ponce Enrile and the armed forces deputy chief of staff, Lieutenant General Fidel V. Ramos, quit their posts, took control of defense headquarters, and called on Marcos to resign.

As these events unfolded in the Philippines, the Filipino crisis was played in the American press like a local story. A few days before the election, Don Regan and I accepted a long-standing invitation to have an off-the-record lunch at the Mayflower Hotel with the top news executives of ABC. Roone Arledge, president of ABC News, asked us to size up Marcos's chances. "There is little or no chance he'll survive," Regan replied. Arledge said he was trying to decide whether to send Peter Jennings to anchor ABC newscasts from Manila, but the ABC brass were worried that the presence of a network anchor could only inflame the situation. "You're covering this thing like the Iowa caucuses," I told Arledge.

Jennings didn't go, but the only campaign debate between Marcos and Aquino took place on ABC's "Nightline" (with the two candidates at separate locations in Manila). And Marcos, in a last attempt to show himself in control, made a surprise appearance on NBC's "Meet the Press" on Sunday, February 23, only hours before he fled, telling the television audience he intended to "hit Enrile and Ramos." That same morning, *The New York Times* carried three stories about the situation in the Philippines on the front page, and seventeen more articles or opinion pieces inside.

President Reagan returned early from Camp David that Sunday afternoon, in time to convene a meeting on the crisis in the Philippines at 3:00 P.M. in the White House Situation Room. The administration's top foreign policy advisers were present as the President, still wearing his western shirt and boots, entered the room. He stopped us short as we pushed back our chairs and rose, our customary ritual whenever the

President entered a room. "Please don't," he commanded. "Let's get right down to business."

Reagan sat at the head of the table, with George Shultz to the President's left; Cap Weinberger to Reagan's right, facing Shultz; and Vice President Bush, CIA director William Casey, Don Regan, and several others seated around it. At the opposite end from the President was John Poindexter, his ever-present pipe clenched between his teeth. No one but Poindexter smoked, although from time to time someone would walk over to a table beside the door, where sodas, coffee, and tea had been placed on a silver tray.

The President nodded around the table and singled out a key player, Ambassador Philip Habib, diplomatic troubleshooter extraordinaire. "Welcome home. I'm anxious to hear what you have to say," Reagan said to an obviously weary Habib, who had returned from a whirlwind trip to Manila only hours earlier.

But intelligence briefings always came first at these meetings, and it fell to Poindexter to lead off. "We have a tough situation facing us, Mr. President. And we'll have to move fast. Intelligence tells us that Marcos is preparing to move against the generals [Enrile and Ramos]." Poindexter outlined a stern message that U.S. Ambassador to the Philippines Stephen Bosworth had been directed to deliver to Marcos a short while earlier. Bosworth had warned Marcos not to use violence in order to stay in power. "You will alienate your people," the message read, "and make it difficult for us to help you." Marcos's reply to Bosworth was, "I will sleep on it."

Director Casey, who had slumped in his chair while Poindexter spoke, straightened up and placed his elbows on the table when Poindexter finished. "Mr. President, it does not look good," Casey declared. "General [Fabian] Ver [Marcos's right-hand man, whom many suspected of carrying out the assassination of Benigno Aquino on orders from Marcos] has called for all the Marcos forces in Manila to join together to crack down on the generals. I say again," Casey added with unusual emphasis, "we have a bad situation on our hands." Casey reported that Marcos had 12,000 loyal troops, backed by armor, prepared to move against the anti-government forces holed up in their military barracks. "The situation is made worse because as many as 500,000 people are expected to gather outside the camps, keeping a vigil"; they could become victims if firing broke out, Casey added.

The President looked next to Habib, who minced no words: "The Marcos era has ended, Mr. President." Reagan appeared stunned, but said, "Go on, Phil."

"The society is polarized," Habib continued. "The economy is in ruins. The military is disorganized, not well trained and definitely divided in its loyalty." Turning to the issue of Marcos himself, Habib reported, "His mind is okay, but he is feeble in his motions. This has clearly taken a physical toll. Marcos cannot run the country the way he used to."

George Shultz echoed Habib with uncharacteristically blunt language. "Can Marcos govern? Not a person believes he can. He's had it." Shultz's words helped drive home the message to Reagan. Clearly, now, his advisers were forming a solid front to let the President know that we must push Marcos out immediately. Shultz himself stressed the urgency: "It is a fast-moving situation and the U.S. must act promptly if it is to have influence. The passage of time reduces our options."

Shultz also referred to previous disasters in our foreign policy, noting that "The United States has not done well in transitions in the past in Vietnam, Iran, and Nicaragua." He then detailed his plan: a hardline public statement to be delivered from the White House, threatening the cutoff of U.S. aid; a private message from Reagan to Marcos, making use of the rapport that Paul Laxalt had established with the Filipino president; and, finally, the promise of U.S. dollars to a post-Marcos government.

Now it was Weinberger's turn. He outlined our military situation, which struck me as pitifully weak. There were 625 U.S. Marines at Subic Bay, where the aircraft carrier *Enterprise* was in port. It was scheduled to leave the next day, and an early departure in the event of serious trouble—or the necessity of using our air power to protect our bases there—was virtually impossible. At Clark Air Force Base, only a small contingent of military police was available. The other carrier in the region, the *Midway*, was sailing in the Gulf of Thailand, and a strike force of 2,000 Marines was hours away in Hong Kong. Meanwhile, on the ground in Manila, the situation was precarious. "The rebels have only 1,500 men in camp. They can't prevail and they could be wiped out," Weinberger concluded.

Weinberger's words were sinking in around the table when the Situation Room duty officer, a CIA intelligence expert detailed to the White House, pushed open the heavy sliding door to the conference room and handed Poindexter a message. "This is urgent," the CIA man told Poindexter.

Poindexter read the message silently to himself, then aloud: "Military forces are moving on the crowd outside the headquarters camp. They are pushing through a chain-link barricade. Attack helicopters, six APCs [armored personnel carriers], and tanks. Moving toward the camp." He added that the crowd of citizens in front of the camp numbered in the thousands. They were led by Catholic nuns, their arms interlocked as they stood in the front ranks.

"That's all we need," the President said. "One of those nuns is killed and we have a Joan of Arc." His fist slammed down on the table, startling the imperturbable Shultz. Clearly, Reagan was frustrated, but, more than that, he was angry.

The President's anger served only to underscore the need for prompt, decisive action. Everyone agreed on what must be done, but we needed a consensus on exactly how to get there.

Don Regan had sat silently throughout the meeting, carefully making notes and biding his time. Now the moment had arrived for him to have his say. "Let me play devil's advocate. If we move without a clear-cut successor to Marcos, there is a distinct possibility—God forbid—that we could end up with a government unfriendly to the United States. Are we certain we are ready for this step?" he asked. Regan recognized that he was no expert in foreign policy, but his role here was clearly defined: to make certain every alternative had been explored. He summed up with some words of caution: "If we push Marcos out and in three or four days there's no one there, we could end up in a far worse situation."

Weinberger answered Regan first—"We have to consider more than just getting Marcos out." Shultz directed him back to his three-point plan and its urgency: "Marcos acts under pressure and does not act under persuasion."

President Reagan, who had remained silent for most of the meeting, finally spoke up: "Marcos is clearly stubborn. We have asked him; now we need to tell him." Reagan continued, "But let me caution you— Marcos is a proud man. He must go with dignity or there will be bloodshed. The whole place will go up in flames."

The President suggested we follow the "Laxalt Route," using the Nevada senator as his emissary. Reagan's choice of Laxalt for the earlier mission to Marcos was to pay dividends now, as we struggled to force Marcos out without violence.

The meeting was interrupted for a second time, at 4:05 P.M., by an intelligence update that underscored the urgency of a decision. "An attack [by the Marcos forces] is expected in twenty-five minutes," Poindexter announced.

Decision time had arrived, and President Reagan told us what it would be: "We will move ahead with the points that Secretary Shultz has outlined. Our message to Marcos has to be that we are asking him to leave for his safety and for the good of the country. We will offer to be of help, but we won't be able to provide assistance to the Filipino people unless

Marcos cooperates." As notebooks closed, the President emphasized his orders—"It must be in exactly those words, or it won't work."

As the meeting concluded, I quickly reviewed my notes. One thing stood out: "VP:————." There was a blank following Vice President Bush's name. He had spoken, I know, but what he had said had not been worth my recording. With his background as CIA director and ambassador to mainland China and to the United Nations, Bush was uniquely qualified to be of help in a situation like this, yet he had offered no insightful opinion, no sage advice. It was disappointing that Bush had come to believe that it wasn't his place to offer his opinion to the President.

This was typical of Reagan's crisis meetings. He was primarily a listener, letting his trusted advisers have their say, and then announcing our course of action. He never dominated these sessions, believing there was no sense in meeting with his advisers unless he listened to what they had to say. Contrary to the impression of him that has been presented by numerous journalists—none of whom *ever* attended one of these meetings—the President was decisive. He listened; he was well-informed on the important points; and once he had received the counsel from his top appointees, he acted.

The President's previous encounters with Marcos allowed him to understand how to deal with Marcos, even through emissaries. One of the things he knew about Marcos was that his dignity had to remain intact, which is why he emphasized that we must let Marcos think he was making up his own mind, instead of forcing something upon him. Reagan said we should offer Marcos a carrot, not a stick: couch our message in terms of "You want to avoid violence and we want to avoid violence, so why don't you come to the United States, where we will provide you with a safe haven and medical care?" and not in terms of, "Do what we tell you and resign at once, or else we will have nothing more to do with you." Based on Reagan's knowledge of how Marcos operated, we handled this situation with kid gloves for many days in order to avert violence by nudging Marcos along to leave peacefully. It was our diplomatic efforts, a lot of them from our own press room, that helped Marcos reach the decision to leave peacefully.

As the meeting broke up, I huddled with Poindexter to hammer out the statement we would issue. We checked the words with President Reagan and George Shultz, both of whom approved. Shortly after five o'clock, as I headed toward the briefing room, the Situation Room duty officer stopped me in the hallway with an ominous message: "The situation in

Manila remains precarious, as pro-Marcos forces continue to prepare for an attack."

Rushing to the briefing room, I delivered a message to the press, but it was really aimed at an audience of one, Ferdinand Marcos. "The American people are watching with concern and compassion the events unfolding in the Philippines." My brief statement cited the need for peaceful resolution of the tense situation, followed by the punchline: "We cannot continue our existing military assistance if the government uses that aid against other elements of the Philippine military." "That means you might cut off aid," a reporter summarized. "Exactly," I replied.

At the same time, top-secret talking points were being prepared for Ambassador Bosworth to deliver to Marcos in an hour or two, when it would be Monday morning in Manila and the Filipino President would awaken for his last full day in office. Bosworth was to make it clear that he was speaking for Reagan and tell Marcos, "It doesn't matter how strongly you feel about having won the election. You do not have the support of the people. We want to help and we are deeply concerned. But we must have a plan from you for a transition to a new government. There must be no violence. You hold the future of your country in your hands."

Those of us who had participated in the crisis meeting on the Philippines left the White House that Sunday night hopeful that our decisions had been wise and that Marcos would heed our advice. But we were far from certain.

It was five o'clock the next morning when the White House line in my bedroom rang, awakening me an hour before my alarm was set to go off. I knew it meant trouble. The White House operator's words, "Sir, Admiral Poindexter and Mr. Regan are on the line," confirmed it. The two of them, still at their homes, had looped me into their telephone conversation. "Matters have come quickly to a head," Poindexter declared. He explained that although Marcos was trying to avoid violence, General Ver had publicly broken with Marcos and was preparing to lead an armored column to storm the compound where the anti-Marcos troops were barricaded.

"We've got to say something immediately," Poindexter said. "Can you do it?" "Yes," I replied, "I can call the wires from here. That's the quickest way they'll read the message in Manila." I jotted down Poindexter's words, and, as I asked the White House switchboard to connect me with reporters from the Associated Press, United Press International, and Reuters, I started to dress for a quick trip to the White House. At five-thirty, speaking from my bedroom, I read the statement that would be found on Marcos's desk after he fled:

"We have received disturbing reports of possible attack by forces loyal to General Ver against elements of Philippine forces that have come to the support of General Ramos and Minister Enrile. We urge those contemplating such action to stop. . . . Attempts to prolong the life of the present regime by violence are futile. A solution to this crisis can only be achieved through a peaceful transition to a new government."

We had cut the umbilical cord.

After my calls to the wire services and networks, I headed for the White House and gave several interviews for the morning television news programs in the United States. I pointedly remarked that Marcos was "an old friend and a longtime ally of the United States," adding, "There has been no request for asylum, and no offer of asylum nor offer of any safe haven on military bases in the Philippines. But we have expressed our willingness to be of assistance to an old friend and ally should he make a decision in any fashion." By midday, it became apparent that the message had had its desired effect—and Ver's troops backed down from the throng.

Time was now running out on the Marcos presidency. Nine hours after I issued the White House's early-morning ultimatum to Marcos, at two o'clock Monday afternoon Washington time (3:00 A.M. Tuesday in Manila), Paul Laxalt and other key members of Congress were attending a briefing by George Shultz on the Philippines in Room S-407 at the Capitol, a secure room where members of Congress often discuss sensitive issues. Laxalt received word that Marcos was calling him. Marcos wanted to know if Shultz, Ambassador Bosworth, and other State Department types whom he did not trust were trying to force him out, or if President Reagan truly wanted him to step down. "Is there a possibility for a coalition government with Mrs. Aquino?" Marcos inquired. Laxalt told Marcos that my statement calling for "a peaceful transition to a new government" represented President Reagan's way of thinking. Laxalt said he would have to find out what Reagan thought about a deal for Marcos to share power with Aquino and call Marcos back.

Laxalt and Shultz ended their meeting on the Hill and sped to the White House, where at 3:52 P.M. they met with the President, Poindexter, and Regan to decide what Laxalt should say to Marcos. That meeting lasted thirteen minutes, and then Laxalt went into Poindexter's office and placed the call to Manila, where it was now 5:00 A.M. Tuesday. When Marcos came on the line, he asked Laxalt what he should do, and Laxalt gave him an unmistakable answer, as diplomatically as possible: "Cut and cut cleanly. The time has come."

Laxalt later said there was such a long pause that he wondered if Marcos was still on the line. Finally, Marcos said slowly, "I am so very, very disappointed." Laxalt described Marcos as "a desperate man, clutching at straws," and as someone "reaching for a life preserver." When he gave Marcos the word that the time had come, Laxalt told those of us who were monitoring the situation, "All the spunk went out of him."

Even though he had apparently decided to leave office, Marcos went ahead and had himself sworn in as president. So did Mrs. Aquino, at a separate ceremony, after which she named Enrile her defense minister and Ramos her chief of staff.

About 9:00 P.M. Monday our time, 10:00 A.M. Tuesday in Manila, we received the first indication that Marcos had decided to resign, when Imelda Marcos called the U.S. Embassy in Manila to ask for details about how we would get them out and where we would take them. She also placed an unusual, unexpected, and not entirely welcome call to Nancy Reagan, who had been kept fully abreast of the situation in Manila. Mrs. Reagan told Imelda Marcos that she and her family were welcome in the United States. We would have preferred for them to go somewhere else, but no other country would accept them, and there was no alternative but to invite them to Hawaii. Nor did we expect Marcos to become a permanent resident of the U.S., but it turned out he never could go elsewhere.

It wasn't until the next morning, Tuesday, February 25, at 6:15 A.M. Washington time, that the Marcoses finally agreed to accept our offer. Right up until the last minute they were seeking to at least be allowed to remain in the Philippines, perhaps in Marcos's home province. Marcos himself was in a state of tremendous agitation. Events were just closing in on him so fast that he was overwhelmed. By 7:00 A.M. Washington time, when four U.S. Air Force helicopters landed at Marcos's palace to pick up Marcos and his entourage of nearly one hundred and carry them to Clark Air Base, he was almost a passive observer at his own ouster.

Leaving with Marcos were his family, servants, guards, friends, and even General Ver and his family. From Clark they flew to Guam and on to Hawaii. By 9:45 A.M. in Washington George Shultz, after talking to President Reagan, was able to walk into the White House briefing room and announce that the U.S. had formally granted recognition to the Aquino government. He also praised Marcos for his "reason and compassion." As Philip Habib had concluded at the critical meeting with President Reagan and the other key advisers less than forty-eight hours earlier, the Marcos era had ended.

*   *   *

Marcos's departure made us two for two in the month of February 1986 in the department of bringing pressure to bear that helped ease out foreign dictators. On February 7, Haiti's "President for Life," Jean-Claude Duvalier, influenced in part by pressure from the Reagan administration, exerted via our embassy in Port-au-Prince, fled into exile in France aboard a U.S. Air Force plane. Although our presence and our influence in Haiti did not compare to our clout in the Philippines, our offer of safe transportation had helped Duvalier reach the decision to step down.

Duvalier's downfall was not without embarrassment for me. Early on the morning of January 31, as the President flew to Houston for a memorial service for the seven astronauts who had died in the *Challenger* explosion three days earlier, I informed reporters on Air Force One that Duvalier had quit and hurriedly left Haiti. My report was correct, although, unfortunately, it was premature by seven days. It was based on bum information from the State Department, and we soon had to retract the Duvalier story.

What happened was that at 7:23 A.M. that day the State Department notified the NSC people in the White House that Duvalier had been toppled. John Poindexter passed the word on to Don Regan, and at 8:00 A.M., before we left the White House, Regan briefed several senior staffers, including me. The President himself was given the news at eight-forty, just before he left the White House for Andrews Air Force Base and the flight to Houston. I went to the rear of Air Force One at nine-ten, a few minutes after we took off, and told the five pool reporters that "the White House was informed shortly before 7:30 A.M. that the government of Haiti had collapsed and the leadership, including Duvalier, had fled the country." AP and UPI immediately filed the story from Air Force One, setting off wild celebrations in the Haitian exile communities in New York and Miami. Two hours later, however, UPI called Helen Thomas, who was on the plane with us, and asked if we were certain about Duvalier's fall. She asked me, and I told the pool reporters the latest word was that the situation "is not as clear as we first thought it was." A little while later I told Helen and the other pool reporters that the news of Duvalier's fall apparently was untrue.

When Duvalier actually did surrender power and go into exile, coupled with Marcos doing the same thing two and a half weeks later, it was a double-barreled triumph for the Reagan administration, which was sorely needed in the aftermath of the *Challenger* accident.

For once our good work did not go unnoticed in the press. As William

Raspberry of the *Washington Post* observed, this made "two in a row for President Reagan, indeed two in a short month." Marcos, wrote Raspberry, had joined Duvalier in the "slowly growing ranks of out-of-work dictators." It was nice to receive such praise, especially from someone like Raspberry, who was often critical of Reagan. Almost without exception, the news media spoke approvingly of the administration's role in the ouster of Duvalier and Marcos.

The end of the Ferdinand Marcos regime in the Philippines was, in my opinion, the most severe test of the Reagan administration's foreign policy prior to the Iranian arms crisis in late 1986. Most of the other emergencies we had to deal with—the Korean Air Lines incident, the bombing of the marine barracks in Lebanon, the TWA hijacking, the capture of the *Achille Lauro*, and the arrest of *U.S. News and World Report* correspondent Nicholas Daniloff by the Soviets—created situations that had to be resolved after the fact. In those instances we could only react, not act.

With Marcos, however, we had the opportunity to decide carefully what we wanted to do and to plan how to do it. Our goals were fourfold:

- We wanted the Philippine government to be the one that had the most legitimate popular appeal among the Filipino people.
- We wanted to be on good terms with whichever regime was in power, with assurances that we could maintain our two military bases there.
- Assuming Marcos had to leave, we did not want to desert him and make him into a Flying Dutchman, a man without a country, as the Carter administration had done with the Shah of Iran.
- And we wanted to avoid creating another Iran, where one of our staunchest allies became one of our most bitter enemies.

In fairness to the Carter administration, I should say that we had the benefit of their handling of the Shah to learn from, and there was a viable alternative for power in the Philippines: Corazon Aquino. It is possible that the United States could have propped up a military regime to succeed the Shah in Iran, but as a practical matter, there were only two real choices for power, the Shah and the Ayatollah Khomeini. We put all of our chips on the Shah, and we lost.

In the Philippine situation, you might equate Marcos with the Shah of Iran, while the Communist rebels, the Filipino New People's Army, took the role of Khomeini as the worst of all worlds from the U.S. standpoint. Fortunately for us, it did not come down to a choice between Marcos and the Communists, whom we never could have thrown our support to. Mrs. Aquino may not have been exactly to our liking, but she had popular support without being a monster like the Ayatollah. Moreover, once President Reagan got to know her during her visit to the United States in September 1986, he developed a genuine respect and affection for her.

And so I look back on the ouster of Marcos as our finest hour in foreign policy. Not only did we accomplish all of our goals, with the press office playing an instrumental role, but we dealt the Soviet bloc a major foreign policy defeat. The Soviet Union was the first nation—and one of the few—to offer congratulations to Marcos after his election "victory." And after Marcos fled, a telegram from the president of Czechoslovakia was found on his desk. It read, "Excellency, please accept my sincere congratulations on the occasion of your election to the post of President of the Republic of the Philippines." Neither the United States nor any of our allies were so foolish as to accept Marcos's vote count.

The Marcos episode also showed exactly how the most important decisions were taken within the Reagan White House. Everyone had their say; George Shultz gave the best advice—and this time it was accepted; Don Regan raised the bottom-line questions to make sure we were on the right track; and Ronald Reagan made the correct choice.

It was the Reagan White House—at its best.

14
Beat the Press

For my six years as White House spokesman, it was Us Against Them. Us was a handful of relatively underpaid but dedicated public servants in the White House press office. Them was the entire White House press corps, dozens strong, many of them Rich and Famous and Powerful. My job was like that of anyone in the public relations business, to tell the press only what my client, in this case the President of the United States, and his top aides wanted me to, while the job of the press was to try to find out everything, and I do mean everything, including the most intimate details about President Reagan's health. We had our innings and they had theirs.

To give credit to the reporters who covered the White House, they were a talented group who ferreted out stories so efficiently that almost everything leaked out before we were ready for it to, and we had very few scoops that hadn't already broken in the press. The press, however, did miss out on the biggest story of the Reagan administration, the diversion to the Nicaraguan Contras of money from our sales of weapons to Iran, which didn't become public until Attorney General Edwin Meese announced it to a shocked group of reporters in the White House briefing room on November 25, 1986. Of course, that story also caught most of us within the Reagan administration by surprise. Among the other major stories that had not become public in advance of our announcing them were the appointment in 1981 of Sandra Day O'Connor as Associate Justice of the Supreme Court; the 1982 resignation of Alexander Haig as secretary of state; the Don Regan–Jim Baker job swap in 1985, which saw Regan move from secretary of the treasury to White House chief of staff and Baker go the opposite way; and the resignation of Chief Justice Warren Burger in June 1986, with William Rehnquist replacing him and Antonin Scalia taking Rehnquist's seat on the Supreme Court.

President Reagan sometimes became frustrated because most of his major announcements had already been reported in the newspapers that morning or on television the evening before. He would often say, "It's a total mystery to me how I can say something here in the Oval Office, and before I turn around it's out in the press." Occasionally, he would facetiously address the chandelier as if there were a microphone there. He would look up and say, "Get that, *Washington Post*, and be sure you get it right!"

One round that went to us was on September 24, 1986, when the President traveled to Omaha for a campaign rally. It was during the height of the Daniloff crisis, when *U.S. News & World Report* correspondent Nicholas Daniloff was under arrest on espionage charges in Moscow. President Reagan wanted to avoid having to discuss the Daniloff arrest, and he boarded Air Force One so fast for the flights to Omaha and back that the press people could only report how they were unable to get answers to the questions they always shouted at him. I told the assembled multitudes from the media that we had invented a new game. It was called "Beat the Press," and definitely not "Meet the Press."

Once, in frustration, I gave a memorable retort to the press that became known as "Speake's Law." ABC Television's art department even had it made into a sign that I put on my desk: "You don't tell us how to stage the news and we don't tell you how to cover it." They did tell us how to run our operation, as they had every right to, of course, but now I get to turn the tables and give a report card on the reporters and the institutions who regularly covered Ronald Reagan from 1981 until I resigned in 1987. Many of the reporters, to be sure, *were* institutions in their own right. But don't take my word for it; just ask some of them.

First among institutions, at least in his own mind, is George Will. There's no question that Will, a columnist for the *Washington Post* and *Newsweek* and a regular on the David Brinkley show Sundays on ABC, is a heavyweight. Some people take success in stride; others, who affect bowties, don't. Will is the most pompous and arrogant among a whole legion of egotists, prima donnas, and problem children who report on the White House. I sometimes tried to goad Sam Donaldson into puncturing Will's ego when the two of them appeared together on the Brinkley show.

I have always felt that George is a pseudo-conservative, that while some of his philosophy is conservative and he achieved his fame by being a rare species—that is, a conservative with some intelligence—a lot of the conservatism he espouses is a false conservatism. I contrast Will to Hugh Sidey of *Time* magazine and Emmett Tyrell of the *American Spectator*, both of whom obviously are conservative, but who make no bones about their conservatism and their endorsement of Reagan and his policies. I just have no respect for someone like Will who tries to play the game both ways.

I think Will felt the need to overcompensate from time to time for his closeness to the Reagans, and his criticism of the President for his handling of Daniloff's arrest was one of those times. It always galled me that Will would have these tête-à-têtes with Nancy Reagan over lunch and then turn around and bite the hand that literally fed him. It was sometimes the same with Lou Cannon of the *Washington Post*, who had covered Reagan since he was governor and had become friendly with the Reagans, Ed Meese, Mike Deaver, Bill Clark, and other members of the inner circle: You were too close to the emperor, so you periodically reestablished your credentials as an unbiased observer by saying that the emperor had no clothes on.

Reagan never did understand that, but he was somewhat detached from the press and how it worked. Even with pet reporters, Reagan seldom picked up the phone and called to stroke them or plant a story, the way Kennedy and Johnson had. Reagan occasionally would call Hugh Sidey or James J. Kilpatrick, but usually he just wanted to congratulate them for sticking it to Carl Rowan or Martin Agronsky on the "Agronsky and Company" television show. The President and Mrs. Reagan's favorites among the press corps, in addition to Will, Sidey, Kilpatrick, and Tyrell, were Bill Plante of CBS; Gary Schuster of the *Detroit News* and later of CBS; and, for a time, Chris Wallace of NBC, because Nancy liked his father, Mike Wallace of CBS. But she eventually closed the door on Chris—in spite of all the access she gave him, his reporting was consistently the nastiest among the three networks.

Will's preparing the President for the debate with Jimmy Carter in 1980 and then doing commentary on it on ABC didn't seem to bother his conscience. Of course, scoops come from who you know, but I think if you're prepping a candidate for a debate, it's a conflict of interest to go on TV and say that candidate won the debate. Will's role in the 1980 election was clearly off-base for a journalist, and it's a wonder his fellow members of the press corps didn't come down on him harder.

But I believe I know how Will justified that conflict of interest, at least to himself. One of the very strange things about Will is that he apparently doesn't consider himself a journalist. Will was once invited to a Christmas party hosted by Vice President and Mrs. Bush. His secretary phoned to inquire, "Will press be present?" The answer was yes; after all, the party was *for* the press. Will's secretary then said, "Mr. Will does not attend social events where press are invited." As we used to say in Mississippi, "Six months ago I couldn't even spell 'reporter,' and now I are one."

Underlying our whole theory of disseminating information in the White House was our knowledge that the American people get their news and form their judgments based largely on what they see on television. We knew that television had to have pictures to present its story. We learned very quickly that when we were presenting a story or trying to get our viewpoint across, we had to think like a television producer. And that is a minute and thirty seconds of pictures to tell the story, and a good solid soundbite with some news. So when Reagan was pushing education, the visual was of him sitting at a little desk and talking to a group of students, or with the football team and some cheerleaders, or in a science lab. Then we would have an educators' forum where the President would make a newsworthy statement. We knew very quickly that the rule was no pictures, no television piece, no matter how important our news was. If we saw nothing on the President's schedule that would make the evening news that night, we would say, "No coverage." And if the press didn't like it, the press didn't like it. There was no need to have cameras in there and reporters trying to ask questions that would embarrass the President unless we could get our story on T.V.

Before we entered the White House we had decided that the sole focus of the first year was to be the President's economic program. Part of it was the strike-while-the-iron-is-hot theory: Everybody is interested in whatever the President does during his first year in office. And we were changing the parameters of the debate. Under Reagan, the operative question would be, not how much are we going to spend, but how little are we going to spend? Almost no news item, no speech, no trip, no photo-op whatsoever was put on the President's schedule during 1981 unless it contributed to the President's economic program. The day Reagan was sworn in, he went to a private office in the Capitol and signed an order directing a reduction in force throughout the federal government, which was carried on live television. Ordering a cutback in the number of federal employees on the first day was a dramatic, although probably hollow action, but it looked good.

Throughout the Reagan years, we not only played to television, we based all of our television judgments strictly on audience size. If ABC's "Good Morning, America" was the leading morning show, which it was during most of Reagan's term, they got our number-one person on a given subject, like George Shultz on foreign policy. On the evening shows, when Dan Rather was the leader, we'd put our number-one guy on there. So we played entirely to the ratings, and made no bones about it. Sunday shows were the same way. If you wanted to make an impact, you would go with ABC's David Brinkley show on Sundays. No doubt mistakenly, we kept "The MacNeil-Lehrer NewsHour" on PBS about third or fourth in our priorities, because the viewership wasn't that much. I say mistakenly, because more movers and shakers watched "MacNeil-Lehrer" than any other news show. We hardly ever made the President available for that show, and the same with the Shultzes and the Caspar Weinbergers. "MacNeil-Lehrer" generally got the second tier, the assistant secretaries, and that was not wise on our part.

Foremost among White House television reporters—foremost among all reporters, for that matter, with a reputation for being obnoxious—is ABC's Sam Donaldson. Sam's notoriety is well-deserved; put him within a mile or so of *any* President and he will shout a question. Sam's just boisterous. I always referred to him as, "Shoot from the Lip."

Donaldson's rules of engagement were, "Shout first, worry about it later." But I found Sam to be the brightest television reporter to cover the White House. He covered it by instinct. He didn't work terribly hard, didn't make a lot of phone calls. He felt at the end of the Carter administration that he'd served his time in the White House, and he wanted to get out, but he had no place to go. In the T.V. news business, the funnel is upside down; it's exceedingly narrow at the top.

Two or three times a week I'd get a five or six o'clock call from him, which I would always handle, whether we were in good humor with each other or not. He would say, "Here's the way I see it. President Reagan's going to do such and such." And I'd say, "You've got it." Or I'd say, "Don't go quite that hard on it." He'd say, "Fine, thank you." It was a thirty-second conversation. At six-twenty-eight, two minutes before air time, he'd go out on the White House lawn, tape what he had to say, and it would be the lead story on the broadcast. Sam's the only reporter who is not edited by his network. Generally the reporters have to present a story idea, then a story script, then it's checked by a Washington producer, then by the bureau chief or the assistant bureau chief, and then it has to be fed to New York, where someone may want to change it. But Sam is his own editor.

One tactic I warned the President to look out for during press conferences was that Sam was very prone to shoot misquotes or misstatements at you to try to get you to comment. Donaldson is very smart, and I'm sure it was a deliberate effort on his part to distort things in order to provoke an answer.

Sam was always in hot water, although it was hard to hold his antics against him. He was like the bad boy who's always disrupting class. One of his first escapades on my watch occurred when British Prime Minister Margaret Thatcher visited the White House a month after Reagan took office. The President and Mrs. Reagan were waiting just inside the front door while Mrs. Thatcher's limousine ceremoniously pulled up for a South Lawn arrival. There was a press stand three tiers high, crammed with cameras and microphones and reporters, and Sam was at the very top of it. The color guards and the bands were arrayed on the lawn, all set to do their thing. As Mrs. Thatcher's motorcade came around the curved drive, there was dead silence—until Sam shouted at the top of his lungs, "Bring her on!" I got so angry that I left the ceremony, went inside, and called Bill Knowles, the ABC bureau chief, and I said, "Bill, this is awful. He disrupted the ceremony. It was an absolute disgrace, a reflection on ABC." But Bill replied, somewhat sadly, "Sometimes, Sam is bigger than all of ABC."

Sam surely left an indelible impression on Mrs. Thatcher. At the economic summit in Versailles in 1982 the press was allowed into the dining room and he shouted a question at her. She raised her eyebrows and said, "I do not do questions at luncheon." Sam, for once, was at a loss for words. I only wished Reagan could handle people like that.

Sam's aggressiveness nearly got him fired on November 15, 1981, after Deaver agreed to let the President attend the dedication of the new ABC studio near the Mayflower Hotel. Roone Arledge, president of ABC News; Leonard Goldenson, ABC's board chairman; and all the top brass came down from New York for the occasion. Standing behind the anchor desk in the studio, the President made a few remarks, and that was supposed to be the end of it. But Sam was crouched right in front of the President with a microphone. He sprang up and asked the President a question about David Stockman, whose unfortunate remarks on the Reagan economic program had just appeared in *The Atlantic*. Sam was entirely out of line. He later admitted that Arledge and the other top managers were so mad that he thought they might fire him. They might have, had President Reagan not laughed it off, saying, "That's all right, that's just the way Sam is." On the elevator Deaver said very coldly to Arledge, "You blindsided us on this." And the ABC people apologized. Sam was chastised, but he lived to play another day.

Sam's final gaffe on my watch occurred as the Iranian story was breaking in November 1986. On the November twenty-third David Brinkley show, Sam referred to Mrs. Reagan on the air as a "smiling mamba," or snake, which made both her and the President angry, and, prudently, he wrote a letter of apology to her.

In spite of Sam's shenanigans, our analysis consistently showed that Sam and ABC were the fairest and straightest of the networks. We always felt that CBS had a little extra zinger against the President. You could never really quarrel with it, but the knife was just a little bit sharper on Dan Rather's lead-ins.

To give Dan credit, though, he was always receptive to my phone calls about their coverage. I would see the networks' six-thirty feed of their evening news shows, and many times I saw something awry and called Dan's producer and said, "This just won't do. You've got it wrong," or "This is unfair." Often Dan himself would call me back during the six-fifty-eight-to-seven-o'clock period—it happened once during the Iran-Poindexter story in late 1986—and he said, "When you call, I'll listen. I'll change it because of what Larry Speakes says. But this Poindexter, I don't trust him." Like me, Dan had not had any faith in Poindexter since 1983, when Bill Plante of CBS asked me if we were invading Grenada and Poindexter told me we weren't, which was a lie.

During the coverage of the Iran arms deals in late 1986, Dan made a mistake in reading his script and he said "President Nixon" instead of "President Reagan." I was sort of amused by it. But the next afternoon Don Regan called me and asked, "What have you done about that?" I told him I hadn't done anything, but Don insisted: "There are a couple of people up at Camp David tonight who are quite interested in what Dan is going to say." There was no mistaking who he meant. I called Dan, and he was apologetic: "You know it was a bad mistake and I did screw up. Sometimes those things happen. But I honestly think it's better that we don't correct it because it just calls attention to it." I said, "I understand." I called Regan back and explained Dan's response to him, but Regan demanded that I call Rather again. "The Reagans are expecting it,"

Regan said. So I got Dan again, and I said, "Dan, you're playing to an audience of two." His reply: "Good advice leads to good decisions." And he came on and apologized for it.

Bill Plante and Lesley Stahl initially took turns for CBS. Lesley was the most tenacious, hard-working reporter on the White House beat, and she is tireless on the telephone. But I always thought she got where she was because she was blond and attractive and female. Lesley's looks worked against her in a way, at least early on in the Reagan administration: The President always used to get her confused with Judy Woodruff of NBC.

Lesley had a habit of writing down virtually every word I said, even on the most routine things. She would ask me, "Will there be a photo opportunity today?" I would say, "No photo opportunity today," and she would copy down, "No photo opportunity today." Everything had to be written down. One of her CBS colleagues once told me, "You'd be surprised how many times I've heard your briefing played back to me verbatim by Lesley, and then I'd have to tell her if there was any news." Very often the only question Lesley could ask on a given subject was "Why?" And many times there are no whys. Lesley's insistent "Why?" would drive me up the wall—and, regrettably, I let it show a time or two.

One of the classic examples of how she did her job occurred in December 1981, when Polish ambassador to the U.S. Romuald Spasowski and his wife defected to this country, in a dramatic protest against their government's crackdown on the Solidarity union. Spasowski and his wife were giving up their whole lives—their family, their friends, and all their belongings. The ambassador, a tall, lean, and somber man, and his wife, Wanda, a tiny woman, came to the Oval Office for a meeting with the President. During the meeting, Mrs. Spasowski sat next to her husband on a couch, just shaking with sobs. Before I ushered the press into the Oval Office I reminded the reporters that this was a very emotional time for the ambassador and his wife and I asked them to conduct themselves properly. They filed in, and the President and the ambassador were talking quietly, with Mrs. Spasowski sitting there crying. Lesley immediately leaned over the couch, saying loudly, "Mr. President," and Reagan and the ambassador continued talking. "Mr. President," and the two of them kept on talking. I finally whispered, "Lesley, they're talking." And she said, "Oh, I didn't notice." She was so anxious to get a question in that she simply ignored the sensitivity of the situation.

I became exasperated with her and I zinged her a few times in the briefings, which led her to conclude that I was anti-female. That just wasn't true. My idea was if they do their job, man or woman, then they should be treated professionally. But in her case I do think she too often took a simplistic approach to the news. Many television reporters, including her, approach their stories with an attitude of "This will get me on the air." Quite frankly, they weren't worried if they later learned it was off base. "If it's wrong, nobody will remember by tomorrow night," one T.V. star told me. Television never bothers to correct. But print reporters were much more careful, because their mistakes were part of the permanent record. I've heard that when Abe Rosenthal was editor of *The New York Times*, he used to make his reporters write their own corrections, to impress on them that they had to get it right the first time.

I will say that my personal respect for Lesley grew tremendously when she showed genuine concern for Reagan at the time of his cancer surgery in 1985. She stood out from the rest of the press corps because her concern was personal, not just professional; she was interested in the man as well as the news. After that she and I became friendly, and when CBS asked her if she wanted to leave the White House beat and become a national correspondent, she came to me and asked if I thought it was a good decision. And I told her it was, because where do old White House correspondents go? They don't go anywhere unless they become network anchors. She has done a good job running "Face the Nation," and I appeared there for an enjoyable Sunday interview the Sunday after I left the White House.

Bill Plante was a good reporter, who had excellent contacts. Both of the Reagans liked him, and he and Mike Deaver were very close. Most every Thursday afternoon they would have a wine-tasting in Deaver's office. They were both known as great wine connoisseurs, and would sample some of California's best, as a taste-test for wines that would later be served at State dinners. Of course, no one, including Plante, had an inkling then that Deaver had problems with alcohol. Plante was the kind of guy who was in the know but was fair with his reporting. He eventually had to become a Sam Donaldson, because only aggressive reporters succeed in television. Plante was getting criticism from his office, and contract time was coming up. He was always in competition with Lesley. There was always the threat that CBS would drop the dual approach and have Lesley as the sole reporter. So he became a shouter. But by and large he was a good and fair reporter.

NBC fell in the middle, neither as objective as ABC nor as hard-nosed as CBS. But NBC's lead White House correspondent, Chris Wallace, combined the worst qualities of Sam Donaldson and Lesley Stahl: He was both obnoxious and a bit slow on the uptake.

Wallace's version of the Sam Donaldson act almost cost him his press credentials during the 1984 summit in London. The British threatened to lift his credentials for the summit when he shouted a question at President Reagan and Margaret Thatcher as the two of them walked together outside St. James's Palace. Mrs. Thatcher bristled noticeably and when they got inside she told her press secretary, Bernard Ingham, that she wouldn't tolerate being asked a question like that. Ingham called me and said it was very serious and they wanted to take Wallace's credentials, which meant he wouldn't be able to cover the summit.

I thought that would be the greatest thing that could happen because it might teach him and the other reporters that although they behaved that way in the United States, the host country's protocol is different. But I felt I had to make some half-hearted gesture on his behalf, just to defend the rights of our press, and the British never acted on their threat. However, I spoke to Ray Cullen, who was NBC's senior producer at the summit, and he and I agreed that we would both be laughing up our sleeve if Wallace's credentials got jerked.

I never forgave Wallace for accusing me of lying in February 1983 over how much I knew about a White House investigation of a scandal at the Environmental Protection Agency. Our briefing exchange was testy:

WALLACE: You were unaware of any investigation, but you were aware that everybody was being asked to turn over information on contacts?
SPEAKES: Sure.
WALLACE: I don't consider that a candid answer.
SPEAKES: Well, screw you then.
REPORTER: Was that on the record, Larry?
SPEAKES: Now wait a minute. That's the most serious charge that you could level at me. It was not a lie. As far as I'm concerned, you are out of business.

That phrase became famous in succeeding years. It meant I would not return a reporter's calls and would try to keep other people in my office from talking to them. Chris was the first of an honored few whom I put out of business, but he was the only one I put a life sentence on. He toughed it out for a few weeks and then sought a meeting, which I refused. Finally I agreed to see him. He came in, but he never could bring himself to admit that he was wrong to accuse me of lying. The best he could do was, "I'm sorry it happened." Which to me was not sufficient. So I told him, "Okay, Chris, we'll try to work together," which *was* a lie of the little white variety; I had no intention of cooperating with him in the future. I usually answered his questions in a briefing as politely as I thought necessary, but I told my secretary, Connie Gerrard, to put the "three-time rule" into effect for Chris. That meant that he'd have to telephone three times for every call I'd take.

Sometime later, Chris and I had another squabble. "Chris no longer has a life sentence," I told Pete Roussel. "He now has a death sentence." "What does that mean?" Pete asked. "That means I won't talk to him until after he's dead."

Chris was a fairly good reporter, but he was a lot like Lesley Stahl. He would literally take down almost every word I said in a briefing. Sometimes I'd nod over to my staff to look down at Chris, who was taking notes on something that anybody ought to be able to remember.

The NBC team of Chris Wallace and Andrea Mitchell, another shouter, was enough to drive a man to distraction. In fact, they drove out two of their own network people. Ray Cullen, a longtime producer who had covered Reagan since the 1980 campaign, left and said he just couldn't handle any more of those two. He went to Houston for NBC. And Emery King, who was number three on the White House beat for NBC, left to become an anchor in Detroit. Emery used to refer to Chris as "Junior"—making the point that Chris was the son of a more famous father—and do a great imitation of Chris.

Of all the network correspondents, Barbara Walters was the best personality interviewer, as opposed to hard news interviewer. Of course, she wasn't around the White House that much, but when she was I always treated her with a healthy respect, not only because of her skill, but because I felt she was something of a shark. She would pretend to be friendly, and then save up some real zingers to end an interview with. My respect for her was so great that I readily accepted an offer of a farewell interview with her on ABC's "20/20" when I left the White House, and made it an exclusive.

In dealing with the daily newspapers, our starting point was always the *Washington Post*. It had a slight edge in importance over *The New York Times*, simply because it hit the doorstep first, and all of Washington spun off the *Post*—including Congress, the Supreme Court, and everybody in the administration.

The *Post*'s White House team consisted of the veteran Lou Cannon and a young reporter, David Hoffman. Cannon had covered Reagan when he was governor, had gotten close to him, had written a book about him, and is working on another. But he seemed to overcompensate for his closeness; often he'd zing Reagan for no apparent cause, especially after Cannon's main sources, Bill Clark and Ed Meese, left the White House and Cannon was no longer such an insider. After a spate of negative stories by Lou, the President finally got fed up: "I wish nobody in the White House would even say 'Good morning' to Lou Cannon." Also, we always thought that *Post* editors went out of their way to select photographs that were as unflattering as possible to President Reagan.

David Hoffman, who has shared the White House beat with Cannon for the last few years, is probably the best reporter to cover the White House during the entire Reagan term. Not just from the *Post* or from the print media, but the best reporter, period. He developed sources, wrote solid stories, and checked all his points. I respect him even though he and I got off to a bad start when he was with Knight-Ridder before he joined the *Post*. There's something about Knight-Ridder reporters that makes them hot dogs, "show-off" questioners, performing for their colleagues. Owen Ullman was the same way. And Saul Friedman, too. One thing I liked about Hoffman by the time he was with the *Post* was that he would call about four or five in the afternoon and say, "We're looking at going with this. Does that make sense to you?" Or he would call at six-thirty and say, "We've got this. I just want you to know you're going to get hit with it when the paper hits the street at ten, so you can get a head start on it."

Overall, Cannon and Hoffman were extremely fair, even though just before I left, the two of them really got the hatchet out for Don Regan. Between Hoffman's skill and Cannon's incomparable contacts from having covered Reagan for so long, the two of them were undoubtedly the most effective team that covered the White House during my six years with Reagan.

The New York Times also had a tremendous amount of influence, because the lead story in the morning would very likely be the lead story that night on the television news. Reporters in Washington would get ideas from the *Post*, but producers in New York would get their story ideas from the *Times*. The *Times* and the *Post* were of course quite different in their approaches. We in the press office felt that the *Post* engaged in boutique journalism, or personality journalism, while the *Times* dealt in much deeper issues—although they did adapt some of the *Post*'s approach by instituting their gossipy Washington page.

Steven Weisman, who covered the White House for the *Times* in the early days of the Reagan administration, was something of a whiner, complaining incessantly about press logistics. Gerald Boyd and Bernie Weinraub, who succeeded Weisman, turned out to be very solid reporters. It was interesting to watch Boyd and Weinraub in action. They generally didn't react to everything the *Post* did. Many times they would look at a *Post* story and say, "My editors were upset by this, but I can look at it and see there's nothing in it." And very often there wasn't. But the *Post* seemed to feel it always had to react to *Times* stories, which were often important scoops based on very serious leaks.

I was always wary in my dealings with William Safire, the *Times* columnist. He would call looking for a quote, and he is such a master of language that he could use it to devastating effect in his column. I also had a running battle with Bill Kovach, the *Times* Washington bureau chief, but we are both southerners and it was always friendly banter. Every once in a while the *Times* would get holier than thou and refuse to participate in official government-sanctioned background briefings with an assistant secretary of state or someone. On one occasion their reporters walked out, saying, "Why does this have to be on background?" "Because it does, that's the way we do business," was my answer. "Well, we won't participate." "Fine, there's the door, go." I went upstairs after that briefing, picked up that day's *Times*, and circled in red ink the number of unattributed source stories they had—"Administration officials," "high White House sources," and so forth. It came out to about twenty-five. I wrote a letter to Kovach and sent it by messenger, and said, "When you guys stop picking up information from mid-level bureaucrats on street corners, then you can walk out of officially sanctioned government background briefings." I never had any more trouble with the *Times* failing to attend backgrounders after that.

I was accused from time to time, particularly toward the end, of catering to the big newspapers. I would never have admitted it publicly, but obviously we did, because the *Post* and the *Times* had the most influence with opinion makers. The ones that were left out, particularly Gannett, Knight-Ridder, Newhouse, and the *Baltimore Sun*, were mad at the biggies who got the scoops, but they were even madder at us for perpetuating the system.

But the *Times* and the *Post* didn't get the lion's share of the scoops only because they were so big and powerful. They also had the best reporters, and would have done very well whether we played favorites or not. There was hardly an afternoon when at least one reporter from both the *Times* and the *Post* didn't call and say, "We've got this story. Would you like to comment on it? Does it make sense to you? Is it on target?"

I had to keep reminding myself and my staff that newspaper groups like Gannett and Knight-Ridder were important because of their circulation. Many times I would tell people in the White House that one Gannett interview, one Knight-Ridder interview, was worth ten *New York Times* interviews in terms of circulation all over the country. And indeed if we were trying to reach small-town America, that was the place to go.

After the *Post* and the *Times*, you really looked toward the wires. But they had almost no influence in Washington, and they were reduced almost to handout organizations. There was seldom a scoop on any wire. They generally followed, not led. But you couldn't ignore them for their influence in Middle America.

As I had first observed the day Ford pardoned Nixon, Helen Thomas of UPI had great instincts. Before one of Reagan's early hospital visits for a urinary tract infection, Deaver and I went to the Oval Office and the President said, "Why do they [the press] have to know everything? I'm just going out for a little test, that's all it is." And we said, "Mr. President, you can't go to Bethesda Naval Hospital unannounced without absolutely driving the stock market bonkers and having the Russians on full-scale alert." He got fighting mad. "Well, I'm just not going to do it." An hour or so later we went back to try again. "Mr. President, we just have to announce this." And he said, "Damn it, what do they want me to do? Go down to the press room and drop my pants and say, 'Here it is'?" I was going back and forth all day between my office, Deaver's office, and the Oval Office, and Helen finally said, "What's going on?" I said, "Nothing." But she sniffed it out. "Is the President all right?" she finally asked. And I just said, "Hang on," and before long I was able to make the announcement. But she had already sensed it.

The *Wall Street Journal* had its own wire service, the Dow Jones Wire, but they didn't staff the White House beat like the other wire services. Rich Jaroslovsky, the *Journal*'s White House reporter at the start of the Reagan administration, also covered the White House for the Dow Jones news wire. He'd come to my morning and noon briefings, but in the afternoons he wanted us to call him at the bureau office and read him any news releases we had about economics and business. I said to him, "Look, if you're going to be a wire service, you have to stay here. AP and UPI and Reuters are here. They get the news. We don't have to call it to them."

Although the *Journal* is a great paper, I was disappointed by the low-caliber reporters they assigned to the White House. I guess they just didn't regard politics as important as business. Al Hunt, the *Journal*'s Washington bureau chief, is one of the best and most canny political reporters of all, but the people he sent to the White House weren't very good. White House staffers regarded Jaroslovsky as a joke. We just didn't think he was a good reporter, that he didn't understand the issues. In the last couple of years the *Journal* assigned Jane Meyer and Ellen Hume to the White House, and they were even less politically sophisticated.

*   *   *

During Reagan's first term we devoted an inordinate amount of time to the weekly news magazines, *Time, Newsweek*, and *U.S. News & World Report*. Every news magazine would see every senior official for thirty minutes every week. No newspaper or network enjoyed that privilege. The senior White House staff liked the idea that they could remain totally anonymous, that they would never identify you. And there was a feeling of ego, that you were writing history.

Larry Barrett of *Time*, whom I always called the "Rent Man" because he looked like the guy who would come by every week and say, "I'm here to collect the rent," was a good reporter. I liked the way *Time* covered the White House. They wouldn't take up my time unless they really needed to talk to me for a story they were working on. But the reporters from *Newsweek* and *U.S. News* would obviously be given a shopping list of questions at the first of the week, and they would have to get answers to all those questions. Ninety-nine times out of a hundred you never saw anything they asked you in print. Dick Darman finally gave up and said, "No more magazine interviews." I couldn't indulge in that luxury because I was the point man in dealing with the press, but when there was a choice of seeing a news magazine or seeing somebody else, I would generally see the somebody else. I just didn't think the news magazines were worth my time.

Tom DeFrank of *Newsweek*, who had covered the White House since the Ford administration, was a good reporter with a lot of sources in high places. But he seemed to be most interested in gossip, especially gossip that I was on my way out, which never turned out to be true. I would call him and say, "Tom, where are you getting this stuff? You're spreading it all over town again." Eleanor Clift, his partner, was the most negative reporter who covered the White House. She and Tom would come to my office, sit next to each other on the couch, and flip open to the first page of their notebooks, where they had written down the subjects they wanted to ask about. Eleanor would have a constant stream of "Didn't the President look bad this week? Is his health all right? He really did stumble over that. You guys really did screw up on this thing." I finally stopped seeing them. Tom came by and asked me why, and I told him, "Tom, I've got to level with you. I do not need thirty minutes every week of this negative stuff from Eleanor. Now if you can figure out a way to come by yourself, I'll be glad to see *you.*"

U.S. News was number three among the news weeklies in the quality of their reporters, as well as in circulation. The last good reporter *U.S. News* sent to the White House was John Mashek, a veteran political correspondent who has since left the magazine for the *Atlanta Constitution*. *U.S. News* was always the one that got squeezed out when there wasn't enough time to see everyone. One of their reporters, Jim Hildreth, was a motormouth whose questions always took longer than my answers.

Picture the White House at Christmastime: beautiful decorations, a festive atmosphere, and, at the annual Christmas party for the press, an open bar; a lavish buffet featuring shrimp, roast beef, and ham; an open bar; individual photographs of each member of the press and his/her additional guest posing with the President and Mrs. Reagan; an open bar; gifts like Christmas ornaments or ski caps with a White House emblem on them; and an open bar.

Judging by some of the imaginative requests we got for invitations, not being invited to the Christmas party was akin to not being asked to the senior prom.

The annual White House Christmas party actually became the annual White House Christmas parties on my watch; the guest list grew so large that we had to hold the party on two nights. By the time of my last Christmas party in 1986, we had to invite five hundred journalists and their guests each night. Posing for 250 pictures a night with some of their harshest critics was about all the Reagans could handle.

The transition from a one-night Christmas affair to two nights, like almost every other logistical question involving the press, was not without controversy. No matter which night they were invited, some people were unhappy, and rumors began circulating that we had an A list and a B list. That just wasn't true. After the White House social office said the size of the press corps had grown too large for us to hold our Christmas party on one night, the Reagans agreed to have it on two nights, and we simply went down the list at random, assigning one person to the first night and the next to the second night. The White House reporters made such a big deal about A lists and B lists that I finally started having some fun at their expense. When a reporter would ask me, "Which night is for the A list?" I'd say, "Which night are you coming?" They'd innocently reply, "Tuesday," and I'd catch them with "Oh, I'm so sorry, but Wednesday night is for the A List."

Planning the Christmas party for the press was always a nightmare. My secretary, Connie Gerrard, would start in August, reviewing the press list to see who should be invited. The goal was to limit it to people who actually covered the White House regularly. Each network would have four correspondents, which was okay, but then they would rotate camera crews once a month so that over the course of a year you would have six or eight cameramen from each network. Moreover, the networks obtained White House press credentials for virtually everyone in their Washington bureaus—150 to 200 per network. And, naturally, everyone from the bureau chief to the file clerks would want to come to our Christmas party.

Hard-working though the members of the media were, they always found time to call us and beg for invitations. Some of the more memorable attempts at making the guest list:

- "My parents are dying, and it would mean a lot if I could bring them to the Christmas party." (That one never worked.)
- "I've been invited every year," from reporters who had *never* been invited. (Didn't they think we kept a record of who we invited?)
- "I've been invited every year," Part Two, from reporters who had been invited regularly while they covered the White House but no longer were on our beat, and in some instances had even been transferred out of town. Our answer: "You'll get an invitation when we see you covering the White House again."
- "My boss won't let me be off on Christmas and New Year's unless you invite him, too." This one, from Candy Crowley of the Associated Press, worked one year. After all, she *was* a White House regular, and we didn't want to play Scrooge, even if her boss was threatening to.
- "Please, please let us have an invitation for one of our reporters, Kevin Delaney." This request, from ABC, also worked, even though Delaney was their Hong Kong correspondent.
- "I'm calling to R.S.V.P. the invitation you sent to my husband, the reporter. He and I have split up, but I'll be there with my boyfriend." We had to tell this poor victim of a broken marriage that she and her lover weren't welcome, and then we sent the husband's invitation to his new residence. We did make a point of inviting him for the second night, just in case his ex-wife showed up and somehow got by the guards on the first night.

Members of the Fourth Estate would come to the Christmas party looking their best, wearing suits and ties and nice dresses and high heels, which for many was their annual exception to their own dress code. You would expect those who had won the prestigious assignment of covering the President of the United States to dress and conduct themselves accordingly. You would be wrong.

I had a running battle with the press corps over their attire, which had deteriorated tremendously during the four years between the time I left the White House in January 1977 and returned in January 1981. At a

White House event there would be a roomful of people in business suits or black tie, and the press would come in grimy T-shirts and jeans, unshaved, and with their hair uncombed. There were really some scruffy types among the regulars.

One of the first things I did was to require the reporters to wear business suits for White House dinners, in or out of the White House, and black tie when there was a black-tie event. But that didn't apply to informal, everyday occasions. The windows in the Reagans' living room overlooked the lawn on the north side of the White House, just outside the West Wing, where the press would gather to see who was going in and out. The reporters would lounge around out there in the sun, sometimes take their shirts off, sometimes have their lunch out there, and just make a mess. Eventually, we built a fence to keep them off the lawn, and we insisted that when they were on the White House grounds, they wear shirts.

A lot of the news media's harshest criticism of Ronald Reagan has been directed at his perceived lack of contact with the press. During the approximately 2,000 days I worked for Reagan, he had "only" 535 sessions with the press—more than one every four days. His press contacts consisted of 257 interviews; 216 question-and-answer periods in the Rose Garden, on his way to or from various other meetings, or going to an airplane or helicopter; thirty-nine full-fledged press conferences, and twenty-three other news conferences, which usually took place in the White House briefing room.

But reporters apparently believed he should have spent approximately one hundred percent of his presidency in consultation with them. What upset them the most was his relatively small number of press conferences, at least by their definition; they gave him credit for only the thirty-nine full-scale conferences in the East Room of the White House, refusing to count the other twenty-three. I constantly pushed for Reagan to hold more press conferences and conduct interviews on a regular basis, but other advisers always found excuses to scratch them from the President's schedule.

Reagan did hold far fewer full-fledged press conferences than most of his predecessors, and there's a good reason for it: Press conferences no longer serve the presidency or the press, and are in danger of becoming obsolete unless reporters decide to use them as information-gathering sessions, which is what they're intended to be. More and more, the reporters present in the East Room are second-stringers, while the first-stringers are back in the office watching on television, particularly those that are facing A.M. deadlines or wire deadlines.

In the wake of Watergate and Vietnam, press conferences have deteriorated into a game of "How can I trip him up?" and "I gotcha." Instead of asking legitimate questions on matters of importance, most of the reporters who attend press conferences are there only to try to trap the President. They are trying to make news, not report it. The incredibly arrogant television networks even go one step further—when they show excerpts from the news conference afterwards, they generally try to use only the questions that come from their own correspondents and ignore the rest. It's a case of "It wasn't important unless we asked it."

One thing to remember about press conferences is that they are strictly theater. The press is asking questions that they've written down beforehand, and the President is giving answers he has developed during a rehearsal. There's no spontaneity.

As a result, press conferences are in danger of becoming a waste of time. They no longer serve the President, the press, or, more important, the public.

Despite news media claims to the contrary, Reagan himself did not object at all to press conferences. The preparation for press conferences was always tedious, but he didn't mind standing there and answering questions. He would kid a lot about going out in front of "my friends in the press corps," or say, "Here we go again for my favorite pasttime," but he always said at the end of press conferences, "I wish we could figure out a way that we didn't have to leave so many hands uplifted when I leave the room. It just kills me to have to leave the room with everybody wanting to ask another question." But there were time constraints, both on him and on the networks, who didn't want to devote an entire evening of prime-time to something that didn't bring in revenue, like a press conference.

The audacity of the networks was unbelievable. Before our second press conference, in March 1981, we decided to use a lottery to select which reporters would be called on to ask questions. The President drew the names out of a big jug in the Roosevelt Room. The irony was that he drew about forty names—all fair and square—before he ever picked the name of a network reporter. So the network stars said they were not going to attend, since they weren't going to get to ask a question. In the end, they did attend, but we never used that method again. I used to joke with one of my assistants, Mark Weinberg, that the Washington bureau chief of each network had it written into his contract that he had to protest one slight per day and make one major protest a week; they were always complaining about something.

The television reporters tended to dominate both the press briefings and Reagan's press conferences. There were some that he knew by sight and would call on frequently, like Bill Plante, Andrea Mitchell, Sam Donaldson, and Gary Schuster, who got his CBS job by the way he posed questions at presidential news conferences when he was at the *Detroit News*. The President often called on Andrea simply because her shouting drew his attention. So you would have to say that being obnoxious does have its rewards.

The careers of television reporters often could rise or fall on their performance at a press conference. It became an unwritten rule that each of the three networks, as well as the two wire services, would get to ask a question at a press conference. You could see Lesley Stahl losing it if the President forgot to call on her after calling on reporters from the other two networks. There would be sheer panic in her eyes.

Reagan's briefing material for press conference preparation was usually presented in a Q-and-A format: "Mr. President, what about the shipment of Soviet helicopters to Nicaragua?" He would be given an answer of three or four sentences, sometimes along with information—only items, like the helicopters are capable of doing this or that. He didn't have the luxury as I did of reading from a piece of paper—he had to really know the material.

It makes me angry whenever I hear people say that Reagan was not adequately prepared for his press conferences. If he did do badly, I would fault myself, and ask myself how I could have prepared him better. Usually there weren't many things you could have done: You would tell the President what to say, and if he said it, he said it, and if he didn't, he didn't. I don't say that as a disinterested observer; I was in charge of preparing him.

We would set a tentative date for a press conference, ten days to two weeks in advance, and we would send word out through my office to the departments and agencies that we would appreciate questions and answers on the subjects that they thought might come up. Then we would put together a briefing book by the Friday before a press conference, for the President to take with him to Camp David and study over the weekend. It would have several dozen domestic and foreign topics, with questions and answers on each topic.

If the press conference was scheduled for Tuesday night, we would have our first rehearsal Monday afternoon at two in the family theater in the upstairs part of the White House. There would be a presidential podium, television-type lighting, a microphone, a public address system, and three or four of us at a table, acting as reporters and posing questions. Others, like Stockman, Meese, Deaver, and Baker, would sit in to observe and evaluate the President's performance. We would fire questions, we would follow up, and we would try to trap him; we would try to play the exact role of the press. We would spend forty-five or fifty minutes on domestic questions and then break for ten minutes to critique: "Mr. President, on Aid to Dependent Children, you could have mentioned that in 1982 we did increase the budget in this area by ten percent." Or, "the budget figure you quoted was $900,000 and it should have been $9 million." The President took criticism very much in stride. Occasionally he would debate an answer with you or say, "That's a good idea." Then we would do the same thing on the foreign policy side. And we would have a repeat rehearsal for two hours Tuesday afternoon before the President went upstairs to rest for the press conference.

That may seem like a lot of preparation, and in truth it was, but you have to remember that Nixon would shut down totally for forty-eight hours in advance to prepare himself for a press conference. Press conferences, after all, are—or, at least, should be—one of the primary ways in which a President communicates directly with the American people, and there's nothing wrong with trying to make sure you're properly prepared for one.

In press conferences, out of thirty questions and follow-ups the press would ask, we might fail to anticipate one. And often we could even predict which reporters were going to ask which questions. In spite of all our groundwork, we never could tell how Reagan would do. Many times the dress rehearsal bore no resemblance to the actual event. Sometimes the rehearsal would be bad and you would be living in fear that the President was going to make a series of major mistakes in a press conference and he'd be absolutely brilliant, or you might feel entirely comfortable after the briefing sessions and the final act would be riddled with mistakes.

One thing about President Reagan, he was not good at remembering names. Mike Deaver told me that during the Sacramento years he had prepared flash cards with the legislators' pictures on one side and their names on the other, and Reagan's son, little Ron, would hold them up, and Reagan would have the hardest time identifying them correctly. I wound up preparing flash cards that had the major reporters on them, and

I gave them to Reagan for him to study. He knew a few people like Gary Schuster and Bill Plante from the campaign, and Sam, and Andrea, who was so pushy that he finally got to know who she was, and Lou Cannon and Helen Thomas.

To help Reagan get ready for press conferences, I prepared seating charts for the President on a huge board. There was a little sleeve where each seat was and I would slip each reporter's Secret Service identification photo into the sleeve, so that before press conferences the President could actually study where each person would be sitting. He would use that board during rehearsal on the day of the news conference. That worked fine, except for the time he called on a reporter by name and nobody stood up. And the President waggled his finger quite confidently and said, "Bob." No response. "You, Bob Thompson." No response. Bob Thompson, a veteran White House reporter from Hearst Newspapers, was at home, watching on T.V. What happened was, the guy told us in the afternoon that he was coming, and he didn't let us know that he wasn't.

We carefully controlled seating at press conferences. I was accused of telling Reagan who to call on, which was true to some extent, but more often than not, I would tell him who *not* to call on. The reporters who got assigned to the rear often felt they were being punished, but we never assigned people to the back row as punishment, except for pests like Lester Kinsolving; Trudy Feldman, who represented several minor news organizations; and corporate gadfly Evelyn Y. Davis, who had obtained press credentials. Always, immediately before the President would enter the East Room where the press conferences were held, he and I would stand in the nearby Blue Room, and we would have the White House producer pan the audience so he could see who was sitting where. I would say, "Mr. President, there's Trudy Feldman, wearing a blue dress," so that he could identify her and not call on her by mistake.

We also tried to identify people who might ask softball questions, and I would put three or four people on the right-hand side of the front row. I would tell the President, "If you get battered from the left or the center, go to your right." At one press conference it became unbelievably obvious that I had lined these people up for that purpose. It got written up and I had to quit because it was embarrassing not only to Reagan and me, but to the reporters who were put up there as patsies.

When Jim Baker or Don Regan and I would go up to the White House living quarters to get the President a few minutes before a press conference began, there would be as much tension as there would be if he were getting ready to enter the ring for a prize fight. Mrs. Reagan would be there in a bathrobe—she would watch it on live T.V.—and there would be this long farewell between the two of them. Sometimes their good-byes would last so long that I would be afraid we'd be late for the news conference. She would hold his hand, wish him luck, tell him to do well, and remind him, "Now when Helen [Thomas] says, 'Thank you,' you leave," and he would say, "I will, honey." Then they would kiss and he would be off to his fate, waving to her as he got on the elevator.

As we walked over to the press conference, I would always repeat the First Lady's admonition, urging Reagan to zip out of the East Room as soon as Helen said her "Thank you." "It's always the last question that gets you," I would tell him. "If we could figure out when it was coming and quit just before it was asked, you'd bat 1,000." But, nice guy that he is, the President would linger as reporters surged up around him for another shot at making news. Often, they'd begin with a softball question, like, "When are you going to hold another press conference?" Then the gut punch: "What about the Israeli invasion of Lebanon?"

Once, as we made our way out of the East Room, we had a frightening moment. The President was walking down the aisle between rows of reporters on the way to the door, when Laura Chasen, a reporter from the operation headed by extremist Lyndon LaRouche, shot by a half dozen reporters and headed directly toward President Reagan with her hand outstretched. Was this to be another John Hinckley incident? Before either the Secret Service or I could react, she latched onto the President's arm and demanded, "When am I going to get my personal interview?" That prompted Richard Nixon, who was watching on television, to make one of his occasional calls to the White House and suggest that the whole mob scene at the end of press conferences "looked unpresidential." After the Laura Chasen episode, we altered the configuration for East Room press conferences so that the President could exit from doors directly behind the podium.

As soon as a press conference ended, I would do what the press got to calling "the spin patrol," where I would circulate among the reporters from AP, UPI, Reuters, and the networks, and they would say to me, "How do you think he did?" No matter what, I would say, "Great." I guess I could have made front-page news by saying, "He really screwed up, didn't he?" Which probably would have led to another front-page story about me the next day: "White House Press Secretary Resigns."

Reagan's Saturday radio broadcasts, which started in April 1982, at the suggestion of longtime Reagan aide Joe Holmes, were one of our most effective public relations instruments. Saturdays usually are slow news days, and more than fifty percent of the radio addresses made front-page news and virtually all of them were carried somewhere in the Sunday papers. Originally, the radio addresses were to have run for ten weeks, but they were so successful that they've been on ever since, for six years now. Of course, Reagan had done a masterful job on his syndicated radio broadcasts when he was out of office from 1975 until the 1980 campaign began, so we expected him to do well on these Saturday addresses.

Once in a while, when we were to be out of the country or aboard an airplane on Saturday morning, which meant that we would be unable to do the broadcasts live, we would tape them in advance. In that situation we would give the tape to the press on Friday afternoon, with the understanding that it wouldn't be broadcast until Saturday.

Ironically, the only person who violated the broadcast embargo was a former White House press secretary, Ron Nessen, who had become head of Mutual News. About five o'clock one Friday afternoon in the fall of 1986 an AP radio guy stormed up to inform me that Mutual had just broadcast excerpts from our tape. I got Nessen and I said, "What is this? Why are you breaking the embargo?" His answer was, "You've got news in there." I said, "Since when does it being news allow you to break an embargo?" And he said, "That's big news and I'm not going to hold it until tomorrow." I said, "Ron, you've been in this business long enough to know that that's when you do impose an embargo—when there's news in it. You don't need an embargo if there's not any news in it." "No, absolutely not," he said, and I told him, "Well, as far as I'm concerned, you and your reporter are out of business with me." The poor Mutual reporter was caught in the middle because of Nessen's aggressive action.

Another reporter who got put out of business, through no fault of his own, was Jeremiah O'Leary of the *Washington Times*. The *Times* had a gossip columnist named Diana McLellan, better known as "The Ear," who had written previously for the old *Washington Star* and the *Washington Post* before joining the Moonie-owned *Times*. For some reason, Ms. McLellan thought I made good copy, and it seemed that whenever she had space to fill, she would write that I was on my way out because Nancy Reagan was down on me. McLellan's stories were false, and she never called to give me a chance to respond in advance.

I finally called in the *Times* White House team, headed by O'Leary, and told them they were "out of business" until their columnist apologized in print for her wicked ways. Days went by, and O'Leary, an old and dear friend of mine, was rightfully angered by the sentence I had unfairly pronounced on him. "You've got the wolf at my door," O'Leary protested.

I called off the hounds a few weeks later, when Arnaud de Borchgrave, editor in chief of the *Times*, phoned to inform me that "that woman's contract is not being renewed." I don't take credit, but I did rejoice that I would no longer be faced daily with her notoriously inaccurate column.

Being the principal White House spokesman was a wonderful job, and I wouldn't trade that experience for anything. But it was also six years of being on the hot seat. I don't mean that to sound self-serving; an expert witness, who happened to be a frequent antagonist of mine, Sam Donaldson, wrote:

"The job of [White House] press secretary is a very tough one. You have to go out there every day and walk a tightrope, sometimes with inadequate information; you have to answer the phone at all hours of the night and on weekends; you have to fight to hold on to your turf and your office's integrity in the shark tank of the White House bureaucracy; you have to support decisions loyally even though you may not fully agree with them; . . . and you have to put up with reporters like me."

That pretty much sums up the job. My workday, which averaged fourteen hours, began at 6:00 A.M., when the radio would wake me up with four headlines and the weather. Those four headlines gave me enough information to know whether I wanted to put my head back under the pillow and call in sick (which I never did), or bounce out of bed and go to work. I would shower and come downstairs for a breakfast of cold cereal. Over breakfast I would go through the *Washington Post* and make notes on a yellow legal pad, listing the issues I anticipated for the day. I can attest that that's not conducive to good digestion. I tried to read the paper as thoroughly as I could at the breakfast table; John Chancellor once gave me some of the best advice I ever received: "Read the *Washington Post* before you leave home. The whole town revolves around what's in the *Post*. If you don't read it before you get to work, you'll never get a chance."

I would leave for work about seven, arrive at the White House at seven thirty, and park my four-wheel-drive truck there on West Executive Drive outside the White House. One of the chief barometers of power in the White House was how close your parking space was to the door, and gradually I moved up. For my last two or three years my parking place was right at the foot of the steps to the door of the West Lobby.

From the moment I entered my office until the moment I left for home, usually about 8:00 P.M., I had hardly any free time. I would have to deal nonstop with the phone calls that came in on my two dozen telephone lines, as well as with the dozens of reporters present in the

White House. We once tallied the daily calls to the four secretaries who answered all incoming lines in the press office and found that they handled an average of 1,850 calls a day, over four hundred each. No wonder they liked to travel aboard the press plane, where there were reporters, but, mercifully, no telephones.

I usually briefed the press twice a day; altogether, I conducted 2,000 briefings over the course of six years. Those were undoubtedly the hardest part of the job. They amounted to being cross-examined twice daily by reporters who considered themselves the journalistic equivalent of Edward Bennett Williams and F. Lee Bailey all rolled into one. The briefing room for the press had forty-eight seats, which were usually full, with some of the hardest cases—the reporters from the networks and the wire services—in the front row. I used to joke that if I ever did write a book, the title was going to be *Everybody Wants to Be Press Secretary, but Nobody Wants to Go into the Briefing Room*.

The briefings lasted anywhere from two minutes to an hour and a half. I made it a practice once the briefing was over to shoot directly out of the briefing room, not linger to catch any questions. That's the most dangerous time in a press conference, when you've finished and you're leaving the briefing room—they would pepper you with questions, and there would be no transcript of the questions and answers to back you up. So the best thing to do was to avoid the questions entirely.

Aside from the briefings, the face-to-face conversations with reporters and the countless phone calls, I sat in on virtually every presidential meeting I had time for, especially during my last two years. That way, I would know what was said and what was not said, and if some participant later reported it differently, I would know the facts. I was there whether it was a congressional leadership meeting or a Cabinet meeting or a press interview.

My lunch hours were usually spent jogging, and on many occasions I would finish running and lie down on the Ellipse, across the street from the White House, where there were several softball diamonds. Sometimes I'd actually go to sleep in the grass, as a means of breaking the tension, and at least twice people woke me up and asked, "Sir, are you saving this spot for the softball game?"

My blood pressure had run borderline high during the Ford administration. It dropped significantly during the Carter years, when I was in the public relations business, so it was clearly caused by the stress of working in the White House. When I came back to the White House the second time, I vowed to keep a close watch on my blood pressure. The doctors told me to watch my weight and keep up my running.

One day during Reagan's cancer stay at Bethesda Naval Hospital in 1985, I asked White House physician John Hutton to take my blood pressure. He took it in a little examining room next to the President's bedroom, and got a reading of 160 over 110, which is very high. Hutton asked Ken Lee, another White House physician who was a cardiologist, to retake it, and Dr. Lee got the same reading. He and I talked it over and then I said, "Well, I'll be headed home in a little bit." Dr. Lee said, "You're not going to play tennis or anything like that, are you?" And I said, "Well, I was thinking about running." His instructions were simple: "Don't!"

Working in the White House also helped make me one of Johnson & Johnson's best customers—I went through bottle after bottle of Tylenol, to relieve headaches caused by tension.

I certainly can't blame all the stress on the media. One of the main sources of pressure on me was a fellow White House aide, David Gergen. I had known Gergen since I went to work for Nixon in 1974 and Gergen was in the speechwriting shop. Right from the start of the Reagan administration, with Gergen in the job of staff director to White House Chief of Staff Jim Baker, he tried to horn in on the press office. One time before Jim Brady got shot I told him that Gergen had said "he doesn't want us to do this," and he said, "You tell Dave Gergen he's not the press secretary."

I felt that from the minute Brady was shot, Gergen set his eye on that job. In fact, while Brady was lying at death's door in the hospital, Gergen went to Baker and suggested that he be given the title of press secretary in place of Brady. Baker was receptive to many of Gergen's foolish ideas, including this one, and passed Gergen's proposal along to Dr. Arthur Kobrine, Brady's brain surgeon. When Kobrine mentioned it to Brady, Brady, who was hardly able to talk during that period, replied, "They just want to make me a vegetable."

Kobrine relayed that stark comment to Baker. When I heard about it, my own determination to hold on to the job was reinforced. At that point, those of us in the press office still clung to the hope that Brady could some day return. Gergen, meanwhile, retrenched and came up with Plan B, which Baker did accept: Gergen was named director of White House communications, with control over the speechwriting unit and the out-of-town press corps, while I was appointed deputy assistant to the President and principal deputy press secretary. This was a bizarre arrangement that had me dealing with the Washington reporters for out-of-town newspapers, while Gergen dealt with reporters from the same newspapers who called from their home offices. Under Gergen's plan, he and I also shared briefing room duties, with me briefing the press three days a week and him two.

Gergen was extremely disorganized and usually late. I felt the key to a press operation was to be cool, calm, organized, and on time. Ninety percent of the time, all the press corps saw was the press operation. They didn't see the President. They didn't see the chief of staff. They didn't attend the important meetings. So the only impression they would have would be the way the press office performed. I thought the train ought to run on time. A twelve o'clock briefing ought to be at twelve o'clock. If it isn't, the press asks why, and you say, "Well, we don't have all the information we need." And the next thing, they're reporting that "the White House is in disarray."

I considered it my initial job to keep Gergen out of Brady's job, to keep Brady's seat warm in case he came back. Guerrilla warfare broke out almost at once between Gergen and his staff and me and mine. He was always trying to stab me in the back, telling Baker that "Speakes didn't get this quite right." But Baker would pass that on to me, so I was aware of what Gergen was up to, and I had my guard up. Gergen had an aide he would send to my briefings; he would stand in the back and I knew he was there only to give an immediate report to Gergen on what I said. After a couple of days I confronted Gergen's guy and told him, "If you want to come to the briefings you're perfectly welcome. Why don't you just stand up front with the rest of the staff?" He never came back.

My staff and I retaliated with tactics of our own. The most effective was my dubbing the six-foot-four Gergen "The Tall Man." It got shortened to "Tall," which is how people in the White House started referring to him. At one point *The New York Times* reported that that there was a joke within the White House that Gergen had been kidnapped as a child and raised by giraffes. That made him look foolish to Baker, and helped grease the skids. We used Gergen's height against him in another way: The podium in the briefing room is motorized so that you can adjust its height. Before Gergen would brief, Mark Weinberg of my staff would go out and drop the podium to its lowest height. Then Gergen would go in and tower over it like Ichabod Crane. He never was able to figure out why the podium struck him well below the waist.

In a classic case of Washington in-fighting, we threw virtually every booby trap in his way that we could, planted every story, egged the press on to get down on him. It took a couple of years before Baker saw that Gergen's system was not working, and he told Gergen so. Also, I was able to drop hints to Baker that Gergen was responsible for leaks to the press alleging that Baker had not joined in the effort to oust the controversial

James Watt because their wives were involved together in an evangelical Christian program. That was the last straw with Baker, that Gergen would leak information about his family. Gergen finally left the White House in early 1984 to become a Washington consultant and then editor of *U.S. News & World Report*.

Since Gergen left the White House there has been no more animosity between the two of us, maybe because our contact with each other is limited. Our paths have crossed every so often; one such occasion came a year or so after Gergen resigned, when he accompanied Mort Zuckerman, who had bought *U.S. News*, and seven or eight of their reporters and editors to the Oval Office for an interview with Reagan. Gergen and the others sat there mostly in silence while Zuckerman asked ninety percent of the questions; one of Zuckerman's reporters later characterized it as "the $160 million interview." That's about what Zuckerman had paid for the magazine, and the reporter said that Zuckerman could go away happy and leave them alone since he had had his interview with the President.

15

The White House

Follies

News item: "OUAGADOUGOU, BURKINA FASO, OCTOBER 16, 1987—Captain Thomas Sankara and twelve other officials were executed and buried today after Sankara's chief adviser ousted him as president of this impoverished West African nation, an official source said.

"The source, speaking on condition of anonymity, said Sankara and a dozen other officials, including *the presidential press secretary* [emphasis added] and a senior police official, were shot and buried this morning in a mass burial outside Ouagadougou, the capital."

I've played some tough rooms in my time—notably, the White House briefing room—but I have to admit that I was never threatened with the fate that befell my counterpart in Burkina Faso. And at times my job had its lighter side. As I look back over my six years as White House spokesman, I think of some of the lowlights—the flaps over the bunny suit and the pronunciation of the White House economic adviser's name, the open mike controversies—and the highlights: my Japanese "Tea Dudes," the April Fools' jokes we played on the press, and having bystanders salute me or moon me during presidential motorcades, just because they thought I was the President as I rolled by in the dummy presidential limousine.

246

Take the Modigliani mix-up, please—as Henny Youngman might say. Professor Franco Modigliani of MIT, who had criticized President Reagan's balanced-budget proposal as "a Mickey Mouse approach" that could become a "formulation for disaster," won the Nobel Prize for economics in October 1985. When I was asked for a White House comment on the award, I said I had "nothing" for the press, adding, "I thought he was the feller that painted the Sistine Chapel." It was quickly pointed out to me by my more cultured sparring partners in the press that it was Michelangelo who painted the Sistine Chapel—back in the sixteenth century—while Amedeo Modigliani was a late-nineteenth and early-twentieth-century artist. I was even accused of being anti-Italian. "Couldn't be," I countered. "I eat spaghetti twice a week."

I got into hot water over another matter relating to economics, only this one wasn't funny at all. Martin Feldstein, a Harvard economist who was chairman of Reagan's Council of Economic Advisers, was under fire in late 1983 because he repeatedly criticized the budget deficits that kept growing throughout most of the Reagan administration. At a press briefing on November 30, 1983, I tried to let the media know that Feldstein had better shape up or ship out. It was a raucous session, with both the reporters and me making jokes about how precarious Feldstein's job security was; at one point, noting that he was attending an administration luncheon on economic matters, I mouthed the words "last supper" to the press, hoping not to be quoted.

The next day, however, Steven R. Weisman wrote a front-page story in *The New York Times* implying that I was anti-Semitic because I had switched back and forth between two pronunciations of Feldstein's name: "Mr. Speakes today repeatedly pronounced Mr. Feldstein's name two different ways—STEEN and STINE (Mr. Feldstein uses the latter pronunciation)—provoking laughter from some reporters." In fact, I had always inadvertently mixed up the pronunciation, and, although I did poke fun at him, I meant no disrespect toward him by saying his name both ways. A check of a recording of the briefing revealed that I had mispronounced his name twice, while reporters had done it four times, and that the press corps had made four times as many quips about him. Punchlines from the press included: "Did he take a taster to the lunch?" "I think they're eating fried Feldstein." "I'd advise Feldstein to commit suicide." Altogether, I made ten quips about Feldstein to thirty-eight by the press, with thirteen from Sam Donaldson alone, yet I was the one whom Weisman presented as prejudiced. The frivolity of the ladies and gentlemen of the Fourth Estate, who were sometimes downright mean, went unreported.

The Feldstein incident wasn't the only time I got in trouble with the New York press. After the New York Mets won the World Series in 1986, they were invited to visit President Reagan at the White House. A celebration of their victory at the New York restaurant run by their former teammate, Rusty Staub, had gotten a bit out of hand. Before the Mets called on Reagan, I publicly expressed the hope that they wouldn't tear up the White House the way they had Staub's restaurant. My remarks received heavy play in the New York tabloids, and New York Mayor Ed Koch fired off a telegram to President Reagan, demanding my resignation.

Another incident better forgotten—although hardly anyone has—is the Barbara Honegger/Easter Bunny flap. Honegger, then the deputy assistant attorney general for civil rights, wrote an article in August 1983 in the *Washington Post* blasting the Reagan administration for its alleged lack of commitment to the interests of women. She quickly resigned, and when asked for a White House comment on her criticism, I replied, "The last time I saw her, she was the Easter Bunny at the White House Easter Egg Roll." Catching myself on the verge of inserting my foot in my mouth, I tried to smooth it out, adding, "It's not easy to dress up in a hot bunny suit. I've never done it, sort of ashamed to admit it." It turned out she had dressed up as a bunny on two occasions, the last for a get-well picture for Jim Brady, but not for the White House Easter Egg Roll. (It was Ed Meese's wife, Ursula, who traditionally donned the bunny suit at Easter egg time.)

My statement quickly became a cause célèbre. The *Washington Post*, for example, reported the story under the headline, "The Fur Flies on the Bunny Trail." The morning after the flap broke, Reagan and his entourage were leaving Los Angeles for San Diego, and the President said to me, "Who is this you've got dressed up in a bunny suit?" He said it in a joking way, but I knew he wasn't happy. "Oh, yes," I answered, "that's something I probably shouldn't have said." Mrs. Reagan remarked sharply, "No, you shouldn't have." I added, "But I feel very strongly this woman is doing a disservice to the President," and they agreed. I didn't remind Reagan that he himself had committed a similar faux pas several weeks earlier, when he tried to score points with female critics by commenting, "If it wasn't for women, us men would still be walking around in skin suits, carrying clubs." His remark hadn't gone over any better than mine.

I have to admit my bunny suit remark was a cheap shot that added to the controversy, and it probably would have been better if I had ignored her outfit or used different language. But I was attempting to put down someone who had gotten out of line.

The bunny suit controversy wasn't the only time I received a firsthand lesson on how protective Nancy Reagan could be of her husband and his image. During the 1984 election we made a campaign stop at a wildlife refuge in Maryland. It was to have been a great all-around photo opportunity, as well as a chance for Reagan to score some points with environmentalists who had never forgiven him for his remark to the effect that if you've seen one redwood you've seen them all—not to mention his choice of James Watt for Secretary of the Interior.

Right before our campaign outing, however, Reagan had appointed another controversial environmentalist, or anti-environmentalist, if you will—ousted Environmental Protection Agency administrator Anne Burford—to a relatively minor post, head of the National Advisory Committee on Oceans and Atmosphere.

The press was not content with providing the T.V. audience with beautiful pictures from the wildlife preserve. They had better fish to fry. As a Park Ranger concluded a painstaking and a horribly boring briefing for the President, the three network correspondents erupted in a verbal explosion that would have made the biblical Tower of Babel sound like a diction class. I stepped forward, hands outstretched, to try to restore order. Too late! Sam Donaldson, Chris Wallace, and Bill Plante were in a verbal horse race, knowing full well that the first to quit shouting would lose and that the loudest and longest-winded would get to question the President. "My guardian says I can't talk," declared Reagan. That was bad enough, but then my picture, with a puzzled President Reagan looking on from behind me, ended up on Page One of the *Washington Post*—five columns wide.

I thought I was just doing my job, keeping the President out of trouble, but after I was pictured fending off the cameras, Jim Baker suggested that I not step in anymore. He implied that Nancy Reagan was behind his "suggestion." It was sort of a damned-if-you-do and damned-if-you-don't situation. If you didn't step in and cut the press off from badgering the President, then the Bakers and the Nancy Reagans would say, "Why isn't Larry doing his job?" If you did step in, it appeared you were trying to manipulate and shield the President, and you got criticized because it looked like you were ordering him around. For a long time after that I didn't step in at all and just let the President worm his way out as best he could.

I guess I should have followed the example of Lyn Nofziger, who had perfected the art of cutting the press off when he was Reagan's main press person while Reagan was governor. Lyn used to crouch right in front of the press, looking back at Reagan, and when Lyn was ready to break it up, he would rise in front of the press corps so that all the cameras could pick up would be Lyn's backside. Of course, Lyn had a little more to work with than I did.

Another time I ran afoul of the President was in October 1981. Mrs. Reagan, mercifully, was not present when this happened, or else she, too, would have chewed me out. We had just finished a couple of days of intense preparations for a presidential press conference, and I had an appointment with Marty Schram, then of the *Washington Post*, later with the *Chicago Sun-Times*. Marty was working on a story on how the President prepared for his news conferences. His expert interrogation led me right down the primrose path; before I knew it, I was talking when I should have been listening, and I made it sound as if Reagan did little more at press conferences than deliver answers we had pumped into him. Schram's devastatingly accurate piece appeared the next day, without identifying me or Pete Roussel, whom Marty had also interviewed. Nevertheless, my fingerprints were all over the story, and after our senior staff meeting that morning Chief of Staff Jim Baker took me aside and said, "I want you to go into the Oval Office and apologize to the President." I went in and sheepishly told the President that I had made a mistake—"a big one," I admitted—and I would never repeat it. He was obviously humiliated and hurt by what I had told the *Post*. "That's all right," he said, "but you made me look like Charlie McCarthy." He was referring, of course, to the puppet that belonged to the late ventriloquist Edgar Bergen. We learned our lesson and never again spoke to a reporter about the preparation of the President for press conferences.

We always had a spare limousine in the motorcades in case one broke down. As threats of terrorism increased, the Secret Service started running the two limousines together in order to confuse anybody who might want to attack the President. The two cars were identical, both with flags, antennas, and other trappings of presidential power. The President's personal aide and I rode as a matter of course in the backup limousine, functioning as decoys for the President. Kind of Presidents without portfolios, you might say.

The public would always cheer the first limo, where we were riding. As we waved back at the crowds, Kodak Instamatics would flash wildly. I often wondered how many people looked at their newly developed pictures and said, "Who's this?" The attention we got certainly convinced us that the plan was working and that we would be the ones hit by a terrorist attack.

In the latter stages of the 1984 campaign, David Fischer, Reagan's personal aide during the first term, brought along both Ronald and Nancy Reagan masks. He used to put on the Ronald Reagan mask during motorcades, and during a visit to an air force base these air force guys were saluting the President's car all along the route—or so they thought. Then Fischer lowered it and it dawned on the air force people that it wasn't Reagan to whom they had delivered their snappiest salutes. They just wilted. We also had the Nancy Reagan mask with us, but neither of us had the courage to put it on; if she had found out, she probably would have fired both of us.

On our trip to the economic summit in Germany in 1985, Jim Kuhn, who had succeeded Fischer as Reagan's personal aide, and I were riding in the decoy limousine in a motorcade. The Reagans and Chancellor Kohl and his wife were in a limousine directly in back of us. All at once Kuhn and I noticed about four kids who were getting ready to moon the President. The instant we passed, the quartet spun around, backsides poked in the air, and dropped their trousers, thinking our car was the one that had the President in it. The President's car was so close behind, he couldn't have missed it. But he never said a word about what surely must have been an historic first.

Then there was the hot day in Madison, Wisconsin, during the 1984 campaign, when a girl on the shoulders of some big guy in overalls dropped her halter top to her waist. The President missed the show, but we certainly didn't. Someone called it "the two biggest events" of the campaign.

Reagan was caught unaware by another incident that had sexual overtones. He was reviewing a group of Lippizaner stallions as horsemen from the Vienna Riding School put them through their paces one day on the South Lawn of the White House. The President must have wondered if he had unwittingly said something funny, because laughter rippled through the press area, and, as he continued, it erupted into loud guffaws. Women, red-faced, turned their backs. Just as the President declared, "And we have only seen just a tiny bit of what they actually do in their exhibitions," one of the stallions—all of which were extremely well endowed—chose to display his maleness.

Jim Baker and I made a rapid retreat back into the White House. "I'm not responsible for scheduling this event," Baker laughed. "Where is Deaver?" The videotape of the horse, displaying himself while a straight-backed Austrian rider sat astride him, plumed hat and all, made the rounds. It was complete with the President's remark—spoken, of course, to the stiff assembly of Austrian diplomats—but, in reality, an uncanny narration of the offending stallion. Another White House first: an equine porno film.

Speaking of animals reminds me of Joe Canzeri's dog. Canzeri, the head advance man in the White House during Reagan's first few years, bought a dog one New Year's while we were in Palm Springs. For the flight back to Washington, Canzeri insisted that his dog be flown on the press plane. After being told that the dog would have to travel in the baggage compartment, Canzeri got on a White House radio at the foot of the stairs of Air Force One, called Bob Manning, who headed the White House transportation unit, and declared, "Damn it, I want my dog upstairs on the topside of the plane—in the cockpit, if you have to!" The dog flew in the cockpit.

When the plane arrived at Andrews Air Force Base outside of Washington, Mark Weinberg and David Prosperi from my office went up to Jim Kuhn, who was then an advance man working for Canzeri, and said, "We have bad news for you. The dog didn't survive the flight." Jim turned white and might have died himself, but Mark and David quickly confessed that they were just joking.

Another tale from the animal world concerned a goodwill mission to the Philippine President Ferdinand Marcos that Reagan once made on behalf of President Nixon. The Reagans were staying in a big fancy room at Marcos's palace, but there was a problem: Nancy Reagan, who was afraid of bugs, saw a huge cockroach in their bedroom. The Reagans called for one of Marcos's servants, who came running in with a big spray can and killed the roach. "Don't worry about it," he assured the Reagans, "they just come from the kitchen." Somehow, that didn't make them feel any better.

Reagan loved to tell jokes, but sometimes his clowning around got him in trouble. I'll never forget a Saturday in August 1984 out in Santa Barbara, just before one of his weekly radio addresses, when he quipped into a microphone that he thought was dead, "My fellow Americans, I am pleased to tell you today that I've signed legislation that will outlaw Russia forever. We begin bombing in five minutes." Not to mention the time in July 1985, just after the Americans taken hostage on the TWA plane in the Middle East had been released, when he warmed up for his nationwide address on the crisis by saying into a mike he again thought was closed, "After seeing *Rambo* last night, I know what to do next time this happens."

I had a running battle with the networks over that; the time-honored rule was that they should treat as off-the-record anything the President said before his broadcast actually began. They saw it differently, pointing out that as a veteran broadcaster, he should have been able to tell whether or not his words were being transmitted out of the room he was in. And those two times, the networks won. Looking back, I'm not so sorry they did; his remarks really were funny, and the world didn't come to an end because they were reported. The President actually found the whole furor amusing, and he started joking about it in his speeches. However, never knowing what he might say next, we had a huge old-style "ON THE AIR" sign made, which would light up when the mike was hot. At least that way he would know when his quips might become news.

Reagan's habit of ad-libbing often got him into trouble. He would tell a joke that didn't go over well; or he would cite one of those *Reader's Digest* stories that he had read, which might be wrong or come out wrong; or he would remember scenes from movies as if they had happened in real life. Don Regan and I started trying to discourage the President from ad-libbing. Many times, as the President was going into a speech, Regan would say, "No ad-libs!" and shake his finger at him.

Quick as he was ordinarily, President Reagan sometimes missed a cue. In April 1986, Reagan attended the Baltimore Orioles' opening game as the guest of team owner Edward Bennett Williams. Reagan and Williams were sitting in the Orioles' dugout, and I knew a photo opportunity when I saw one. I had a White House advance man grab a hot dog vendor and escort him down to the dugout. With a flourish, the vendor said, "Hot dog, Mr. President?" The cameras and microphones were poised, but our ever-honest President replied, "No, thanks. I've already had lunch." Seeing my P.R. coup about to go down the drain, I nudged Reagan, and he finally caught on. He ordered three hot dogs—one for himself, one for Williams, and one for Oriole manager Earl Weaver. (No one offered me a hot dog, but I didn't need one anyway, as long as Oriole first baseman Eddie Murray was in the dugout.) Reagan then added to his gaffe by whipping two dollars out of his pocket to pay for the three hot dogs. Three hot dogs may have cost that much fifty years ago when he was a baseball broadcaster, but these days that would hardly pay for the mustard. No one told him that wasn't enough, and the vendor pocketed the money, kept his mouth shut, and left, chalking up his loss to the honor of the occasion.

Reagan also made a national security revelation of sorts that day to an unlikely person, Orioles' catcher Rick Dempsey. The ballgame was on April 7, a couple of days after one of our soldiers was killed in the nightclub bombing in West Germany that was traced to Libya. During his visit to the dugout, Reagan started discussing the attack with Dempsey and told the ballplayer that he would like to "nail his [Qaddafi's] nuts to that log over there [pointing to the Orioles' bench] and push him over." We bombed Libya a week later.

We had a number of celebrities make guest appearances during press briefings, but the only one who was invited back a second time was another sports figure, Los Angeles Dodger manager Tommy Lasorda. Lasorda's second visit occurred just before the 1985 Geneva summit, at a time when one of the major news stories was the defection to the U.S. of KGB officer Vitaly Yurchenko, who changed his mind after a brief stay here and returned home. Sharing the podium with me, Lasorda was asked as a joke what he thought of the Yurchenko affair. "Oh, yes, I remember him," was Lasorda's answer. "Bobby Yurchenko, rightfielder, San Diego Padres, 1968."

We often brought Hollywood figures to the briefings, and we paraded one out on an April Fools' Day. He was a dapper, somewhat portly gentleman with a pencil-thin mustache and a walking cane. He looked the epitome of a diplomat, which is how I introduced him—Monsieur LePieu from France. I told the press corps that our guest expert had met with the President to discuss the international economic situation and would report on his conversation with Reagan.

"Laaadiees and gentlemon," the visitor began, "I have had zee dee-stinct privileege to meet with Monsieur le Presi-doont, Rrrronald Rrrrea-gan, this day. And here ees what he told me (pause):

" 'Errrr. What's up, doc? Heh! Heh! Heh!' "

Pencils dropped throughout the briefing room, as all of us roared with laughter. My mystery guest was Mel Blanc, the voice of Bugs Bunny and many other cartoon characters.

Music has always been a way of life for me, especially the country music of my boyhood. But I appreciate all forms of music, and some friends in Switzerland once sent me an Alp horn, the instrument herdsmen use to call to each other from mountaintop to mountaintop. This one was so large that it reached all the way across the room when I stood behind my desk and played it. I'd tune up in the late afternoons with a *"Woooooh. Woooooh. Woooooh."* One day a visitor on his way home from work poked his head into my office, and I looked up to see the familiar face of Ronald Reagan. "It sounds like there are three lovesick mountain goats in here," he solemnly informed me.

The Japanese sure know how to pamper a guy. At the economic summit in Tokyo in April 1986 I had the best personal setup of my six years in the White House. My office was about the same size as the entire first floor of my home outside Washington. In addition to a desk, I had a conference table that would put the one in the White House Cabinet Room to shame. Each morning when I came in there would be three Japanese, two in tuxedos and one in a white coat. They would be standing more or less at attention, lined up at the door, as I walked in. They would bow, and I would bow. Then they would bow again, and I would bow again, and then we would get down to business. They would stand by my desk and whatever was my heart's desire I could have, whether it was eggs and bacon, a traditional Japanese breakfast, or just tea and toast. They would disappear silently and come back with a silver cart and a silver service. The guy in the white coat would pour the tea and one of the guys in the tux would serve the tea to me. I took to calling them the "Tea Dudes." I finally told the staff that I wanted those three guys to travel with us everywhere we went from then on.

We had come to Tokyo after a week in the air—flying from New York to L.A. to Honolulu to Bali to Japan—and I was pretty well out of clean clothes. Japan, of course, is ultra-expensive, and on my thirty-dollar-a-day

White House per diem, I couldn't afford to spend seven or eight dollars to have a shirt cleaned. But I had forgotten something that's traditional at all summits: All members of the official party are entitled to have their expenses paid by the host government. That meant cleaning, food, everything. So I became the most generous host in the world, making sure all the members of my staff were well fed and comfortable, at Japanese expense. And my entire wardrobe was cleaned and pressed when I arrived back home. It was our contribution to the war against the trade deficit.

That was one of several trips where those of us in the press office carried food with us in the aluminum boxes that we used for transporting typewriters, supplies, and other office equipment, so we wouldn't have to spend money for it over there. We would take peanut butter, crackers, cookies, little jars of jellies and jams, and a carrot cake that Sally McElroy's roommate (Sally worked in the press office) baked for us. We would also grab bread and other stuff off the Pan Am charter in order to be able to eat on these trips, because our per diem wouldn't buy a ham sandwich in a place like Tokyo or Paris.

From a sartorial standpoint I was at my best on that trip, one of my last major tours with President Reagan. When I arrived in Hawaii it was so hot that I went out and bought one of those loud flowered Hawaiian shirts and briefed the press in it. Ten days later at the summit in Tokyo, Canadian Prime Minister Brian Mulroney, seated around a table with the leaders of the seven summit nations, said in his booming voice, "Larry, where's that shirt you had on in Hawaii?"

One of the hazards of our business is reporters who can read upside down. I've come to believe they taught them how to do it in journalism school. Nothing on our desks was safe. I finally told my staff, "Let's set up a scam."

Mark Weinberg, a master of phony memos, drafted one saying that we had decided to move the press out of the White House and over to the Executive Office Building (a "gotcha" that played on their worst fear, of being evicted from their coveted West Wing quarters). We even began the memo at "Page 2," picking up right in the middle of a sentence, as if it was a page that had accidentally been left on a desk.

Saul Friedman of Knight-Ridder was the biggest offender, and we hoped we would catch him in our trap. But the one we ended up trapping was Jim Hildreth of *U.S. News & World Report*, who found our memo in a stack of papers on the desk of Flo Taussig, an assistant who sat closest to the press room door. Hildreth not only read it, he swallowed it hook, line, and sinker. He called Margaret Tutweiler in Jim Baker's office to complain. She didn't know anything about it, and she called me. I said, "This guy's bitten like a snake. He has really fallen for our trap." Hildreth made a few more phone calls within the White House, and he was about to go with a story in the next issue of *U.S. News*. Finally, on Thursday of that week, just before his deadline, I called Hildreth and told him, "You've been a victim of your own stupidity. That memo isn't true." "Are you sure?" he asked me. "Of course, we just did it to trap people like you." Hildreth was furious, and even accused *me* of dishonesty.

The press office gang also pulled the phony memo scam on one of our own, Mort Allin, the deputy press secretary for foreign affairs. If ever there was a fellow who loved his car, it was Mort. He sputtered up West Executive Avenue to his parking place outside the White House every morning in his ancient Volkswagen bus. We circulated an official-sounding memo that read, "Due to the extreme sensitivity of the balance of trade issue and the use of imported manufactured items by some members of the Reagan administration, effective immediately, all vehicles manufactured outside the continental United States shall not be allowed to park on West Executive Avenue." Mort raged at every top White House official until he found out it was a hoax.

Mark Weinberg also was the target of some of our pranks. He was immensely loyal to me and to the Reagans, and seldom took a day off, even devoting his weekends to serving as press officer at Camp David. In 1983, after two years on the job, he decided to spend a weekend with his parents in Cleveland. Upon his return he vowed, "Never again." We'd removed every notebook, pencil, and book from his office. In its place were all the office belongings of press officer Robin Gray. Mark found his every possession neatly arranged on a secretary's desk.

Mark cherished his Camp David weekends, a time when he developed a particularly close relationship with the Reagans. He spent so much time there that his social life in Washington was practically nonexistent; on the rare weekends when the Reagans stayed in Washington, Mark had little to do. During one of the annual standoffs with Congress over the budget, we faced another shutdown of the entire government for lack of funds. All nonessential personnel were to be relieved of their government duties until funds were appropriated. Heading home from a trip aboard Air Force One, we sent the President's military aide back to Mark's seat to inform him, "I'm sorry, we cannot let you fly on Marine One [the President's helicopter] to Camp David this weekend." Mark countered, "Well, get me a White House car to take me to my apartment when we land." "That's not possible either. Budget," the major replied. Mark went into a funk. When we landed at Andrews Air Force Base he wandered aimlessly on the tarmac while we tried to persuade him it was all a joke. The President finally had to come over and personally escort Mark to the waiting helicopter.

But the quick-witted Weinberg was usually the perpetrator, not the victim. One morning we were confronted with one of the occasional stock market rumors that the President had suffered a heart attack. I strode into the press room to announce that the President was "vigorous and virile, hale and hearty, . . . and somewhat bemused that he has pulled another Mark Twain. Rumors of his death are somewhat premature." The press, taking it more seriously than I, zeroed in on how we handled the rumor, which had begun on the Tokyo stock exchange at 2:00 A.M. Washington time. "Dr. Weinberg was in charge of press relations at that hour," I declared, summoning Mark into the briefing room.

"How did you determine that the President was all right?" the press asked. Weinberg didn't miss a beat. "I picked up the phone, rang the President, and said, 'Mr. President, did you have a heart attack?' He said, 'No,' and I said, 'Okay, go back to bed and phone me if you do.'"

The mainstream reporters—Sam Donaldson, Lesley Stahl, Lou Cannon, et al.—had their foibles, but for the most part were fairly solid citizens. It was the ones from the fringe organizations who tended to be flaky. The courts have ruled that under the First Amendment, we had to issue press credentials to anyone passing as the representative of a news organization, including the most obscure and limited circulation newsletters, unless they posed a threat to the safety of the President. We were not even able to exclude one would-be press person who had been arrested five times for rape. Not that we expected him to try to rape the President, but he had an established pattern of violent behavior. I guess that theoretically, if you claimed that you needed to cover the White House so that you could write a letter to your parents, your girlfriend, or whomever, we would have to admit you. The way the system worked, people would apply to my office for credentials, and, assuming their claim had any validity at all, we would pass them on to the Secret Service, who would investigate their background and then issue their White House press pass. The number of people holding press credentials averaged 1,700 throughout the Reagan administration.

Naomi Nover, a large, white-haired older lady, covered the White House under the banner of the "Nover News Service." If Naomi was printed in a single newspaper anywhere, we couldn't find it, but she was a fixture in the press room, and particularly on our foreign trips. Her husband, Barnett Nover, had founded the Nover News Service, but he died many years ago and Naomi replaced him. From time to time we challenged her on who she wrote for, and she would dig up clippings— ones that always had the date cut off, so we didn't know when or where they had been published. But she was harmless and her husband had been one of the regulars at the National Press Club bar, so no one objected very strenuously to having her around.

So much did Naomi miss and respect her late husband that she donated a refrigerator to the White House press room in his memory during the Ford administration. When Ford made his first appearance in the press room in September 1974 to announce the appointment of Ron Nessen as his new press secretary, Naomi nabbed him. "Will you dedicate the new refrigerator?" she asked. Ford hadn't the foggiest idea of what Naomi was talking about, much less how one goes about dedicating a refrigerator. Nevertheless, we arranged for a presidential dedication—by letter.

Naomi's legend continued to grow during the Reagan years. During our April 1984 trip to China, she was attempting to work her way past a Chinese guard to observe the President viewing the ancient terra cotta figures that had been unearthed by archeologists at Xian. The guard knew no English and certainly had no idea who Naomi was. He wasn't about to budge until Gary Schuster of CBS flashed a dollar bill. He pointed to the engraving of a bewigged George Washington on the bill and then gestured to Naomi, who, with her white hair carefully gathered into a bun on the back of her head, resembled the first President. "Important person in America," Schuster said. "Her picture. On our money." The Chinese guard quickly stepped aside.

One thing I will never forget about the Chinese is that as we traveled through the countryside the officials would have arranged for the residents to turn out to watch us, and these peasants were totally expressionless. Just a complete blank wall. Occasionally when we waved we would get a tentative wave back from someone in the crowd, but that was rare.

I had the same Chinese driver the whole time I was there. The drivers were assigned through the U.S. Information Agency, and you always suspected they were intelligence people. But the guy never spoke a word, never appeared to understand a word of English. One day some of us were sitting in the backseat and someone said, "Gosh, it's hot in here." And the driver immediately lowered the windows.

I was well-known in the world's most populous nation long before we visited there. During a 1981 press briefing I referred to the "government of Taiwan," which does not exist, as far as the People's Republic is concerned, since Taiwan is viewed as merely a province of the mainland.

The New China News Agency observed that "The remarks of Mr. Speaks are both ludicrous and stupid." Well, nobody's perfect.

Another of the stellar characters in the press room was Lester Kinsolving, who had been an Episcopal minister but had hung up his cleric's robes to heed a higher calling, that of correspondent for an obscure outfit called the Globe Syndicate. Kinsolving was a thorn in the side of press secretaries dating back to Ron Ziegler, and his attempts to steal the show at press conferences and briefings didn't win him any friends in the press corps, either.

Once, when we were traveling with President Ford during the 1976 campaign, Kinsolving had a run-in with ever dapper NBC radio correspondent Russ Ward, who was attired that day in a dazzling white suit that would have made Colonel Sanders envious. We'd picked up some sandwiches on the press buses as we worked our way across Ohio in a motorcade. Kinsolving stomped a plastic catsup container and the catsup shot out with such force that it splattered all over Ward's suit. Kinsolving claimed it was an accident, but he couldn't convince the usually mild-mannered Ward, who shouted at Kinsolving (this was back while Kinsolving still was a minister), "You're nothing but a gorilla in a priest suit!"

That's not the end of the story. The sandwiches had come from one of our stops, where the ladies' club from the local church was selling them. Someone whispered to me that Lester had taken the sandwich without paying. Shortly before our next stop, I got on the microphone at the front of the bus and announced, "The Secret Service has informed us they have an inquiry from the Sheriff's Department. Someone failed to pay for their lunch at the last stop. We will not be allowed to cross the county line unless the culprit comes forward to confess and pay the ladies of the church." Silence. Again I made the announcement, adding, "We're a mile from the county line." Kinsolving sheepishly came forward and forked over the money as the boys and girls on the bus roared with delight.

Lester continued to distinguish himself during the Reagan years. He caught the attention of the President himself at press conferences because he would often ask Reagan a question, no matter whom the President had called on. Reagan finally remarked, "My finger must be crooked—every time I point at somebody, Lester Kinsolving starts asking a question."

Lester also enlivened one slow summer briefing in August 1982, when he started asking me about a report that the government hired people regardless of their sexual preference. He and I had the following exchange:

KINSOLVING: Does President Reagan believe that the United States should be represented by all the many kinds of announced sexual preference or not?

SPEAKES: I haven't heard him advocate a quota system of sexual preferences for federal employees.

KINSOLVING: I understand that. Does he believe that you should hire all kinds of sexual preferences? I mean, there is a wide variety.

ANOTHER REPORTER: How many kinds are there, Lester?

KINSOLVING: Well, there is necrophilia, bestiality, sodomy. . . . I just want to know, where does the President stand on this?

SPEAKES: Is there a serious question anywhere here?

But Lester did get the best of me once. He used to wear this huge tape recorder, suspended by a strap around his neck, and it hung down to his stomach. He looked like an organ-grinder, and I always used to ask him where his monkey was. I must have asked him that question once too often, because he finally responded, "I don't need a monkey as long as you're here."

Kinsolving never lacked for imagination. Once, taking his cue from the theory that female reporters who wore Nancy Reagan's favorite color, red, would get the nod for questions during press conferences, he showed up for a news conference clad in a fire-engine-red jacket. It worked; the President called on him.

Johanna Neuman of *USA Today* quickly caught on. When she raised her hand during a press conference, she was wearing a red glove. She, too, got to ask a question.

Another one who often managed to get called on, even though she didn't wear red, was Evelyn Y. Davis, the bane of many corporate stockholders' meetings, who had obtained press credentials. I used to seat her behind some potted plants at the rear of the East Room, and show the President where she was sitting, so that he wouldn't call on her. Invariably, though, he would recognize her for a question. "Why did you call on her?" I'd ask him. "I don't know," Reagan would say. "I know I made a mistake, but she just jumped out from behind those potted flowers."

The press has a reputation for mooching, and it's well-deserved. I used to serve coffee and pastries to the press corps every Friday morning, and Jerry O'Leary of the *Washington Times* would stuff them in his pocket and eat them all through the day. Another notorious scavenger was Helen Thomas, who used to work from 7:00 A.M. until 8:00 P.M. nearly every day and was always looking for something to eat. I once gave her a lollipop that had jalapeño all through it and would leave a burn in your mouth for days. That stopped Helen from scarfing around for food for a while.

My tenure at the White House wasn't all fun and games. During Reagan's vacations in Santa Barbara, all sorts of California crazies started crashing the press briefings, which were held in an unguarded room at our hotel. Once, while I stood behind the podium, T.V. lights limiting my vision to the first few rows of press, someone shouted from the back of the room, "Larry Speakes speaks lies." I made out a shadowy figure menacingly pointing an extended arm out of the darkness directly at me. Then, to his left, someone else shouted, "Larry Speakes speaks lies." And again, until a dozen figures were shouting at me. As they exited the press room, they splattered a red liquid over their T-shirts, symbolizing blood, and chanted against our Central American policy.

On our next visit to Santa Barbara, a similar chant erupted—this time on the street outside the press room. As the briefing continued, the "Larry Speakes speaks lies" got closer and closer. Suddenly, the protesters pushed open a door at the side of the press room. A half-dozen newsmen, putting aside their devotion to the First Amendment, threw their bodies against the door. As the protesters sought to crash the briefing, the press guys, whole-heartedly on my side for a change, manned the barricades and kept them out.

Fame has its moments, but I quickly learned that all press secretaries must look alike. Congressman John Duncan of Tennessee profusely praised my deft handling of the press once as he flew aboard Air Force One on a trip to his home state. "You've got to be the best there ever was, *Ron*," he told me. I never found out whether he thought I was Ron Ziegler or Ron Nessen.

Another time, during a trip to Los Angeles, a lovely couple stopped me outside the hotel. "I know who you are. You're Jody Powell," they said, almost in unison. They asked for my autograph, and not wanting to disappoint them, I signed, "Best wishes, Jody Powell."

It seems fitting that I should wind up on Wall Street. One of the biggest goofs while I was White House spokesman concerned the stock market. We were flying down to New Orleans on Air Force One and I stopped by the press area for my usual chitchat. The subject quickly turned to the Federal Reserve Board and whether the board members might raise or lower interest rates when they met the next day. Later, a transcript of our conversation was given to me and I scanned it without paying much attention. I let it run as it was, and when we landed in New Orleans, it was distributed to the other reporters who had flown down on the press plane.

When I got to my room at the hotel, my phone was ringing. It was Pete Roussel calling to ask me, "What have you said?" Now, those are the most chilling words a press secretary can hear. I had no idea what had happened, until Pete informed me that "the stock market has gone up ten points in the last ten minutes." I tossed the phone on my bed and made a beeline for the press room, where I discovered that the pool report, written by Sara Fritz of the *Los Angeles Times*, had quoted me as saying that the Federal Reserve was going to take steps to reduce interest rates. That was ridiculous on its face, because nobody had any way of knowing what they were going to do. Meanwhile, though, Reuters had picked up Fritz's report and moved a story about my alleged remarks. I confronted Fritz in what developed into a very loud argument over the accuracy of the pool report. I think she just got it wrong and refused to admit it. She would not change the pool report, but she agreed to do an addendum, saying that I denied predicting that rates would go down.

Immediately after my misquote was corrected, the market dropped eight points. Little did I realize my power in financial circles. We made two points on the Larry Speakes rally.

16

Seeds of

Catastrophe

During the 1980 campaign, Ronald Reagan made a promise that he would live to regret. He told voters he would downgrade the position of national security adviser. It was a pledge he set out to keep, but all he succeeded in doing was to allow two of his foreign policy directors, Bud McFarlane and John Poindexter, to get out of control.

Not only did Reagan attempt to diminish the role of the National Security Council director, but most of his selections for the post were poor ones. None of the first four NSC directors under Reagan—Richard Allen, William Clark, McFarlane, and Poindexter—had a forceful personality or the stature to help Reagan conduct foreign policy properly.

At the same time, strong-willed Cabinet officers like George Shultz and Caspar Weinberger were constantly at odds over foreign policy, leaving the Reagan administration in a quagmire of feudal bickering on such issues as arms control, U.S.-Soviet relations, the Middle East, Central America, and South Africa. You name it, Shultz and Weinberger would debate it—often in a debilitating public controversy that sent alarming signals of disarray to friend and foe abroad. Our allies, in particular, wondered why we couldn't get our act together, and the press had a field day.

Ideally, the NSC director should have been able to exert a positive influence, but Reagan's first four were too mediocre a lot to be of help.

264

And he changed them like he would change underwear. In the first thirty-eight years after the post of national security adviser was created in 1953 to help the President and the National Security Council coordinate foreign policy, ten people held the job. Each one averaged nearly four years of duty.

In less than seven years, through late 1987, Ronald Reagan had no fewer than six directors of national security. Allen, Clark, McFarlane, and Poindexter averaged less than a year and a half on the job. Considering their talents, it's a blessing for the country that they didn't last longer. It wasn't until January 1987, when Reagan appointed Frank Carlucci, that he filled the job of national security director with someone who had the proper qualifications.

Carlucci undoubtedly would have served the remaining two years of Reagan's term with distinction had he not been tapped to move over and replace Cap Weinberger as Secretary of Defense when Weinberger resigned in November 1987. And it appears that the President and his chief of staff, Howard Baker, didn't learn a lesson from past mistakes; to succeed Carlucci as NSC director, they promoted Carlucci's deputy, Lieutenant General Colin Powell.

As the first black to head the NSC, Powell may prove to be a wise choice, but he fits exactly the same pattern as two of his predecessors, Bud McFarlane and John Poindexter, career military men who were moved up from the number-two job at the NSC, with unfortunate results. (Congress recognized the problem with having people like McFarlane and Poindexter as NSC director, and, in the wake of the Iran-Contra affair, recommended that a career military officer not be placed in the job.)

The President's appointment of Powell was the lazy man's approach, the same as when McFarlane and Poindexter were promoted: "I don't think much of this job, and you happen to be sitting there in the number-two spot, so I'll take the easy way out and make you number one." More thought should have been given to selecting a national security director each time the job was open, especially at the start of the Reagan administration, when someone like Carlucci or former NSC director Brent Scowcroft should have been picked; either of them likely would have remained for all or most of Reagan's term. As it was, having six different NSC directors has caused a real lack of continuity in a critical position.

Moreover, the President and his top aides—Jim Baker, Ed Meese, Mike Deaver, and Don Regan—had such low regard for the position of NSC director that they paid little attention to those who held the post. Without proper supervision, the NSC heads were left free to do their own thing.

For one national security adviser, Bud McFarlane, doing his own thing meant sending weapons to our archenemy, Iran, in the misguided hope of freeing Americans who had been taken hostage in Lebanon. McFarlane's successor, John Poindexter, made a bad situation worse by permitting an aide, Ollie North, to take millions of dollars the Iranians paid for arms and divert it to the Nicaraguan Contras. The result was the worst foreign policy blunder of the entire Reagan administration.

Making the national security adviser a technician without adequate supervision led to chaos. President Reagan failed to compensate for his own inexperience—and sometimes his downright disinterest—in foreign policy.

The Reagan approach was entirely different from that of two other recent Presidents: Nixon, who dominated foreign policy in his first term, along with Henry Kissinger, his national security director, leaving Secretary of State William Rogers out in the cold; and Jimmy Carter, who had a similar arrangement with Zbigniew Brzezinski at the expense of his first secretary of state, Cyrus Vance. You don't have to like Kissinger or Brzezinski or approve of their method of operation to appreciate their raw intellectual talent and their ability to see the world from a strategic and historic perspective.

In Washington, more than anywhere else, proximity is power. There are three crucial differences between the secretary of state and the national security adviser—location, location, and location, as they say in real estate. The office of the national security adviser is in the White House, just down the hall and around the corner from the Oval Office, while the secretary of state is over at Foggy Bottom. Although the State Department is only a few blocks away, it's light-years in Washington terms.

Reagan's NSC directors started off without clout, but their proximity to the President did give them access, and, eventually, more power than Reagan had intended. Starting in 1982, a thirty-minute block of time was set aside daily for the national security adviser to see the President. By contrast, Reagan's first secretary of state, Alexander Haig, had to ask Mike Deaver for an appointment to see the President, and Haig's successor, Shultz, got two thirty-minute meetings a week with Reagan only after Shultz threw a tantrum.

There was one more key element that led to the Iran fiasco. No one in the foreign policy turf battle trusted anyone else. All of the key players in the Iran initiative—Reagan, McFarlane, Poindexter, North, and CIA director William Casey—were obsessed with secrecy. I was kept in the dark, when a discussion of the impact of public disclosure of some of their unfortunate actions might have prevented these disasters from occurring.

Without a coordinated plan for the public relations side of foreign policy, the Reagan administration became a veritable sieve of leaking information. Top-secret plans were splashed across the front pages of the *Washington Post* and other newspapers almost daily. State blamed the White House, the White House blamed Defense, and the CIA blamed everybody.

With all the elements for catastrophe in place, Bud McFarlane had the germ of an idea: a strategic opening to political factions in Iran, which had officially been branded a terrorist nation by the State Department and a country that, along with Libya, was blamed for nearly every act of terrorism against the U.S. since Reagan took office.

McFarlane proposed following tenuous links that *might* lead us to moderates in the Iranian government, moderates who *might* rule the strategically located nation in the post-Khomeini era. Shultz and Weinberger quickly saw McFarlane's plan for the folly it was—a recipe for disaster in American foreign policy. They made their arguments to the President, but he was obsessed with the fate of American hostages, and he ignored their pleadings. Shultz and Weinberger then opted out—or, more to the point with Shultz, he was cut out by Poindexter, who didn't trust him.

Thus, President Reagan was deprived of the advice of his two most senior and capable Cabinet members who knew the most about the issues. And the execution of the Iran opening—which McFarlane thought might rival Kissinger's successful overture to China—was left in the hands of two foreign policy novices, McFarlane and Poindexter, the second of whom turned the whole thing over to a swashbuckling marine lieutenant colonel who had even less experience.

No wonder the whole thing blew up in our faces!

The Big Three during Reagan's first term—Jim Baker, Ed Meese, and Mike Deaver—couldn't have agreed more with the President's decision to reduce the role of the NSC director, since that left them with one less competitor. Having decided to diminish the power of the NSC director, the troika quickly found the right men for the job. First there was Richard Allen, a veteran of the conservative elements of academia, like the Center for Strategic and International Studies at Georgetown and the Hoover Institution at Stanford. He had established his credentials with Meese and other Reaganites by advising Reagan on foreign policy during the two years leading up to Reagan's election in 1980. Allen was the first NSC head in many years who did not have direct access to the President; he had to report through Meese. Allen himself outlined the emasculation of his role when he met with the press right after he got the job and told reporters, "You're seeing a disappearing act right now."

Allen was a right-wing ideologue whose disdain for the press was obvious. So the reporters were always looking to bring him down, and they finally found what they had been searching for. The day after the Reagans moved into the White House in January 1981, Nancy Reagan granted an interview to a Japanese magazine, which Allen helped arrange. The editors of the magazine gave Allen $1,000 in cash as a token of their "gratitude." Allen said he thought he would offend the Japanese if he declined the money, but he knew he couldn't give it to Mrs. Reagan and he knew it would be wrong for him to spend it, so he just put it in the safe in his office, and forgot about it. The following September someone cleaned out his safe, found the money, and notified the FBI, which started investigating Allen. Allen was cleared of wrongdoing over receiving the money, but then it turned out he had accepted several watches from another Japanese friend and he had put some incorrect information on his financial disclosure forms. The press wouldn't let the story die, and Allen was forced to resign right after New Year's of 1982.

I always thought the Allen controversy was unfair and overblown. Allen told the truth about the $1,000 payment on the first day, and his story still stood up six months later, after the most thorough FBI investigation. And the watches and the problem with his disclosure form were small-time stuff. But Reagan had to let Allen go because the press was after him.

Allen may have used bad judgment, but not bad enough to lose his job. Nevertheless, he was the first person in the Reagan administration to be hounded out of office by the press. Reporters resented Allen's arrogance and his refusal to talk to them, and they were determined to get him. That was the beginning of the 6:00 A.M. stakeout outside the target's home, which the press later perfected as an art form with Ollie North and Don Regan. When you saw the cameras outside your home at dawn, you could start counting your days.

When Allen was forced out, the Baker-Meese-Deaver team found an even more lackluster replacement, William Clark. Clark was another decent man, but he had absolutely no experience in foreign affairs. Clark was basically a California rancher and a small-time lawyer, but Reagan made him his chief of staff when he was governor and appointed him to three California judgeships, capped off by the state supreme court. And then, right after he entered the White House, Reagan named Clark to a key foreign policy post, as the number-two guy at the State Department—and Clark embarrassed both himself and the administration during his Senate confirmation hearings in February 1981.

During those confirmation hearings for the job of deputy secretary of state, Clark admitted that he did not know the names of the leaders of Zimbabwe or South Africa; he couldn't list which of our European allies were reluctant to have nuclear weapons based on their soil; and he was unable to articulate any personal opinions on a wide range of foreign policy topics. Clark was confirmed, but the overseas press had a field day: An Amsterdam newspaper called Clark a "nitwit"; the headline in the London *Daily Express* was "Ask Me Another"; another London paper, the *Daily Mirror*, mentioned Europe and added, "Europe, Mr. Clark, you must have heard of it"; and Tass said that Clark "knows nothing about foreign policy." I was just thanking my lucky stars at the time that I wasn't Clark's press secretary.

In spite of Clark's lack of expertise in foreign policy, he was named to succeed Allen, and his long association with Reagan gave him enough clout to demand that, unlike Allen, he would report directly to the President. But in picking someone as unqualified for the job as Bill Clark, the troika again made sure that the new NSC director would never present a challenge to them. One thing Clark did do, and this was a big plus: He kept the President fully briefed on everything, almost overbriefed. That was in contrast to when Dick Allen was on the job and he was not around Reagan enough to keep him sufficiently briefed.

Still, Clark was in over his head, as I witnessed personally. The only time I was questioned by the FBI as part of an investigation into a news leak occurred in 1982 or 1983 as a result of one of the first secret missions to the Middle East by Bud McFarlane, then Clark's deputy. We in the White House were keeping mum about Bud's trip to Beirut for fear that he might become a target of the terrorists, but Lou Cannon reported in the *Washington Post* that Bud was over there.

Clark was determined to find the leak. As I reconstructed events, I discovered that what had happened was that Lou had written a front-page story on the issue of the day—White House debates on Middle East policy—but Chris Wallace of NBC, not Lou, had actually gotten the scoop about Bud's trip. Chris had a story on the evening news at six-thirty, a few hours before the early editions of the *Post* came out, quoting "White House sources" as saying that Bud was in Lebanon. It was quite obvious to me that Lou had written an article on the same general subject without reporting Bud's whereabouts and then Lou wrote a new lead for his story after seeing Wallace on NBC News. I stressed that to the FBI agents who questioned me—although they weren't sophisticated enough about the news business to understand the point I was making. The FBI and Clark didn't even know that the story had been on NBC first. I thought it was Dave Gergen who had leaked the story to Wallace, because Gergen talked so much to Wallace, and I gently steered the FBI agents in that direction, without any success. In any event, they never did find out who was responsible for that leak—or for any other leak, and, God knows, the Reagan White House was fertile ground. Ironically, the two FBI agents who talked to me looked at my schedule and my phone logs for that day, and Lou Cannon happened to be on my phone log, but he had called me on something else.

Clark's attempt to discover who tipped Cannon about McFarlane's trip to Lebanon was typical of the thinking among the NSC's top staffers throughout my six years in the White House, and it contributed mightily to the atmosphere that culminated in the Iran arms scandal. In 1986, when John Poindexter was head of the NSC, he and his aides drafted a national security directive on how to control leaks and punish them. Poindexter's people even talked about polygraphing to detect leaks, and they wanted to create a strike force of FBI agents to investigate leaks. Of course, such a strike force wouldn't have been much of a threat to the leakers or to the recipients of their stories, unless the FBI agents assigned to it were a lot sharper than the ones who had questioned me.

Don Regan and I joined forces to kill Poindexter's anti-leak campaign. Given the way people like to gossip and cultivate the press, there was no way you could completely shut off the leaks, and Poindexter's plan, if put into effect, would itself have become public and been a major embarrassment to the administration. At a very high level meeting on the issue, George Shultz—who was violently opposed to the use of lie detectors and in December 1985 had threatened to quit rather than submit to a polygraph examination himself—sided with Don and me, while Poindexter and Bill Casey wanted to do everything possible to muzzle the leakers and the press.

Allen, Clark, McFarlane, Poindexter, and Casey, as well as Jim Baker, Meese, and Deaver, were obsessed with the idea of keeping the press in the dark. I wish that they had consulted me on things like the Iran-Contra arms deal, to find out how it would play if it did get into the press. I would have told them that most Americans would *never* have stood for sending arms to Iran, which had held our embassy people hostage for more than a year before Reagan entered office and has been our worst enemy for years. The American people had accepted the need for giving military aide to unsavory characters like Ferdinand Marcos and the Shah of Iran, but the idea of sending weapons to the Ayatollah just boggles the mind—or at least the mind of anybody who understands public opinion.

But this was another instance, like Grenada, where my role was untenable. The White House press corps viewed me as their adversary, as someone who was a mouthpiece for the administration. Unfortunately for me, many top officials at the White House also viewed me as an adversary, as a reporter who represented the press corps. I once told Jim Baker, "I'm not the UPI. You've got to understand that." But Baker, Meese, and later McFarlane, Poindexter, et al. had a built-in attitude that the press office is the press. I could only say what they told me, so if they didn't tell me much, I couldn't say a lot to the press. They had no understanding that what I was authorized to say would only get me past the first question and not past the ninety-nine that would follow.

The press corps was correct; my job was to speak for the White House. It was the NSC directors, along with Casey, Baker, Meese, and Deaver, who were mistaken; I was part of their team and should have been treated as such from the start. But Reagan and his top advisers, dating all the way back to 1967, when he became governor of California, had always viewed the press with attitudes ranging from suspicion to downright hostility.

Even the troika had to admit after almost two years that Bill Clark was the wrong man for the job of NSC director. They finally moved him over to replace James Watt as Secretary of the Interior when Watt was forced out in October 1983.

Whenever I think of the man whom Reagan and the troika picked to succeed Clark as national security director, I still can't believe it. Al Haig, who had worked with McFarlane back in the Nixon administration, once arched his eyebrows and said to me with astonishment, "Bud McFarlane, the NSC adviser?"

You would assume that someone who was at least nominally in charge of national *security* would undergo the most thorough security investigation before being approved for the job. Yet that must not have been true in Bud McFarlane's case, for he was one of the most bizarre characters I ever met.

Bud was a career marine officer whom I had first known in the Nixon and Ford administrations, when he served as military assistant to Henry Kissinger and as a national security aide in the White House. I think Bud wanted desperately to be a Kissinger or a Brzezinski. He liked to project a thoughtful, ponderous image, as they did (although he lacked the accent, of course), but he couldn't bring it off. He used so many twenty-five-dollar words that one suspected he took the dictionary and read through it to prepare himself for White House meetings and sessions with the press. Not long before he resigned, he dropped the word "prescience" on an unsuspecting press corps during a briefing. Unfortunately, he underscored the fact that prescience was not a regular part of his vocabulary by pronouncing it "pre-science" instead of the correct *"pres*-e-ence." McFarlane also had a habit of inserting the occasional Latin phrase into his conversations, and he loved to back up and give historical and strategic perspective, with long pauses and a very deliberate style of speech. Members of the media told me that as a result, they found many of his briefings extremely boring.

I got to know Bud very well and had a chance to observe him at close range, because during the two-plus years he was NSC director, he and I spoke almost every morning to discuss how to present foreign policy matters to the press. We spent an especially large amount of time together during the TWA hijacking in June 1985, when he was assigned to give me detailed reports of the meetings involving the President and the advisers who were working on that crisis.

The mention of Bud's name brings a number of vignettes to mind:

- Bud's strange behavior during overseas trips. He would hang around the press room late at night, for no apparent reason. Oftentimes during these press-room visits he would make erratic statements about what was happening on the trip. I often wondered if he'd had too much wine at a state banquet. Sometimes he'd spill a lot of beans that he wasn't supposed to. Once, during the London Economic Summit in 1984, he was highly critical of Margaret Thatcher, which was totally out of line.

Then there was the incident during the President's visit to Portugal in 1985. Rick Burt, the assistant secretary for European affairs at the State Department; Peter Sommer, one of Bud's aides; and I were in a car, riding over to the palace where the summit talks were held. Rick was incensed about leaks that were coming out of the meetings. He asked me who was doing the leaking. I said it was Bud, and Rick agreed. A short while later, at a luncheon hosted by Portugal's prime minister in a palace atop a mountain overlooking the sea, Bud walked up to me and said angrily, "I understand you think I've been talking to the press too much. Well, you can just take this and shove it," and he handed me a note I had written to him that read, "They want you for an interview on Cable News Network."

• One New Year's Day when we were in Palm Springs, my phone rang very early, and he said, "Larrrry?" with his measured tone. I had no doubt who it was, and I replied, "Buuuud." Then Bud hit me with what I guess he thought was a blockbuster: "I've spent the last two or three days contemplating our foreign policy goals." I said to myself, "Well, that's what you get paid to do." He went on, "I'm not sure we're articulating them well to the press corps, particularly to television. Do you think it would be a good idea if we gathered some of the television types together for an off-the-record briefing?"

I hung up the phone and called Bill Plante of CBS and I said, "Plante, I don't know whether you want to do this or not. Bud has come up with this idea. I don't want to fool with it, and I imagine you don't either, but he wants to have this session. Do you want to gather your troops?" Plante got a few of the network correspondents together and they went into the bar of our hotel, where McFarlane launched into a long discussion; eventually, they had to adjourn to the lobby because the bar was too noisy. This extraordinary, off-the-record interview proceeded, an informational thing, in which Bud dumped on the workability of the MX missile system, the strategy of arms control negotiation, and so forth. Everything we were pursuing, he knocked down. The people who were there told me it was really odd. Sam Donaldson figured out a way to circumvent its being off-the-record. He told Jody Powell about the session with Bud, and Jody wrote a whole column on what Bud had said.

McFarlane was also the subject of rumors that he was having an affair with a T.V. correspondent. The stories started when we were traveling, maybe in the '84 campaign. One night Bud and the woman reporter were down at the end of the bar in this long, intimate conversation. I'm sure that conversation was nothing more than a discussion of foreign policy. But that led to speculation. Then later, there were times, many times, when somebody would ring up from the White House pressroom around five or five-thirty in the afternoon, and say, "Guess what, Bud's in the briefing room." Many times he asked a reporter for change for the cigarette machine. The trouble was, Bud didn't smoke. Or he would ask a reporter for change for the candy machine, when he could have sent his secretary down to the mess to get whatever he wanted. So he was making excuses to come to the press room.

The reporter, meanwhile, seemed to have a pipeline into the White House. She seemed to know a lot that none of the other reporters knew. She used to preface her questions to me with things like, "Some in your administration are saying," and that "some" could only be Bud; Bud was a super source for her at the very least. Bud, in his strange and naive way, may have thought she was receptive to our message, which to some extent she was, that she was intelligent, which she was, and that this was a good reporter to cultivate as an avenue to put out information.

Once, Secretary Shultz was addressing the press corps on a sensitive foreign policy decision. The woman asked a tough question and Shultz declined to answer. He did reply, "When we make our decision, I'm sure you'll be the first to know."

Finally, on a trip to California, Bud asked if we could talk for a few minutes. I knew what was coming. "Have you heard these rumors about me?" he asked me. I said I had. He asked, "What do you suggest I do about them? There's absolutely nothing to them." I said, "Well, I don't doubt that, Bud. Quite frankly, I would confront them head-on, privately, off the record. Sam is one of the main guys who's stirring things up, so you ought to talk to Sam and tell him it's not true." And I think he did. Sam had led the press corps, really whipped them about the alleged affair. The television reporters were the main ones who had been victimized by the leads she was getting, and Sam had actually confronted his network rival about it.

- Shades of Al Haig: Bud was miffed during the Geneva summit conference with Gorbachev in November of 1985 because he didn't get to ride in the right limousine and wasn't seated at the proper place at the conference table. In Haig's case the snubs were real, but in Bud's they were just perceived. Even so, Bud resigned soon after the summit. I told Don Regan that that was clearly not the real reason why Bud left. I told Regan, "For a man to give up being foreign policy adviser to the President of the United States because he thought he wasn't seated properly at the table strikes me as an awfully weak excuse." And Regan agreed. Bud quit a very powerful and visible job, and quit without a job in hand, because of pure fatigue, I think. He just got tired of refereeing spats between Shultz and Weinberger and Shultz and the White House.

Regan was accused of forcing McFarlane out of office, but he was completely baffled by Bud's departure. He said over and over, "I didn't do anything to him." Regan was also said to have been behind the rumors about Bud and the T.V. reporter, but that just wasn't true. There wasn't even that much friction between Don and Bud, except over the time Bud scheduled King Hussein's session with the press, and over the times that Bud slipped things into the President's daily intelligence briefing without Don's approval.

- Something I didn't witness personally, but was certainly in keeping with what I did observe: The Reverend Benjamin Weir, who was one of the American hostages in Lebanon, and his wife, Carol, wrote in their book about Weir's ordeal *(Hostage Bound, Hostage Free)* that Bud acted very erratically at the time of Weir's release in September 1985, after Weir had spent sixteen months in captivity. Mrs. Weir reported that "Mr. McFarlane started out in a controlled voice, telling me that the government had spent millions to get Ben released. He accused me of being difficult and ungrateful. Finally he shouted, 'I'm tired of you, young lady!' [a puzzling thing for Bud to have said, because Mrs. Weir is several years older than Bud] and slammed down the receiver." Bud may have been agitated and under severe strain when he spoke to Mrs. Weir, but imagine how traumatic the situation was for her, having had to worry about her husband all that time.
- November 20, 1986, when the *Washington Post* reported that Bud said the Reagan administration had made a "mistake" by sending arms to Iran in hopes of obtaining the release of the hostages. Those of us in the White House just couldn't believe Bud had said something like that; it was he who had devised the arms-for-hostages scheme when he was national security adviser.

About eight-thirty the morning the *Post* story broke, my phone rang and it was Bud. He was out of town giving a speech somewhere, but his wife had called him and read him the story. He gave me some explanation that was so convoluted it was unbelievable. This was obviously Bud's first self-examination of what he had done and some of the problems caused by the sale of arms to Iran. He kept emphasizing that the arms deal had been well-intended, and insisted that the *Post* story misrepresented his views. I think Bud had spoken to Lou Cannon without realizing how what he said would look in the cold light of print. I got off the phone and told my staff it was the doggonedest phone conversation I had ever had. I had no earthly idea what he was trying to tell me.

- Finally, and tragically, Bud's taking an overdose of Valium in a suicide attempt in February 1987, while he was under investigation about the Iranian arms deal. Bud was the kind of guy who would hold his hand over a candle and let it burn, to show his commitment to the cause. My guess is that as all the details about the Iran-Contra affair came out, he decided to take all the blame himself.

Bud was bright, a hard worker, and, above all, patriotic. He was probably the best of the bunch of NSC directors—the initial foursome of him, Allen, Clark, and John Poindexter—but Bud certainly was no superstar.

After McFarlane quit in December 1985, John Poindexter was named to replace him. Like McFarlane, Poindexter was a career military officer, a vice admiral, who was being promoted from deputy director of national security to the top job. In addition to his other shortcomings, Poindexter was a poor manager and had little understanding of the care and feeding of members of Congress.

One thing I want to emphasize is that both McFarlane and Poindexter had direct access to the President without going through Regan. Whether or not McFarlane and Poindexter told the President what was happening on Iran is one question, but Don Regan has been unfairly blamed for the Iranian scandal; he was outside of the loop on a deal like that. Ironically, Regan recommended Poindexter to the President for the job when McFarlane resigned, believing that Poindexter was an easygoing guy who would be a team player, would not seek the spotlight—as Bud had done, we thought, a little too much—and would not be a maverick NSC director who would give him problems.

Regan generally did not intervene in foreign policy—I never saw him try to shape foreign policy in any of the meetings, because he did not consider himself an expert. Generally in meetings of the NSC or the National Security Planning Group, which included the President, Vice President Bush, Casey, Weinberger, Shultz, the NSC director, and Regan, Regan would withhold comment until the end. Then he would usually play devil's advocate, saying "Let's be sure before we make a final decision here that we have considered everything."

Regan didn't hire anybody for the NSC, he didn't know the people who worked for Bud or John, and he was not directly involved in the whole Iranian arms deal and the diversion of funds to the Contras.

Poindexter was forced to resign on November 25, 1986, the day the White House disclosed that funds from the Iran arms sales had been diverted to the Contras. Frank Carlucci was named to succeed him. On credentials alone, Carlucci was by far the best choice among the six Reagan has made for NSC director. He was fifty-six when he was appointed, and he was not only several years older than his four predecessors, Allen, Clark, McFarlane, and Poindexter, were when they got the job; he was wiser as well. He had the kind of varied background, much of it in foreign policy, you would look for in a national security adviser. Carlucci had been a foreign service officer; ambassador to Portugal under Ford and Carter; and a high-ranking official at the Office of Economic Development, the Office of Management and Budget, the Department of Health, Education, and Welfare, the CIA, and the Pentagon. He had also held a top post in the private sector, as president of Sears World Trade. I didn't get to know Carlucci that well because he came aboard just one month before I left the White House, but, in view of his background, I'm not surprised that there were no major screwups on his watch.

When they selected Carlucci for the job, Reagan and Regan finally locked the barn door. But the horse was already out.

17

Arms to Iran,

Dollars to the Contras

At the moment Ronald Reagan took office as the forticth President of the United States on the West Front of the Capitol on January 20, 1981, I was standing behind the podium in the White House briefing room. I was conducting the first press briefing of the Reagan administration. The subject: Iran. The fifty-two American diplomats, held hostage for fifteen months, were aboard an airplane poised for takeoff at the end of a runway at Teheran's airport.

Six years and 1,999 press briefings later, I met with the press for the last time on January 30, 1987. The subject: Iran. Several Americans had been kidnapped in Lebanon and held by Iranian-backed terrorists, and renegade members of the Reagan administration had shipped arms to Iran in hopes of securing the captives' release.

As the Reagan years progressed, the number of Middle East terrorist incidents aimed at the United States mounted. President Reagan became increasingly frustrated and ever more determined to gain the hostages' freedom. "I pray every day that all Americans will be released," he told the Reverend Benjamin Weir, a Presbyterian missionary, when Weir visited the Oval Office on September 19, 1985, several days after Weir's release from sixteen months of being held hostage by radical Shiite Muslims in Lebanon.

In private moments, the President put it more bluntly: "The bastards—we ought to string them up in a public square." The incidents that concerned him the most were the bombing of the Marine Corps barracks in Beirut in 1983; the hijackings of the TWA plane and the *Achille Lauro* in 1985; and the March 16, 1984, kidnapping of William Buckley, the CIA station chief at the U.S. Embassy in Beirut. The Islamic Jihad group brutally tortured Buckley for more than a year before he died in their custody in June 1985, and our intelligence operatives had obtained video-tapes and still photos of Buckley wasting away under torture, which the President and many of us in the White House viewed with horror.

A few weeks after Buckley's murder, as the President emerged from anesthesia following surgery at Bethesda Naval Hospital to remove a malignant tumor from his intestine, Reagan authorized National Security Council director Bud McFarlane to ship weapons to Iran via Israel, in hopes of securing the release of Americans held hostage in Lebanon. That was the first of several times in 1985 and 1986 that President Reagan gave approval to McFarlane and his successor, John Poindexter, to send arms to Iran.

Reagan's justification for the arms shipments was that they would gain us leverage with the so-called moderate elements in Iran. I know that the President and perhaps McFarlane and Poindexter really believed that, but almost everyone else involved—Americans, Iranians, and Israelis—recognized the shipments for what they were: bribes that were intended to lead to the release of the hostages. The arms shipments undermined America's credibility with other nations, especially our allies, whom we had enjoined never to cooperate with terrorists.

When the phone rang in my room at the Sheraton Santa Barbara at three o'clock on the morning of Sunday, November 2, 1986, I wasn't surprised that my caller was a reporter, Cable News Network correspondent Frank Sesno, with an urgent inquiry about stories from the Middle East that one of the American hostages was being released. Based on discussions I had had with National Security Director John Poindexter shortly before midnight about the impending release of what we thought would be two hostages, I told Sesno that the White House could not comment, but I added unofficially that there was probably a ring of truth to the story.

Soon after my conversation with Poindexter, he had had a courier from the White House Communications Agency deliver me a note in his handwriting that read, "Larry, *eyes only.* I called the President at 12:09 [A.M. Sunday] and told him we had one [David Jacobsen, the director of the American University Hospital in Beirut, who had been kidnapped on

May 28, 1985] and were awaiting a second. I told him we would announce either one or two depending on the circumstances. Here's the announcement and background for answering questions. I will call you when it's time to release." In fact, the first draft of the President's statement said, "I am pleased to announce that *two* of the American hostages in Beirut have been released." We initially thought that one of two other American hostages, Thomas Sutherland or Terry Anderson, might be freed with Jacobsen.

The key questions were whether we had given up anything in return for Jacobsen's release, and whether we had negotiated with his captors. At that time, Poindexter hinted about a much bigger operation, but he gave absolutely no details. He seemed to be alluding more to intermediaries who had put pressure on the captors, rather than to bargaining. I assumed that Poindexter's aide, Ollie North, was talking to one of the dozens of shadowy Middle East groups that we had pursued over the years, and that North's contacts were talking to people who could release the hostages. Poindexter gave me no hint of an Iranian connection.

I asked if Terry Waite, who had been negotiating with the terrorists on behalf of the Archbishop of Canterbury in hopes of getting the hostages released, had helped us. Poindexter's answer was, "No, but you have got to praise Waite. We would much rather people think that Waite did it instead of knowing the method that was used." Poindexter pointedly avoided telling me "the method that was used." He was using Waite—who had recently returned to the Middle East—as a smokescreen for Jacobsen's release; when a reporter asked at a briefing that Sunday morning about Waite's involvement, I replied that there were several intermediaries who had played a role and that we were "appreciative of the efforts that Terry Waite has made over the last year to secure release of not only American hostages but those of other countries." I did deny that Waite was representing the U.S.: "He's not working for the U.S. government, he's working for the Archbishop of Canterbury."

Very early in the briefing I was asked about Islamic Jihad and responded that some new approaches had been made by the United States. "What were the new approaches?" and "Have there been any changes in U.S. policy, any concessions, any negotiations?" a reporter demanded. My answer, on instructions from Poindexter, was, "There has been no change in U.S. policy. We continue our policy of talking to anyone who can be helpful, but we do not make concessions, nor do we ask third countries to do so. We have not changed our policy at all." I was also asked if we had had any direct contact with Islamic Jihad, but my reply was, "I don't want to answer that question." That was a tipoff that I was already suspicious that we were trying to make a deal with the terrorists. Little did I know that Ollie North was in Cyprus, awaiting the hostage release, which would only have confirmed my suspicions.

Our flight from Los Angeles to Washington on Election Day, Tuesday, November 4, was eventful from the moment we lifted off the ground. Cable News Network reported that Air Force One was in trouble because our landing gear did not retract shortly after takeoff. The first I heard of the incident was when Mark Weinberg, still on the ground with the press, phoned me on Air Force One. I checked with the pilot, Air Force Colonel Robert Reddick, who told me the landing-gear doors were kept open longer than usual to cool the brakes after a short flight to L.A. from the Point Mugu Naval Air Station near Santa Barbara with a full load.

On board Air Force One, the pool reporters started asking questions about the circumstances of Jacobsen's liberation. Poindexter and I were the only two senior staff people on the plane with the President. I went to where Poindexter was sitting and said, "John, we're going to have to have something more on Jacobsen. 'No comment' is getting pretty thin." "I'll write something," he said calmly, and took out a yellow legal pad. Poindexter wrote two or three false starts, then ripped them up. I thought that peculiar, since all that was required was a restatement of our policy on not dealing with terrorists. "I want to get this right," Poindexter declared. Near the end of the flight, he finally handed me a sheet with a carefully worded, handwritten memo. One question he posed was: .

"Does the U.S. still have an arms embargo against Iran in the Iran-Iraq Gulf war?"

"Answer: As long as Iran advocates the use of terrorism the U.S. arms embargo will continue. Moreover, the U.S. position on the Iran-Iraq war remains that the fighting should stop and that the two sides should reach a negotiated settlement of their dispute. We favor an outcome where there are no winners and no losers."

"Follow-up: Does the U.S. still embargo arms to Iran?"

"Answer: Yes."

It was artfully constructed. "Does the U.S. still have an embargo on arms to Iran?" "Yes, we do." His words allowed for the fact that we had raised the curtain a time or two, although Poindexter didn't admit it, and I had not even the slightest suspicion. I passed on Poindexter's answers to the reporters in the press pool, but this time I made it clear that Poindexter was the source and that I was not offering any opinion on whether what he said was true or not. Senator Eastland had taught me years earlier always to attribute information to its source if you couldn't personally vouch for the facts. I, of course, had not trusted Poindexter since Grenada three years earlier.

As the flight across country continued, the White House press office sent word to me that the official Iranian news agency was carrying a report from Teheran that the head of the Iranian parliament, Hashemi Rafsanjani, had said that Bud McFarlane and four other Americans had visited Iran disguised as air crewmen and brought with them two planeloads of military spare parts and a message from President Reagan. They were supposedly arrested, held five days as an illegal diplomatic mission, and later expelled. I tended to discount that report, but it added to my suspicions, and I handed Poindexter the message from the ground to see what his reaction would be; he maintained a poker face, betraying no reaction at all. In retrospect, he gave an Academy Award–winning performance.

As the Iran-Contra scandal unfolded, we heard a lot about Ollie North's numerous "strategy sessions" with President Reagan. One example: An article in *The New York Times* on December 3, 1986, reported that North had told a delegation from the United Methodist Church the previous February that he personally briefed the President twice a week on terrorism in Central America.

I was present at several of North's meetings with the President. One meeting, at one-thirty on the afternoon of November 7, 1986, was typical of North's contact with Reagan. Several other Reagan aides and I watched as North, who had prepared a document giving the President background information on Jacobsen and his captivity, ushered David Jacobsen and his family into the Oval Office so that Jacobsen could thank Reagan for his efforts to free Jacobsen and the other hostages. North's entire conversation with Reagan was as follows: "Mr. President, I'd like you to meet David Jacobsen."

Following that "intimate discussion" with the President, North walked over to where I was standing. He had that little sly grin of his and I said to him, "Ollie, why don't we just let you walk out of here and brief the press yourself?" and we both laughed.

After North became a fixture on the front pages, I had the President's appointment logs checked. They showed that there were less than two dozen meetings in which Ollie and the President were both present, most of them in 1985 and 1986, and none of the meetings included just Ollie and the President. As far as Reagan was concerned, North was a staff guy—and only a mid-level one at that.

* * *

The shadow of Ollie North hung over the entire Iran-Contra deal. My own encounters with North throughout the time I worked for Reagan were as few and far between as I could make them.

Pete Roussel, my deputy, reminded me after the scandal broke that the first time Ollie came to my office, early in the administration, I smelled a rat. North had come to give me some background for a briefing. After Ollie left, I turned to my staff and said, "You guys, take anything that guy gives you and cut it by half."

There was just something about North; what really put me off from day one was that he was so cocksure and assertive. North appeared to be a little bit too glib; you just sensed you weren't getting exactly the straight story from him. As a result, I never relied on anything he told me when I went before the press, unless he could give me irrefutable proof or I could confirm it with another source. I concluded early on that he would have me lie to the press if it would serve his ends.

Ollie prevailed on me in early 1986 to call the *Washington Post* and ask them to keep his name out of the paper. The *Post* had notified the NSC that they were going to run a story identifying North as "the key figure in implementation of U.S. policy in Central America." Ollie was widely known among reporters as the administration's chief operative in that area, but he told me he had never been identified publicly and that the *Post* was about to blow his cover. "I'm afraid for my children," North pleaded with me. "They [his enemies, whom he implied were lurking everywhere] have already slashed the tires on my car and poisoned my dog." The *Post*'s deadline was fast approaching, so I phoned Len Downie, the *Post* managing editor, and argued Ollie's case. At one time national security considerations might have kept a story out of print, but those days had long since passed. The only thing that might do the trick was to plead that someone might get killed if a story ran. That's the point I used with Downie. "Ollie is actually afraid something might happen to him or his family," I said. Downie agreed to consider my appeal, and phoned back in an hour to say the paper would hold off printing Ollie's name, but would "take another look tomorrow." The next day, Downie, a real straight-shooter, called to say the Associated Press had carried Ollie's name in a dispatch ten days earlier, and the *Post* was going to go ahead with their story. I had no argument. Incidentally, testimony before Congress later revealed that North's dog had not been poisoned but had died of cancer.

Little did I realize when Ollie used me to try to keep his name out of print that he had an intimate reporter-source relationship with many

Washington journalists. After all my years as a newspaperman and press spokesman, I still believed that those who were involved in secret operations would be the last to reveal them to the press. Sometimes, however, they are the first to break the code of silence, hoping they can use the press to achieve their own goals. Ollie was that way, and over the years, dozens of reporters printed stories that he had given them.

I really drew the line on Ollie after it was reported in March 1986 that Nicaraguan government troops, the Sandinistas, had conducted a cross-border raid into Honduras and were actually operating in that nation. Less than forty-eight hours earlier the House had rejected the administration's $100 million aid package for the Nicaraguan rebels, the Contras, but there were indications that the House would vote on it a second time and the Senate was debating Contra aid when the Sandinistas crossed into Honduras. My announcement on March 25 that the Sandinistas had invaded Honduras caused a firestorm among the press, who thought it was contrived to help us get our Contra aid package through Congress.

I didn't have many facts about the Sandinista invasion, and I was suspicious of what I had been told. I called North and said, "You've got to come over here and give me more facts. And I want you to bring some documentation." He came over with these huge military topographical maps stamped "Top Secret" that had troop positions marked on them. He opened one up, spread it out on my coffee table, pointed to those very jungles where the Nicaraguan troops had crossed into Honduras, and said, "Now, right here is where these people are. Believe me, I've been there, and I *know!*"

I was really questioning North closely, asking him for facts, numbers, military unit identifications, whatever he could provide to make it credible. I was encouraging him to write it out; I wanted to read the press a statement from him, not from me. Even though North did have a wealth of facts about the invasion, I was even more suspicious of him from then on than I had been previously. He used to call me, sometimes a couple of times a day, and I would ignore the calls. Whatever he was trying to sell me, I was not buying. Once North said to me, "I never can get through to you," and I answered, "Oh, gosh, I've just been busy"; I tried to play it low-key instead of telling him I didn't trust him, because, after all, we both were members of the President's team.

There would be periods when you would see Ollie every other day in the hallway, always wearing that boyish little sly smile that said, "I've been up to something highly secretive that I can't tell you about," which was often true. You wondered if he had been in Central America or wherever. It was always a joking thing: "Where have you been, Ollie, and when did you get back?" Ollie always looked as if he had a day's growth of beard, as if he hadn't had time to shave. He also had circles under his eyes, as if he hadn't had enough sleep. He loved to operate big in the Situation Room. When there would be a terrorist incident he liked to show off his knowledge. He would dominate the normally sedate Situation Room, standing in the middle of the floor, a phone at each ear, barking cryptic orders to some faraway operative. The SitRoom professional staff—CIA and foreign service officers on loan to the White House—would turn to their computer consoles and shake their heads. Ollie was more of a know-it-all than a macho type of guy.

I always had the impression that Ollie could see himself in a movie, that as he flew across the country he could visualize a camera on him, and although nobody knew who he was and his mission was secret, the whole thing was being made into a movie. He seemed to be play-acting, almost as if he could see the script being written as he operated. I sized Ollie up as a patriot, a brazenly zealous one, a man who genuinely believed he was doing the right thing.

North unquestionably cut a dashing figure among the rather drab cast of characters in the Reagan White House. Fawn Hall, North's secretary, also attracted more than her share of attention. She was certainly one of the best-looking women in the White House, and some male staffers not only would talk about what a knockout she was, they would make excuses to visit Ollie in his Executive Office Building quarters across the street, just to get a glimpse of her. But hardly anybody in the White House knew her well.

White House staffers enjoyed talking about North and speculating about whether his tall tales were true. But he was not highly regarded among Reagan aides, other than Poindexter and those who worked directly for the NSC.

Soon after the Iran controversy broke, I found out firsthand exactly how Nancy Reagan felt about North. One night in mid-November I went over to Reagan's study in the family quarters of the White House to read him an announcement I was going to make. He and Mrs. Reagan were sitting there in their robes, and he must have just come out of the shower, because his hair was slicked back. The two of them were in front of the television, eating dinner from silver trays on T.V. tables, and they had taken their contact lenses out and were wearing glasses, which made both of them look decidedly older. I walked into the darkened room and eased into a chair next to Mrs. Reagan. They were concentrating on the television, and it took a minute before she looked around and said, "Oh, Larry, I didn't realize you'd come in."

This was in the period when Ollie was doing those curbside interviews out of his car in front of his home. As the Reagans and I sat there, Ollie appeared on the screen and a reporter asked him if he was going to seek immunity from prosecution. Always glib, just as he was whenever I spoke to him, North quipped, "Immunity? If I had immunity, I wouldn't have this bad cold."

Mrs. Reagan looked over at me and then back at the screen, and she declared, "Not funny, sonny!" I knew right then that Ollie was no national hero in her mind.

By mid-November the Iran story was dominating the front pages, and President Reagan realized it was imperative that he tell his side. On Wednesday, November 12, he summoned the congressional leadership to the Cabinet Room to tell the whole story—as he knew it. He didn't realize that Poindexter and a tiny group at the NSC had withheld many of the facts from him. "We have not negotiated with terrorists," Reagan told the congressional delegation. "We have not broken any laws. . . . It was a covert operation . . . designed to advance our strategic interests in the Middle East."

Poindexter then took the floor and outlined the three goals he hoped the shipment of arms to Iran would accomplish: "First, to make contact with moderate, pro-U.S. elements in Iran and to help them gain power; second, to stop Iranian support of terrorism; and third, to secure the release of hostages."

The admiral went on to confirm the stories about McFarlane's trip to Iran, which he said had occurred in May 1986. He said Bud had told the Iranians that the Soviets were making preparations to support Iraq in the Persian Gulf war, but that the U.S. recognized the reality of the Iranian revolution and was not trying to turn back the clock. McFarlane, he said, told them they must change their policy on terrorism and work with us to secure the release of the hostages. Then Poindexter got down to details. "We transferred to Iran with the assistance of the Israelis 1,000 TOW anti-tank missiles and 240 units of spare parts for Hawk air defense missiles." He said the Iranians paid for them in cash. "We also provided intelligence to Iran to show them the futility of the war against Iraq," he said. Poindexter added that Bud's trip and other approaches to the Iranians had been successful because three of our hostages were released, no other Americans had been kidnapped, and at least some Iranian leaders had become more aware of the Soviet threat and more favorably disposed toward us.

Republican leader Bob Dole wasn't satisfied with Poindexter's explanation. Dole asked, "Why do overtures to the Iranians not constitute dealing with terrorists on the hostages?" Reagan himself broke in: "We would have continued on this track with Iran even if no hostages existed."

George Shultz then interjected something that was very telling, revealing the battles within the administration that had preceded Reagan's approval of the arms shipments. Shultz said he had been in two meetings with the President where the whole situation was discussed. He said the arms shipments had to be conducted by somebody, but once a decision was made, "the State Department had nothing to do with it." Democratic Senate leader Robert Byrd asked, "Were you opposed?" and Shultz replied, "I never discuss the advice I give to the President." Jim Wright said, "That's okay, we understand," and Byrd commented dryly, "You were left out."

Byrd was not finished. He challenged Poindexter, pointing out that the release had not taken place as anticipated, since only Jacobsen had been freed. "The whole thing was a serious mistake," Byrd declared. "It gave the appearance of us exchanging arms for hostages and hurt our credibility."

There were countless strategy sessions on how to deal with the unfolding scandal. One of the stranger attempts to provide advice to the President occurred shortly after the scandal broke. Mike Deaver, who had left the White House by then, engineered a bipartisan meeting for the President with a pair of senior statesmen. Deaver invited Democratic honcho Bob Strauss and William P. Rogers, a Republican leader who had served Eisenhower as attorney general, Nixon as secretary of state, and Reagan as head of the commission that investigated the January 1986 *Challenger* explosion. They were an odd couple if ever there was one. Rogers and Strauss had dinner with Reagan in the White House living quarters; Deaver hoped they could advise the President to admit he had made a mistake. But Rogers, who is a friend of mine, later told me it was the weirdest thing he had ever been to. Any frank advice to the President about what he ought to do would have probably found its way into the newspapers immediately, and Rogers was reluctant to speak frankly.

My own advice to the President, which I gave him several times, was to admit that he had made a mistake. What I wanted him to do was sit up and say, "I was wrong. I take full responsibility, and I apologize." I thought that would have helped bring the whole matter to an early end. The uproar over Iran reminded me of Watergate; I'm still convinced that if Nixon had taken responsibility and apologized early on, there never would have been an attempt to impeach him.

Dennis Thomas, Don Regan's chief aide, shared my view about what Reagan should do, and he repeatedly wrote a presidential apology into speech drafts. But the President was reluctant. He finally agreed to acknowledge that "mistakes were made" and to take responsibility, but he never could bring himself to say that *he* had made a mistake. It was just the makeup of the man; he did not think he had done anything wrong and was not about to concede that he had, as a matter of principle. It was the same thing when the subject of pardoning people like North, Poindexter, and McFarlane came up. Reagan said he wasn't going to consider any pardons, not because it was politically bad, but because he didn't think any crime had been committed, so no pardons were called for. He later modified his views somewhat when Mike Deaver faced a jail term for perjury and many thought he would pardon Deaver.

After my experience with Ford's pardon of Nixon, I always shied away from using the word "pardon." When the press asked me after the Iranian scandal broke if any pardons were contemplated, I insisted on using the term "Executive clemency," which I said is an option that is always available to any President of the United States.

The daily drum beat of bad press mounted throughout November. Poindexter summoned McFarlane back to the White House to help him and North try to construct a plausible story. As I went to Poindexter for answers to the barrage of questions I was getting, he seemed to be crumbling from the weight of criticism that was hitting us from all sides—the press, Republicans as well as Democrats on Capitol Hill, and even foreign governments. "There weren't many records of these contacts," Poindexter confided in me. "I'm trying to get clear in my own mind what we did." I got the impression that Poindexter had not been on top of North's operation, leaving the gung-ho marine with virtually a free hand.

Dennis Thomas and I, joined by Pat Buchanan, hammered at Don Regan with the message that "We must get our story out." Regan agreed that we had to move quickly, and he asked for suggestions on the best way. "The President could go down to the briefing room, but that would mean a lot of tough questions from the press," I said. "Or he could bring a small group of reporters into the Oval Office for a statement and a few questions." The best course, I told Regan, would be for the President to deliver a prime-time address to the nation. "That's the way to do it," I advised him. "Go straight to the people—but only if we are certain we have the whole story."

The President and Regan finally decided at mid-morning on November 13 that Reagan would speak from the Oval Office at eight o'clock that night. I announced to the press at my noon briefing that the President would address the nation. As usual, even on serious occasions like these, the banter flew back and forth. Somebody asked me, "What about Cosby?," a reference to NBC's top-rated Bill Cosby show, which was scheduled for eight o'clock. I didn't understand about Cosby at first, but then I replied, "He better be tuned in too." Then someone from ABC spoke up and said, "What about 'Our World'?"—which also came on at eight and was at the opposite end of the ratings from "The Cosby Show." Everyone laughed as I answered, " 'Our World.' Oh, gosh, let's change the time for the national address."

At the time of Reagan's address, we thought we were disclosing all the facts. Only later did we learn that many of the facts had been withheld, and that some of what the President said in the speech was incorrect. Bearing in mind that the NSC staff wrote the original draft of the President's speech, and that Poindexter and North then polished it up, a number of glaring inaccuracies stand out:

- "The charge has been made that the United States has shipped weapons to Iran as ransom payment for the release of American hostages in Lebanon, that the United States undercut its allies and secretly violated American policy against trafficking with terrorists. Those charges are utterly false."
- "I authorized the transfer of small amounts of defensive weapons and spare parts for defensive systems to Iran. . . . These modest deliveries, taken together, could easily fit into a single cargo plane."
- "Our government has a firm policy not to capitulate to terrorist demands. That 'no concessions' policy remains in force. . . . We did not trade weapons or anything else for hostages—nor will we."

The President had walked out on a limb that was about to be sawed off.

One significant bit of evidence that the NSC was running the whole Iran-Contra operation was a seemingly innocuous set of questions and answers on the Iran arms sale that Rodney McDaniel, executive secretary of the NSC, sent to Nicholas Platt, executive secretary at the State Department, on November 15. The Q's and A's were to be dispatched to embassies overseas "immediately." Normally, the instructions for ambassadors to use in their diplomatic contacts with their host countries would have been issued by the State Department and we would have gotten a copy at the White House. But this time the information originated in the NSC, which was calling the shots.

The NSC described our policy as making a "limited exception" to the arms embargo in order to bring about an honorable end to the war. "To further the dialogue . . . we decided to provide a limited quantity of defensive arms." The weapons were a "small token of our seriousness in pursuing the dialogue." McDaniel also said that U.S. policy had been effective in preventing terrorism, that the Iranians had aided in the release of the hostages from TWA Flight 847, and that no additional hostages had been taken by groups associated with Iran.

Anything that came out of the NSC depended on Poindexter's credibility, which wasn't that great with the press after the Grenada episode. I continued to take pains to attribute my information to Poindexter or others, instead of putting my own credibility on the line. At one briefing as the scandal unfolded, Sam Donaldson, who was determined to nail the admiral, noted that Poindexter had perhaps deliberately misled the press several times in the past and asked why they should believe him now. "There's no basic track record for us to trust him or the administration when he's involved," Sam added. I had no answer.

I did have one revealing encounter with Poindexter after Walter Pincus of the *Washington Post* wrote a story on November 14, 1986, reporting that President Reagan had ordered secret arms shipments to Iran the previous spring upon being told that was the only way to get Iran's help in freeing five U.S. hostages who were then held in Lebanon. The President had disregarded warnings from Shultz and Weinberger that such action would undermine his public stance against dealing with terrorists, according to the *Post*. Pincus had hit the nail on the head.

November 14, the day Pincus's story was published, I met with Poindexter and scribbled down his responses to my questions about the story: "Pincus does not understand everything involved. About a year ago [there was] a [presidential] finding, covert, limited distribution (original), no one else aware of objectives. Iran did not have control of hostages, does not hold them." So Poindexter was claiming that since Iran did not have control of the hostages, we were not dealing directly with the captors. What was really significant was that he was admitting, if in somewhat cryptic fashion, that we had been shipping arms to Iran for at least a year—which was about as candid as he was capable of being. He also referred to the formal presidential memorandum notifying Congress, which he had locked away in his safe—and later destroyed when the scandal broke.

In spite of my own bad experience with Poindexter, I was astonished by the number of lies he both told and encouraged, to keep the plot going and to cover it up later:

- When Shultz confronted Poindexter during the May 1986 summit in Tokyo about rumors that we were still shipping arms to Iran, Poindexter claimed there wasn't "a shred of truth" to those stories.
- After North reported to Poindexter that he had lied when he told the House Intelligence Committee in August 1986 that he was not involved in helping the Contras, Poindexter complimented him on a job "well done."
- After Ed Meese started his investigation in November 1986, Poindexter told him he didn't know the details of diversion of money to the Contras—which Meese bought hook, line, and sinker. North flatly contradicted Poindexter, testifying that Poindexter approved the diversion and declared, "This had better never get out."
- Poindexter assisted North and McFarlane in the preparation of the false chronology of events after the scandal became public—the "Ollie Chronology," we called it within the White House. Peter Wallison, who had become the President's counsel, advised me never to use the chronology in my press briefings. He said it was so far off base that the press would shoot holes through it in a minute.
- As has been widely noted, Poindexter, who was famous for his photographic memory, said 184 times during his testimony before the congressional Iran-Contra investigating committee in 1987 that he was unable to recall the answer to a question posed to him.

In contrast to Poindexter, George Shultz covered himself with glory, both during the crisis and in his testimony before Congress last summer. Shultz had been the most forceful opponent of the arms shipments during early discussions with the President, to the point that he annoyed Reagan. But it has since been shown that Shultz was right. Moreover, unlike Poindexter, Shultz has always told the truth. I was extremely impressed that he showed up without a lawyer for his congressional testimony during the investigation of the Iran-Contra affair. It was his way of saying, "What do I need an attorney for? I'm just here to tell the truth."

When the story broke in November 1986, however, Shultz was under fire within the White House for his opposition, both private and public, to the President's policy. The knives were really out for Shultz after he appeared on "Face the Nation" on November 16 and expressed his opposition to sending arms to Iran, said he could not speak for Reagan or the administration, and refused to deny that he had considered resigning.

Many of the people close to Reagan, from the First Lady on down, felt that Shultz should resign or shut up. Casey, for one, sent the President a note suggesting he needed a "new pitcher" at the State Department. And Don Regan commented to me, "I don't know what's gotten into George. If he doesn't like it, he should quit." Shultz, who was usually a bit cantankerous, seemed morose during this period, and it puzzled Regan and me. The President, always reluctant to have a confrontation or fire anyone, directed me to tell the press he didn't want Shultz to resign, which I did.

I have to admit that at the time I thought Shultz was wrong to air his views in public. If he thought it was such a bad policy he could have left the administration back in 1985 in order to bring about a change, but that wouldn't have served the President or the country. I felt that the secretary of state should be loyal to the President in public, or not say anything at all. I felt the same way I did with Jerry terHorst and Bernard Kalb: If you disagree with policy or if you're losing a policy battle, you either ought to get on board or, if you feel strongly enough about it, you quit. But you don't criticize the President publicly. You fight your battles within and then you shut up if you lose. Knowing all that I do now, however, I believe Shultz was correct in making his case to the President that we should own up to our mistakes and stop shipping arms to the Iranians. But Shultz was getting nowhere, so he had no alternative but to go public in hopes of persuading the President to bring the controversy to an end.

One thing that strikes me is the comparison between Shultz and his predecessor, Al Haig. Haig said he was quitting without meaning it, but Reagan said, "Fine." But the much shrewder Shultz was careful not to issue any Haigian ultimatums, and he remained on the job. His decision to stay on was an act of patriotism, knowing that Reagan and the country needed him.

By November 19, the night President Reagan held a press conference that we knew would be dominated by questions on Iran,* administration officials had acknowledged several times that Israel had shipped arms to Iran with our approval and that we had promised to restock Israel's arsenal.

We held full-scale rehearsals for the press conference in our customary

---

*Iran did dominate the news conference, to the extent that when one reporter interjected, "Mr. President, could we turn to U.S.-Soviet relations for a moment, please?" Reagan's response was, "I'd be delighted."

place in the White House family theater, both on November 19 and the day before. My staff and I had prepared a couple of dozen questions and answers for Reagan; question number eight in the Iranian section was, "What role have third parties played, and particularly Israel, in the arms shipments to Iran? Do third-party shipments continue and will the United States do anything to block these shipments?" The President answered it incorrectly both days by saying, "No third parties," and Poindexter corrected him both times. I added, "Mr. President, there have been many stories outlining Israel's role, but we have never said so officially."

This was one occasion when the President's poor performance during rehearsals was repeated at the press conference. When Bill Plante of CBS raised a question during the news conference about the fact that "the U.S. apparently condoned [arms] shipments [to Iran] by Israel . . . as an ancillary part of this deal," Reagan responded, "Bill, everything you've said here is based on a supposition that is false. We did not condone, and do not condone, the shipment of arms from other countries."

When I heard Reagan deny that any third country was involved, I slipped out of the press conference and stepped into the Blue Room, where Regan, Poindexter, Pat Buchanan, and several other top aides were watching on television monitors. They knew we had a major goof on our hands, but no one seemed to know what to do, so I turned back toward the East Room, where the news conference was continuing. Just as I reached the doorway I heard Reagan add to his mistake in response to another question about arms shipments: "We, as I say, have had nothing to do with other countries or their shipment of arms or doing what they're doing." I spun on my heels, went back to the Blue Room and told Poindexter, "You've got to get up a statement and have it ready when we walk out of the press conference that says, 'I was wrong,' and explain why."

By the time the news conference ended, Poindexter had drafted a correction for the President to read: "There may be some misunderstanding of one of my answers tonight. There was a third country involved in our secret project with Iran. But taking this into account, all of the shipments of the token amounts of defensive arms and parts that I have authorized or condoned taken in total could be placed aboard a single cargo aircraft.* This includes all shipments by the United States or any third country. Any other shipments by third countries were not authorized by the U.S. government."

No sooner did the President and I leave the East Room than Poindex-

---

*Poindexter was still promoting the one-airplane story, which was not only false but irrelevant; you could ship dozens of nuclear bombs on one cargo plane.

ter was there with his handwritten draft of a correction. The President looked it over and muttered, "Gosh, I didn't realize I'd said that." He added that he must have given the wrong answer because he was carefully trying to avoid mentioning Israel by name. Reagan immediately approved what Poindexter had written, ordering me to "Get it out, by all means." Twenty minutes after the press conference ended, I was able to release Reagan's correction to the press.

A short while later, several of us settled down in my office for a review of the videotape of the press conference, using the White House internal replay system, and a post-mortem. Among those present were a two-man tag team from the NSC: Howard Teicher, their expert on the Middle East, and Ollie North, the designated hitter on terrorism. Ollie made a big point of saying, "The press is just after us," laying the Us-Against-Them bit on heavily. He recited to me a number of instances where the Iranians had been helpful since we had started selling them arms.

As we turned to walk out of my office, Ollie put his arm around me and, referring to the fact that I never returned his calls, said, "We don't have a problem, do we?" And I said, "No, Ollie, we don't." But he was fired six days later, and that was the last time I ever spoke to him.

Since my first couple of years with Reagan, I had skipped his trip to California at Thanksgiving, and 1986 was no exception. I preferred to take one of the few short vacations I got each year and stay at home with my family. In 1986 Jeremy and I went deer hunting. For much of the cold, rainy Thanksgiving weekend, though, I sat at home watching the revelations that were coming out of Santa Barbara on Cable News Network, as well as reading newspaper stories like the one the *Los Angeles Times* broke on Thanksgiving day that North had shredded documents. Finally, after seeing coverage from California where Don Regan got pushed and shoved all over the place during an interview on CNN the day after Thanksgiving, I called Pete Roussel, who was in Houston for the weekend with his mother, and said, "Pete, this won't do. What we ought to do is come in Monday morning and tell 'em we're quitting." It was obvious that there was more to it than I had ever realized. It was a lousy thing that had happened, and a lot of things had gone on that smelled, and smelled badly.

I also placed a call to Dan Howard, who was the senior person from the press office with Reagan in Santa Barbara, and told him to stay off television as much as possible. I added, "Don't issue any statements on this in your own name. Say, 'So-and-so tells me.' Don't get yourself or the

President in trouble by denying something when you don't know whether it's true or not true." I didn't want my office to have its credibility on the line when there was obviously a lot going on that we didn't know about.

Right after the press corps returned to the White House from Santa Barbara, I held a series of one-on-one discussions with the White House T.V. correspondents and wire service reporters. I told them how I would handle stories during the Iranian crisis: "If I know something to be the truth on my own, I will say so. If I receive something from someone else and can't vouch for it, I'll tell you who told me. And in a case where I have no way of knowing, I will simply say I don't know." The best example being, did Ollie shred documents? I did not know, nor did I have any way of knowing. I had not seen him do it, and I had no access to the FBI investigation to learn what they were finding.

During the next week I made final arrangements with Merrill Lynch and on December 4, one week after Thanksgiving, I told Regan and then the President that I was leaving, and announced my departure to the press. The Iranian fiasco simply locked in my decision to leave, although the Merrill Lynch job was too good to pass up in any event. I had been negotiating with Merrill for two months and *Newsweek* had even reported on October 26, before the Iranian scandal broke, that I was considering the Merrill job.

The fact is, I probably would have left the White House anyway, but the Iranian thing forced me to make my decision. Seeing what was coming out on Iran, I said to myself, "This won't do." As far as I was concerned, the Three Stooges—Poindexter, North, and McFarlane—had ruined the Reagan presidency. I was really angry about it, and I could see there was going to be nothing but agony and antagonism with the press for months to come. I wanted to be fair to the President, and since Don Regan asked me to stay on until February 1, and Merrill Lynch was agreeable, I did.

It has become a cliché since Watergate, but it's still fair to ask, what did President Reagan know about the Iranian-Contra deal, and when did he know it?

First, there's no doubt that he wanted the hostages back and that he was prepared to sell arms to Iran in order to accomplish that. He gave oral approval to McFarlane and Poindexter and signed three secret intelligence findings—on December 5, 1985 (Poindexter's first day as NSC director); January 6, 1986; and January 17, 1986, authorizing the shipment of weapons to Iran in return for the hostages' release. Reagan was even willing to go to the limits of his power if it would get the hostages back; as he told Shultz and Weinberger on December 7, 1985, "the American people will never forgive me if I fail to get these hostages out over [a] legal question." Moreover, Don Regan testified that during the Geneva summit in November 1985, McFarlane told him and the President about the shipment of arms to Iran via Israel and the cover story of calling the cargo "oil drilling equipment" if the arms deal became public.* The important thing to remember is that the Iranian embargo was imposed by Reagan and that he was legally free to raise the curtain at any time if he believed it was in the national interest and reimpose it as he saw fit.

The second question is, what about North's giving $4 million to the Contras, beginning in 1985, from the $12 million in profits from the arms sales to Iran?† Although Reagan knew about and approved the arms deals with Iran, no one—not congressional investigators, not the special prosecutor's team, and not the press—has ever been able to find a "smoking gun" showing that Reagan knew about the diversion of funds to the Contras. And the reason for that is simple: Reagan didn't know. The evidence shows that at least one of Ollie North's memos about the diversion had a space for the President's signature, and that space was left blank. It was clearly a draft for Poindexter's review that was never sent to Reagan.

Whenever the subject of the diversion of funds from the Iranian arms sales to the Contras came up between Reagan and me, and it did several times, the President always said to me, "I knew nothing about that."

One particularly strong denial by the President came after his interview with *Time* magazine in which Reagan called North "a national hero." *Time* came out on Monday, December 1, 1986, and I found the press up in arms during my noon briefing. They pounded away on the key question: Did the President know much earlier about the diversion of funds to the Contras? I went straight from the briefing room to the Oval Office and asked Reagan when he found out about the Swiss bank account and the diversion of funds. "You can tell them flat out that I had no knowledge whatsoever of it until Ed Meese briefed me last Monday afternoon [November 24]," he declared.

I'm just convinced that the President would not have approved the diversion of funds to the Contras. I don't buy the theory that the Presi-

---

*Altogether, 2,008 TOW anti-tank missiles and over two hundred Hawk anti-aircraft missiles were shipped to Iran by Israel, with us replenishing Israel's stocks; one shipment of five hundred TOWs from Israel to Iran took place two days before David Jacobsen was released, and we sent an identical number of TOWs to Israel five days after he was freed.

†The remaining $8 million was deposited into Swiss bank accounts controlled by North and his associates, former general Richard Secord and arms dealer Albert Hakim.

dent nodded and winked on it. He just wasn't that kind of guy. I've seen him answer the question too many times, and I've discussed it with him privately too many times. Frankly, I don't believe the man can tell a lie. The man can make a mistake and the man can hear something so many times that he believes something is true when it really isn't, but he simply isn't a liar.

I have no doubt that North *thought* the President knew what was going on, but North was wrong. One statement of North's that I believe is his testimony that it wasn't until November 21, 1986, after the diversion of money to the Contras had become public, that Poindexter told him the President didn't know about it. North had given Poindexter five different memos on the diversion, expecting Poindexter to pass them on, but Poindexter didn't. I think North knew that the President had three goals—to get the hostages back, to support the Contras (which had been our policy since March 1981), and to establish relations with moderates in anticipation of the post-Khomeini era in Iran—and North just mixed all three of those into one pie and decided that anything he did to reach Reagan's goals was all right. To be sure, the President was signaling just that. For example, on our way back from Tokyo in May 1986, Reagan told Poindexter that he wanted to help the Contras even if Congress wouldn't appropriate money for them, and I'm sure Poindexter must have passed that on to North.

I regard North as the ultimate military functionary; I can visualize him testifying at the Nuremberg war crimes hearings that "I was just following orders." I think he had every reason to assume that Reagan approved what he was doing, but this is where the whole thing broke down: Poindexter took it on himself to mislead both the President and North, failing to inform Reagan what North was up to, and failing to inform North that the President didn't know about it.

Nevertheless, when the President disclosed the departure of Poindexter and North on November 25, he announced that Poindexter had resigned and that North had been fired. Not only was North publicly fired, but Ed Meese let Poindexter off the hook and placed the blame on North when Meese appeared in the White House briefing room that same day to take questions from the press about the scandal. Meese declared, "The only person in the United States government that knew precisely about this . . . was Lieutenant Colonel North. Admiral Poindexter did know that something of this nature was occurring, but he did not look into it further."

North may have broken the law by diverting money to the Contras and he may have been overzealous, but he unfairly took the fall. Not so much for Reagan as for Poindexter, who, in my opinion, was much more to blame than North was.

As details of the scandal trickled out, Don Regan and Nancy Reagan started crossing swords, sowing the seeds for his ouster. Regan was pushing the First Lady hard to get the President to come forward and acknowledge personally that he had made a mistake with the Iranian initiative, and Don and Mrs. Reagan had rip-roaring arguments over the telephone that sometimes ended with her slamming down the phone in his ear.

The press had been out to get Regan from the start of his tenure as White House chief of staff in 1985. They zeroed in early on his arrogant, know-it-all style, and when Iran weakened him, they were ready to take advantage. From the time the Iran story broke, reporters would gather around congressmen who visited the White House and ask them, "Do you think somebody ought to be fired over this?" Some congressmen demurred, but others would answer, "Yes." The follow-up question was usually, "Should it be Regan?" Mrs. Reagan got wind of this, and she began to sound out friends of hers and the President's, like Mike Deaver and Stu Spencer, a California political consultant and longtime Reagan loyalist. It became a vicious circle, with reporters also calling Deaver and Spencer, and the two of them saying that Nancy was upset with Regan. Mrs. Reagan finally turned up the heat full blast, sending word through her friends to NBC's Chris Wallace that Regan had to go.

Regan survived the first push to oust him in early December of 1986. A month later, however, Senator David Boren of Oklahoma, a respected Democrat who often sided with the President, reopened the controversy on a weekend radio show, saying that Regan should resign. Boren and Regan soon ran into each other at the annual black-tie bash for politicians, business leaders, and the press, the Alfalfa Club banquet, on January 31, and Regan said to Boren, "I hear you've been mentioning my name." An embarrassed Boren admitted it was true. That again turned up the heat on Regan, but the last straw came four weeks later, on February 27, when the Tower Commission Report on the scandal gave Regan the bulk of the blame for "chaos" in the White House. Nancy Reagan decided that Don had to go.

The Reagans didn't even do Regan the courtesy of informing him of his ouster before CNN reported it. Frank Carlucci, who had just come on board as NSC director in place of Poindexter, heard the news on television and rushed over to Regan's office to tell him that he was out and Howard Baker was in. Regan really let go of his legendary temper, dashed off a two-line letter of resignation, and was out the door and through the gates of the White House within fifteen minutes.

I sympathized with Regan, feeling that he was an outstanding chief of staff who had become another in a long line of Washington's sacrificial lambs. He had only tried to do what was best for the President, but he pushed too hard, crossed the fiercely protective First Lady, who didn't like him anyway, and paid the price. It was necessary for someone at the top to go in order for the President to put Iran behind him and move on to something else. And Regan was the one; the scandal had happened on his watch.

The uproar over diverting money to the Contras proved once and for all what I have always believed: that Central America is not an issue you can sell to the American people. Beginning with El Salvador in 1981, we were never successful in convincing the American people that what we were doing down there was right or worthwhile. By all rights we should have been able to. We were talking about democracy, about keeping the Communists off our doorstep, but it never sold. It's interesting that public support for our program in Central America rose dramatically after a guy like Ollie North was out on national television during the congressional hearings in the summer of 1987. I think it was probably because the news media filtering prevented us from ever getting our message across. Atrocities committed by the other side never got the amount of publicity that the ones by our guys got. In our own briefing room, any discussion of Central America would boil down more to a debate on it than to a news session. There was just a strong bias against American policy in Central America within the press corps. But once you removed the filter and had Ollie North speaking live and direct to the American people for a week, there was a dramatic change in public support for our Central American policy.

Part of the problem is that the American people don't understand Central America. I would bet that ninety-nine out of one hundred couldn't look at a map and tell Costa Rica from El Salvador. Also, it was confusing because we were on the government side in El Salvador and with the anti-government forces in Nicaragua.

Add Iran to the mix, and you had a disaster waiting to happen.

18 *Assessing*

Ronald Reagan

For six years I spoke out on behalf of Ronald Reagan. Now the time has come for me to speak out for Larry Speakes. In assessing Reagan, let me emphasize that I am not a longtime member of his entourage; aside from the brief talk Bob Dole and I had with Reagan during the 1976 Ford-Dole campaign, I had never met Reagan until Jim Brady introduced us on January 19, 1981, the day before Reagan was inaugurated. My observations on Reagan are offered in an objective sense, from someone who, in effect, had the opportunity to cover him on a daily basis the way a reporter with almost unlimited access might have.

In the end, when the results of Reagan's eight years in office are tallied, I am convinced that he will be recognized by history as a great President. His term in office will be regarded as a watershed of American political and governmental history—a time when America took stock, sized up its obligations as a nation and its abilities as a people, and showed again the mettle that has made us what we are, a truly great nation. Reagan brought with him a new approach to government. He showed us that there are limits to what the federal government can do, and that state and local governments, private business, and individual Americans must do their fair share. His philosophy changed our philosophy. His accomplishments, particularly in reviving our economy and establishing a breakthrough in relations with the other superpower, the Soviet Union, will ensure his place in history. Iran broke Reagan's stride as he headed into the final turn, but, in the end, it will amount to more sound and fury than long-term significance—a small, although critical, stumble in eight years of success.

While I share Reagan's conservatism and consider his presidency—at least before the Iran-Contra arms scandal—to be a wonderful and momentous one, I was not blind to the man's flaws and weaknesses.

First, Reagan's strengths:

He truly is a Great Communicator. One of my first impressions of Reagan from a distance during the 1976 campaign, when I was on the opposite side with Gerald Ford, was his knack for cutting the usual political lingo and getting straight to the issue that mattered the most to the voter, his pocketbook. He impressed me with his ability to reach the average voter and get his philosophy across. He has been a very effective President, not only because his philosophy struck a chord with most Americans, but because his skills as a communicator enabled him to lead and motivate them. Those of us who worked for Reagan never apologized for his background as an actor. Communication is the starting point for leadership. If you can't communicate, as Carter couldn't, then you can't motivate and you can't lead.

Reagan approached the modern presidency with goals as clear-cut as anyone since Franklin Roosevelt. And his goals were very basic: a strong economy and a strong national defense. Our biggest step toward achieving these goals was setting one priority item for the first year: the economy. If the first year was successful—and clearly it was—it would set the tone for the remaining years.

One reason for Reagan's success was that, while he knew what he wanted, he was also flexible and willing to compromise in order to attain his goals. During his first year, he accepted a slightly smaller tax cut than he had sought, but that was the only way to get any tax cut through Congress. The President was a master of timing when it came to compromising. He often said that some of the ultraconservatives would rather have him jump off the cliff with a flag in each hand. He said he believed it better to get half a loaf today and come back and get the rest tomorrow or next year. That was his legislative philosophy.

To me, the economy is the best measure of the success of the Reagan Revolution. When Reagan took office, interest rates, inflation, and unemployment were out of control. A few figures are in order here:

- The prime rate, which was 20.5 percent in January 1981, was reduced to single digits.
- Inflation has virtually come to a halt under Reagan. The primary indicator of inflation, the Consumer Price Index, was a whopping 12.4 percent in 1980; it declined during the Reagan years to as low as 1.1 percent in 1986, and was about 4.4 percent for 1987, one-third what it was the year before Reagan took office.
- Unemployment, which was 7.4 percent in December 1980, Jimmy Carter's last full month as President, dropped to 5.8 percent in October 1987, the lowest level since mid-1979. Moreover, studies show that American living standards have risen substantially under Reagan, and 14 million jobs have been added to the economy in the last five years.
- Since Reaganomics helped the country emerge from a recession (the foundation for which Reagan inherited from Carter) in late 1982, the economy set a peacetime record by growing in every month for five years.
- Even in the aftermath of the stock market collapse on "Black Monday"—October 19, 1987—the Dow Jones Industrial Average was twice as high as it was when Reagan took office. At its peak of over 2,700 in August 1987, the Dow had tripled during the Reagan years.

Reagan has been criticized, justifiably, for the record budget and trade deficits that occurred during his two terms. Nevertheless, the budget deficit was trimmed substantially in 1987, and he believed our balance of trade would improve as more of his economic medicine—reducing the value of the dollar—was administered. Reagan's critics have said that the twin deficits will eventually catch up with the country and ruin the economy after he leaves office. They may be right. But they may also be wrong; only time will tell. What we do know is that when Reagan took office the economy was in dire straits, and that his presidency has coincided with an era of almost unprecedented prosperity.

Reagan has also proved that a strong military is essential for a strong foreign policy. With a strong U.S. military, we gain respect from our allies as well as our adversaries. A key factor in the success of his foreign policy has been his determination to see that the Strategic Defense Initiative (Star Wars) is funded by Congress through its research and testing stages until it is ready for deployment. Not only does Reagan believe in the dramatic possibilities of a missile defense like SDI, but I am convinced that his insistence on retaining Star Wars did more than anything to cause an about-face in the Soviet approach to arms control. I saw it at both

Geneva and Reykjavik—the U.S. having SDI technology scared the day-lights out of the Russians. In spite of all the propaganda about what nice guys Gorbachev and the Soviets are in the wake of the Washington summit, we must remember that they are not our best friends and that the only way for us to get concessions out of them is for us to negotiate from a position of strength.

Reagan's personal charm has enabled him to forge warm relation-ships with allied leaders, from Margaret Thatcher to Yasuhiro Naka-sone. In my opinion, our ties to our allies are stronger than at any other time since World War II, in large part because of the personal contacts Reagan established with leaders of the other industrial nations. The first thing he did was to get on a first-name basis with them. In 1981 they regarded him as a newcomer and something of a lightweight because he was a former actor. But by 1984 François Mitterrand and the others were asking how we were able to create all those new jobs and still hold inflation down. Reagan and Thatcher, of course, are extremely close, but he and Nakasone were also unusually close. Each tried to outdo the other with gestures of personal closeness; Nakasone even took us to his home village several miles north of Tokyo, which was a rare display of affection by a Japanese leader.

Reagan also had a much better grasp of details than he was generally given credit for. I tried for a couple of years to sell Baker and Deaver on the idea that the President needed more contact with the press on an intimate level. I proposed that we have cocktails with just five or six reporters over at the presidential residence, and let them talk to the President totally off the record. Finally, in 1984, Baker and Deaver agreed to do it. We started meeting at five-thirty for an hour or so. The press was amazed at his depth of knowledge on a given issue. He divulged many secret details that would have made headlines had these sessions not been off the record. He would give impressions of Gorbachev, or launch into details of his Central American policy, and other issues. The press, even those that liked to ridicule him for his lack of knowledge, would leave those meetings and tell me that they were absolutely amazed at what the President knew. "You ought to do more of these, he was great," Lou Cannon, who was there, told me after one such meeting. But those sessions, unfortunately, were a low-priority item for Baker and Deaver.

I do have mixed feelings about Reagan's management style. Reagan is a manager who doesn't get involved in details. He sets the policy and just assumes he has competent people to carry it out. But he wants to hear issues aired, and they were, sometimes very bitterly. Decision meetings usually lasted an hour, with plenty of give and take.

At Cabinet and staff meetings, the President was generally a listener. He would walk in and say, "All right, tell me what you think." That's not to imply in any way that he was not in charge or that he was not decisive or that he was not a leader, but he saw it as his job to hear out his Cabinet officers and then make decisions. The buck stopped with him, but it did not necessarily start with him. Many times, though, he would offer an idea out of the clear blue, saying, "Why can't we do this?" or he would have a gleam in his eye and say, "I've got an idea." More often than not, Reagan's suggestion had merit and was something the policymakers hadn't thought of.

It may sound simplistic, but Reagan's approach to traffic laws gives the perfect example of how he sees the role of government. He opposed the mandatory helmet law for motorcyclists in California when he was governor. He felt that if somebody wanted to ride a motorcycle without a helmet and kill himself, he should have the freedom to do so, as long as he didn't hurt anyone else. To him, drunken driving was different, because a drunken driver could come across the center of a highway and kill somebody. That sums up his entire approach to government.

As for his weaknesses, some of the business about his lack of attention to detail was true. But that was just his style. His theory was you hire good people and let them do the job. "Surround yourself with the best people you can find, delegate authority, and don't interfere," was the way Reagan described his philosophy of management in a widely read cover story in *Fortune* magazine in September 1986. Some leaders like to hire weak people for fear that strong people would show them up. Reagan would get deeply involved only in issues that interested him, like the Contras' valiant battle against the Communist-backed government in Nicaragua. Arms control, on the other hand, was a very, very complex issue that he didn't know that much about to begin with and only mastered in its basic principles and broad outlines. He wanted—and got—a breakthrough arms control agreement with the Soviets, but he left the details to the experts.

Some of his strengths were also weaknesses. His ability to cut through the political clutter down to the *Reader's Digest* item often backfired, especially with that collection of three-by-five cards he kept containing facts or quotes. A lot of those "facts," although they had been reported in the press, were incorrect, but when he saw something he thought was a good idea he would file it away and use it. His statement that trees cause as much pollution as automobiles was something he had read somewhere.

A lot of those facts would get locked in and then would come out at inopportune times.

Mike Deaver used to say that you had to be very cautious with the President right before a press conference because the last thing you put in was the first thing that would come out. Reagan had an actor's ability to memorize. He had a propensity to deal in figures and percentages in order to illustrate his stories. But if you confronted him with a blizzard of numbers at the very last minute, he might get confused and screw up. So we had a rule that you just didn't clutter him up with a heavy dose of minutiae at the last second. Generally we would quit about three o'clock on the afternoon of a press conference, to give him time to rest and absorb all he had learned during the preparations.

One person I watched very closely at the beginning of Reagan's term was Jim Baker, who, like me, had not worked with Reagan before. Baker had a real ability to communicate with the President. Baker spoke in short sentences, used anecdotes to illustrate his points, and repeated what he said, and I tried to do the same myself whenever possible, in order to get my views across to the President.

Another Reagan weakness was that he wouldn't fire anybody. He was too nice a guy in some respects. Every politician tends to be loyal to a fault to his staff and his friends. Any politician worth his salt believes what Senator Eastland told me: "In politics, loyalty is everything."

Al Haig quickly became a problem, but there were pros and cons: What's the trauma of firing a secretary of state compared to putting up with him? It's too bad that Dick Allen had to go, but, since he did, he should have gone long before he did. The same with Don Regan, Ray Donovan, and Anne Burford. But Reagan firmly believed these people were not guilty of any wrongdoing, that they were victims of politically inspired or press-motivated campaigns. So he would not do anything to hasten their departures, which would have put a stamp of guilt on them that he felt they did not deserve. David Stockman should have quit after the Greider story, which clearly showed that Stockman didn't believe what he was out there saying. Why he stayed on, I'll never know. But since he chose not to resign, he should have been fired. However, Reagan just wasn't tough enough on him.

All that changed when Don Regan replaced Jim Baker as chief of staff. Regan got no credit for being decisive, but he was, especially on personnel matters—unlike Baker. Baker generally went along with people forever, as did the President.

The difference between Regan and Baker was best brought home to me in February 1986, when reports surfaced in the *Wall Street Journal* that John Fedders, head of enforcement at the Securities and Exchange

Commission, had repeatedly beaten his wife. To make it worse, Fedders was a six-foot-ten former college basketball star, and his wife was a tiny woman. The day the news broke, Regan called Fred Fielding and me to his office. Fred had interviewed some people who knew Fedders and confirmed that the allegations in the press were true. Regan looked at me and said, "Do you think we should let him go?" And I said, "The quicker the better." Regan instantly said, "Do it," and Fielding immediately set in motion Fedders's "resignation." Without Regan to push the President, that situation no doubt would have lingered on indefinitely.

Another problem, a long-standing one, which Regan had inherited from Baker, was Margaret Heckler, the secretary of health and human services. She had been a tough case all along, constantly making mistakes in congressional testimony and statements to the press, and generally being a pain to work with. Regan just gave her the big nudge and finally, in October 1985, he came up with the job of ambassador to Ireland for her, which she accepted—very, very reluctantly. The Heckler problem had been festering for several years, but nothing was done about it until Don Regan made a decisive management move.

President Reagan was simply too much of a good guy. It extended to scheduling as well as personnel matters. He didn't say to his staff as often as he should have, "Now, wait a minute, I don't want to do that." He made no secret of it—"They tell me what to do," but, of course, "they" hadn't been elected President. It was like Dole saying when he ran for V.P., "All indoor work and no heavy lifting." Dole sought the prize, but he belittled it. In a way, Reagan belittled his own capacity as President. Where his schedule was concerned, Reagan should have asked, "Why am I seeing all of these people?" Instead, he said, "Each morning I get a piece of paper that tells me what I do all day long."

Also, on appointees, if there was poor staff work, Reagan wouldn't say, "Hey, go back and do a better job." Nominating Sandra Day O'Connor to the Supreme Court was a brilliant stroke, but some of the other nominations weren't as good, including his first two selections for the Supreme Court in 1987—Robert Bork and Douglas Ginsburg. Once again, it was Ed Meese's fault, but the President almost always sided with Meese—even to the point of literally embracing Meese in the press room after Ginsburg's nomination had to be withdrawn following press reports that he had smoked marijuana, which Meese, who had championed Ginsburg, had failed to find out. Ray Donovan was another mistake, nothing more than a political payoff. Aside from his legal problems, he was never effective as secretary of labor, because, as someone said, he had never met with an AFL-CIO official in his life. Jim Watt was another political liability who could have been weeded out with better staff work in check-ing out his history. Again, he wasn't an expert in his field. Guys like him and Donovan enjoyed no respect within the area that was assigned to them.

You could call Iran Reagan's Bay of Pigs. It was something he was sucked into, and then it simply got out of control. His attempt to make a strategic opening to Iran rapidly became an arms-for-hostages deal. The thinking was, a few arms here, a few arms there, what will that hurt if we can get our hostages back? We were trying to show the powers-that-be in Iran that the Iranian "moderates" had some clout, by providing the moderates with weapons. You could deny that it was arms for hostages, although it really was. Reagan himself simply rationalized it by saying, "We were supplying arms to someone—Iran—who might influence those terrorists who were holding our hostages," just as he convinced himself in 1985 that he didn't really have cancer. It's all in the eye of the beholder.

Reagan's critics say that if he did not know about the diversion of funds to the Contras, he should have. But the point is, he didn't delegate that authority; it was a cowboy operation from the start. How do you ride herd on every mid-level staffer like Ollie North? How can you know about what you don't know? Whom do you ask if you don't even know to ask? So I don't fault the President. I fault North and his boss, John Poindexter. The bottom line is that by diverting profits from the Iranian arms deals to the Contras, North, McFarlane, and Poindexter were running a rogue operation. They saw to it that the buck stopped with them, not with the President. What they did was wrong, and there was nothing that Presi-dent Reagan could have done about it, because he did not know about it. But in the final analysis one thing is crystal clear: The President—in fact, any President—must accept full responsibility for the actions of his administration.

There are two separate issues here: arms shipments to Iran and the diversion of funds to the Contras. On Iran, people often forget that overtures from political factions there dated back to 1981, when Dick Allen was national security adviser. When new overtures were made in 1985 and 1986, President Reagan, after very deliberate consideration, decided that we would pursue these openings. This is where Shultz and Weinberger broke with the President. Reagan discussed the matter thoroughly with his advisers; Cap and George disagreed and bowed out; and Reagan went ahead and did what he thought was right.

As for the Contras, Poindexter was always saying that something had to be done about the freedom fighters. I would hear the talk in the White House, "We've got to keep those poor fellows alive. They're down to two days of ammunition, they have to go into the field with only five bullets, no uniforms have been bought for the last two months." I believe these reports were exaggerated and that even the intelligence gathered by the CIA was doctored to distort the Contras' plight.

Things like that were being fed to the President, making a deep impression, and he authorized the solicitation of funds from third countries and private U.S. citizens. Poindexter has speculated that the President would have approved the diversion of funds had he known about it. Well, here is some speculation of my own, which is equally valid:

Had John gone to the President and said, "Mr. President, we want to take the profits from the Iranian arms sale and give them to the Contras," the President would have thought that was novel and ironic and a real comeuppance to the Ayatollah, and would have smiled and nodded and said, "Why not?" But, had Poindexter added, "Mr. President, we have some doubts about the legality of this," the President would have demanded a full investigation by his legal, diplomatic, military, and political advisers, and would have concluded that no one in the U.S. government could send money to the Contras unless Congress approved it.

Of the last six Presidents, I have worked for three of them: Nixon, Ford, and Reagan. I was in Washington when Johnson and Carter were President, and, like many people of my generation, I studied Kennedy closely. Here is how I would rank the six of them:

First, Ronald Reagan. He knew where he wanted government to go and how it should get there. He straightened out the economy, got our foreign policy back on the right track, and restored our pride in being Americans. Iran was the exception to his success.

Second, Richard Nixon. He was a brilliant political and foreign policy strategist. We're still reaping the benefits of his opening to China and his mastery of U.S.-Soviet relations. The negatives, which culminated in Watergate, were that he was cold and isolated.

Third, Lyndon B. Johnson. He was a superb legislative strategist, the last American populist. The Great Society attuned Americans to the needs of the poor, the sick, and minorities. Vietnam was an albatross.

Fourth, John F. Kennedy. He motivated Americans to strive for greatness and he rekindled our spirit as a nation, much like Reagan did twenty years later. What would he have achieved had Camelot not ended in Dallas after less than three years?

Fifth, Gerald Ford. He was a man for the times who healed the wounds of Watergate. He was vastly underrated and would rank much higher if he had had more than two and a half years to achieve his goals. It really is unjust that the Ford presidency has become an asterisk in history.

Sixth, Jimmy Carter. He was earnest and honest, promising "I'll never tell you a lie," but that wasn't enough. He was, unfortunately, unable to lead. Domestically, he left the economy in shambles. Diplomatically, the Camp David accord was his only real achievement, but it had little effect in the long run. Moreover, his policies led to the loss of Iran as one of our staunchest allies.

Throughout my six years with Reagan, I pleaded with him and his inner circle for more openness in government—more openness to their own press office and more openness to the press and the American people. If the President and Poindexter had not been so obsessed with secrecy on the initiative to Iran and it had been more widely discussed, it might never have happened at all. Had there been no arms shipments, there would have been no profits from them to funnel to the Contras.

On the other side of the equation, however, just as the White House has to change its ways of dealing with the press, the news media needs to treat the presidency differently. I recall the time back in January 1983 when the press all but went into a feeding frenzy over the President's proposal that the corporate income tax be abolished. I finally accused the White House reporters of "licking your chops and clapping your hands and doing back flips" over the story. When President Reagan heard what I had said, he shook my hand.

First and foremost, let's restore what is potentially one of the most important institutions of democracy in the television era, the presidential press conference, to what it should be: an information-gathering device, not a tool for establishing journalistic reputations. The time has come when each and every reporter who covers the President must stop thinking of himself or herself as Bob Woodward, and must stop asking variation after variation of the old question, "When did you stop beating your wife?" Many reporters come to *create* news, not to *cover* it.

Politicians and the press corps have an adversary relationship, as they must in a democracy, but it doesn't have to be an "I gotcha!" relationship. Let the reporters ask questions about subjects they truly need information on, instead of approaching press conferences as a vehicle for making headlines themselves. It's time to abolish the cult of personality in the press corps itself. If reporters think they can do a better job of running the country than those who are in power, let them run for office themselves.

The White House and the press can work together to bring about two much-needed improvements:

- Let's cut down on the number of live telecasts of what are often non-events. A live broadcast used to be reserved for a declaration of war, or, at the minimum, a presidential address to the nation. But live coverage has become the rule, not the exception. Everything nowadays is trumpeted as bulletin material. We run the risk of lulling the public into a ho-hum response to stories that are essential to their well-being. We're in danger of creating a modern equivalent of the little boy who cried "Wolf!"

- Let's send that omnipresent, omniscient public official, the informed source, into a long-overdue retirement. Let government pledge to tell the story on the record, and let the press promise to report it on the record. Too often, the public official who declines to speak for attribution has an axe to grind, a score to settle, or a need to puff his own self-importance to a reporter. Tell it on the record, or don't tell it at all; report it on the record, or don't report it at all.

If political officials and the press treat each other with a little respect, both sides will benefit—and so will the American people.

19

Moving on

to a New Life

On the afternoon of Monday, November 3, 1986, the day before the congressional elections, I was standing backstage with the Reagans at the final campaign rally for Republican candidates at the Pacific Amphitheater near Anaheim. As President Reagan had crisscrossed America to campaign for his fellow Republicans in Congress, he had made the Reagan administration and his policies the issue. This was the last time Ronald Reagan would ask the public, in effect, to endorse him for office. I had already started talking to Merrill Lynch, and I knew it was likely to be the last campaign rally for both Ronald Reagan and me.

Struggling with my own feelings, I observed Reagan very closely as he stood there, holding Mrs. Reagan's hand, which he often did, while he waited to enter the stage. There was a kind of eerie silence. Reagan usually said something to relieve the tension before he went to make a speech— even on historic occasions. But this time he said nothing, not a word. Mrs. Reagan was also silent, understanding what her husband was feeling; she just looked up at him and squeezed his hand, as he bounced up on stage for The Final Act.

The rally itself was a real circus. We did everything from fireworks to balloon drops to flag-waving parachutists jumping out of airplanes. As I stood there at the corner of the stage, the words from Reagan's "Last Campaign" speech really moved me:

"There are really no last, no final campaigns. Each generation must renew and win again for itself the precious gift of liberty, the sacred heritage of freedom." The band broke into a rousing, "California, Here I Come," which added to my sense of finality.

By early December, the people at Merrill Lynch and I had had considerable discussions about the job—senior vice president for communications—and the terms of the contract. I had been talking to them since late September.

The job was right, and it was an opportunity to join one of Wall Street's most prestigious firms. An old friend, Harold Burson, the country's premier public relations executive, had recommended me to the folks at Merrill. We quickly concluded a deal.

The first person I talked it over with at the White House was Don Regan, the former Merrill Lynch chairman and a Wall Street legend. He said, "I am in a quandary. If I tell you to go, the President gets mad; if I tell you to stay, my pals at Merrill get mad." But in the end he advised me to take the offer. He joked, "If they offered me this, I would go back."

With my contract finalized, I told Regan on December 4 that I had decided to accept the offer and that I would like to announce my departure at his and the President's convenience. He said, "Well, my idea is to announce it as quickly as we can. Let's just be sure the press doesn't think you are leaving over the Iranian thing."

Right after talking to Don, I went in to see the President. I told him, "Mr. President, I've made a decision that I hoped I'd never have to make. That is to leave before the end of your term. I had hoped to stand with you on the Capitol steps when you turned the presidency over to your successor on January 20, 1989, and left to go to California for the last time. But I have been presented with an opportunity that is very difficult to refuse, and I have made up my mind to accept it."

"I understand," he said—almost the same answer Senator Eastland had given me more than twelve years before when I left Capitol Hill to come to the White House for the first time. Reagan said he was sorry to see me go, but he didn't want to stand in my way of accepting such an opportunity. The President was like that. He always felt that if you had a good reason for leaving, you ought to go ahead and do what was best for yourself.

The growing controversy over Iran was very much on both our minds. I figured that two months would be sufficient to find my successor, and, naively, that that would be enough time "to put us on an even keel on the Iranian matter," as I told the President. He agreed, and February 1, 1987, was set as my departure date.

I sat in the chair beside the President's desk, and he pushed his chair back and turned so that he was facing me. We were alone in the Oval Office, and it was a moment of rare informality that I had seldom experienced with Reagan—which made my leaving that much more difficult.

We talked some more, and I said, "It has been a great privilege to serve you. As a kid growing up in a town in Mississippi of seven hundred, I never expected to meet a President, much less work with one." He smiled and replied, "Well, what do you think about a kid growing up in a small town in Illinois?" And we both laughed. It suddenly struck me that nearly thirty years ahead of me, he, too, had been a kid growing up in a small town in Middle America. Our roots were the same.

I went back to my office, roughed out my statement, and walked into the briefing room at noon to announce my own resignation, much as on January 19, 1981, I had announced my own appointment as deputy press secretary.

On February 1, 1987, a Sunday, Laura and I left Washington. As our flight lifted off from National Airport and banked to the east, we looked back on the city where we had been newlyweds more than eighteen years before. The sun was breaking through the clouds, casting its rays on the Capitol, the White House, and the marble city below. We flew into the clouds until they closed under us and Washington disappeared.

Minutes later, we flew into New York, took the turn out to the east, and then flew back to land at LaGuardia Airport, with Manhattan in the distance. New York's skyline—the World Trade Center and Wall Street and the Empire State Building—was silhouetted against the setting sun.

It was the perfect way to end one chapter of my life and begin another.

Index